A Practical Guide to Libel and Slander

N.K.

A Practical Guide to Libel and Slander

Jeremy Clarke-Williams, LLB (Hons)
Partner, Russell Jones and Walker, Solicitors

Lorna Skinner, MA (Cantab)
Of the Middle Temple, Barrister, 1 Brick Court

Print on Demand Edition

Tottel
publishing

Published by
Tottel Publishing Ltd
Maxwelton House
41-43 Boltro Road
Haywards Heath
West Sussex
RH16 1BJ

ISBN 13: 978-1-84592-417-1
ISBN 10: 1-84592-417-7
© Reed Elsevier (UK) Ltd 2003
Formerly published by LexisNexis Butterworths

Reprinted by Tottel Publishing Ltd 2006

British Library Cataloguing-in-Publication Data.
A catalogue record for this book is available from the British Library.

Typeset by Letterpart Ltd, Reigate, Surrey
Printed and bound in Great Britain by
CPI Antony Rowe, Eastbourne, East Sussex

Preface

Defamation has gone through a bewildering number of changes and developments over the last few years. Apart from the Defamation Act 1996, there has been the impact of the Civil Procedure Rules, the Human Rights Act 1998, and the availability of conditional fee agreements. Meanwhile, important judgments have included the overhaul of the defence of qualified privilege and the introduction of guidelines on the appropriate level of damages.

This activity has been difficult enough for those who specialise in defamation to absorb and adapt to, let alone those practitioners who deal with libel and slander claims less frequently. Others outside the legal profession have also had to try to keep track of what has been going on, in particular those who work in the media and all those whose work involves what might be categorised as 'reputation management'.

Lorna Skinner and I, for our sins, spend every day of our working lives pursuing or defending libel and slander claims for clients, she as a barrister in a leading defamation chambers, and myself as a solicitor in one of the busiest defamation firms. We have endeavoured in this book not just to summarise what the defamation law is but also to supplement this with some practical guidance based on our experiences at the coal face.

Researching, preparing and writing a book of this sort inevitably requires considerable co-operation and assistance from others involved in the process, from the first blank sheet of paper through to the publication itself. For my part, I owe a huge debt of thanks to the following people.

First, to my secretary of the last 14 years, Karen Leiper, who has converted my handwritten hieroglyphics into superbly formatted and ordered text; if the content matches her efforts, the book will be worthwhile indeed. Second, to my colleagues in Russell Jones & Walker's defamation department, Jacqueline Young and Theresa Ryan, who added their skills to key sections of the book and their helpful comments to the draft proofs.

Third, to my wife Cynthia and our sons, Douglas and Adam. They have uncomplainingly put up with more weekends and evenings than I care to mention with me closeted away writing this book. Their support has been unfailing and hugely appreciated.

Finally, I am told it is considered bad form to include any sort of acknowledgment to one's publishers in an introduction. However, I would like to break with tradition to thank Mark Wilson and Shaun Thorpe at Butterworths for their patience, understanding and courtesy throughout the lengthy gestation period of this book, so often interrupted by the demands of my day job.

We have sought to reflect the state of the law as at mid-November 2002.

Jeremy Clarke-Williams
Partner, Russell Jones & Walker
London WC1

In addition to those mentioned by Jeremy, to whom I also owe a huge debt of thanks (with the exception, I suppose, of his family!), I would like to thank Ben Mawson, a talented new recruit to Chambers, for his much-valued contributions to key areas of the text. I would also like to thank my husband, Stephen, and in particular my sons Isaac and Elijah, for all their interruptions and disruptions, which provided me with a near-constant reminder that there is more to life than work and books.

Lorna Skinner
Chambers of Richard Rampton QC
1 Brick Court
Temple
London EC4Y

Acknowledgments

Solicitors' Practice Rules 1990 and Solicitors' Costs Information and Client Care Code 1999 are reproduced with the kind permission of the Law Society. © The Law Society.

Bar Council CFA Guidance written by members of the Bar Council's Conditional Fee Agreements Panel and reproduced with the kind permission of the General Council of the Bar.

Press Complaints Commission Code of Practice reproduced with the kind permission of the Press Complaints Commission.

Broadcasting Standards Commission Code on Fairness and Privacy reproduced with kind permission of the Broadcasting Standards Commission. www.bsc.org.uk.

Section 2 of the ITC Programme Code is reproduced from the January 2002 edition of the ITC Programme Code.

Contents

Table of Statutes

Paragraph references printed in **bold** type indicate where the statute is set out in part or in full.

Table of Statutory Instruments

Paragraph references printed in **bold** type indicate where the Statutory Instrument is set out in part or in full.

Table of Cases

C

R

S

An action for defamation in the High Court: overview of standard procedural steps to trial

DEFAMATORY PUBLICATION

LETTER OF CLAIM

RESPONSE TO LETTER OF CLAIM

ISSUE OF CLAIM FORM
Within one year of defamatory publication.

SERVICE OF CLAIM FORM
Within four months of issue – no response required.

SERVICE OF PARTICULARS OF CLAIM
Within 14 days but no later than the latest time for serving a claim form.

FILING OF PARTICULARS OF CLAIM
Within seven days of service together with certificate of service.

FILING OF ACKNOWLEDGMENT OF SERVICE or FILING AND SERVICE OF DEFENCE
Within 14 days of service of particulars of claim.

FILING AND SERVICE OF DEFENCE
Within 28 days of service of particulars of claim if acknowledgment of service filed.

SERVICE OF ALLOCATION QUESTIONNAIRE BY COURT
On filing of defence.

FILING OF ALLOCATION QUESTIONNAIRE AND FILING AND SERVICE OF REPLY
At least 14 days after date of deemed service of questionnaire, by date specified in questionnaire.

ALLOCATION TO MULTI-TRACK

CASE MANAGEMENT CONFERENCE
At least three days' notice.
May be fixed any time after claim allocated.
Case summary may be required.
Held whenever it appears to the court that it cannot properly give directions on its own initiative.
Legal representative familiar with case and with sufficient authority to deal with likely issues must attend.
Likely topics: (a) clarity of claim; (b) amendments required; (c) necessary documentary disclosure; (d) expert evidence; (e) disclosure of factual evidence; (f) arrangements for giving clarification/further info and putting questions to experts; and (g) split trial/preliminary issue.
May well fix timetable to trial including trial date or trial period and if it does so will also specify date by which a pre-trial checklist must be filed by the parties.

SERVICE AND FILING OF PRE-TRIAL CHECKLIST
Unless dispensed with will be sent by court for completion and filing by the date given in directions at the case management conference and in any event not later than eight weeks before trial date or start of trial period.
Court will serve questionnaire at least 14 days before.
Court may then require a further hearing in order to determine what directions to give in order to complete preparation of the case for trial.

PRE-TRIAL REVIEW
At least seven days' notice.
Likely to be held in all cases where trial estimated to last more than ten days.
To achieve settlement/set trial agenda.
Legal representative familiar with case and with sufficient authority to deal with likely issues must attend.
Should be attended by trial advocates and someone authorised to settle.

TRIAL

Chapter 1

Introduction

1.01 This chapter sets out in brief, summarised form the elements of a claim in defamation and the available defences. Alternative dispute resolution and funding are also considered at the conclusion of the chapter. All of these matters are dealt with in greater detail throughout the course of the book.

What is a defamatory publication?

1.02 A claimant is defamed if words are published about him which tend to lower him in the estimation of right thinking members of society generally[1].

1   *Sim v Stretch* [1936] 2 All ER 1237 at 1240, per Lord Atkin.

Libel or slander?

1.03 Publication of defamatory material in writing or some other permanent form is a libel; publication in spoken words or some other transitory form constitutes a slander.

In the case of a libel, the law presumes that the publication complained of has caused damage, but that is not the position in slander (with certain exceptions).

Burdens of proof

1.04 The claimant must show that the material of which he complains:

(a)   is defamatory of him;
(b)   refers to him;
(c)   has been published to a third person.

There are two important presumptions which tend to benefit a claim-ant in a claim for defamation:

(a)   he is presumed to be of good reputation, by which it follows that the defamatory material is presumed to be untrue and the defendant must prove otherwise;
(b)   it is presumed the material has caused him damage – he does not have to prove that it does.

Defences

1.05   If it is claimed that a publication has defamed a claimant then there are a number of defences which the prospective defendant can utilise to try to defeat the claim. These can broadly be divided into two categories:

(a)   technical defences – which address the question of whether or not the essential ingredients for a claim in defamation are satisfied;
(b)   legal defences – where the ingredients for a claim are present and correct, then the law recognises various defences which, if any one is made out, then the claimant's claim will fail. These range from the obvious (the words complained of were true) to the obscure (volenti non fit injuria).

The defences to a defamation claim are dealt with in detail later in this book[1], but they can be summarised as follows.

1   See Chapters 11–16.

Technical defences

The words complained of are not defamatory of the claimant

1.06   If the words complained of do not lower the claimant in the estimation of right thinking members of society generally, then no cause of action accrues.

The words complained of do not refer to the claimant

1.07   If the claimant is not named and no picture of him appears, he will have to demonstrate that the words complained of are about him.

Evidence from witnesses who saw the publication and who, independently, without it being drawn to their attention, understood it to refer to the claimant will be needed.

The words complained of were not published to a third party

1.08 In other words, you can make the most appallingly libelous allegations about someone to whom you are writing a letter, but if that letter is addressed to the target of your allegations and read only by him, then he has no cause of action in defamation against you (within the jurisdiction of England and Wales at any rate).

Legal defences

Limitation

1.09 The Defamation Act 1996 (DeA 1996), s 5 amends the Limitation Act 1980 (LA 1980), s 4A in so far as it relates to defamation (and malicious falsehood) actions, which means no action may be brought 'after one year from the date on which the cause of action accrued'. Note that the court is given a discretion to exclude the time limit under the amended section 32A of the LA 1980 'if it appears to the court that it would be equitable to allow an action to proceed'.

Note also that the limitation period remains three years in Scotland.

Innocent dissemination

1.10 This was introduced by the DeA 1996, s 1. The effect of the statute is to remove from liability for a defamatory publication some of those who previously found themselves caught within the liability loop but who did not themselves bear any responsibility for the defamatory nature of the publication. If you are not the author or editor of the words complained of (eg a printer, distributor or retailer), you took reasonable care in relation to its publication, and you did not know and had no reason to believe that what you did caused or contributed to the publication of a defamatory statement, then you can avail yourself of the protection of this defence.

It is this defence which tries to deal with the relatively new and burgeoning area of libel on the Internet and in electronic media

3

generally, something which may have been bolstered by the freedom of expression provisions of the Human Rights Act 1998 (HRA 1998)[1].

1 See Appendix 5.

Justification

1.11 If the words complained of are true then the defendant has a complete defence to a claim in defamation. The burden of proving them to be true falls on the defendant, the public policy view being if you are not sure of your facts, then do not publish. The defendant's position is eased somewhat by the requirement that only the 'sting' of the libel need be proved to be true and errors in more peripheral facts will not necessarily be fatal to the defence.

Fair comment

1.12 This defence is traditionally summarised as 'fair comment made in good faith and without malice on a matter of public interest'. In other words, this defence protects the expression of honestly held expressions of opinion on matters of public concern. It does not just apply to the 'why oh why' columns which pepper newspapers; it is available to any one as long as the criteria are satisfied. Taxi drivers and pub philosophers have the same entitlement as Anne Robinson and Richard Littlejohn. The separate elements of the defence are important, however, and the defendant must:

(a) persuade the court the subject matter was a matter of public interest;
(b) prove the expression of the opinion was based on a true factual background;
(c) satisfy the jury that the comment was an opinion an honest minded person could make on the facts. 'Honest comment' would be a more accurate title for the defence because fairness is not actually a requirement;
(d) not have acted maliciously – in other words, not have expressed his comments dishonestly and with the dominant or sole motive of harming the claimant.

Absolute privilege

1.13 This is a complete defence which is necessary to enable society to function. There have to be occasions where people can say precisely what they want without any fear of legal action regardless of how extreme, damaging or malicious their words may be. The following are the main categories of absolute privilege:

(a)   statements made in the course of Parliamentary proceedings;
(b)   statements made in the course of judicial proceedings (which includes certain communications between lawyers and their clients);
(c)   statements made in the course of state proceedings;
(d)   statements of other public officials, protected by statute;
(e)   fair and accurate reports of Parliamentary proceedings published contemporaneously;
(f)   fair and accurate reports of judicial proceedings published contemporaneously;
(g)   other occasions where absolute privilege is extended for public policy reasons – eg actions based on material acquired as part of the disclosure process in litigation tend to fail on this basis.

Qualified privilege

1.14   Qualified privilege is the most flexible and disputatious defence in the defamation canon. As with absolute privilege, it sets out to protect certain occasions of publication from successful actions in defamation, but, unlike absolute privilege, a qualified privilege defence can be defeated by showing the defendant was actuated by express malice. The defence exists for 'the common convenience and welfare of society'[1] and it is the occasion on which the words are published which is protected, not the communication itself[2]. It is a defence which arouses strong emotions both among those who wish to advance freedom of expression and those who wish to place some limits on the propensity of some parts of the media to shoot first and ask questions later. This is because in essence it protects untrue publications (if they were true, the defence of justification could be used), and the definition of the borders where protection does or does not apply is contested in numerous applications in defamation actions.

The formidable technical and legal issues which can and do arise in the application of this defence are dealt with later in this book[3]. At this point, it will suffice merely to set out the broad classifications of qualified privilege occasions:

(a)   statements made in pursuance of a legal, moral or social duty;

(b)   statements made in the protection or furtherance of an interest, either private or public;

(c)   statements made in the protection of a common interest;

(d)   fair and accurate reports of Parliamentary proceedings, whether or not published contemporaneously;

(e)   fair and accurate reports of judicial proceedings, whether or not published contemporaneously;

(f)   statements published by virtue of the DeA 1996, s 15, either without explanation or contradiction (Part I) or subject to explanation or contradiction (Part II) (as provided by Schedule 1 to the DeA 1996).

The most important case on qualified privilege in recent years was *Reynolds v Times Newspapers Ltd*[4], in which the House of Lords took the opportunity to set out ten factors or circumstances which should be taken into account by the courts in determining whether an occasion attracts qualified privilege. The judgment seemed to nudge judicial sympathy toward publishers and, in particular, the media, in the three key areas of investigative journalism, reporting journalism and opinion journalism. What has emerged in decisions since *Reynolds* is that the court will examine closely the quality of the investigation which led to the publication and that will influence its approach to qualified privilege. However, the court's distaste for over the top tabloid journalism remains undiminished – as the Court of Appeal judgment in *Grobbelaar v News Group Newspapers Ltd*[5] clearly demonstrated. Even when the Court was prepared to take the virtually unprecedented step of overturning the jury's verdict of *Grobbelaar*[6], it was not prepared to rule in favour of *The Sun* in relation to qualified privilege in respect of its coverage of the Grobbelaar allegations.

There is nothing to suggest that qualified privilege will not continue to be the area of defamation which taxes lawyers and which baffles clients more than any other.

1   *Toogood v Spyring* (1834) 1 Cr M & R 181 at 193, per Parle B.
2   *Adam v Ward* [1917] AC 309 at 348, HL, per Lord Shaw.
3   See Chapter 15.
4   [2001] 2 AC 127.
5   [2001] EWCA Civ 33, [2001] 2 All ER 437.
6   The House of Lords has recently given judgment in this case, reinstating the jury's verdict but substituting damages of £1.00 for the jury award of £85,000.

Offer to make amends

1.15   This is embodied in the DeA 1996[1] and gives an opportunity to a defendant who has got it wrong to put their hands up at an early stage, with what is intended to be a consequent saving of time and costs. It came into force on 20 February 2000.

A defendant making an offer to make amends must include proposals for a correction and apology and the manner of its publication, compensation and costs. If the offer is accepted then the claimant cannot bring or continue proceedings. If he disputes the terms then the redress is an application to a judge, who can determine the level of damages taking into account the adequacy or otherwise of the correction and apology which has been offered or published.

If proceedings are issued because the offer is rejected then the defendant must either stick to the offer to make amends as his only defence, or abandon the offer and plead one of the other defences.

It was perceived in the past that a hard-nosed claimant with a cast iron case could bully a defendant by ignoring pre-action concessions of error and proposals to settle and plough on with proceedings which led to the payment of higher damages and costs than were merited in order to stop litigation where the defendant had no realistic defence to a claim. The offer to make amends, especially combined with a well-judged CPR Pt 36 offer, can put real pressure on a claimant with the prospect of adverse costs consequences if he ignores what is on offer and insists on litigation.

1   The DeA 1996, ss 2–4.

Res judicata

1.16   A claimant cannot bring a successful action if judgment has already been given in respect of the issues between the same parties. In other words, a claimant cannot sue twice on the same publication.

Volenti non fit injuria

1.17   If the claimant has provided the material to the defendant with permission to publish, he cannot then sue for defamation on it. In other words, if you have consented to publication, you cannot then recover damages for defamatory allegations contained therein.

Accord and satisfaction

1.18 If the defendant can prove that the claimant has surrendered his cause of action in exchange for valid consideration or a document executed under seal then that provides a complete defence. This may be somewhat obscure, but beware the claimant suing a number of defendants who brokers a deal with one intending to pursue the others. The common law rule is that a cause of action is indivisible and so there is a risk that letting one defendant off the hook could discharge all the others from liability as well[1].

1   *Duck v Mayeu* [1892] 2 QB 511, CA; *Cutler v McPhail* [1962] 2 All ER 474.

Vulgar abuse

1.19 This is not technically a separate defence but an aspect of meaning. However, it tends to be treated as a defence so it is worth mentioning it in this context. If the words complained of are clearly recognisable as hot tempered abuse, and the reasonable person to whom they were published would have recognised them as such, then a defamation (in this case almost always a slander) action will fail. The legal point is that a right thinking member of society would not think less of a claimant who was simply on the receiving end of a torrent of abuse.

Judge and jury

1.20 Unusually, despite being civil actions, defamation trials are generally held before a judge and jury. At trial, the judge's role is to determine questions of law and the jury's role is to determine questions of fact. A critical issue in defamation cases is frequently what the words complained of mean. The judge decides whether the words are capable of bearing the meanings which the parties attribute to them, and the jury decides what meaning the words in fact bear.

Remedies

1.21 Historically, the law recognised only two ways in which a claimant can be compensated for the damage caused to his reputation by defamatory material:

(a)   an injunction to prevent repetition or republication of the words complained of; and
(b)   damages to reflect the damage caused.

The jury determines the level of damages awarded to a claimant following guidance from the judge and persuasion from the advocates for the parties.

The level of jury awards has caused controversy in the past, and has been the subject of much criticism by the media (which is most directly affected by high jury awards). The most telling criticism was the inconsistency of jury awards, particularly where household name celebrities were concerned. Awards to 'stars' seemed to occupy a different universe to the sums awarded to less well-known litigants. These concerns resulted in the Court of Appeal issuing judgments containing guidelines about the amount of damages which were appropriate in defamation cases. For example, in *Elton John v Mirror Group Newspapers Ltd*[1], it was held that juries could be directed to awards approved or made by the Court of Appeal, and it raised the previous prohibition on comparisons being made to damages in personal injury cases. It also allowed counsel and the judge to indicate what an appropriate award of damages might be in the event of a finding for the claimant.

The Court of Appeal's willingness to intervene in the verdicts reached by juries in defamation cases reached its most dramatic conclusion in *Grobbelaar v News Group Newspapers Ltd*[2], when it overturned the jury's verdict in favour of the former Liverpool goalkeeper against *The Sun*, describing it as 'an affront to justice' and 'a miscarriage of justice which this court can and must correct'. On appeal to the House of Lords, the jury verdict in favour of Mr Grobbelaar was reinstated but his damages were reduced to £1.00 (from £85,000).

The DeA 1996[3] introduced provisions for the summary disposal of defamation actions before a judge alone. The judge's powers under these provisions go well beyond those of a jury. The judge can award summary relief, which can include:

(a)   a declaration that the statement was false and defamatory of the claimant;
(b)   an order that the defendant publish or cause to be published a suitable correction and apology;
(c)   damages not exceeding £10,000;
(d)   an order restraining the defendant from publishing or further publishing the material complained of.

In addition, if the parties cannot agree on the terms of publication of the apology, the judge can intervene and give directions[4].

A party can apply for summary disposal at any stage of the proceedings.

1   [1996] 2 All ER 35.
2   [2001] EWCA Civ 33, [2001] 2 All ER 437.
3   The DeA 1996, ss 8–10.
4   The DeA 1996, s 9.

Alternative dispute resolution

1.22 Lord Woolf was quoted as saying a year or so after the implementation of the Civil Procedure Rules 1998, which were born from his Access to Justice civil review, that trials are a breakdown in the civil process.

The concept of the pre-action protocol was an important cornerstone of the CPR. It was hoped and intended that in every area of civil litigation a framework and procedure could be established to govern and guide the pre-action exchanges between parties. A defamation pre-action protocol was implemented in October 2000, and includes a requirement for parties to consider, as part of the pre-action steps, whether there are alternative means of resolving their dispute than litigation. If parties launch straight into proceedings, then the courts may punish them with punitive costs orders at a later stage. The civil litigation culture has been changed and parties, however aggrieved they may be, cannot ignore this fact.

Before the present Labour Government was re-elected in May 2001, its spokesmen indicated its intentions to continue the programme of legal reform started in its first term. One imagines this will inevitably include the continuing development, refinement and encouragement of alternative dispute resolution ('ADR').

Funding

1.23 Legal aid has never been available for defamation and nothing is going to change that situation.

Consequently, the most important development in the area of litigation funding has been the availability of conditional fee arrangements ('CFAs'). The legislative history of CFAs began with the Court and Legal Services Act 1990 (CLSA 1990), which came into force in 1995. In 1998, CFAs were extended from personal injury, insolvency and human rights claims. In 1999, the Access to Justice Act (AJA 1999) was passed and relevant rules of court and practice directions came into force in July 2000.

If the CFA complies with the Conditional Fee Agreement Regulations 1995 and 2000, then no risk of 'maintenance' arises. However, it is essential that a CFA be in the right form, because all other contingent fees are either unlawful or unenforceable. The indemnity principle is not dead and perhaps inevitably this has spawned a new area of satellite litigation.

A CFA will normally provide that if the claimant succeeds in his claim, then his solicitors will be entitled to recover their fees in the normal way from the defendant together with a success fee of up to 100%. However, if the claim is unsuccessful, the claimant will not be required to pay his solicitor/client fees – although he will still be liable for his disbursements and for his opponent's costs and disbursements (if subject to an adverse costs order).

A CFA can be backed with insurance which, for example, will protect against the risk of paying your opponent's costs. If successful, the insurance premium can be recovered from the defendant.

Insurance (which is routine in personal injury claims conducted on CFAs) has proved less attractive in defamation because the cost of premiums has been prohibitively expensive – between 15% and 40% of the sum to be insured. A fully contested defamation action which goes all the way to trial can easily generate legal costs of more than £1 million. The arithmetic for the costs of a premium on that basis explains why insurance is still the exception rather than the rule in defamation.

1.24 The availability of CFAs still leaves a potential defamation claimant with a very difficult decision to make before deciding to take action against, for example, a well-resourced media organisation. If the action is defended and goes to trial, and the costs on each side are, say, £500,000, then if the claimant loses, even with the benefit of a CFA which protects him from paying his solicitors' costs, he still faces liability for his counsel's fees and other disbursements (which may represent, say, £150,000 if counsel is not also on a CFA) and his opponent's costs and disbursements. Many claimants may feel that going under with a liability of £650,000 is little different in its consequences than going under for £1 million. The bottom line is still that you should not start a defamation action unless the advice you have received on the merits and prospects of success is extremely positive. It means that the availability of CFAs has not led (and will not lead) to a huge increase in frivolous defamation actions.

Note that CFAs are also possible with one's counsel, if the barrister is willing, and that involves a further contractual arrangement (between solicitor and counsel) which needs careful scrutiny and consideration.

Details of the utmost importance in preparing a CFA include defining precisely what a 'win' means and what success fee should be applied.

The critical process within the solicitor's office is that of risk assessment. Getting it wrong is expensive for all concerned.

What increases the problems in defamation is that risk assessment must somehow assimilate the unpredictable 'X' factor which is a jury. It explains why defamation solicitors will rarely rate even the best case as having a higher than 75% prospect of success. In other words, if you take four excellent defamation cases to trial, you are likely to lose one of them! It is this which also helps to explain the high insurance premiums in the defamation market.

Chapter 2

The ingredients of a prima facie case

2.01 This chapter deals with the three essential ingredients of a claim for defamation: reference, defamatory meaning and publication. The three essential ingredients of a claim in defamation are:

(a) Were the words published about the claimant?
(b) Are the words defamatory?
(c) Were the words published to a third party?

These were mentioned at the very start of this book but it is now time to consider each of these elements in more detail. If any one of these elements is missing, the claimant has no claim for defamation.

Reference/identification: were the words published about the claimant?

2.02 The prospective defamation claimant must be identifiable as the person defamed in the words he complains of. It does not matter whether he is named or not in the words complained of provided he is identifiable from those words. The test is: 'Are [the words] such as would reasonably lead persons acquainted with the claimant to believe that he was the person referred to?'[1].

1 *Syme v Canavan* (1918) 25 CLR at 238, per Isaacs J.

Considerations where the claimant is referred to by name

2.03 If the claimant is referred to by name then he has been defamed to all persons who read the words complained of. Issues such as whether or not they actually knew of him or would be able to recognise him if they passed him in the street are completely irrelevant.

Where the claimant is identified by name, he is not required to plead facts and matters which prove that readers understood the words to refer to him, even if he is not the intended subject of the publication. However, the preceding statement is subject to two caveats. First, where the group of defamed persons is large, for example where the subject of the publication is 'John Smith', the law will not permit the claimant to maintain an action for defamation unless he does plead facts and matters establishing that readers understood the words to refer to him, as opposed to any of the many other John Smiths. Second, where the defamation is unintentional, the defendant may plead facts and matters to establish that in fact no reasonable reader understood the words to refer to the claimant. In such a case, the claimant would again be well advised to plead particulars of reference.

Considerations where the claimant is not referred to by name

2.04 Where the claimant is not referred to by name the particulars of claim should set out every fact and matter in support of the contention that ordinary sensible readers or any portion of them would be of the opinion that the words complained of referred to him.

In cases where the claimant does not allege that all readers understood the words to refer to him, but that only some of them did, he will in theory only be permitted to recover damages for publication to those persons.

Other matters of general importance on reference

2.05 It is important to note that the question of whether or not the words complained of identified the claimant is one for the jury – it is not technically necessary for the claimant to call witnesses who read the words and identified him from them. Having said that, it would be folly of a high order not to call a selection of 'reference' witnesses where one is acting for a claimant in a defamation claim who was not actually named or pictured in the publication sued upon. A jury lives in the real, not the technical, world!

In every case where identification is in issue, if reasonable people would reasonably believe that the words referred to the claimant, then the publisher will not escape liability even if he tried to disguise reference by using initials or asterisks or a fictitious name or some other subterfuge. The publisher's intention is irrelevant, so even if he selected a fictitious name or other device in an attempt to avoid defaming anyone he will still be liable if in fact he did inadvertently refer to someone who then brought a claim.

Experience suggests that whether or not the claimant is named in a defamatory publication seems to make little difference to the level of damages awarded by a jury if the action goes to trial. Perhaps a jury accepts that litigation is unlikely to have got so far if something as basic as identification is still a real issue. However, whether or not the claimant is named invariably plays an important part in settlement negotiations about damages and is always put forward as a mitigating factor by the defendant's lawyers.

Reference witnesses should be able to give clear and unequivocal evidence that they read the article (or saw the programme) and, without prompting, independently recognised that it referred to the claimant. If the witness can only say that the article was brought to his attention, perhaps with the words 'Have you seen this article about X?' then he cannot give reference evidence. If identification is an issue, then make sure that appropriate evidence is obtained before any claim is made against the publisher. Normally one would expect to plead reference witnesses where the claimant is not named in the words complained of.

If the only reference witnesses are family or friends of the claimant, that does not render their evidence any less valid. There is frequently an implication from defendants in libel actions that reference evidence from friends and family carries less weight than evidence from witnesses less close to the claimant – presumably on the basis that the love of friends and family is such that they will disregard the most appalling slurs made against their friend or relative. The counter-argument of course is that friends and family are in fact the people with whom a claimant's reputation is most precious.

The meaning of the word defamatory: are the words defamatory?

2.06   The traditional test of what is a defamatory allegation is one which tends 'to lower the claimant in the estimation of right thinking members of society generally'[1].

Other classic tests are whether the words would 'injure the reputation of another by exposing him to hatred, contempt or ridicule'[2] and whether the words are ones 'which cause a person to be shunned or avoided'[3].

The fact that these definitions derive from fairly ancient cases and yet are accepted as serviceable for today's purposes bear out the American advice 'if it ain't broke don't fix it'. No phrase which encapsulates the concept of what is a defamatory publication in a more succinct or quotable way has emerged in the last 60 years or so, which means we are stuck with these trusty war horses.

Assessing whether or not a publication is defamatory is usually straightforward – and if it is not then one must be extremely cautious about proceeding with a libel claim. However vehemently your client presses his claim, the fact is that if you cannot really see the defamatory imputation then if the action is not struck out on the way, the jury will probably wonder what all the fuss is about.

It is not always straightforward to determine whether an allegation is defamatory. In those cases there is no substitute for experience and it is better to incur the cost of an advice from libel counsel at this stage than to bash on and hope for the best, leaving your client with a huge bill when the case collapses in ruins somewhere down the line. If the claimant wants you to act under a conditional fee agreement, an advice on merits and prospects of success is an essential part of your risk assessment process and only claims with an extremely good likelihood of success should progress.

EXAMPLE: A woman police constable seeks advice on an article headlined 'Drive on Drink', which reads as follows:

'Nobody approves of drinking and driving these days – and most people are careful.

But there's a new woman PC with a beat in the Dales – and she frightened the whole community. Legend has it that she now pulls at least one foolhardy over-imbiber every night. So, on Xmas Eve would you believe one hostelry which is normally packed could only manage to attract four customers.

And now she is rumoured to have stopped a teetotal Methodist minister. So if you fancy a drink in the Dales, be warned – luv!'

The woman police officer is the only new woman police constable in the Dales area and this article has upset her and she has been experiencing a lot of mickey-taking from work colleagues. Does she have a claim? The advice given was that she did not, because right thinking members of society would not think less of a police officer who was being accused of being over-zealous in the performance of her duties in cracking down on drink-driving. However, if she had been accused of over-zealousness in the performance of her duties in some other aspect of a police officer's job, the advice might well have been different.

1   *Sim v Stretch* [1936] 2 All ER 1237.
2   *Parmiter v Coupland* (1840) 6 M & W 105.
3   *Youssoupoff v MGM Pictures Ltd* (1934) 50 TLR 581.

2.07   Be wary of ancient (and even relatively recent) case law when taking a view on whether a publication is defamatory. For example, there is much historical authority to suggest that an imputation of homosexuality is defamatory. Whether contemporary right thinking members of society would think less of someone against whom such an imputation has been made is an open, and as yet untested, question. The general view is that it would not be, and lawyers have in recent years circumvented any potential problem by pleading an innuendo meaning[1] to the effect that the words imputed hypocrisy or deceit, because the claimant held himself out to be heterosexual.

When assessing whether material is defamatory, practitioners should always have at the forefront of their minds the fact that the test of whether a publication is defamatory depends on the view that right thinking members of society would take of the claimant. Therefore, for example, a claimant who complains that his reputation amongst members of the criminal underworld has been damaged as a result of the publication has no actionable claim for defamation.

Another consideration is that words published about the claimant which are not defamatory in themselves may become defamatory because of their context. If, for example, a big splash headline on page 4 of a tabloid newspapers reads 'Golden boy of business caught snorting coke in vice raid' but does not name the offender and a box in the corner of that page reports the latest business exploits of a top businessman noted for his principled approach to business matters, that businessman may well have an action for libel against the newspaper.

1   See Chapter 3, paragraphs 3.06–3.07.

Publication: were the words published to a third party?

2.08   The third essential element for a claim in defamation is that the defamatory allegation or act must have been read, heard or seen by someone other than the maker of the allegation and the subject of the allegation. The third party must also have communicated to him the defamatory 'sting' of the words or actions.

What this means is that if you receive a sealed letter making the most appalling untrue allegations about you then you have no claim in defamation against the writer of the letter because you have suffered no injury to your reputation. (The fundamental principle of the law of defamation is that one should be allowed to seek redress at the law if one's reputation has been unfairly attacked and your reputation is the opinion held of you by others not by yourself.) In *Sadgrove v Hole*[1] the court held that defamatory allegations written on a postcard sent to the subject of the allegations had been published because the writing was visible to everyone through whose hands the card passed.

Burden of proof: The claimant merely has to prove facts from which it can be reasonably inferred that the words complained of were brought to the attention of a third party. He does not have to prove that the allegations were brought to the actual attention of a third party.

1   [1901] 2 KB 1.

Unintentional publication

2.09   The defendant will be liable even if the defamatory material was published unintentionally if he is unable to demonstrate that he took sufficient care to prevent publication. If he can show that publication was unintentional and that he took sufficient care, then he will not be liable for the publication, eg a defendant would escape liability for defamatory allegations made in a diary which someone reads without permission when the diary was kept in a drawer by the defendant's bed.

Liability for publication

2.10   Section 1 of the DeA 1996 has addressed the question of responsibility for publication. Previously, liability for publication arose from any involvement in, or authorising of, the publication process. This meant, in respect of a newspaper article, the following participants might have been potentially liable if that article made defamatory allegations: journalist, features/news editor, editor, publisher, printer, distributor, newsagent and the man on the corner selling the paper from his box to workers returning home. Some of those are fairly included in the loop of liability, but it was always felt unjust that some of the others were potentially liable for the contents of an article in respect of which they had played no part in writing or authorising and which they did not even read and, indeed, may not even have been aware of. The DeA 1996, s 1 seeks to introduce a new statutory defence of innocent dissemination. Quite apart from rectifying what was seen by many as an unfairness, the DeA 1996 had to do something to deal with an area of publication which is assuming enormous importance – the Internet (and electronic mail generally).

Republication

2.11 The law on this is straightforward: 'Every republication of a libel is a new libel, and each publisher is answerable for his act to the same extent as if the calumny originated with him'[1].

This makes sense: if this was not the case then a claimant would be bound to sue only the first publisher of a defamatory allegation and subsequent publishers could defame him with impunity. An unpleasant libel which appeared in a small circulation specialist magazine read by a small number which was picked up by a mass-circulation tabloid would lead to the unfortunate claimant suing only the magazine while the tabloid escaped liability even though its republication probably caused far greater damage to the claimant's reputation.

However, the victim of republication does have a choice. Either he can sue the republisher, or he can sue the original publisher and seek to make him liable for the republication as the natural and probable result of the original publication. In theory he could sue every publisher, but because of the rule against double recovery this will seldom be advisable. Whether the republication was the natural and probable result is governed by the ordinary principles of the law of tort on causation and remoteness of damage. The route chosen by the claimant will inevitably depend upon the identities of the respective publishers, the depth of their pockets, and issues such as whether the original publication or indeed the republication is, or is likely, to be protected by any defence of privilege[2].

1   *Morse v Times-Republican Co* 124 Iowa R at 717 (1904). This gives rise to the rule against repetition, or the repetition rule, which requires republishers to defend the statement as if it were they who first made it. They are prohibited from relying on asserting that they were merely repeating the statement of another.
2   As to which see Chapters 14 and 15.

Chapter 3

Form and meaning

3.01 This chapter deals with issues arising from the form of the publication complained of and the defamatory meaning which the publication is said to convey.

Analysing the publication

3.02 Analysing the publication is the first – and in some ways the most important – job for the legal adviser. You will be concerning yourself with two questions initially:

(a)   What form is the publication in?
(b)   What does it mean?

Form of the publication

3.03 Normally defamatory allegations are published in words – either spoken or written. However, there are many other activities or objects which can constitute a defamatory publication. For example, photographs, pictures, cartoons, signs, gestures and effigies have all been held capable of conveying a defamatory meaning, so do not dismiss a potential claim simply because it has not been spoken or written. A good example (in an unreported case) was an incident in which a woman in her local supermarket (where she was well known) was intercepted while leaving the shop by security guards and frog-marched to a back office where she was accused of having stolen some meat pies. These actions, published as they were to other shoppers in the supermarket at the time, clearly constituted a slander. A claim was made, and settled by the supermarket. The important thing is to bear in mind at all times the three essential elements of a claim in defamation – that the words or actions were published about the claimant, that they were published to a third party, and that they were defamatory of her.

Meaning

Natural and ordinary meaning

3.04 The natural and ordinary meaning of the words (or other publication) complained of is the meaning which the words would be reasonably understood to bear by ordinary people using their general knowledge and common sense. An example is the allegation that Hitler was a brutal dictator responsible for countless deaths. The meaning of these words is plain and obvious on their face.

The natural and ordinary meaning includes 'any implication or inference which a reasonable reader guided not by any special, but only by general, knowledge and not fettered by any strict legal rules of construction would draw from the words'[1]. Laymen (and lawyers) often mistake inference for innuendo (which is discussed at paragraph 3.06 below). An example of a statement which gives rise to an inference would be that 'X has a surprisingly lavish lifestyle for an accounts clerk', which may infer that X is embezzling. It should also be noted that the meaning intended by the publisher is irrelevant to the legal definition of meaning (although it may well be relevant to the question of damages).

When deciding what might be inferred or implied from words complained of, the court has in mind the typical reader who has been described as 'the reasonable man of normal intelligence, possessed of such a high degree of knowledge of the current circumstances as it may be proper to infer in the circumstances of the case'[2]. It is accepted that ordinary people do not read words in the same way as lawyers and that their capacity for implication is much greater – particularly where the words are derogatory.

1   *Jones v Skelton* [1963] 1 WLR 1362 at 1371, per Lord Morris.
2   *Holdsworth v Associated Press* [1937] 53 TLR 1029 at 1033, per Scott LJ.

3.05 The case which came to be regarded as the leading case on meaning is *Rubber Improvement Ltd v Daily Telegraph*[1]. It is certainly the case the bones of which are most often picked over in applications made prior to trial for rulings on meaning. In that case, the newspaper had published a report that the City of London Fraud Squad was investigating the affairs of R Co and that Lewis was the chairman of the company. Lewis and R Co brought libel proceedings, claiming the report meant they were guilty (or at least suspected by the Fraud Squad to be guilty) of fraud. The House of Lords held that while the words were defamatory they were not capable of meaning the claimants were guilty of fraud but could mean that they were suspected of fraud. The ordinary reasonable reader would not conclude guilt because one who did would be unduly suspicious or unfair in his approach, and therefore unreasonable.

Burden of proof: Where the words complained of are defamatory in their natural and ordinary meaning, the claimant is now required to plead the meaning or meanings which he alleges the words conveyed, and so technically must prove this as well as their publication[2]. It is then up to the defendant to plead and prove from the circumstances in which the words were used, or the manner of their publication, or other facts known to those to whom the words were published, that the words would not be understood by the reasonable reader to convey the imputation which a straightforward reading of the words would convey. For example, the defendant might assert that the words were understood by everyone to whom they were published as a joke, perhaps if the words were published in a television comedy programme. The defendant's task is to satisfy the jury that reasonable people who read or heard the words would not understand them to bear the meaning claimed[3].

1   [1964] AC 234.
2   CPR Pt 53 PD, para 2.3(1)(a).
3   See also paragraph 3.08 below.

Innuendo meaning

3.06 The law of defamation recognises that some words have technical or slang meanings which depend on some special knowledge possessed not by the general public but by a limited number of persons. It also recognises that ordinary words can sometimes bear a special meaning other than their natural and ordinary meaning because of some extrinsic fact or circumstance. The words are then said to carry an innuendo.

A claimant seeking to rely on an innuendo meaning has to plead and prove the facts or circumstances including, where appropriate, the technical terms which give the words a special meaning which is to be found not in the words themselves, not based on the general knowledge of the ordinary man, but which depend on facts and circumstances known only to some persons or some classes of persons giving the words an innuendo meaning[1].

EXAMPLE: A photograph was published on 21 April 1992 in a local newspaper showing a queue of people waiting to buy tickets for Leicester City v Cambridge United – a key promotion clash. On 30 April 1992, the same photograph was published again (in error), this time captioned 'On Queue: the City faithful queue outside Filbert Street for tickets to Saturday's big match against Newcastle'.

X was a police officer who worked in plain clothes, largely under his own supervision, while on duty. He queued for tickets for the Leicester v Cambridge game and his face was clearly visible in the photograph which appeared in the local newspaper.

However, the only time he could have queued to purchase tickets for the Leicester v Newcastle game was when he should have been on duty. When the photograph of the queue for the earlier game was wrongly republished purporting to show the queue for the Newcastle game, his police colleagues saw the photo, saw X's face in the queue and taunted him for skiving off his police duties to buy tickets for the big game. Copies of the photo were pinned on various station noticeboards with appropriately derogatory captions.

X pursued a claim against the local newspaper in libel and a swift settlement including damages, an apology and costs was secured.

This is a graphic example of an innuendo meaning. The newspaper had made a mistake and had no intention to defame X. The republication of the photo captioned as it was only conveyed a defamatory meaning to those individuals who not only knew X but also knew that he could only have queued for the Newcastle game when he was on duty. Anyone else seeing the photo would not only have seen nothing defamatory in it concerning X but could never have guessed what defamatory content the photo might have had in respect of X.

1   See CPR Pt 53 PD, para 2.3(1)(b) and 2.3(2).

3.07 The group of people to whom an innuendo meaning is conveyed does not have to be as small as in the example above – it could include virtually every member of the population and still remain an innuendo meaning. For example, a gossip column could publish of a politician that he has been as loyal to his wife as was the Prince of Wales to his. Just about every adult member of the population in the jurisdiction would know that the Prince of Wales had admitted to adultery during his marriage and so would understand the innuendo meaning of the comment.

Important points to remember are:

- a claimant relying on an innuendo meaning only has to show that some of the people to whom the words were published knew the facts;
- a claimant cannot rely on facts or circumstances occurring or becoming known after publication to support an innuendo meaning;
- a claimant does not have to show that any person knowing the special facts or circumstances actually understood the words complained of to be defamatory (and indeed would not be permitted to call evidence to that effect);
- (as pointed out in the example above) a defendant need not know the facts giving the words their special meaning;
- where an innuendo meaning is pleaded and proved, the claimant cannot recover damages for all publications, but only those publications to persons who had the knowledge from which the innuendo meaning was divined.

The converse of innuendo meaning is that it is open to a defendant to rely on extrinsic facts to show that words defamatory in their natural and ordinary meaning did not in fact convey a defamatory meaning, or conveyed a lesser defamatory meaning[1] to those to whom they were published. Such a meaning is known as a 'reverse innuendo meaning'. However, to do so, the defendant must demonstrate that every person to whom the words were published understood those special facts.

Burden of proof: The onus is on the claimant to show there were extrinsic facts or circumstances known to one or more of the people to whom the words were published which would mean the words conveyed the defamatory imputation he relies upon to a reasonable person with that knowledge. As mentioned previously, he need not prove that anyone actually understood the words in the sense he claims.

1   Which he will then seek to defend as justification or fair comment. As to which, see Chapters 12 and 13.

Deciding the question of meaning

3.08   A defamation action is generally tried before a judge and jury and the question of meaning is divided between the two. The judge decides whether the words are capable of bearing the meaning alleged by the claimant. The jury then decides whether the words actually bear that meaning. No evidence can be adduced by either party as to what the words mean. Where innuendo meanings are pleaded, witnesses may be called to give evidence of their knowledge of the special facts relied upon, but those witnesses are not permitted to give evidence about what they understood the words to mean. In summing up, the judge will simply ask the jury to apply the test: what meaning (or meanings) would the words convey to ordinary reasonable persons? This really boils down to asking the jury what it thinks the words complained of mean.

If meaning is disputed

3.09 If the meaning of the words complained of is in real dispute, then either party (though usually this will be the defendant) may apply to the court for a ruling on meaning[1]. CPR Pt 53 PD, para 4 provides that the court may at any time decide whether a statement complained of is capable of having any meaning attributed to it in a statement of case, and/or whether the statement is capable of being defamatory of the claimant, and/or whether the statement is capable of bearing any other meaning defamatory of the claimant[2]. Paragraph 4.2 of the Practice Direction provides that an application for a ruling on meaning may be made at any time after the service of the particulars of claim. However, it also says that such an application should be made promptly. Any failure to do so is likely to be penalised in costs. Though the Civil Procedure Rules appear to permit such an application to be made to a Master, because a ruling on meaning is substantive and binds the trial judge, it is advisable to ask for the application to be released by the Master to be listed before the judge in charge of the jury list. Following a ruling on meaning the court may exercise its power under CPR 3.4 (power to strike out a statement of case)[3]. The litigant should also be aware that the Civil Procedure Rules permit the court to rule on meaning on its own initiative, although experience has shown that such proactive behaviour, provided for elsewhere in the Civil Procedure Rules, is very rare indeed. *Mapp v News Group Newspapers Ltd*[4] is a useful starting point for any party considering making such an application.

The CPR provisions are the direct result of the courts' clear reluctance to allow meaning disputes to become long-running sagas. In *Hinduja v Asia TV Ltd*[5], Lord Justice Hirst said of the immediate predecessor to CPR Pt 53 PD, para 4[6]: 'This rule is intended to lay

25

down a swift and inexpensive procedure in chambers to eliminate meanings which the words are plainly incapable of bearing'.

This view was adjusted somewhat in *Geenty v Channel Four Television Corpn*[7], where Lord Justice Hirst conceded that the Court of Appeal should be more prepared to interfere with a judgment which has ruled out a meaning for once and for all than a judgment which has preserved a pleaded meaning so leaving it to the jury to make the final decision.

1   See Chapter 22.
2   Note that the DeA 1996, s 7 prohibits the previous practice of asking the court to rule on whether words were arguably capable, as opposed to capable, of bearing a particular meaning or meanings.
3   CPR Pt 53 PD, para 4.4 (see Appendix 4).
4   [1997] EMLR 397.
5   [1998] EMLR 516.
6   CPR Sch 1, RSC Ord 82 r 3A.
7   [1998] EMLR 524, CA.

3.10 The consensus is that the introduction of the concept of proportionality in the Civil Procedure Rules has added weight to the desire of the courts to discourage appeals against meaning rulings made by judges. This will probably manifest itself by making it very much harder to get permission to appeal.

One possible option would be to use clause 3.7 of the defamation pre-action protocol and suggest to one's opponent, where meaning is hotly disputed, that the issue be put before a nominated and jointly agreed libel QC or retired libel judge for determination, with the parties agreeing in advance to accept that determination. That could be a swifter and cheaper process than an application and perhaps appeal (although of course on a court application the parties are not required to pay the judge to determine the issue!). It may be particularly appropriate when the determination on meaning will effectively determine the claim. It is certainly an option which may appeal to litigants who wish to avoid the delay and expense of lengthy interlocutory battles. This procedure is likely to find increasing favour as a method of resolving 'logjam' issues between parties.

Chapter 4

Who can sue and be sued

4.01 This chapter sets out those persons and entities whom the law allows to sue or be sued for defamation (ie who has 'legal capacity'). It then sets out the circumstances in which the law will make a person or entity with legal capacity liable for the publication of defamatory matter and the practical considerations applicable in each case.

Introductory

4.02 Since an action for defamation is a personal action, the only person entitled to bring the claim is the person defamed. Persons not defamed who suffer damage as a result are not entitled to sue, though other causes of action may be available to them. Where persons are jointly defamed, they may bring an action for defamation together or individually.

The person defending an action should be the person who published, or caused or authorised to be published, the defamatory words or the person vicariously liable for the publisher's actions in accordance with the principles of vicarious liability of general application to the law of tort. Where more than one person published the defamatory statement, the claimant may choose to bring proceedings against them all jointly, or any of them may be sued separately[1].

1 See Chapter 2, paragraphs 2.09–2.11.

Legal capacity

4.03 The general rule is that any natural person or organisation with legal personality may sue or be sued for defamation. The corollary of this is that in general any entity to whom the law does not accord legal personality cannot sue or be sued. Note that where the claimant is not human, for example a company, it cannot recover damages for hurt feelings. It can only recover for damage to its reputation and, if applicable, goodwill.

Specific categories (in alphabetical order)

Alien enemies

4.04 Alien enemies are persons or companies domiciled or registered in states with whom the country is at war. The term therefore includes British nationals or nationals of a state not involved in the war, who are resident or carrying on business in an enemy's country. Alien enemies have no capacity to sue, but can be sued.

Bankrupts

4.05 Since an action for defamation is a personal action, bankruptcy does not prevent a person bringing or continuing proceedings. However, where the publication has caused special damage, the right of action for that damage will pass to the trustee in bankruptcy. A person's status as a bankrupt does not prevent proceedings being issued against him. However, such proceedings would normally be inadvisable for the obvious financial reasons.

Charities

4.06 A charity may sue or be sued for defamation. Where proceedings are brought by a charity, they should be brought in the name of the trustees. When proceedings are brought against a charity, it is common practice to name an official of the charity (as opposed to the trustees) who is sued 'on behalf of Charity X'.

Children and patients

4.07 Neither status has any effect upon the ability to sue or be sued for defamation. However, the procedural rules require that proceedings brought by or against children and patients must be conducted by a litigation friend. A child is a person under 18 years of age. A patient is a person who by reason of mental disorder within the meaning of the Mental Health Act 1983 is incapable of managing and administering his own affairs. A person may become a litigation friend without a court order if he satisfies the requirements of CPR 21.4. The procedural steps are set out in CPR 21.5. and in the Practice Direction to CPR Pt 21. Otherwise, a court order is required.

A claimant may issue and serve a claim form against a child or patient who does not have a litigation friend. The claimant should then apply to the court for an order appointing a litigation friend under CPR 21.6. If he does not do so, any further step taken in the proceedings will have no effect unless the court orders otherwise.

Settlement

4.08   A child or patient will not be bound by any out of court settlement without the approval of the court. A party settling with a child prior to commencement of proceedings should apply to the court for approval of the settlement under Part 8 of the CPR. Once proceedings have commenced, the application for approval should be made under CPR 23.

Companies and corporations

4.09   Companies and corporations may bring or defend proceedings for defamation in the same way as an individual. To be defamatory of a company or business the words complained of must go further than mere disparagement of its products and reflect upon its trading reputation or mode in which its business is carried on. Companies must sue and be sued in their full registered name. The words 'public limited company' or 'limited' are part of a limited liability company's name, and must be included.

The Crown

4.10   The Crown cannot sue for defamation. However, it is theoretically possible to sue the Crown.

The dead

4.11   Because defamation is a personal action, a deceased person's estate cannot sue or be sued for defamation. If the claimant dies during the course of proceedings for defamation, his claim dies with him. The same applies to a defendant, although the claimant may pursue the claim against any other defendants still living. However, once a verdict has been given or issues of fact found, judgment may given notwithstanding.

Diplomats

4.12   A diplomat may bring proceedings for defamation. However, a diplomat who does so waives his immunity in respect of any counter-claim brought against him which is directly connected with his claim. Otherwise, with certain very limited exceptions, no proceedings for defamation or indeed any other civil claim may be brought against a diplomat. A diplomat is immune from suit.

Employer's associations

4.13   An incorporated employer's association has legal personality and may therefore sue and be sued for defamation. The ability of an unincorporated association to bring proceedings for defamation is uncertain, being analogous to that of a trade union (as to which see paragraph 4.23). Proceedings may be brought against an unincorporated employer's association in its own name.

Firms

4.14   Although not a separate legal entity from the partnership, the law permits partners to sue and be sued in the name of their firm. They can also sue or be sued individually. The fact that a party is a partnership is disclosed in the title to proceedings by adding the words '(a firm)' after its name.

Foreign persons and companies

4.15   Foreign persons and companies may bring proceedings for defamation. Proceedings may also be brought against them, but the permission of the court to serve the proceedings outside the jurisdiction may be required.

Foreign states

4.16 It seems likely that a foreign state will not be permitted to bring proceedings for defamation, at least where its governmental functions are said to have been impugned. Proceedings cannot be brought against a foreign state where they relate to anything done by it in the exercise of its sovereign authority. The foreign state is immune from suit. However, proceedings can be brought against a foreign state where they relate to anything done by it not in the exercise of its sovereign authority.

Friendly societies

4.17 A friendly society is a voluntary association of individuals subscribing for provident benefits. A friendly society may be incorporated, registered or unregistered. An incorporated friendly society has the capacity to sue or be sued by virtue of its corporate status, as to which see paragraph 4.09. A registered friendly society may sue for defamation and must do so in its registered name. Likewise, proceedings against a registered friendly society should be brought against it in its registered name. An unincorporated, unregistered friendly society has the same status as any other unincorporated association, as to which see paragraph 4.24.

Government

4.18 Institutions of central or local government, such as government departments or local authorities, have no right at common law to maintain an action for defamation. However, proceedings for defamation may be brought against such entities.

Groups

4.19 A general reference to a group of people distinguishable by race, creed, colour or vocation will not give rise to a cause of action to any person within that class. So, for example, the statement 'all lawyers are thieves' will not afford any lawyer a cause of action. However, a person or persons within that group may bring proceedings if he or they are pointed to by the words complained of. For proceedings against groups, please refer to paragraph 4.24 below.

Married persons

4.20 A married person may bring or defend proceedings against their spouse, but proceedings for defamation may not be brought over a publication by one party to a marriage to the other.

Political parties

4.21 A political party, regardless of whether it has legal personality, cannot sue for defamation because it is contrary to the public interest[1]. The capacity of a political party to be sued for defamation will depend upon whether it has been incorporated or not. If it has, then it can be sued in its own name. If it has not, then the considerations dealt with at paragraph 4.24 in relation to unincorporated associations apply.

1   *Goldsmith v Bhoyrul* [1998] QB 459.

Sole traders

4.22 A sole trader must bring proceedings in his own name. Where the defamatory material complained of refers only to the claimant's trading name, it is advisable for him to bring proceedings as, for example 'Michael Brown (trading as Big Shoes)'. He will also need to plead particulars of reference in his particulars of claim. When proceedings are brought against a sole trader, the defendant should be identified as, for example, 'Keith Stevens (trading as Little Shoes)'. If the claimant does not know the defendant's own name, the procedural rules permit him to bring proceedings against the defendant in his trading name as, for example, 'Little Shoes (a trading name)'.

Trade unions

4.23 It is not certain whether a trade union can sue in its own name for defamation but it is likely to be the case that it can. However, it is clear that proceedings for defamation may be brought against a trade union.

Unincorporated associations

4.24 An unincorporated association has no legal personality and therefore cannot sue or be sued in its own name. Where individual members of the association are identifiable from the words complained of, they may bring proceedings in their own names. Likewise, where individual members of the association can be identified as responsible for publication, proceedings must be brought against them in their own names.

Liability for publication

Who should you sue?

4.25 This is not such a straightforward question as it may appear. Most actions in libel are brought against newspapers, magazines, television companies, book publishers and radio broadcasters. In such cases a number of people and companies are involved in the publication of the words complained of – and the liability for publication arises from either participation or authorisation. In the average claim arising from a newspaper article, the claimant could consider suing the publishing company, the editor and the journalist responsible for the story. Until the advent of the DeA 1996, the claimant could also pursue anyone involved in the printing, distribution or sale of the newspaper, from the distribution company to the vendor selling the paper from behind his box in the high street.

The choice of defendant introduces various tactical considerations. For example, if the offending publication appeared in a newspaper, and you want disclosure of the reporter's notes, you may wish to join him as a defendant – otherwise you may find that he was a freelance and the newspaper publisher (who you have sued as having ultimate responsibility for the words complained of) has no power to require the notes to be produced for inspection. If you are pleading malice then it may present problems if you sue the editor who may have had very little to do with the publication in reality. Each case must be judged separately and this theme will be developed throughout the book.

The 'distributors' defence'

4.26 Section 1 of the DeA 1996 has addressed the question of responsibility for publication. Previously, liability for publication arose from any involvement in, or authorising of, the publication process. This meant, in respect of a newspaper article, the following participants might have been potentially liable if that article made defamatory allegations: journalist, features/news editor, editor, publisher, printer, distributor, newsagent and the man on the corner selling the paper from his box to workers returning home. Some of those are fairly included in the loop of liability, but it was always felt unjust that some of the others were potentially liable for the contents of an article in respect of which they had played no part in writing or authorising and which they did not even read. The DeA 1996, s 1 has introduced a new statutory defence of innocent dissemination. Quite apart from rectifying what was seen by many as an unfairness, the Act had to do something to deal with an area of publication which is assuming enormous importance – the Internet (and e-mail generally).

Chapter 5

Injunctions

5.01 This chapter deals with those occasions where a claimant wants to restrain a defendant from publishing defamatory material or from publishing further defamatory material.

Introduction

5.02 If a claimant issues defamation proceedings, he is entitled to claim for two remedies – damages (for the damage caused to his reputation by the words complained of) and a final injunction (restraining the defendant from further publishing the allegations complained of in future). Note, however, the summary disposal provisions in sections 8–10 of the DeA 1996 which give the judge the power to declare a statement 'false and defamatory' and in effect the power to order an apology[1].

Most defamation claims settle before trial and, if settled in the claimant's favour, the remedies obtained will usually include an apology in one form or another, and it should be the hope of obtaining an apology which will help to vindicate his character that usually motivates a claimant to embark on a defamation claim. However, if proceedings run their course to trial, the jury can only award damages and an injunction. And there is no doubt that of the two, the injunction is the poor relation of the remedies. Usually its availability is not even mentioned during trial, the jury is not asked to consider its application, and the judgment of the court will ignore it. By the time the parties have got to trial, injunctive relief is unnecessary and well past its sell-by date.

Where injunctions assume a much greater importance is at the very outset of the claim, and indeed your client's first request may be to demand that you stop a publication or terminate a sequence of publications in mid-flow.

1 See Chapter 22.

5.03 The first thing to emphasise is that obtaining a defamation injunction is difficult, and the implementation of the HRA 1998 has had the effect of making them even harder to obtain. This is because two fundamental rights come into opposition when a claimant seeks a defamation injunction – his right to protect his reputation from false and defamatory allegations against the defendant's rights to freedom of speech. The courts have historically dealt with this by refusing to grant an interim injunction to the claimant if the defendant genuinely intends to plead a defence of justification[1] or fair comment on a matter of public interest, or qualified privilege where there is no evidence of express malice.

The HRA 1998, s 12 seeks to give a greater weight to the Article 10 freedom of speech rights than to the Article 8 rights to respect for family life, home and correspondence. Section 12(4) of the HRA 1998 provides: 'The court must have particular regard to the importance of the Convention right to freedom of expression . . .'. Setting aside the arguments about the validity of a country subscribing to the European Convention on Human Rights seeking to give greater weight to one Convention right over another, the upshot is likely to be that defamation injunctions will be even rarer beasts in the future, particularly where media defendants are involved.

It is also the case that legal considerations applicable to interim injunctions in defamation cases have always differed from the law relating to injunctions generally. The standard authority setting out circumstances where an injunction may be granted[2] does not apply in defamation, as the Court of Appeal has repeatedly made clear[3]. The reason for this has its roots in history: an injunction cannot be granted unless the words complained of are defamatory, and whether or not the words are defamatory is a question which has, since Fox's Libel Act 1792, been a matter for the jury. The court is very reluctant to interfere in an area which should properly be left to the jury. The recent Court of Appeal decision in *Safeway plc v Tate*[4] reasserted the importance of the jury's role in deciding whether there was 'libel or no libel'. In the light of the recent judgment of the House of Lords, the Court of Appeal judgment in *Grobbelaar v News Group Newspapers Ltd*[5], where the jury's verdict was overturned as perverse, now seems to represent a one-off attack as opposed to a change of direction in attitude towards the role of the jury.

1   The rule in *Bonnard v Perryman* [1891] 2 Ch 269, CA.
2   Set out by the House of Lords in *American Cynamid Co v Ethicon Ltd* [1975] 1 All ER 504, HL.
3   For example in *Herbage v Pressdram Ltd* [1984] 1 WLR 1160.
4   [2001] QB 1120, CA.
5   [2001] EWCA Civ 33, [2001] 2 All ER 437.

Procedure

5.04 An injunction can be granted by a judge at any time after a claim form has been issued.

This means it can be granted before the claim form has even been served on the defendant.

It can be granted ex parte (in the absence of the defendant). Indeed an injunction can be granted by telephoning a judge at home if the matter is sufficiently urgent and publication is imminent.

The judge will want to know why the claimant has not notified the defendant of its application and, if the application is successful, the usual practice is to grant the injunction for a limited period of about five days with leave to apply to continue the injunction until trial. This then gives the defendant the opportunity to apply to have the injunction lifted.

The court will order an injunction when it is satisfied that there is a reasonable apprehension that unless it is ordered the defendant will publish or continue to publish the words complained of. It will not grant the injunction unless it is satisfied that if the publication were to go ahead it would result in immediate and irreparable injury; neither will it do so if the claimant can be fully compensated in damages[1]. The court must be satisfied the words complained of are untrue and there is no defence available – a pretty high hurdle for the claimant to overcome.

1   *Monson v Tussauds Ltd* [1894] 1 QB 671, CA.

5.05 Generally an application for an injunction, whether made ex parte or on notice, will be governed by CPR 25.

It can be made without notice 'if it appears to the court that there are good reasons for not giving notice'[1]. Urgency is the usual reason in defamation. CPR Pt 25 PD, para 4 sets out the provisions for urgent applications and those made ex parte. The claimant will need:

(a)   a claim form – either issued or in draft with an undertaking to issue immediately or in accordance with the court's direction;

(b)   an application notice;

(c)   evidence in support;

(d)   a draft order (also on disk).

These should be filed whenever possible with the court two hours before the hearing. The supporting evidence should explain why no notice has been given to the defendant and must make full disclosure of all relevant matters and material facts[2]. The order must specify precisely the acts which the defendant must do or be restrained from doing[3].

An application will be made on notice either in a less urgent case or in a hearing subsequent to an ex parte application, for example where the interim injunction has been granted for a limited time and the claimant wishes to continue the restraint. Each party is required to file at court and serve copies of all the written evidence on which they intend to rely. CPR Pt 25 PD, para 2.2 stipulates that the application notice and evidence in support must be served as soon as possible after issue and no later than three days before the hearing date. Once again, a draft order should be filed with the application (and should be available on disk).

1   CPR 25.3(1).
2   CPR Pt 25 PD, para 3.3.
3   CPR Pt 25 PD, para 3.

Undertaking as to damages

5.06   The undertaking as to damages is now dealt with in CPR Pt 25 PD, para 5.1(1). Self-evidently, if an injunction is granted, then the court is giving the claimant a remedy before the merits of his case have been finally decided. Consequently, the claimant has to give an 'undertaking as to damages', which means he has to promise to pay his opponent compensation if he later fails to establish his entitlement to the injunction. The undertaking is to the court, not one's opponents.

In a defamation action, this can have serious implications. If, as a result of an injunction, a claimant succeeds in 'pulling' a front page tabloid story or the broadcast of a well-trailed television programme, then the damages payable if the claim subsequently fails could be quite substantial.

The court will conduct an inquiry into what loss the defendant suffered because of the injunction. Damages are then assessed on the basis that the claimant has covenanted with the defendant not to prevent the defendant doing what he was in fact restrained from doing by the terms of the injunction[1]. The court has a discretion whether or not to enforce the undertaking given to it.

If the claimant's claim involves having to show special damage, for example a slander claim (subject to the exceptions), then he will not obtain an injunction unless he can show he has already suffered such damage. The risk of damage is not enough.

In defamation, an application for an injunction will normally be made to prevent repetition of defamatory material. To prevent a threatened publication is much more difficult because the claimant will have to detail as best he can the actual words complained of which he wants to restrain and it is unlikely that such detail will be available to him.

1 *Hoffman-La Roche v Secretary of State for Trade and Industry* [1975] AC 295.

5.07 The risk to a claimant in applying for an injunction lies in the undertaking as to damages discussed above.

The risk to a defendant in contesting an injunction on the basis that it will be able to justify the allegations is that if the defendant ultimately fails to do so, then the claimant is likely to recover higher damages from a jury at trial. Robert Maxwell was awarded £50,000 exemplary damages against Private Eye when it could not justify its allegation that Maxwell had funded an African tour by then Labour leader Neil Kinnock in the hope of getting a peerage. It had asserted that it could justify the allegations when contesting Maxwell's application for an interim injunction.

Robert Maxwell is usually cited as the enemy of freedom of speech because of his predilection for what were called 'gagging writs' to prevent defamatory material being published about him. However, he failed three times to restrain publication of Tom Bower's book about him[1] because Bower said he could justify the material and, ultimately, he dropped his action. For those not involved in the Maxwell litigation over the years, it seems curious that more media defendants did not contest injunctions obtained against them on the basis they could justify what they were publishing.

A more prosaic example of the way in which injunctions might be obtained in libel actions occurred in *Taylor v Chapman*[2], in which a local scrap metal merchant began a placard campaign in Oswestry against a local police officer. An injunction was obtained to halt the ongoing campaign pending the trial at which the claimant was awarded £2,500 damages. This was a down-to-earth example of the court awarding an injunction to prevent repetition of defamatory material.

The key to obtaining an interim injunction in a defamatory action is promptness. A court is most unlikely to be sympathetic to a claimant who has delayed in his attempts to restrain a defendant. History also suggests that it is businesses and businessmen who have most success in obtaining injunctions, partly perhaps because the courts err on the side of caution where business is involved and partly because such claims often include other causes of action, for example breach of confidence.

1   *Maxwell: The Outsider* (1988) Aurum Press.
2   (1992) unreported.

Chapter 6

Choice of counsel

6.01 This chapter deals with the 'other lawyers' who will be a critical element in your client's defamation claim or defence – counsel.

Choice of counsel

6.02 Despite the supposed glamour and profile of defamation litigation, there are only two sets of chambers which specialise in defamation work. These are both to be found in London: at 1 Brick Court, Temple, and 5 Raymond Buildings, Grays Inn.

Both are long established and both contain many excellent barristers. Every defamation action will find members from these chambers involved, often representing all the parties.

Where their monopoly occasionally falters is in the choice of leading counsel. Individual silks from other chambers have established excellent reputations, most notably of course, the late George Carman QC. There are also good juniors who maintain a defamation practice in sets such as Matrix Chambers, Doughty Street Chambers and Farrar's Buildings.

Critical to their continued standing is the knowledge and guarantee that if one instructs a barrister at either 1 Brick Court or 5 Raymond Buildings, and your opponent instructs another barrister in the same chambers, then an impenetrable 'Chinese wall' will exist ensuring confidentiality. That is a tribute in part to the clerks at those chambers.

Qualities needed in defamation counsel

6.03 A defamation barrister has to be a highly skilled hybrid. Essential requirements include accomplished drafting skills, the ability to present complex legal submissions, a sensitivity and willingness to empathise and engage with a client who may be under very considerable stress, and advocacy skills before a jury.

All these must be overlaid with a 'street wisdom' – a remote, academic manner and approach is of little use in defamation where one's preparations are ultimately geared to what will appeal to and persuade a jury of 12 men and women who are not lawyers. At the same time, there must be an awareness of the way the media work and the public perception of it.

The top defamation barristers are an impressive amalgam of all these qualities.

When to instruct counsel

6.04 The effect of the Civil Procedure Rules and the defamation pre-action protocol is to encourage early and full preparation of your case whether you are a claimant or defendant.

The availability of conditional fee agreements also means that many claimants will want to know whether their solicitor is prepared to take on their case on a 'no win no fee' basis.

These developments combine to increase the wisdom of involving counsel at an early stage. A solicitor will not entertain a CFA with a client without a clear idea of the merits of his case and its prospects of success. The comfort of counsel's opinion to back (or defy) one's own judgment is not only an important security blanket, but probably a necessary step in any event if one's client is intending to back his CFA with insurance. The insurers will certainly want a counsel's opinion before agreeing to insure, and in defamation an advice from a barrister in one of the leading sets often means insurers are satisfied and will not seek their own separate opinion.

You may also be seeking a CFA with counsel; in which case, the barrister will certainly want to be involved in the case as early as possible so he or she can decide whether he or she is prepared to risk a 'no win no fee' deal.

6.05 The requirements of the defamation pre-action protocol stipulate the information which should be included in the letter of claim and the defendant's response. In both cases, the protocol suggests it is desirable for the claimant and the defendant to identify the meaning(s) which he attributes to the words complained of. This was the compromise which emerged from the working party's debates on this area precisely because solicitors were reluctant to commit themselves to a meaning in the letter of claim which counsel might subsequently disagree with. That could lead, for example, to an embarrassing distinction between the meaning set out in the letter of claim and the later pleaded meaning in the particulars of claim – something which might be exploited by the defendant's counsel at trial.

Clearly one way of resolving this concern is to instruct counsel to settle the letter of claim, and, in more complex defamation claims, that is the prudent way to proceed. In defamation actions, more than in any other area of litigation, the letter of claim is effectively 'the first pleading'. Indeed, arguably, it is more important than the particulars of claim if the action goes to trial because it is a document which the jury will almost certainly have in their bundle (unlike the statement of case). The tone and content of the first letter is of critical importance and it will assist in setting the mood for the jury. A reasonable approach is more likely to put them on side than a tirade of anger and vent spleen.

It is not unreasonable to ask counsel to settle this letter. The cost of doing so is almost invariably recoverable on assessment.

A further reason for involving counsel at an early stage is that it enables them to have a say in the tactics and strategy to be adopted. If you have ploughed off in a particular direction and only instruct counsel at a later stage, there is a danger that your barrister might respond with the old saying, 'I wouldn't have started from here'!

Summary of counsel's possible involvement in a complex defamation action

6.06 Counsel's role in the action may include some or all of the following:

- giving advice on the merits and prospects of success;
- settling the letter of claim/defendant's response to the letter of claim;
- settling the particulars of claim/defence;
- settling the reply;
- settling the request for further information/response to request;
- giving advice on disclosure and witness evidence;
- settling notice to admit facts;
- deciding on a QC and arranging a conference with client;
- representing the claimant/defendant at interlocutory hearings on, for example, contested meaning, qualified privilege, attack on pleadings, inadequate disclosure (note: interlocutory hearings are extremely common in complex defamation actions and can occur at any stage after the issue of proceedings);
- attending the case management conference;
- attending the pre-trial review;

- giving advice on trial bundles, witness evidence to be called at trial, legal applications to be left to the trial judge;
- being briefed for trial;
- giving advice on appeal.

Throughout the proceedings there will also be conferences with solicitors and clients. The number and timing of these will vary case by case.

Junior and leading counsel

6.07 Defamation is unusual in civil litigation in that virtually every trial is a major event with high stakes and higher costs riding on the outcome.

What this means is that in practically every defamation trial you will find leading counsel briefed for both claimant and defendant.

The choice of which QC to use will be determined by a combination of your junior counsel's suggestion, your own experience, the type of case you are involved in and the client you represent, and availability.

In a large defamation action, it is sensible to choose your leader and organise a conference quite early on so that he gets a feel for the case and everyone gets a feel for each other! It is extremely important to have a QC the client trusts and whom he believes is as committed to his cause as he is. It is likely that the junior will have had plenty to do with the client, will have a very detailed knowledge of the ins and outs of the case, and will have won the confidence of the client. The QC has to demonstrate that he or she is bringing something extra to the case, and the first conference fulfils a very important function in that regard.

The downside of the omnipresence of leading counsel at defamation trials is that most junior defamation counsel have very little experience at trial work. They build up their skills at complicated interlocutory hearings on points of law before masters and judges, but have little opportunity to develop jury skills during their junior careers other than by observation. It is possible that if the summary disposal procedure under sections 8–10 of the DeA 1996 becomes as popular as Lord Hoffman hoped it would[1], then there may be an increase in the number of 'smaller' libel actions, and so junior defamation counsel will increase their trial experience. However, summary disposal is before a judge alone, so there is still no prospect of gaining valuable jury experience.

1 Mr Justice Hoffmann (as he then was) prepared a Bill in 1989 proposing the introduction of a quick procedure for 'smaller' defamation claims. It was not enacted but influenced the formulation of the summary disposal provisions which emerged in the DeA 1996, ss 8–10.

Chapter 7

Funding and costs

Introduction

7.01 Much attention has been paid over the years to the level of legal costs in defamation claims. Legal aid has never been available in defamation and, therefore, it used to be said that pursuing a claim in libel or slander was the preserve of the wealthy, the foolish or the insane. This is because the only options to fund either the pursuit or the defence of a defamation action were to pay for it yourself or to find some benefactor (whether a union or some supporters) who would indemnify your costs in the event of you being ordered to pay them.

That position has changed since section 58 of the CLSA 1990 introduced the concept of legally valid conditional fee agreements ('CFAs'), a concept significantly developed by the AJA 1999, which came into force on 1 April 2000.

The Conditional Fee Agreements Order 1995, SI 1995/1674 allowed personal injury, certain insolvency proceedings and proceedings before the European Court of Human Rights to be conducted under a CFA.

7.02 On 30 July 1998 the Conditional Fee Agreements Order 1998, SI 1998/1860 extended the categories of proceedings which could be conducted under a CFA to all work except those originally prohibited by the CLSA 1990 (namely criminal and family proceedings). This meant that, as from that date, defamation proceedings could be conducted on a CFA.

The next significant piece of legislation in this area was the AJA 1999 and this introduced the following key changes to the CLSA 1990[1] which were implemented as from 1 April 2000:

(a) the recoverable success fee[2];
(b) the recoverable insurance premium[3];
(c) the removal of CFAs from the common law[4];

(d) the extension of CFAs to all proceedings for resolving disputes (not just court proceedings)[5];

(e) the facilitation of different forms of CFA with different conditions, eg collective CFAs[6]; and

(f) the recoverability of costs by membership organisations[7].

Two changes which have not been commenced to date are:

(a) litigation funding agreements[8]; and

(b) facilitating the abolition of the indemnity principle[9].

It is appropriate to concentrate on the background to the CFA legislation in this introduction to costs because the availability of CFAs has transformed the ability of individuals of moderate means to contemplate pursuing defamation claims. However, one must also consider the full range of funding options available in addition to CFAs. These are discussed below.

1   The AJA 1999 substituted the original section 58 of the CLSA 1990 with sections 58, 58A and 58B (see Appendix 7 for full text).
2   The CLSA 1990, s 58A(6), as inserted by the AJA 1999, s 27.
3   The AJA 1999, s 29.
4   The CLSA 1990, s 58(1), as substituted by the AJA 1999, s 27.
5   The CLSA 1990, s 58A(3)(b), as inserted by the AJA 1999, s 27.
6   The CLSA 1990, s 58A(3)(b), as inserted by the AJA 1999, s 27.
7   The AJA 1999, s 30.
8   The CLSA 1990, s 58B, as inserted by the AJA 1999, s 28.
9   The AJA 1999, s 31.

Funding options

Privately paying client

7.03   This is the traditional method of funding legal work. The client pays for the work as it is done on the basis of agreed terms of retainer. The solicitor delivers bills for the legal work done on the basis of an hourly rate for his fees and by passing on the disbursements which have been incurred on the case, for example counsel's fees, expert's fees, travel and photocopying costs. In the past solicitors would generally agree a basic hourly rate (the 'A' rate) with the client but would indicate that in addition a 'mark-up' of up to 100% (the 'B' rate) would be added to this basic figure for the care and conduct applied to the work, taking into account certain established criteria now contained in CPR 44.5. These comprise:

(a)   the conduct of the parties;
(b)   the amount or value of money or property involved;
(c)   the importance of the matter to the parties;
(d)   the complexity of the matter or difficulty or novelty of the questions raised;
(e)   the skill, effort, specialised knowledge and responsibility involved;
(f)   the time spent on the case;
(g)   the place where, and circumstances in which, the work or any part of it was done.

The basic cost represents the true cost of the solicitor's time (in other words, how much it costs his or her firm per hour to employ him or her, including salary and all overheads). The mark-up represents the profit element.

It has become more common in recent years for solicitors to agree an hourly rate with their clients which is inclusive of the mark-up element. This practice is preferred under the new Costs and Information Code[1] and conforms with the CPR requirement for the submission of bills.

1   Solicitors Practice Rule 15 and the Solicitors' Costs Information and Client Care Code 1999. See Appendices 14 and 15.

7.04   The old 'A' and 'B' rates and the description 'care and conduct' are likely to fade into history before too much longer. It is now essential that solicitors consider at the outset of a case what is the right rate for the job. With an inclusive hourly rate a case which seemed simple at the start but turns into something complicated cannot be dealt with by an escalating mark-up for care and conduct. One suspects that what a client gains in the ability to understand better the arcane way in which lawyers charge for their work, they lose in agreeing to all-inclusive hourly rates which are likely to assume a high combination of the 'B' factors listed above out of commercial caution. Indeed, most solicitors will charge the same hourly rates (which will vary depending on the seniority of the lawyer) on every case regardless of any consideration of what is the appropriate care and conduct element to be included in the all-inclusive rate for that particular case.

In defamation, as in other areas of the law, the following points should be borne in mind by both solicitor and client before entering into a privately funded retainer:

(a) The client is primarily liable for the fees – so even if they win and obtain a costs order in their favour, if the order cannot be enforced for whatever reason, they still have to pay their solicitor's bill.

(b) Can the client afford to pay the solicitor's fees? Questions about a client's credit worthiness, requests for money on account of costs and rendering interim bills do not do much to further the image of the legal profession, but every firm of solicitors has a bad debt mountain because of unpaid solicitor/client bills.

(c) Interim bills – litigation can take years, especially in large defamation cases where visits to the Court of Appeal over interlocutory issues are a regular occurrence and can add months to the length of a case. To preserve some sort of cash flow solicitors are likely to require a client's agreement to the rendering of interim solicitor/client bills at regular intervals.

(d) Challenging the solicitor/client bill – just because a client agrees an hourly rate does not mean he cannot dispute the number of hours a solicitor tries to charge him for. The details of a client's rights are found in the Solicitors Act 1974 (SA 1974), s 70[1].

(e) Fixed fee – agreeing a fixed fee in a defamation case is the equivalent of betting on the length of a batsman's innings in cricket, ie an exercise in futile speculation. It could, and indeed inevitably will, backfire badly on either the solicitor or client. There would have to be astonishingly good reasons for entering into such an arrangement.

(f) Capped fees – if it is agreed that the solicitor's fees be capped at a particular figure, then it places a wholly unacceptable risk on the solicitor without any compensatory reward if the case is won. For these reasons, there appears to be no instance of either fixed or capped fees occurring in defamation cases. There is also the question of the indemnity principle to consider.

(g) Indemnity principle – a solicitor cannot recover more from his opponent in costs than he has charged his own client – except under the terms of a legally effective CFA. The indemnity principle is still alive and, like Mark Twain, rumours of its demise have been greatly exaggerated.

1 See Appendix 6.

Contingency fees

7.05 A contingency fee is any fee contingent upon the result of the case. It is defined in Solicitors Practice Rule 18(2) as 'any sum (whether fixed or calculated either as a percentage of the proceeds or otherwise howsoever) payable only in the event of success in the prosecution of any action suit or other contentious proceeding'. Practice Rule 8 prohibits contingency fees where a solicitor is 'retained or employed to prosecute or defend any action suit or other contentious proceeding'. A CFA is the statutory exception to this prohibition.

Legal expenses insurance

7.06 Judge Michael Cook says in *Cook on Costs 2001/02*: 'The gate keepers to justice are now the lawyers and the insurers. They decide not only who is to be admitted through the portals of justice but (also) the price of admission'.

That is certainly true in, for example, personal injury litigation but perhaps not yet in defamation on the claimant's side. Insurers undoubtedly play an important role in the 'price of exit' from a defamation case because media defendants are often backed by insurers who assume responsibility for the conduct of the defence and, of course, the damages and costs to be paid in a lost or settled case. It is possible for a claimant to purchase 'after the event' insurance for a defamation claim but the premiums are prohibitive because the risks are more difficult to assess than in almost any other area of litigation. Apart from all the usual litigation risk factors, defamation concerns the nebulous question of the value of a reputation and it incorporates an additional imponderable by requiring that a jury decide the outcome. Small wonder insurers compensate by loading the one area over which they do have control – the premiums. These tend to be between 15% and 40% of the sum to be insured. In a large defended libel case where each party's costs and disbursements can easily reach £500,000, it would mean that to insure against the risk of paying your opponent's costs in the event of a defeat, a client would face payment of a premium of between £75,000 and £200,000.

Media organisations generally do carry defamation insurance and the premiums they pay are dictated by their claims history. The national newspaper groups tend not to be insured, which enables a newspaper to retain control over when to fight and when to flee if confronted with a defamation claim. It means they can fight a case as a matter of principle which commercially minded insurers would be inclined to settle.

Many household or credit card policies carry legal expenses insurance for employment and personal injury claims but none will insure against the risk of being defamed. Any application would need to be made individually and it is almost inconceivable that anyone would carry 'before the event' insurance for a claim in defamation, so the application will be made after the decision has been taken to pursue a claim on the words complained of. Research will be needed to identify the small number of insurers with a 'defamation product'.

7.07 When considering legal expenses insurance, some important points should be borne in mind:

(a)   The contract is between the insurer and the client. There is no contractual relationship between the solicitor and the insurer. The contractual terms should be scrutinised closely.

(b)   Contracts are, self-evidently, subject to the principles of insurance law.

(c)   The client remains primarily liable for payment of the legal costs and the insurer's obligation under a contract of indemnity is to make good the insured's loss.

(d)   There will be rigorous reporting requirements imposed on the client/solicitor. This means, for example, that an unfavourable counsel's or expert's opinion must be disclosed immediately.

(e)   The insured will be under a duty to mitigate his loss. Insurers will not hesitate to intervene if they believe the luxury of their cover is being exploited.

(f)   The scope for conflicts of interest is much more pronounced when insurers are involved in litigation. The solicitor must remember who is the client and fulfil both the duty to take instructions (from the client) and the duty to disclose (to insurers).

(g)   Solicitors are not brokers – you open yourself to potential problems if you recommend a particular policy to a client.

A client does not have to have entered into a CFA in order to apply for and obtain insurance against the risk of losing a defamation claim – but it is more likely that in defamation most insurance policies will arise to back a CFA.

Legal aid (or 'publicly funded legal services')

7.08   The words 'legal aid' disappeared with the AJA 1999. Legal aid was never available for defamation but it was available for malicious falsehood. (However, there is no public funding for that either now.) In terms of defamation, the possibility of legal aid made no difference – but the availability of CFAs introduced an important new way of funding defamation cases.

Conditional fee agreements

7.09 A CFA is a statutory exception to the general prohibition on charging a client by means of a contingency fee, ie a fee dependent on the result of a case. Provided the strict statutory requirements are complied with, and provided the solicitor's risk assessment procedures indicate that the merits and prospects of success are sufficiently good, then a solicitor and a client can agree that the client's case be conducted under the terms of a CFA.

The most common colloquial description of a CFA is a 'no win no fee' agreement. In other words, if the client does not win his case he does not have to pay his solicitor's fees. If he does win his case, then he will normally recover his costs from his opponent and that is how his solicitor is paid.

The reward for the solicitor in agreeing to share the risk of his client's litigation is that if the client does win, the solicitor is not only entitled to his basic charges but also a 'success fee' of up to 100% of those charges. The amount of the success fee is calculated to reflect the risk which the solicitor is taking in running that particular case on a CFA. The success fee is recoverable from the losing party, although this is open to attack on assessment in the same way that basic charges may be scrutinised by a costs judge on assessment.

In defamation, where the defendants tend to be wealthy or well-insured media organisations, where litigation tends to be complex, where contested actions tend to be large, time-consuming and expensive, where much depends on the impression witnesses make on a jury (a notoriously difficult thing to predict) and for other such reasons, it is difficult to think that a success fee of much less than 100% would be agreed with a claimant and incorporated into a CFA.

CFAs between solicitors and defendants in defamation cases will be extremely rare but not inconceivable. In a case, for example, where an important principle of freedom of speech was felt to be at issue for impecunious defendants who might otherwise attract representation on a pro bono basis, it would surely be better for their legal representatives to be acting on a CFA. It would not affect the client's costs liability to the solicitors but if they were to win, it would enable the solicitors to be fully remunerated for their efforts. If it were to arise today, the mammoth libel case pursued by McDonalds against initially five but ultimately two individuals who enjoyed significant pro bono support from solicitors might fall into this category[1].

1   *McDonalds Corpn and McDonalds Restaurants Ltd v Andrew Clarke*: writ issued September 1990, trial started June 1994 and concluded June 1997.

7.10 Legal aid never having been available for defamation, many media defendants feared that the introduction of the availability of CFAs would lead to the opening of a floodgate through which a hugely increased number of defamation claims would pour. That has not happened for a number of reasons:

(a)   Risk assessment – the procedures for establishing the merits and prospects of success of a claim mean that the holes in a potential claimant's case are now examined more rigorously by his own solicitor before that claim is communicated to the defendant, let alone pursued. When solicitors have 'to put their money where their mouth is' they will be much less likely to promote speculative claims.

(b)   The defamation pre-action protocol[1] – the protocol sets out the pre-action requirements for exchange of information about both the claim and the defence, and has inevitably had some impact in reducing the number of issued defamation proceedings either because a good claim is identified as such early on and settled accordingly or a good defence is communicated – so deterring court action.

(c)   Commercial realities for solicitors – a defamation action run for a client on a CFA means the investment of considerable resources by a firm with no ongoing cash flow to support that involvement. Defamation is not high volume/relatively low cost work like personal injury; it is low volume/high cost. Even the lure of recovering a healthy success fee is not going to encourage frivolous speculation by a solicitor – one lost CFA action where no costs are recovered (which is likely to be following a trial) wipes out a large number of successfully recovered success fees on other cases (which are likely to have been settled at an earlier stage than trial). The fact is that most firms will only be able to support a very small number of ongoing defamation actions under CFAs unless they have the support of healthy cash flow from other departments doing other work types (and a cheerful willingness on the part of those departments to indulge their defamation colleagues) or a goose steadily laying golden eggs in a back room! The consequence of all this is that claimant defamation lawyers have adopted a more ruthless approach to turning down cases with only an average prospect of success where the client expects them to share the risk.

(d)   Commercial realities for claimants – 'no win no fee' sounds great, but it does not quite work like that. A losing claimant may not have to pay his solicitor's fees but he is still liable for all his disbursements (including counsel's fees, unless counsel is also on a CFA) and all the legal costs of the successful defendant – unless he has taken out insurance cover (which as mentioned earlier is prohibitively expensive for defamation). If each side's costs are, say, £500,000 (which is not unusual in a fully defended defamation action which goes to trial) then even if all of a claimant's costs are subject to a CFA, he will still face a liability of £500,000 if he loses his action. The difference between a bill of that size rather than £1m is likely to be academic for most defamation claimants of average means. Once this is explained to the prospective CFA defamation claimant, it introduces an acute sense of proportion and responsibility into the decision-making process about whether to take proceedings.

(e)   Commercial realities for defendants – if a claim is notified to a defendant which is subject to a CFA then it tells the defendant two things. First, the claimant's solicitors have conducted and reached a favourable view on the merits of the claim and its prospects of success. Second, that it will be an honest view and not the legal equivalent of a boxer talking up his chances before a bout against a superior opponent. This is because the solicitor is demonstrating he is prepared to put his money where his mouth is. Once the defendant has conducted its own analysis of the case, it may be inclined to bite the bullet much earlier than in days of yore and settle the claim. The CFA era has meant that defendants pick their fights much more selectively than in the past.

The result of all this has been that since CFAs were introduced for defamation, while there has certainly been an increase in the number of potential claimants seeking advice about defamation claims and also perhaps an increase in the number of claims being notified to defendants, there has in fact been an appreciable decline in the number of defamation actions being issued in the courts.

1   See Chapter 8.

Matters to bear in mind when contemplating CFA litigation

7.11 It is not the function of this book to set out the detailed requirements of a CFA, and those contemplating entering into a CFA on a defamation case are strongly advised to refer to the legislation and to the numerous books available which concentrate on conditional fees. However, the following are matters which should be borne in mind by a solicitor considering entering into a CFA with a client:

(a) The essential action at the outset is investigating and establishing the merits of the case and its prospects of success. That will take place before any CFA is signed and will therefore have to be conducted on a privately paying basis or for free. One might be a little wary of a client whose commitment to his case does not extend even to paying to establish whether it has merit and is likely to succeed.

(b) Once the initial investigation is complete, there should be a set procedure and policy to decide whether to take on the case on a CFA, and it should be conscientiously applied in every case. Each firm should prepare its own internal documentation for risk assessment with checklists and guidelines. If possible, objectivity should be preserved by requiring a senior defamation lawyer or lawyers not associated with the case to carry out the risk assessment and decide whether or not to take on the case on a CFA.

(c) If the case is sufficiently large, get counsel involved at an early stage, seeking his opinion and establishing if he would be prepared to conduct the case on a CFA. If not, why not? It could be relevant to your firm's decision also.

(d) Ensure you comply fully with the responsibilities to notify your client of all the information required under the Solicitors' Costs Information and Client Care Code 1999 and the Conditional Fee Agreements Regulations 2000, SI 2000/692[1].

(e) Ensure the form of the CFA itself complies with the conditions in section 58 of the CLSA 1990, as amended by the AJA 1999, s 27[2].

(f) In particular consider very carefully how you define 'success' in the CFA. The definition of success will determine whether or not the solicitor is paid, so take account of counterclaims, negotiated settlements and alternative dispute resolution.

(g)   Comply with the requirements to notify your opponent that your client is funding the case under a CFA with a success fee and insurance premium (if applicable)[3] (Form N251[4]). Failure to do so will mean the additional liabilities are irrecoverable[5].

(h)   If acting for a client whose opponent is pursuing or defending the case under a CFA then you must warn him about the fact that any costs award may include payment of a success fee and insurance premium (or 'provision' or 'notional premium' if it is a collective Conditional Fee Agreement (see paragraph 7.14 below)).

1   See Appendices 10 and 15.
2   See Appendix 7.
3   CPR 44.15 (1).
4   See Appendix 13.
5   CPR 44.3B(1)(c).

Barristers and CFAs

7.12   While good claims on defamation frequently settle without the involvement of counsel following the pre-action protocol exchange of correspondence, it is a rare case indeed in which counsel is not involved once the issue of proceedings becomes inevitable. Since counsel's fees will often be of a similar amount to those of the solicitors in a contested defamation action, the funding of those fees will be a key consideration for any client and solicitor.

In a privately paying case, the client's obligation to pay counsel's fees is the same as for any other disbursement. Provided the solicitor has obtained the client's instructions to use counsel, then the client will be liable to reimburse the solicitor for the fees so incurred. If the client objects to the amount of counsel's fees, the first port of call is likely to be counsel's clerk and a conversation in which the solicitor will try and negotiate a figure more in line with his client's expectations. Usually some form of compromise is achieved, especially if there is an ongoing relationship between the solicitors and counsel's chambers. Alternatively, as mentioned earlier, the client has the right to challenge the solicitor's bill under the SA 1974. On assessment, counsel's fees may be reduced but it must be remembered that the solicitor is primarily liable for counsel's fees, not the client, so if counsel's clerk insists on the payment of the fees in full, it will be the solicitor who bears the shortfall not the client.

Barristers have traditionally prided themselves on a scrupulous adherence to the so-called 'cab rank rule', which means that, as long as he is available to do so, it is a barrister's professional duty to accept any instructions in respect of work he holds himself out as competent to carry out. In other words, he could theoretically find himself representing Mother Theresa one day and Hitler the next. However, the introduction of CFAs has led to an exception to this rule: a barrister is not now obliged to accept instructions where his payment is to be by way of a CFA. It is a matter of preliminary negotiation as between the solicitor and barrister as to whether the barrister is prepared to accept instructions on a case where he is being asked to act on a CFA.

CFAs have, therefore, introduced a new factor into the relationship between solicitors and barristers. A solicitor's CFA is between the client and the solicitor; a counsel's CFA is between the solicitor and the barrister. This triangular contractual relationship links the interests of the three parties inextricably. Each is to some extent placing their destiny in the hands of the other: if the client does not win his case, then neither the solicitor nor the barrister gets paid. It raises issues of trust and confidence as between the solicitor and barrister – a barrister is much more likely to agree to enter a CFA with a solicitor or a firm who he knows well than a solicitor or a firm with whom he has had no previous dealings. Similarly, he may be more willing to accept a CFA case if it is one of a flow of cases on which he is being instructed rather than a one-off. A consequence of CFAs, therefore, is almost inevitably a closer, almost symbiotic, relationship between solicitors and certain sets of chambers.

7.13 A barrister bears any losses in a case personally – he does not have a firm standing behind him, so it is that much harder financially for a barrister to support the litigation risk associated with a CFA case. A large defamation action could easily represent 25–30% of a barrister's income for a whole year, so if he is acting on a CFA and the case is lost, the consequences could be serious. Counsel will therefore want as much evidence, information and documentation as possible before committing himself to a CFA and, once he has signed up to a CFA, he will want a much closer involvement in developments throughout the litigation than might otherwise be the case. In particular, counsel will want to be informed about, and contribute to, any settlement approach and subsequent negotiations. A barrister who will be paid his fees regardless of the outcome can dip in and out of the case according to his instructions; a barrister whose payment depends on a win is justified in feeling entitled to fuss around a case like a mother hen. It remains to be seen whether costs judges will acknowledge this on assessment. Opponents will certainly argue that while a closer involvement by counsel may be reasonable for him to protect his 'investment' in the case, it is unreasonable to expect the opponent to pay for it.

Part II of the AJA 1999, which introduced the development of success fees recoverable from one's opponent in litigation, increased the likelihood of CFAs between solicitors and barristers becoming more popular and common.

A solicitor/barrister CFA is only enforceable if it complies with the provisions of sections 55 and 58A of the CLSA 1990[1]. The agreement must be in writing and must 'not relate to proceedings which cannot be the subject of an enforceable conditional fee agreement'[2]. It must also comply with any relevant regulations prescribed by the Lord Chancellor[3] (currently contained in the Conditional Fee Arrangements Regulations 2000, SI 2000/692, in which the instructing solicitor is defined as the 'client' and the barrister as the 'legal representative'[4]).

It is important to re-emphasise that where additional liabilities are claimed from your opponent(s) – typically a success fee or an insurance premium – one has a duty to notify the existence of a CFA and the additional liabilities. Failure to do so means you cannot recover those additional liabilities. Therefore, if counsel has entered into a CFA with a success fee with his instructing solicitor but, for whatever reason, the solicitor is not acting under a CFA, it is vital that he ensures that the solicitor has provided the requisite notification to the other side[5]. If the solicitor fails to do so, he is probably still liable for the success fee to the barrister but it is unlikely to improve future relations between the two if that sum has not been recovered from the losing opponent and the solicitor has to pay it out of his recovered costs.

1 The CLSA 1990, s 58A(6), as inserted by the AJA 1999, s 27.
2 The CLSA 1990, s 58(3)(b).
3 The CLSA 1990, s 58(3)(c).
4 The Conditional Fee Arrangements Regulations 2000, SI 2000/692, reg 1(3).
5 CPR 44.15.

Collective conditional fee agreements

7.14 The concept of CFAs was always likely to be most attractive to bulk purchasers of legal services, in particular trade unions and insurers. However, the requirement that each separate action should have a separate CFA and the procedural requirements associated with the implementation and notification of a CFA meant the logistical and administrative burden for such organisations was daunting. The Government was keen that CFAs should be attractive to these bodies and so the concept of the collective conditional fee agreement ('CCFA') was introduced[1].

A CCFA is defined as a CFA which does not refer to specific proceedings but which provides for fees to be payable on a common basis in relation to each class of proceedings to which it refers[2]. The 'client' is the person who will receive the services to which the agreement relates[3].

The collective elements of the CCFA are set out in a distinct document signed by the legal representatives and the funder[4] – a requirement which does not apply where the parties are a legal representative and additional legal representatives[5]. This is relevant where solicitors may be considering entering into a CCFA with a particular set of barristers' chambers for a category of work such as defamation.

Under a CCFA, the client is to be informed of the circumstances in which he might be liable to pay the lawyer's costs[6] and also such further information, explanation and advice about this as he may require[7]. (Again, this does not apply where the CCFA is between legal representative and further legal representative.) The lawyer must confirm his acceptance of instructions in writing to the client after accepting individual instructions[8].

A separate risk assessment must be undertaken and preserved for each case where a CCFA provides for a success fee[9].

There is no restriction on who may use collective conditional fee agreements, but realistically they are likely to be most popular among trade unions and other membership organisations for whom one of the prime benefits offered to members is support in defined categories of legal services. The extent to which such organisations support members in defamation claims varies widely – from those which have nothing to do with them, to those which refer such claims to a reputable firm, and from those which provide limited financial backing for pre-action investigative work, to those which offer full support for members (including court proceedings).

1   The Collective Conditional Fee Agreements Regulations 2000, SI 2000/2988.
2   SI 2000/2988, reg 3.
3   SI 2000/2988, reg 1.
4   SI 2000/2988, reg 6(1).
5   SI 2000/2988, reg 6(2).
6   SI 2000/2988, reg 4(2)(a).
7   SI 2000/2988, reg 4(2)(b).
8   SI 2000/2988, reg 4(3).
9   SI 2000/2988, reg 5.

Costs orders and assessment

7.15 The traditional position in the jurisdiction of England and Wales is that in litigation the loser pays the winning party its costs; indeed, this is sometimes referred to as 'the English rule'. This survived the introduction of the Civil Procedure Rules[1] but has been supplemented by the court's entitlement to make a different order[2]. Whether the court chooses to do so will largely depend on the view it takes of the conduct of the parties during the litigation. This flows from the enhanced role the judge is supposed to play in each action as a 'case manager', embodying a more hands-on approach during interlocutory hearings and guiding the parties towards the most proportionate way of dealing with the dispute at issue.

The words 'proportionate' and 'proportionality' are of critical importance under the CPR. The overriding objective set out in CPR 12.1 is for the court 'to deal with cases justly', which includes 'saving expense'[3] and

> 'dealing with the case in ways which are proportionate:
> (i)   to the amount of money involved;
> (ii) to the importance of the case;
> (iii) to the complexity of the issues;
> (iv) to the financial position of each party.'

What this all means is that the ongoing costs of the proceedings are now a central concern of the court – and an influence on the decisions it makes – instead of lurking in the shadows as in the past, only to spring out and horrify the losing party at the conclusion of the case.

It also means that simply because your client has won the case it does not necessarily mean that the loser will be ordered to pay all the costs. Solicitors should make it clear to their clients that the way in which they conduct themselves during litigation may affect the ultimate costs order. For example, if it appears to the court that one party has been over-aggressive and/or has imposed unreasonable deadlines, then it exposes itself to criticism 'on the issue of its entitlement to costs'[4].

1   CPR 44.3(2)(a).
2   CPR 44.3(2)(b).
3   CPR 1.1(2)(b).
4   *Mars UK Ltd v Teknowledge Ltd* [2000] ECDR 99.

7.16 Defamation actions can be conducted very aggressively – perhaps because it is such a personal form of litigation involving as it does the value of a reputation, because the combatants are frequently public figures and media organisations, neither of whom want to be seen to give an inch and perhaps because there are often very important issues at stake such as freedom of speech, privacy, confidence, the public's right to know, and the duties of responsible journalism. It means the litigation is often attritional and can involve numerous interlocutory hearings and more than its fair share of visits to the Court of Appeal. The consequence of this is that, in a contested defamation action, it is the rule rather than the exception that the costs incurred by the parties greatly exceed the damages (if any) which are ultimately awarded.

Generally speaking, on assessment costs judges will consider costs to be disproportionate if they exceed the value of the claim. However, there seems to be a recognition that because a defamation action is not just about money and usually involves a matter of principle which is exceptionally important to the claimant and/or defendant, the court will allow the recovery of costs exceeding the value of the claim.

However, even with the comfort that the costs judges recognise the factors in a defamation claim which tend to make it an intrinsically expensive form of litigation, it is worth taking certain precautions to try and save or minimise costs:

(a) Comply with the defamation pre-action protocol – a party can be punished in costs later in the litigation if it has not.

(b) In particular consider whether alternative dispute resolution might be an option – overcome the natural cynicism of a litigator about 'touchy-feely' mediation; it can work in the right case!

(c) At every stage consider whether there are issues which can be agreed between the parties. For example, defendants invariably dispute identification where a claimant has not been named in the words complained of, but libel trials are not lost because a jury concludes the claimant was not referred to in the words complained of. The costs of maintaining reference as an issue can be substantial as a huge number of witnesses (all of whom will have provided statements) are called to confirm that they identified the claimant, without prompting, from the words complained of.

(d) If you are contemplating an application which is likely to incur substantial costs, then notify your opponent in advance so they have an opportunity to object or to suggest an alternative approach which might be cheaper.

(e) Be open about the level of costs which are being incurred. If you are seen by a costs judge to have played by the rules, to have tried to agree issues to save costs, to have kept your opponent informed about potentially expensive steps you were proposing to take in the litigation and have been open about the level of ongoing costs, he is more likely to be sympathetic when you come to try and recover those costs as reasonable from that opponent at the conclusion of the case.

Summary assessment

7.17 An innovation reinforced by the Civil Procedure Rules[1] was the concept of summary assessment of costs at the end of interlocutory hearings lasting less than a day during the course of the litigation. Formerly, all costs were determined at the end of the case; now the parties should serve and file at least 24 hours in advance of any interlocutory hearing the statements of the costs which they seek to claim from their opponent should they obtain a costs order in their favour. If they do not, the court is likely to award that no costs should be paid.

The court will only carry out a summary assessment if a positive costs order has been made in favour of one party or the other, not if the order is 'costs in the case' or 'claimant's/defendant's costs in the case'.

Summary assessment has not been an entirely smooth innovation to date, particularly in the High Court where many judges have no previous experience of assessing costs. In their previous lives as barristers they would have had little or any experience either of negotiating their fees (a job left to their clerks) or attending a detailed assessment (formerly taxation) and being required to defend and justify their fees (a job left to their instructing solicitors). It is not surprising, therefore, that the summary assessment of costs is seen as something of a lottery by solicitors and as bewildering for clients. The position is somewhat different in county courts, where district judges tend to be experienced in conducting assessments.

It is becoming increasingly common in defamation cases where interlocutory hearings often spread over a number of days, and where the costs claimed by the successful party are substantial, for the judge to indicate that the costs should be the subject of a detailed assessment at the conclusion of the case, but, in the meantime, order the losing party to make an interim payment of a sum of costs less than that claimed to the successful party within a specified time. This seems an entirely sensible development.

1   CPR Pt 44 PD sets out the procedure for summary assessment.

Detailed assessment

7.18   The procedure and rules for the detailed assessment (formerly 'taxation') of costs has been improved and simplified under the Civil Procedure Rules. The procedure is set out in CPR 47. The main improvement is the intention that costs disputes be resolved quickly and that the parties concentrate on identifying the real issues between them for the court to determine. This is achieved by allowing the receiving party to apply for a default certificate if the paying party fails to lodge its objections to the detailed bill of costs within the relevant time period. If the default certificate is set aside, the paying party will still probably be ordered to pay a proportion of the costs immediately. There are also provisions for interim payments to dissuade paying parties from objecting to a bill simply to delay payment.

The costs consequences associated with CPR Pt 36 offers are dealt with in Chapter 26.

Common costs orders made at interlocutory hearings

7.19   Section 8.5 of the Practice Direction supplementing CPR 44.3 contains a useful table of commonly made costs orders at interlocutory hearings and explains their general effect. These are as helpful to have to hand in defamation as in any other area of civil litigation and so the table is set out below:

Term	Effect
● Costs ● Costs in any event	The party in whose favour the order is made is made is entitled to the costs in respect of the part of the proceedings to which the order relates, whatever other costs orders are made in the proceedings.
● Costs in the case ● Costs in the application	The party in whose favour the court makes an order for costs at the end of the proceedings is entitled to his costs of the part of the proceedings to which the order relates.
● Costs reserved	The decision about costs is deferred to a later occasion, but if no later order is made the costs will be costs in the case.

Term	Effect
• Claimant's/defendant's costs in the case/application	If the party in whose favour the costs order is made is awarded costs at the end of the proceedings, that party is entitled to his costs of the part of the proceedings to which the order relates. If any other party is awarded costs at the end of the proceedings, the party in whose favour the final costs order is made is not liable to pay the costs of any other party in respect of the part of the proceedings to which the order relates.
• Costs thrown away	Where, for example, a judgment or order is set aside, the party in whose favour the costs order is made is entitled to the costs which have been incurred as a consequence. This includes the costs of – (a) preparing for and attending any hearing at which the judgment or order which has been set aside was made; (b) preparing for and attending any hearing to set aside the judgment or order in question; (c) preparing for and attending any hearing at which the court orders the proceedings or the part in question to be adjourned; (d) any steps taken to enforce a judgment or order which has subsequently been set aside.
• Costs of and caused by	Where, for example, the court makes this order on an application to amend a statement of case, the party in whose favour the costs order is made is entitled to the costs of preparing for and attending the application and the costs of any consequential amendment to his own statement of case.

Term	Effect
• Costs here and below	The party in whose favour the costs order is made is entitled not only to his costs in respect of the proceedings in which the court makes the order but also to his costs of the proceedings in any lower court. In the case of an appeal from a Divisional Court the party is not entitled to any costs incurred in any court below the Divisional Court.
• No order as to costs • Each party to pay his own costs	Each party is to bear his own costs of the part of the proceedings to which the order relates whatever costs order the court makes at the end of the proceedings.

Chapter 8

The defamation pre-action protocol

Background

8.01 The Civil Procedure Rules endeavour to introduce a new culture to the civil justice system in which litigation is the last resort. One of the key innovations embodied in the CPR is the concept of pre-action protocols. These have gradually been introduced in most areas of civil litigation – usually as a result of the efforts of specialist practitioners in each area followed by a consultation process with the profession as a whole and other interested parties.

The Protocols Practice Direction states at paragraph 1.4 that the objects of the protocols are to:

(a) encourage the early and full exchange of information about a prospective claim;
(b) enable parties to settle claims without litigation; and
(c) support the efficient management of any proceedings that are issued.

In his foreword to the pre-action protocol for personal injury claims, Lord Irvine of Lairg, the Lord Chancellor, stated that:

'The protocol aims to improve pre-action communication between the parties by establishing a timetable for the exchange of information relevant to the dispute and by setting standards for the content of correspondence. Compliance with the protocol will enable parties to make an informed judgment on the merits of their cases earlier than tends to happen today, because they will have earlier access to the information they need. This will provide every opportunity for improved communications between the parties designed to lead to an increase in the number of pre-action settlements.'

8.02 The defamation pre-action protocol was developed and drafted by a working party comprising lawyers representing the full range of interests in the field of defamation and with considerable experience in the conduct of defamation claims. It emerged from a series of meetings held mainly at the Law Society (which endorsed the process) between April and October 1999, at the end of which a draft was submitted to the Lord Chancellor's Department. This document was then posted on the LCD website and sent specifically to a large number of individuals, firms and organisations with an interest in the subject as part of a thorough going consultation process.

This yielded a hearteningly modest number of comments and suggestions, none of which had not already been the subject of extensive and sometimes passionate discussion by the working party. The chair of the working party was consequently in a position to respond fully to the matters raised, to the satisfaction of the LCD, at the conclusion of the consultation process in April/May 2000.

The document was then submitted to and approved by the then head of Civil Justice, Lord Scott of Foscote, and was duly embodied in the CPR and became law as from 2 October 2000[1].

1   The defamation pre-action protocol can be found at Appendix 3.

Aims of the protocol

8.03 The defamation pre-action protocol was drafted bearing in mind the fact that, because of the one-year limitation period, time is always of the essence in defamation claims and that the claimant will almost always be seeking an immediate correction and/or apology as part of the process of restoring his reputation.

The protocol aims to achieve the following:

(a)   to set out a code of good practice which parties should follow when litigation is being considered;
(b)   to encourage the early settlement of a claim;
(c)   to encourage both parties to disclose sufficient information to enable each to understand the other's case and to promote the prospect of early resolution;
(d)   to set a timetable for the exchange of information relevant to the dispute;
(e)   to set standards for the content of correspondence;
(f)   to identify options which either party might adopt to encourage settlement of the claim;
(g)   should a claim proceed to litigation, to assist the court in dealing with liability for costs and making other orders (the extent to which the protocol has been followed both in practice and in spirit by the parties will have an effect here);

(h)   to keep the costs of resolving disputes subject to the protocol proportionate.

It should be noted that letters of claim and responses sent pursuant to the protocol are not intended to have the same status as a statement of case in proceedings.

The protocol itself

The letter of claim

8.04   The letter of claim should be sent 'at the earliest reasonable opportunity'. It was recognised that to impose a time limit following publication would be unfair and unrealistic because defamatory allegations do not necessarily come to the attention of the claimant immediately. This allows some flexibility while imposing an obligation to act without delay.

The information required for the letter of claim includes obvious details such as the name of the claimant, identification of the words complained of (enclosing a copy, if possible, of the offending publication) and the nature of the remedies sought. However, it also requires the claimant to set out 'factual inaccuracies or unsupportable comment within the words complained of' and 'a sufficient explanation to enable the defendant to appreciate why the words are inaccurate or unsupportable'.

Where relevant, the claimant should also detail the facts and matters which make him identifiable from the words complained of and any 'special facts relevant to the interpretation of the words complained of and/or particular damage caused by the words complained of'. This covers publications where the claimant is not named and/or where there is an innuendo meaning[1] and gives information relevant to an assessment of the damages which might be recovered.

Finally, the protocol states that 'it is desirable for the claimant to identify in the letter of the claim the meaning(s) he attributes to the words complained of'. No topic inspired such heated debate at the working party's meetings than the extent to which the claimant should be required to set out his interpretation of the meaning of the publication complained about. On the one hand, it was said how can you contemplate a defamation claim if you are not prepared to say what you contend the words mean? On the other hand, it was said that when the aim was to keep costs proportionate, it was unfair to oblige

67

the claimant to pin his colours to the mast at this stage since if counsel was subsequently instructed to settle particulars of claim and pleads a different or additional meaning then the defendant would use the disparity in the letter of claim to discredit or embarrass the claimant at trial. To impose an obligation would mean claimants instructing counsel to settle the letter of claim to ensure the meaning was fully and accurately particularised – not the idea at all under the CPR. Fair points both, and this clause was the compromise.

1   See Chapter 2, paragraphs 2.02–2.05 and Chapter 3, paragraphs 3.06–3.07.

The defendant's response

8.05   The requirements for the defendant's response to the letter of claim largely mirror those imposed on the claimant in the letter of claim. Indeed, it was the knowledge and acceptance that what was 'sauce for the goose was sauce for the gander' which informed the working party's discussions and assisted their agreement.

Consequently, the defendant must respond 'as soon as reasonably possible' to the letter of claim, but if that is going to take longer than 14 days then the defendant should tell the claimant the date by which he intends to respond.

The response should say whether the claim 'is accepted, whether more information is required or whether it is rejected'.

If it is accepted, then the defendant 'should indicate which remedies it is willing to offer'.

If more information is needed then the defendant 'should specify precisely what information is needed to enable the claim to be dealt with and why'.

If the claim is rejected, the defendant should say why, along with a 'sufficient indication of any facts on which the defendant is likely to rely in support of any substantive defence'.

Again, it is expressed as 'desirable' that the defendant includes his interpretation of the meaning of the words complained of.

The protocol specifically emphasises the need to keep costs proportionate to the nature and gravity of the case, and the stage the complaint has reached, when formulating the letter of claim and the response.

8.06   Finally, the protocol imposes an obligation on the parties to provide evidence to the court (should matters proceed that far) that alternative means of resolving their dispute were considered. It then sets out some options, which include mediation and arbitration. However, the most interesting and perhaps the most relevant suggested option is the 'determination by an independent third party (for example, a lawyer experienced in the field of defamation or an individual experienced in the subject matter of the claim) whose name and fees, along with the precise issues which are to be determined, will have been agreed by the parties in advance'.

This is certainly an avenue which media organisations have been keen to explore – principally as a means of obtaining a 'ruling' on meaning at an early stage with comparatively little expense. It is undoubtedly true that many cases over the years have been contested to trial largely because there has been a fundamental difference of opinion between the parties over the meaning of the words complained of. There are certainly attractions about the idea of the parties submitting to a ruling from a jointly instructed and agreed libel or other expert of an issue which, once determined, might well lead to the resolution of the claim one way or the other.

The Fleet Street Lawyers Association would like to formulate (and perhaps formalise) a procedure to achieve this, and Alastair Brett, the Legal Manager of Times Newspapers Ltd, presented his paper's 'Fast Track Arbitration Rules for resolution of "meaning" or "quantum" disputes in libel actions' at the Protecting the Media Conference in October 2000. These included a list of experts (drawn up by the newspaper's legal team) for fast track arbitration comprising five practising silks and two retired judges with extensive libel experience.

8.07 An example of an issue other than meaning or quantum which might be resolved in this way is as follows. Suppose a radio station broadcast a phone-in programme on which a caller made some very serious allegations about police officers with whom he had recently had dealings and whom he named. The police officers bring a libel claim against the radio station (the caller being a 'man of straw'). The radio station does not suggest there is any truth in the allegations but contends that it is protected by the innocent dissemination defence under the DeA 1996, s 1[1].

Clearly, once this issue is resolved, the case will be capable of resolution. Might not the best approach be for the parties to submit to a ruling from a libel expert on whether the DeA 1996, s 1 defence applies after considering the steps the radio station had taken to prevent defamatory allegations being broadcast in this way, the training staff had received and other such relevant matters?

This will be an area to watch in the development of defamation in the new era and it may be the way in which the costs of this procedure are borne which will determine its success or otherwise. This is particularly the case where an individual of average means is bringing a claim against a wealthy media organisation. The possibility that an individual of modest means may be deterred by the prospect of having to contribute to the cost of ADR seems to be recognised by the media defendants because the Times Newspaper Fast Track Arbitration Rules provide for payment of the arbitrator's fees by the newspaper. The payback is that the claimant limits his damages to £10,000 and legal costs to £5,000.

1   See Chapter 2, paragraph 2.10 and Chapter 4, paragraph 4.26.

The future?

8.08   The success or otherwise of the defamation pre-action protocol lies not in the hands of the lawyers but with the courts.

There is no immediate sanction if you ignore the protocol. Your punishment, if it comes, arrives when the matter is heard by a court and your conduct is reviewed by the judge.

If the judges back up the protocol by penalising parties who ride roughshod over its provisions with heavy adverse costs orders then it will acquire credibility and force. If the courts shy away from such orders, then it will lose credibility and will be ignored. That would be a shame because the protocol was developed by a panel of individuals with every shade of opinion on the libel spectrum and was welcomed by the profession as a pragmatic document. It can play an important role along with all the other recent statutory changes in changing the perception that defamation claims are the exclusive preserve of the rich, famous and foolhardy.

Chapter 9

The letter of claim

9.01 The letter of claim is a document of crucial importance in a libel action. Not only must the content be clear and complete, but the tone must be pitched just right. This is because in a libel trial, while the jury is most unlikely to see the parties' statements of case, you can be absolutely certain that it will see (in the jury bundle) and hear the letter of claim – probably several times. The claimant's counsel will inevitably read out the letter of claim in his opening speech. The defendant's counsel will also refer to it if there is anything in its contents which can be exploited to his client's advantage, for example an inflated demand for damages which suggests the claimant is a gold-digger, or mistakes as to crucial dates which may suggest the claimant is not as concerned about the circumstances of his claim as he makes out. The jury's initial response to the claimant's claim – and indeed to the claimant himself – may well be set by the terms of the letter of claim. Now, in addition, the content of the letter of claim must comply with the requirements of the pre-action protocol[1].

Equally, the jury may well form its important initial view about the defendant from his response to the letter of claim. That too will always find a way into the jury bundle and will invariably be read out by counsel. Again, the pre-action protocol sets standards for the content of the response to the letter of claim, and a defendant ignores these at his financial peril. In the past, one frequently received replies to letters of claim which had clearly been drafted in some haste by the editor while a red mist still surrounded him following receipt of the letter of claim. These were sometimes phrased in such arrogant, dismissive and furious terms that any jury seeing them would undoubtedly react negatively to the defendant as a result. Such letters look more and more crass as the case proceeds and the facts emerge about the damage caused to the claimant and the actual level of investigation undertaken by the defendant before publication.

A claimant might be impressed if at his first meeting his solicitor grabs a dictaphone and rattles off a ferocious sounding letter of claim there and then. Similarly, the editor of a newspaper receiving a letter of claim might think it best to slam back with a barnstorming response. However, almost invariably both parties will be poorly served by adopting that approach.

1 See Chapter 8.

Drafting the letter of claim

9.02 The pre-action protocol requires the claimant to notify the defendant of his claim at the earliest possible opportunity. Since the letter of claim can in many ways be viewed as the first pleading and will often set out the claimant's interpretation of the meaning of the article, one can certainly consider asking counsel to settle the letter of claim. The pre-action protocol mentions the desirability of both claimant and defendant including the meanings they attribute to the words complained of. The cost of this will almost always be recoverable on assessment[1]. However, if counsel does settle the letter, do not be afraid to tweak it when you receive the draft – as has been mentioned, the tone of the letter is crucial.

Consider carefully what you are hoping to achieve with the letter of claim. Generally it should be written in forceful but courteous terms and should make it clear that proceedings will follow if no satisfactory response is received within a stipulated time limit. Before the advent of the Civil Procedure Rules, one could be fairly confident that it would be necessary to follow up the letter with a claim form (or writ as it then was). Experience showed that defendants rarely settled a claim in response to the letter before action. In the new era, claims are increasingly being resolved without proceedings, and the claimant should consider very carefully the remedies he actually wants rather than adopting an extreme stance just to provide a negotiating position. There may be costs consequences if the claimant drops his demands to realistic levels further down the line rather than at the outset. It is in your client's interests to do what you can to promote an early settlement. Ensure that he is fully informed about the options, eg by indicating to him that he may need to waive his entitlement to damages if he wants an apology in agreed form to be published promptly. Make sure your instructions are clear because your client will be exposed to all sorts of difficulties if he changes his stance significantly after his claim has been presented to the defendant in the letter before action.

1 See Chapter 7, paragraphs 7.15–7.16.

Contents of the letter of claim

9.03   Remember that the claimant is presumed to be of good character. The burden of proof lies with the defendant to prove that what is published was true, or that it is protected by some other defence. However, the pre-action protocol does stipulate what must be included:

(a)   Announce who you are acting for and identify the publication in respect of which you have been instructed. Give details of the words complained of, and enclose a copy if possible.

(b)   Explain that the allegations in the article (or broadcast, or letter, etc) are false and defamatory.

(c)   Proceed to explain briefly why the allegations are false. It is in this explanation that hostages to fortune may be offered. Some claimants remember every detail of the circumstances which gave rise to the defamatory publication and communicate these to you clearly and unambiguously at your first meeting. However, more usually there are areas of uncertainty or areas where witness evidence from others or documentary evidence will be needed. One will normally wish to send the letter of claim before one has incurred the expense of seeing all your client's witnesses. Therefore, it is sensible to confine the details in the letter of claim to those facts of which you are certain, rather than to tie your client to an explanation which is later changed or expanded. That gives helpful cross-examination material to the defendant which may ultimately cause a jury to doubt your client's credibility. The pre-action protocol requires a sufficient explanation to enable the defendant to appreciate why the words are inaccurate or unsupportable.

(d)   It is desirable to state the meaning of the words complained of. The meaning will be a key component of the particulars of claim – another reason why counsel should at least approve the letter of claim; it would be profoundly unsatisfactory if counsel did not agree with your interpretation of the words when he came to settle the statement of case.

(e)   Itemise your client's requirements in order to settle his claim. These should be realistic. Gratifying as it might be to the claimant to contemplate the sensitive parts of the anatomies of certain newspaper editors being subjected to the attentions of a vice, it is not a realistic demand! The demands for settlement will normally be all or some of the following:

(i) publication of an apology in a form and with a prominence to be agreed. One will often enclose a draft apology for the defendant's consideration and will suggest where it might be published, for example, on page 3, in a box above the fold of the newspaper. Be realistic about this – even the most serious libel will not get a front page headline apology (although on a very few occasions international celebrities have achieved this 'holy grail')[1]. If the publication complained of is something other than a newspaper article, then the apology demand will vary accordingly – it could taken the form of a broadcast apology (in relation to a TV programme), a personal letter of apology, an e-mail or even a website posting[2].

(ii) an undertaking from those responsible for the libel never to publish the same or similar defamatory remarks in the future. Remember if this stipulation is ultimately embodied in a consent order, it will be seen as an undertaking to the court – and breach could be viewed as contempt.

(iii) joining in the reading of a statement in open court. This normally requires ongoing proceedings and so the issue of a claim form (see paragraph 9.04 below). Statements in open court are dealt with in detail in Chapter 27. The purpose of a statement in open court is straightforward – it is designed to give wider currency to the settlement of the claimant's claim than would be the case if there was simply an apology, eg published in the defendant's newspaper. A statement read in open court attracts absolute privilege if reported fairly, accurately and contemporaneously[3], and so other newspapers or broadcasters can report the statement (which will usually detail the libel before refuting it) without fear of attracting a libel claim form themselves. It is a particularly useful remedy where there is a libel which has attracted a great deal of local publicity. A statement will usually be fully reported in all local newspapers and on local television.

(iv) payment of a sum of damages by way of compensation. Do not mention figures – if you do, you will have established a ceiling from which your client will only ever descend. Do not suggest that the damages should be 'huge', 'enormous', 'vast' or anything similar – the jury will think your client is being greedy, particularly when the defendant's counsel has suggested it for the fortieth time!

(v)   payment of your client's legal costs in full. A schedule of the costs incurred to date should be supplied if you are claiming them. Pre-action costs are an area fraught with uncertainty and peril. The Solicitors Conduct Rules 1996 (Rule 17.03) require you to give the paying party a breakdown of your costs if he requires it in order to make an informed decision about whether or not to pay them. Pre-action assessment of costs is a subject which makes the Gordian Knot look straightforward. The simple advice is that you should try to ensure that any agreement to settle your client's claim includes payment of costs, and agreement of a figure saves much time, cost and angst for both parties. Anything else is inviting unlooked-for difficulties. However, remember that the paying party must be given sufficient opportunity to agree your costs on an informed basis, and if you cannot agree then you must submit to assessment.

(f)   Finally, impose some time limit for a reply to your letter of claim – usually 14 days. Be reasonable if the defendant asks for a bit more time to put together his response. However, leave your client in no doubt that it will be counter-productive to send a letter of claim and not to follow it up with a claim form if no satisfactory response is received. If the defendant calls your bluff and no proceedings are issued, then metaphorical lips could be licked because he knows he can probably libel your client with impunity. The lesson taught by every Hollywood western is a sound one – do not start what you are not prepared to finish.

1   Certainly a newspaper would very rarely agree to it.
2   Where the apology is to be published to persons other than the claimant, the defendant should take care to ensure that he does not libel anyone else! Depending on the circumstances, such a libel may be protected by the defence of qualified privilege (see Chapter 15), but it is better not to run the risk in the first place.
3   See the DeA 1996, s 14(1) and Chapter 27.

When to issue

9.04   Normally one would not issue a claim form for libel on behalf of the claimant before sending a letter of claim, but there may be good reasons for doing so. For example:

(a)   if it is a fundamental objective of your client that a statement be read in open court, then that may only be achieved if there are ongoing proceedings (the procedures for listing and reading a statement in open court are discussed later in this book[1]). Consequently, it demonstrates the seriousness of your client's intent in that regard if the claim form has been issued and accompanies the letter of claim;

(b) if circumstances have conspired so that the letter of claim is dispatched close to the one-year limitation period for bringing libel proceedings, then it might be prudent to issue the claim form and send it with the letter of claim. Apart from demonstrating your client's seriousness in making the claim, it also avoids the scenario where the defendant lulls you into believing that your client's claim will be settled amicably but in fact simply wishes to prolong and deflect the pre-action skirmishes, perhaps with a view to taking them past the limitation period;

(c) if there has already been correspondence between your client and the defendant, then it may be pointless to send yet another letter. Indeed, such a letter may be seen by the defendant as evidence that your client is reluctant to embark on litigation. In this situation, it is often best to indicate early that matters have progressed to a different plane.

1   See Chapter 27.

Responding to the letter of claim

9.05   The response to the letter of claim is another extremely important document because, once again, it is certain to be seen by the jury. If the tone is ill-judged and/or the content is inaccurate, flippant or bullying, then the jury will draw an adverse conclusion from which the defendant may never recover. Much as it irks journalists to trust anyone else with the formulation of words, it is best to allow one's lawyer to prepare the response or, at the very least, to vet the letter before it is sent. The key elements are as follows:

(a) the letter should clearly be seen to be taking the claim seriously;

(b) the tone should be firm and business-like but polite and courteous;

(c) if a time limit has been imposed in the letter of claim then some response must be made within that time limit. A full response is preferable but if you require more time, then ask for it. However, you should note that if the words complained of purport to be a carefully researched and investigated piece of journalism, a jury may be a little sceptical that the newspaper or broadcaster needs more time to make further enquiries when the veracity of the piece is questioned: should not all that research be in a file somewhere?

(d) do not tie yourself to a position which may prove to be more of a hindrance than a help later when the defence comes to be pleaded – another reason for involving the lawyers at an early stage;

(e) finally, if you are in the wrong and it is obvious, then admit it! Humble pie eaten at this early stage is a considerably cheaper dish than the same delicacy consumed six months down the litigation line. As Dennis Healey used to remark: 'If you are in a hole, stop digging'.

Chapter 10

Issue and service of the claim

10.01 This chapter sets out when and where a claim should be started, in accordance with procedural requirements and taking into account tactical considerations. It also identifies what a claim form and particulars of claim should contain.

Issuing the claim form

When?

Procedural requirements

10.02 Proceedings are started when the court issues a claim form at the request of the claimant. Prior to issue, the claimant should be sure that he has satisfied all the requirements of any applicable pre-action protocol[1].

The claim form must be issued before the expiry of the one-year limitation period. After the expiry of the limitation period, the prospective claimant should make a CPR Pt 23 application to the court to exercise its discretion under the LA 1980, s 32A, to direct that the one-year time limit shall not apply[2]. If the claimant does not seek the court's permission to issue proceedings, it is likely that the point will be taken in the defence and an application to strike out will follow.

After a claim form has been issued, it must be served upon the defendant[3]. Within the jurisdiction, the claim form must be served within four months of issue. Outside the jurisdiction, the prescribed period for service is six months[4].

1   See Chapter 8.
2   See Chapter 16, paragraph 16.04.
3   For methods of service, see CPR 6. Note that service upon the legal representative of a party will not be effective unless this has been agreed by the parties. This is the case even where a legal representative has been dealing with all pre-action correspondence on behalf of a party.
4   CPR 7.5.

Tactical considerations

10.03 The historical position was that the first communication a defendant might receive from an aggrieved claimant was a writ (now a 'claim form'). Alternatively, a fiercely-worded letter of claim might set the briefest of time limits for a full response, failing which the writ would be served.

The culture has now changed and this is supported by recent legislation. Since 2 October 2000, parties must comply with the defamation pre-action protocol[1] before issuing proceedings or face the prospect of an adverse costs order in subsequent litigation. The protocol, apart from encouraging the parties to exchange sufficient information to understand each other's cases, also imposes a requirement to consider alternative means of resolving the dispute.

There is also the practical fact to bear in mind that some defamation actions are run on conditional fee agreements. If so, then it would be a foolish or confident lawyer who committed his client to litigation without conducting sufficient pre-action inquiries to determine the merits of the claim and its prospects of success. And surely such inquiries must include in virtually all cases an attempt to ascertain your opponent's case as well as their financial standing?

The principle of proportionality embodied in the CPR[2] also has a relevance here – will the courts endorse a party who shoots first and asks questions later? Almost certainly not.

However, there is only a one-year limitation period within which to bring a defamation action[3] and this reflects the view that if your reputation has been damaged then you will want to act quickly to restore it. Certainly, media defendants have perennially criticised any delay on the part of a claimant bringing his claim, with the implication that if you wait it cannot have been that serious. There is no doubt that the issue and service of a claim form shows you are serious!

It is also the case that if a claim for injunctive relief[4] is an important part of the remedy sought by the claimant, then proceedings must be issued immediately. This comes with the warning that successful applications for injunctions in defamation actions approach hen's teeth in rarity value, and the impact of the freedom of expression provisions in the HRA 1998 is likely to confine defamation injunctions still further.

1   See Chapter 8.
2   CPR 1.1(2)(c).
3   The DeA 1996, s 5.
4   See Chapter 5.

10.04 Finally, a consequence of the court's approach following the advent of the CPR seems to be a greater willingness to strike out claims issued and/or served outside the expiry of the limitation period (and the four-month limit for service)[1]. This means that with such a short limitation period there is a significant incentive on solicitors, with an eye on their professional indemnity premiums, to adopt a cautious approach and ensure that a claim form is issued in good time before the limitation period expires. Minor slips in naming of parties on the claim form may be dealt with more leniently by the courts[2].

The principal tactical considerations are, therefore, to balance the requirements to follow the pre-action steps stipulated by the protocol with the need to comply with the short limitation period and the importance of avoiding the charge of delay.

On the part of the defendant, in most cases there is little to be lost in skilfully stretching out pre-action exchanges to take the sting out of the claimant's anger and to acclimatise him to the formidable demands of pursuing an action. On the other hand, if you are eventually going to settle you are likely to be adding to your ultimate costs bill by this approach, even if by doing so you reduce the damages figure you pay. Also an issued claim form is a public document and will often attract publicity in its own right. The author was surprised after issuing a routine claim form against a small local radio station to receive telephone calls from three national newspapers and a local paper and then to see the action reported in other newspapers too. That unwelcome publicity for the radio station could have been avoided if it had swallowed the bitter pill of settlement during the pre-action exchanges instead of waiting until after issue and service of proceedings.

The issue of pre-action costs, whether they are reasonable and who should be responsible for them, is going to assume a growing importance. It had been a strangely neglected area until the coming into force of the CPR, at least in reported case law. To put your client in the best position, it is prudent to advise your opponent if you are going to incur significant pre-action costs, explain why you contend your actions are reasonable and ask them to notify you in writing their objections, if they have any. That sort of correspondence complies with the new culture and will be useful at any subsequent assessment.

1   In *Smith v Probyn* [2000] All ER (D) 250 – the claimant's solicitors served the defendants' solicitors, but not the defendant. Morland J held that the solicitor did not generally have implied authority to accept service on behalf of the client – indeed it would be a breach of his professional duty to the client. The defendant's solicitors had not misled the claimant's solicitors. The claim was struck out.
2   *Gregson v Channel Four* [2000] All ER (D) 956.

Where?

Procedural requirements

10.05 Proceedings for defamation may not be started in the county court unless the parties have agreed to do so in writing[1]. For that reason, proceedings for defamation are in nearly every case brought in the High Court. The venue for proceedings for malicious falsehood will depend upon the perceived value of the claim; if the claimant expects to recover more than £15,000, the claimant should issue in the High Court[2].

1 See the County Courts Act 1984 (CCA 1984), s 15(2)(c), and CPR Pt 7 PD, para 2.9(1).
2 See CPR Pt 7 PD, para 3.6(ii).

Tactical considerations

10.06 When you have won the toss in a test match, the traditional wisdom is that you think about putting your opponents in to bat and then indicate that you will bat first.

A similar approach prevails in defamation when considering the venue for issuing proceedings. Think about your local county court, the friendly district judge, the convenience for your client and witnesses – and then issue in the High Court in London.

Statute endorses that approach while giving unlimited jurisdiction in most contract and tort cases[1]. Proceedings for libel and slander should be issued in the High Court unless, as mentioned above, the parties consent to a county court venue or the case is transferred to a county court from the High Court[2] (a virtually unheard of step).

Of more relevance is whether one should issue in a district registry of the High Court. If you do, remember there are only relatively few district registries which will conduct a defamation trial with a jury – so the venue assigned for the trial might well be many miles away from where you issued and just as inconvenient for the parties and witnesses as if you had gone down the conventional London route.

There can certainly be good reasons for wanting your defamation action tried in a district registry, from the location of your witnesses and the prospect of a more sympathetic, less cynical jury to the broad regional accent of your client which might be incomprehensible to a London jury. However, even in such cases there must be very good reasons for not issuing in London and conducting all interlocutory hearings in front of the Masters highly experienced in defamation or, more relevantly, the specialist defamation judges. If your reasons are good enough, you could issue in London and, later on, an order can be obtained for the trial to be listed in your local district registry. That may enable your client to get the best of both worlds.

1 The CCA 1984, s 15(1).
2 The CCA 1984, s 15(2).

10.07 It is no coincidence that most of the specialist libel firms and the two specialist libel sets of chambers are located in central London. The fact is that the overwhelming majority of defamation cases are conducted in the Royal Courts of Justice.

As a claimant, you should also bear in mind that most media organisations are based in London, as are their in-house lawyers, solicitors and barristers. If the trial is listed in Hull or Leeds, then you are adding a substantial chunk to your opponent's costs as the entourage comes to town for two or three weeks. That is fine if you win, but if you do not . . .

Malicious falsehood cases are far less common than defamation cases, but the principal practitioners tend to be the same and the same considerations apply.

A final thought relates to damages. A jury bears the responsibility for determining the figure following guidance from the judge and the parties' barristers. Would a London jury invited, for example, to consider making an award which would enable the successful claimant to purchase a new house have a different figure in mind to a Hull jury given the same invitation?

Content of the claim form

10.08 The CPR require a claimant to use Form N1 to start a claim[1]. The claim form and every other statement of case[2] must be headed with the title of the proceedings[3]. The claim form must contain a concise statement of the nature of the claim and specify the remedy the claimant seeks[4]. A claim form for libel must identify the publication which is the subject of the claim[5]. A claim form for slander must so far as possible contain the words complained of, and identify the person to whom they were spoken and when[6].

A claim form should, therefore, state that the claim is for damages, identify the cause of action relied upon by the claimant (libel, slander, etc), identify the offending publication (by reference to its date, title or other identifying criteria), and state that it was published or caused to be published by the defendant. It is usual also to include a claim for an injunction to restrain the defendant from repeating the substance of the offending statement. The claim form must state whether the claimant expects to recover (a) not more than £5,000; (b) more than £5,000 but not more than £15,000; or (c) more than £15,000 or that he cannot say how much he expects to recover[7]. The claim form must be verified by a statement of truth in the prescribed form[8]. Where the particulars of claim are not included in or are not served with the claim form, the claim form must contain a statement that particulars of claim will follow[9].

If proceedings are issued in the High Court, the claim form for a defamation action should contain a statement to the effect that the claim may only be commenced in the High Court by virtue of section 15(2)(c) of the CCA 1984. The claim form for a malicious falsehood action in the High Court should contain a statement to the effect that the claimant expects to recover more than £15,000[10]. For sample claim forms, see Volume 25 of *Atkin's Court Forms*.

1 CPR Pt 7 PD, para 3.1. This form can be downloaded from www.courtservice. gov.uk.
2 Particulars of claim, defence, reply, etc.
3 See CPR Pt 7 PD, para 4 for further details.
4 CPR 16.2(1).
5 CPR Pt 53 PD, para 2.2(1).
6 CPR Pt 53 PD, para 2.2(2).
7 CPR 16.3(2). Unless there is a claim for special damages, the usual statement in a defamation claim form will be to the effect that the claimant cannot say how much he expects to recover.
8 See CPR Pt 7 PD, para 7 and CPR 16.2(2).
9 CPR Pt 7 PD, para 6.2 and CPR Pt 16 PD, para 3.3.
10 CPR 16.3(5) and CPR Pt 7 PD, para 3.6.

Content of the particulars of claim

10.09 The CPR permit the particulars of claim to be included on the same document as the claim form or to be an entirely separate document[1]. In proceedings for libel or malicious falsehood it is usual and advisable for the particulars of claim to set out on a separate document. This is because a claim form is a public document, and a claimant is unlikely to want to re-publish the offending statement to all the world. This used to be the case for slander actions also, but CPR Pt 53 PD, para 2.2(2) now requires a claimant in a slander case to set out the words complained of in the claim form[2].

Where the particulars of claim are recorded separately, they too must be headed with the title of the proceedings[3], and must be verified with a statement of truth[4].

The general provisions of the CPR provide that the particulars of claim must include a concise statement of the facts on which the claimant relies[5]. Specifically, the claimant must specify in the particulars of claim the defamatory meaning which he alleges that the words complained of conveyed, both as to their natural and ordinary, and any innuendo, meaning. In the case of an innuendo meaning, the claimant must also identify the relevant extraneous facts he relies upon to establish that meaning[6].

If the claimant is seeking aggravated or exemplary damages, a statement to that effect and the grounds for claiming them must also be set out[7]. In defamation proceedings, the claimant must give full details of all the facts and matters on which he relies in support of his claim for damages in any event[8].

Usually, particulars of claim will introduce the claimant, then the defendant. They will identify the offending publication by title, date, page, mode, place or any other relevant factor. The words complained of will be set out. If the claimant is not named in the words complained of, it is advisable to set out matters relied upon as causing readers to understand the words to refer to the claimant. The meanings relied upon should follow. The claimant then makes a general assertion of damage to reputation followed by details of all the facts and matters relied upon in support of his claim for damages. A declaration to the effect that, unless restrained, the defendant will republish the defamatory statement follows, and the particulars of claim close with a prayer for the relief sort. For sample particulars of claim see Volume 25 of *Atkin's Court Forms*. CPR Pt 16 PD, para 13.3 provides that a claimant who wishes to may also refer to any point of law on which his claim is based, give the name of any witness he proposes to call and attach to or serve with his particulars of claim a copy of any document which he considers necessary to it.

1   CPR Pt 7 PD, para 6.1.
2   CPR Pt 53 PD, para 2.4 further provides that 'In a claim for slander the precise words used and the names of the persons to whom they were spoken and when must, so far as possible, be set out in the particulars of claim, if not already contained in the claim form'.
3   CPR Pt 7 PD, para 4 and CPR Pt 16 PD, para 3.8.
4   CPR 22. See CPR Pt 7 PD, para 7.2 and CPR Pt 16 PD, para 3.4 for the form of words.
5   See CPR Pt 16 PD, para 9 for a list of general application of matters which must be specifically set out in the particulars of claim if relied upon.
6   CPR Pt 53 PD, para 2.3.
7   Various other provisions apply if the claimant is seeking a specified amount of money or is claiming interest: see generally CPR 16.4.
8   CPR Pt 53 PD, para 2.10(1).

Service of the particulars of claim

10.10   Where the particulars of claim are recorded separately, they may either be served at the same time as the claim form or within 14 days of the service of the claim form. However, the particulars of claim must be served within four months of the issue of the claim form where the claim is served within the jurisdiction, and within six months where the claim is served outside the jurisdiction[1].

1   CPR Pt 7 PD, para 6.1 and CPR Pt 16 PD, para 3.2.

Chapter 11

Defences – generally

11.01 Once the particulars of claim have been served upon the defendant, he is obliged to prepare a document giving his response to the allegation made by the claimant – his defence. This chapter sets out the procedure to be adopted in preparing and filing a defence in general terms, before outlining in brief the various defences to a claim for defamation and the pleading requirements specific to each. Each defence referred to below is dealt with in greater detail in later chapters[1]. Finally, the chapter contains a list of some of the more common misconceptions about what is (but in fact is not) a defence to a claim for defamation, and outlines the next stage following filing of the defence.

1 Readers should note that the rarer defences, applicable to the law generally, such as res judicata, are outside the scope of this book.

Procedural requirements

11.02 A defendant is not required to take any step in a case until he has been served with the particulars of claim[1]. Once the defendant has been served with the particulars of claim he has two options[2]. He may either file a defence[3] or file an acknowledgment of service[4], which buys him extra time for filing his defence. Failure to file a defence or acknowledgment of service (if applicable) within the prescribed time limits could result in default judgment being entered against the defendant[5].

Where a defendant has entered into any funding arrangement[6], before filing any document he must file a notice to that effect in the appropriate form with his first document, whether it be an acknowledgment of service or defence, and must serve copies of it with that document[7].

1 Which may be set out in the claim form or (more commonly) be a separate document entirely: see CPR 9.1(2).
2 CPR 9.2.

3 See CPR 15.
4 See CPR 10.
5 See CPR 12 and CPR 15.3.
6 For example, a CFA: see Chapter 7 and CPR 43.2.
7 On Form N251. See also CPR 44.3B and CPR 44.15. A defendant who enters into a funding arrangement on or after filing his first document must file and serve the notice of funding within seven days of entering into the arrangement: CPR Pt 44 PD, para 19.2.

Time limits for claims served within the jurisdiction

11.03 Within 14 days[1] of service of the particulars of claim, the defendant can either file a defence or he can file the acknowledgment of service[2]. If he files the acknowledgment of service, he then has a total of 28 days from service of the particulars of claim in which to file his defence[3].

1 See CPR 10.3 and CPR 15.4(1).
2 CPR 10.1(3) provides that a defendant may file an acknowledgment of service if he is unable to file a defence within the 14-day limit. 'Filing' means delivery to the court office. The court office will then notify the claimant: CPR 10.4.
3 See CPR 15.4(1)(b).

Time limits for claims served outside the jurisdiction

11.04 Where the court's permission was not required for service of the claim form outside the jurisdiction[1], the defendant has either 21 or 31 days from service of the particulars of claim in which to file an acknowledgment of service or defence[2]. If he files an acknowledgment of service, he will then have either 35 or 45 days after service of the particulars of claim in which to file his defence.

Where the court's permission was required for service outside the jurisdiction[3], the order giving that permission will specify the periods within which the defendant may file an acknowledgment of service or defence[4].

1 See CPR 6.19.
2 See CPR 6.22 and CPR 6.23.
3 See CPR 6.20.
4 CPR 6.21(4).

The acknowledgment of service

11.05   A defendant who wishes to acknowledge service should do so on Form N9[1]. An acknowledgment of service must be signed by the defendant or his legal representative and must include the defendant's address for service[2]. For further information on the content of the acknowledgment of service, see the Practice Direction to CPR Pt 10.

1   CPR Pt 10 PD, para 2.
2   See CPR 10.5. Note that CPR 6.5 provides that an address for service must be within the jurisdiction, and that special provisions apply in relation to acknowledgment of service by a firm: CPR Sch 1, RSC Ord 81.

The defence

Service

11.06   CPR 15.6A provides that a copy of the defence must be served on every other party to the litigation. However, the rules do not say when this should be done or who should do it. It is suggested that the defendant either serve copies direct and, on filing the defence, inform the court that they have done so or, on filing the defence, supply sufficient copies for the court to serve it pursuant to CPR 6.3(3).

Extension of time

11.07   The time for filing the defence may be extended by consent with the claimant up to a maximum further 28 days (56 days from service of the particulars of claim where the claim was served within the jurisdiction), in which case the defendant must notify the court in writing[1]. If the claimant does not consent, or if the defendant requires any further extension, he should apply to the court using the CPR Pt 23 procedure[2].

1   CPR 15.5.
2   See CPR 23.

Consequences of late filing

11.08   In practice, if the time for filing a defence has expired and the claimant has taken no step to obtain judgment in default, the court office will accept the defence, file it and proceed as usual. It will then be too late for the claimant to proceed to obtain judgment in default. However, where at least six months have elapsed since the end of the usual applicable period for filing a defence and the claimant has not entered or applied for default or summary judgment, the claim will be automatically stayed[1]. It is then up to one of the parties to apply to have the stay lifted.

1 See CPR 15.11. In essence, a stay is the equivalent of pressing a 'pause' button.

Content

Mandatory

11.09 The content of a defence to a defamation claim is governed by CPR 16, which is of general application, and the Practice Direction to CPR Pt 53, which applies only to defamation claims. For the form to be adopted, see the sample defences set out in Volume 25 of *Atkin's Court Forms*.

CPR 16.5 provides that the defendant must in every case provide a comprehensive response to the particulars of claim, stating which of the allegations in it he admits, which he is unable to admit or deny, but requires the claimant to prove, and which he denies. Where the defendant denies an allegation he must then go on to state his reasons for doing so, and if he intends to put forward a different version of events from that given by the claimant, he must state his own version. If a defendant fails to deal with an allegation, he will be taken to admit it (unless he has set out in his defence the nature of his case in relation to the issue to which that allegation is relevant, in which case he shall be taken to require that allegation to be proved). The defence must be accompanied by a statement of truth. If the defendant disputes the claimant's statement of value he must state why he disputes it; and, if he is able, must give his own statement of the value of the claim. If he is acting in any representative capacity, he should state what it is. If no acknowledgment of service has been filed, he is also required to give an address for service, which must be within the jurisdiction[1].

The CPR do not in terms state that a defendant should set out his case in mitigation of damage (ie why, if he is found liable, he should not pay as much as the claimant is envisaging). However, the CPR do require the claimant to set out his case in support of his claim for damage and in aggravation of damage[2], and the effect of this, coupled with the provisions of CPR 16.5, is to oblige the defendant to plead his

89

case in mitigation – otherwise he risks being taken to admit what the claimant has alleged. In practice, the defendant's case in mitigation of damage has always been set out in his defence. Some of the most common examples of matters relied on by a defendant in this regard are the fact that he published an apology, that he allowed the claimant a right of reply, or that the publication was not circulated so widely or with such prominence as the claimant contends.

The Practice Direction to CPR Pt 53 sets out what must be included in a defence which pleads any of the following defences: justification, fair comment, absolute or qualified privilege or offer or amends. The rules for each are set out under individual sub-headings below. Additionally, CPR Pt 16 PD, para 14.1 requires the defendant to give details of the expiry of any limitation period relied on.

1   See CPR 6.5.
2   CPR Pt 53 PD, para 2.10.

Optional

11.10   If the defendant so wishes, CPR Pt 16 PD, para 13 provides that he may also refer to any point of law on which his defence is based, give the name of any witness he proposes to call and attach to or serve with his defence a copy of any document which he considers necessary to his defence.

'Holding defences'

11.11   Under the pre-CPR regime, it was common practice for a defendant to serve a 'holding defence', usually consisting of a bare denial that the words published were defamatory and indicating that the full defence would follow. Such a defence would not comply with CPR 16 and in any event the rules specifically provide that such a defence may be struck out under CPR 3.4[1] (assuming that the words published were plainly defamatory).

1   See CPR Pt 3 PD, para 1.6(1).

Specific defences

11.12   'Defences' to a claim for defamation fall into three broad categories: (a) denial of a necessary ingredient of the cause of action, (b) procedural and (c) substantive defences.

Denial of an ingredient of the cause of action

11.13 The necessary ingredients of an action for defamation were dealt with in detail in Chapter 2. In outline they are that the words complained of:

(a) refer to the claimant;
(b) are defamatory of the claimant; and
(c) were published to a third party.

If the defendant contends that one or more of these ingredients is completely absent from the claimant's claim, for example because there was no publication to a third party and the claimant does not contend that there was, the easiest course is for the defendant to apply to strike out the claim under CPR 3.4. If, however, there is some dispute about whether an element of the claim will be established, the defendant should plead this in the defence[1]. So, if, for example, the claimant claims that the defendant slandered him by calling him a 'nasty little thief' in the presence of X, and it is the defendant's case that he did say that to him, but that they were in a lift at the time with no other persons present, he should admit publication of the words complained of and admit that they were defamatory, but deny that they were published to X. He should then go on to give his version of events, ie that they were in an otherwise empty lift at the time he addressed the claimant in those terms. It is not uncommon for a defendant to plead that one of the ingredients of the action is missing[2] (by way of non-admission or denial) and then go on to rely, in the alternative, upon a procedural and/or substantive defence or defences. However, given that trial will probably be by jury, a defendant should be wary of potential pitfalls. It could look very odd, for example, to deny publication of, say, an anonymous note and plead in the alternative that it was published on an occasion of qualified privilege.

1 And then take steps to strike out the claim under CPR 3.4 if appropriate.
2 Prior to the CPR, it was the invariable practice as a matter of form to deny that the words complained of were defamatory. Indeed, it still is and, despite the fact that the CPR now require a defendant to say why he denies any allegation in the particulars of claim (see CPR 16.5(2)), this is never done. It is of course open (and proper) for the defendant to admit that the words were defamatory, deny that they bore or were capable of bearing the meanings ascribed to them by the claimant, and to then set out the meanings which he contends they bore or were capable of bearing.

Procedural defences

Limitation[1]

11.14 Limitation is a procedural defence which exists for policy reasons, namely that defendants should not be perpetually at risk of proceedings being brought, and should not have to defend stale claims. The LA 1980, s 4 provides that the limitation period for bringing a claim for defamation or malicious falsehood is one year from the date on which the cause of action arose. So in a libel claim, if a publication is made on 8 September 2000, the last date upon which the claim form can be issued within the time limit is 8 September 2001 because time does not begin to run for the purposes of calculation until the day following the day on which the cause of action arose. In all cases the court retains a residual discretion to disapply the one-year limitation period in appropriate circumstances, with one exception[2].

Where a defendant contends that the claim was issued outside the limitation period the CPR require him to give details of the expiry of the limitation period in his defence[3]. Where limitation is pleaded in a defence, it is usual to add the contention that by reason of the expiry of the time limit, the claim is therefore liable to be struck out under CPR 3.4. It is submitted that where a defendant is of the considered view that the claim is time barred and that the court is unlikely to exercise its discretion in favour of the claimant, it would be contrary to the overriding objective to go on to incur the substantial costs of assimilating the evidence for and then pleading any of the substantive defences in the alternative. He could plead his limitation defence and expressly reserve his position with regard to any substantive defence or defences and make a prompt application to strike out the claim. In such a case, a judge ruling in favour of the claimant should be prepared to allow a defendant to amend[4]. However, the safest course is to plead any substantive defence in the alternative.

1 See further Chapter 16.
2 The one exception to this is where the claim has been issued but not served within the limitation period and both the limitation period and time for service of the claim form has expired. In those circumstances the court does not have a discretion: *Walkley v Precision Forgings Ltd* [1979] 1 All ER 102.
3 CPR Pt 16 PD, para 14.1.
4 This was common practice prior to the introduction of the Civil Procedure Rules in April 1999.

Consent[1]

11.15 It is a complete defence to a defamation action that the claimant consented to the publication he now complains of. Where a defendant relies on this defence, he should set out particulars of all the facts and matters which he relies upon to establish the existence of the claimant's consent.

1   See further Chapter 16.

Offer of amends[1]

11.16 Where the defence of offer of amends is relied on, no other defence may be pleaded[2]. The fact that an offer of amends has been made but not accepted is a defence to a claim for defamation except where the defendant knew or had reason to believe that the words complained of (a) referred to the claimant or were likely to be understood as doing so, and (b) were both false and defamatory of the claimant[3]. CPR Pt 53 PD, para 2.11 provides that where a defendant relies on an offer of amends, he must state in his defence that he is relying on the offer in accordance with the DeA 1996, s 4(2) and that it has not been withdrawn by him or been accepted, and he must attach a copy of the offer he made to his defence.

1   See further Chapter 16.
2   The DeA 1996, s 4(4). It is assumed that this means no substantive defence, though there is no authority on the point.
3   The DeA 1996, ss 4(2) and 4(3).

The Defamation Act 1996, s 1[1]

11.17 Known colloquially as the 'distributors' defence', section 1 of the DeA 1996 provides a defence for any defendant who can show that: (a) he was not the author, editor or publisher of the words complained of, (b) he took reasonable care in relation to the publication and (c) he did not know, and had no reason to believe, that what he did caused or contributed to the publication of a defamatory statement. A defendant who intends to rely on section 1 should therefore state that he does so in his defence and give particulars of the facts and matters which establish that he comes within the ambit of (a), (b) and (c) above.

1   See further Chapter 16.

Substantive defences

Truth[1]

11.18   Truth, technically referred to as 'justification', is a complete defence to an action for defamation. This means that once it is established that the words complained of are true, all other considerations, such as the motive of the defendant for making the publication, or whether the defendant believed the words to be true, are irrelevant[2].

The defendant pleading that the words complained of are true is not required to defend the defamatory meaning contended for by the claimant. He is entitled to set up and defend his own defamatory meaning, and to ask the jury to find the words complained of to be true on that basis.

CPR Pt 53 PD, para 2.5 requires a defendant who alleges that the words are true to set out in his defence the defamatory meaning or meanings which he seeks to justify, and to give details of the matters upon which he relies in support of the allegation or allegations. These details are known as the 'particulars of justification'.

1   See further Chapter 12.
2   With the exception of spent convictions: see Chapter 12.

Fair comment[1]

11.19   The full name of this defence is 'fair comment on a matter of public interest'. The defence might be more accurately termed 'honest opinion on a matter of public interest', since the essence of the defence is that the words used were such that a fair minded person might have used with reference to the matter in question. The matter in question must be one in which there is a public interest. The defence is not an absolute defence in that it can be lost on proof of malice.[2]

As with justification, the defendant is not required to defend the defamatory meaning contended for by the claimant. He is entitled to set up and defend his own defamatory meaning, and to ask the jury to find the words complained of to be fair comment on that basis.

CPR Pt 53 PD, para 2.6 requires a defendant who alleges that the words were fair comment to set out in his defence the defamatory meaning or meanings which he seeks to defend as fair comment, and to give details of the matters upon which he relies in support of the allegation or allegations. Although the Practice Direction does not so specify, the defendant should also specify in his defence the matter of public interest upon which he relies.

1 See further Chapter 13.
2 See Chapter 18.

Privilege

11.20 The law protects certain occasions of publication, regardless of the truth or falsity of the words published, because for public policy reasons they are deemed to merit such protection. There are two types of privilege – absolute and qualified. In either case CPR Pt 53 PD, para 2.7 requires a defendant who alleges that the words complained of were published on a privileged occasion to specify the circumstances he relies on in support of that contention.

Absolute privilege[1]

11.21 Absolute privilege, as its name suggests, is a complete defence to an action for defamation. Once it is established that absolute privilege attaches to a publication, as with justification, all other considerations – such as the motive of the defendant for making the publication or whether the defendant believed the words to be true – are irrelevant. Some examples of publications protected by absolute privilege are statements made by witnesses, lawyers or judges in court, and statements made in Parliamentary proceedings.

1 See further Chapter 14.

Qualified privilege[1]

11.22 Certain occasions of publication are protected by qualified privilege. The defence applies to a defamatory statement (whether true or false) if it was published on an occasion where the maker of the statement had a legal, social or moral duty or interest in making the statement and the recipient had a corresponding duty or interest in receiving it. Once it is established that qualified privilege attaches to an occasion of publication then that publication will be protected unless the claimant can prove that the defendant was motivated by malice[2] when he made that publication. Occasions of publication protected by qualified privilege are defined both by statute and at common law.

1 See further Chapter 15.
2 See Chapter 18.

Common misconceptions

11.23   The following are not of themselves defences to a defamation claim (unless they are also covered by one of the defences outlined above):

(a)   I published the words in the public interest.
(b)   I did not intend the words to mean X, but Y.
(c)   I did not intend the words to refer to Mr X, but Mr Y.
(d)   The article was written by a fictional character.
(e)   The article was written about a fictional character.
(f)   I intended the words to be a joke.
(g)   I honestly believed the words to be true when I published them.
(h)   I was simply repeating accusations made by others/matters reported elsewhere.

What next?

11.24   Once the defence has been filed, the court will serve an allocation questionnaire upon each party. The parties are required to complete the questionnaire and file it with the court no later than the date specified in it[1]. In that questionnaire the parties must state which 'track' the case should be allocated to: small claims, fast or multi-track. Defamation claims are always multi-track.

Depending upon the content of the defence, the claimant may be required to file a reply (as to which see Chapter 17).

1   CPR 26.3.

Chapter 12

Justification

12.01 This chapter deals with: (a) the requirements for pleading justification as a defence, (b) the burden and standard of proof, and (c) the rules about what will or will not amount to proof of justification.

Justification (truth) is a complete defence to an action for defamation. This means that once it is established that the words complained of are true, all other considerations, such as the motive of the defendant for making the publication or whether the defendant believed the words to be true, become irrelevant[1]. Since the law presumes the defamatory publication to be false, the defendant must plead and prove[2] the truth of the words complained of if he is to successfully defend a claim. Any defendant who is proposing to rely on a defence of justification should be warned that an unsuccessful plea will considerably aggravate the damages awarded to the claimant[3].

1   The one exception is spent convictions: see paragraph 12.14.
2   To the usual civil standard, ie on the balance of probabilities, or, to put it another way, more likely than not.
3   See Chapter 25.

The requirements for pleading justification as a defence

12.02 If a defendant proposes to rely on the defence of justification he must plead this in his defence. Upon receipt of the particulars of claim, the rules allow the defendant up to 28 days to serve his defence[1]. In an ideal world this would present no problems because any publisher of defamatory material who proposes to justify should have all the evidence upon which he proposes to rely at his fingertips at the time of publication. However, this is very rarely the case in reality and, even where it is, the short time limits can impose considerable burdens upon the person drafting the defence (usually counsel) in anything other than the most simple and straightforward case. It is therefore imperative to take instructions from the client at the earliest opportunity so that the pleader has sufficient time to draft a comprehensive defence. If this is not done, there are the invariable costs consequences of applications to amend after service of the defence[2].

CPR Pt 53 PD, para 2.5 provides that where a defendant alleges that the words complained of are true he must (a) specify the defamatory meanings he seeks to justify, and (b) give details of the matters relied on in support of that allegation[3].

1   See further Chapter 11.
2   An application to amend will be allowed where the subject matter of the amendment could not be properly canvassed for the first time in witness statements and it would be a denial of justice to refuse to allow it: see *McPhilemy v Times Newspapers Ltd* [1999] 3 All ER 775, [1999] EMLR 751, CA; and *Mahon and Kent v Rahn* [2000] 1 WLR 2150, CA. Very late applications to amend (ie at or close to trial) run the risk of being refused.
3   Although new to the rules of procedure, this requirement reflects the law since the decision of the Court of Appeal in *Lucas-Box v News Group* [1986] 1 WLR 147, CA.

The defamatory meaning to be justified

12.03   A defendant pleading truth is not required to defend the defamatory meaning which the claimant contends the words bear. If he intends to contend that the words bear a different (usually less serious) defamatory meaning then he must state in his defence what that meaning is. Just as the claimant may plead a natural and ordinary meaning or meanings, and additional or alternative innuendo meanings, so may a defendant plead a natural and ordinary meaning or meanings, and additional or alternative 'reverse' innuendo meanings[1].

At trial, the defendant will seek to defend the words complained of on the meaning or meanings he ascribes to them. It is for the judge to decide whether the words are capable of bearing the meanings contended for by the claimant and defendant[2], but it is for the jury to decide which meaning the words in fact bore[3]. For the defence of justification to succeed it is therefore necessary for the jury to find (a) that the words complained of bore the meaning contended for by the defendant, and (b) that they were true.

Although it is for the claimant to choose which words in the publication he wishes to complain of, the defendant is entitled to use the whole of the publication as context for the meaning he ascribes to those words[4].

1   See Chapter 3.
2   If either party wishes to challenge the other's pleaded meaning on the basis that the words complained of are not capable of bearing that meaning, or indeed if a party

wishes to obtain the court's ruling on his own meaning, he should apply to the court for a ruling on meaning at the earliest opportunity: see CPR Pt 53 PD, para 4 and Chapter 22.

3 *Mapp v News Group Newspapers* [1998] QB 520.
4 But see paragraph 12.08 below.

Details of matters relied on in support of that allegation

12.04 These are known as the particulars of justification, and should be set out as concisely as possible. Basically, their purpose is to tell the defendant's story, as to why he says the allegation made is true. So, in the most simple example, if the words complained of mean that X is a murderer, and X does in fact have a conviction for murder, the defendant will set out in his particulars of justification the facts and matters relating to that conviction. See Volume 25 of *Atkin's Court Forms* for examples of how particulars of justification should be set out in the defence.

In the past it was imperative that the particulars of justification set out every fact and matter upon which the defendant proposed to rely to establish the truth of the words complained of, because at trial the ambit of admissible evidence would be determined by the content of those particulars. If the defendant were proposing to adduce at trial evidence of additional facts and matters not set out in the particulars of justification, he would have to apply to amend the defence. However, this rule has softened as a result of *McPhilemy v Times Newspapers Ltd*[1], in which Lord Woolf MR stated that the purpose of pleadings was to make clear the general nature of a case by marking out its parameters. He disapproved of the then current practice of applying to amend the detail of particulars and said that this could be dealt with in witness statements.

1 [1999] 3 All ER 775, [1999] EMLR 751.

The burden and standard of proof

12.05 In a defamation case the words are presumed false until proved otherwise by the defendant. The defendant is therefore required to prove the truth of the words complained of. The civil standard of proof applies. This means that at trial the defendant must prove on the balance of probabilities (ie that it is more likely than not) that the words complained of are true. It is sometimes said by the courts that a higher standard of proof applies where the allegations made are very serious. What this means in practice is no more than a matter of common sense: if the allegations made are very serious, the evidence required to convince the jury that those allegations are true will need to be all the more persuasive, since it is easier to believe that a person would commit a minor wrong (eg adultery) than a major one (eg paedophilia).

Proof of justification

Statements of fact not opinion

12.06 The defence of justification protects statements of fact. The defence does not apply to statements of opinion. These are protected by the defence of fair comment[1]. Where the words complained of contain a mixture of fact and opinion, justification should be pleaded to the facts and fair comment to the opinion. If there is likely to be any dispute about whether the words are a statement of fact or opinion, it is advisable to plead both in the defence, relying on each in the alternative.

1 See Chapter 13.

Substantial truth

12.07 To allow a claimant to succeed in an action for defamation simply because of comparatively minor errors of fact in the publication complained of would be to contradict the purpose of the tort by vindicating the reputations of those who do not deserve it. For this reason it is only necessary for a defendant to prove that the words complained of were substantially true, or, to put it another way, that the gist or 'sting' of the defamatory charge is met by the evidence provided[1]. However, the sting of the libel will not be met where the statement complained of is that the claimant is guilty of habitual misconduct, and the defendant can only prove one isolated instance of such conduct[2]. Nor will proof of a past conviction or past misconduct meet the sting of the libel if the reference to it in the statement complained of infers a continuing propensity for such conduct[3].

1 *Edwards v Bell* (1824) 1 Bing 403 at 409, per Burroughs J.
2 *Wakley v Cooke* (1849) 4 Exch 511.
3 See, eg, *Sutherland v Stopes* [1925] AC 47 at 74, HL, per Lord Shaw of Dunfermline.

Distinct charges

12.08 The Defamation Act 1952 (DA 1952), s 5, provides that in an action for libel or slander in respect of words containing two or more distinct charges against a claimant, a defence of justification shall not fail by reason only that the truth of every charge is not proved, if the words not proved to be true do not materially injure the claimant's reputation having regard to the truth of the remaining charges. Whether the charges made in a publication are separate and distinct or whether they contain a 'common sting' are questions of law to be decided by the judge.

A recent example of a case where section 5 of the DA 1952 was applied is *Irving v Penguin Books*[1], which was tried by judge alone. The claimant was a military historian specialising in Second World War history and in particular Hitler. He brought proceedings for libel in respect of certain passages in a book published by the defendant entitled 'Denying the Holocaust'.

The judge found to be substantially true charges that the claimant had for his own ideological reasons persistently and deliberately misrepresented and manipulated historical evidence and had portrayed Hitler in an unwarrantedly favourable light (principally in relation to his attitude towards and responsibility for the treatment of the Jews); that he was an active Holocaust denier; that he was an anti-Semitic and racist and that he associated with right-wing extremists who promote neo-Nazism.

The judge found that certain imputations defamatory of the claimant had not been proved to be true, namely allegations that he was scheduled to speak at an anti-Zionist conference in Sweden in 1992 which was also to be attended by various representatives of terrorist organisations such as Hezbollah and Hammas; that he had a self-portrait of Hitler hanging over his desk and that he removed microfiches of Goebbel's diaries from the Moscow archives without permission, thereby exposing them to a real risk of damage. However, applying section 5 of the DA 1952, the judge decided that the failure on the part of the defendants to prove the truth of those charges did not materially injure the reputation of the claimant, having regard to the seriousness of the defamatory allegations which had been proven to be justified. The defence of justification therefore succeeded.

1   [2000] All ER (D) 523, Gray J.

12.09 Section 5 of the DA 1952 only applies where the claimant has actually chosen to complain of two or more distinct charges. Where, for example. the publication alleges that the claimant is (a) a thief, and (b) an uncaring father, and the claimant chooses only to complain of the charge that he is a thief, the defendant is not permitted to defend himself by proving that the claimant is an uncaring father.

A recent illustration is *Cruise v Express Newspapers plc*[1]. The claimants, Tom Cruise and Nicole Kidman, had brought proceedings for libel in respect of an article published in *The Sunday Express*. They reproduced the whole article in their particulars of claim, but complained of only one of two defamatory statements in it. The defendant pleaded justification and sought to rely on the statement which the claimants had not complained of but which, because the article was set out in its entirety in the particulars of claim, formed part of the claimants' statement of case. The claimants contended that the reason why they had reproduced the article in full was because the words containing the sting of which they complained were inextricably mixed with words containing the separate and distinct sting of which they did not complain. The Court of Appeal held that the defendant was not entitled to adduce evidence in justification of the sting of which the claimants did not complain, and nor were the claimants required to attempt to sever words of which no complaint was made, since the whole of the text would be before the jury so that they could see the context in which the words complained of were published. In so far as the defence of justification purported to justify the sting of which the claimants did not complain, it was struck out.

1   [1999] QB 931, CA.

Repetition and belief

12.10   A defendant is not permitted to defend a claim as justified on the basis that what he has written is a true record of what others have said or of his beliefs about the claimant's activities. For the purpose of the law of libel, a hearsay statement is the same as a direct statement and every republication of a libel is a new libel and each publisher is answerable as if he were the originator of the libel[1]. This is known as the 'repetition rule'. Thus if Z writes that 'Mr X is rumoured to be Miss Y's murderer', and Mr X brings proceedings for libel, Z cannot defend himself by proving that such rumours did in fact exist[2]. Likewise, if Z writes that 'I believe that Mr X murdered Miss Y' or where Z repeats the beliefs or claims of others. However, as with all publications, the context of the words will be taken into account in order to determine their meaning.

Where a defendant pleads his defence in breach of this rule, the defence will be struck out either on an application by the claimant or by the court of its own motion under CPR 3.4. In *Stern v Piper*[3] the claimant brought an action for libel against the publishers of a newspaper in respect of an article in its financial pages which made adverse comments about the claimant's conduct, quoting from an affirmation prepared in connection with a pending High Court action for debt against the claimant. The defendants pleaded a defence of justification, relying upon the details of the affirmation made as part of the High Court debt action. The Court of Appeal held that the report in the article of statements in the affirmation, being essentially hearsay, fell directly within the rule that it was no defence to an action for defamation for the defendant to prove that he was merely repeating what he had been told. The plea of justification was struck out. This decision was applied in *Shah v Standard Chartered Bank*[4], where the Court of Appeal held that it was not open to the defendant to justify the existence of reasonable grounds for suspicion by relying on what someone else had told it, since the defendant had to establish that there were objectively reasonable grounds to suspect the claimant (ie some conduct on the part of the claimant which gave rise to the suspicion), not that its information had come from an honest and reliable source.

The only apparent exception to this rule is where a defendant reports that X has issued proceedings. In such a case, the defendant will not be required to prove that the claimant has committed the wrong alleged in the claim form[5].

1   *Rubber Improvement Ltd v Daily Telegraph* [1964] AC 234, HL.
2   *Aspro Travel Ltd v Owners Abroad Ltd* [1996] 1 WLR 132, CA is authority for the proposition that in certain circumstances a rumour may be repeated without suggesting that it is well founded and that proof only of the fact of the rumour may be sufficient justification. However, *Aspro* should be treated with caution since it was doubted by the Court of Appeal in *Shah v Standard Chartered Bank* [1999] QB 241, CA.
3   [1997] QB 123, CA.
4   [1999] QB 241, CA.
5   See *Cadam v Beaverbrook Newspapers* [1959] 1 QB 413, CA; and *Stern v Piper* [1997] QB 123, CA.

Suspected commission of offences

12.11   A statement to the effect that someone is suspected of the commission of an offence, has been questioned in relation to it, or has been arrested for or charged with it does not of itself imply actual guilt[1]. It will therefore not be necessary for the defendant to prove actual guilt in order to succeed in his defence of justification, although he will be required to prove that there were reasonable grounds to suspect, or whatever other meaning he attributes to the words complained of.

1   *Rubber Improvement Ltd v Daily Telegraph* [1964] AC 234, HL.

Facts subsequent to publication

12.12   The defendant is entitled to rely on facts which occurred after the publication of the words complained of provided they support the allegations made as at the time of publication.

Previous convictions

12.13   The Civil Evidence Act 1968, s 13[1], provides that in an action for libel or slander in which the question of whether the claimant committed a criminal offence is relevant to an issue arising in the action, proof of the fact of that he stands convicted of that offence is conclusive evidence of the commission of that offence by the claimant[2].

1   As amended by the DeA 1996, s 12(1).
2   But see paragraph 12.14 below.

Justification and reference to spent convictions

12.14   The one exception to the rule that justification is a complete defence is where the statement complained of makes reference to a spent conviction. In such a case, the defendant will lose the protection of the defence if the claimant can prove that the publication complained of was made with malice[1].

The Rehabilitation of Offenders Act 1974 makes certain provisions which are intended to allow persons with 'minor' criminal convictions to live down their past. Following conviction, after a specified length of time known as the 'rehabilitation period', the Act says that the conviction becomes 'spent'[2]. Once a conviction becomes spent the person with that conviction is to be treated as someone who has never committed or been charged with or prosecuted for or convicted of or sentenced for that offence. It is for this reason that section 8(5) of the Act provides that a defence of justification will fail on proof of malice.

1   See Chapter 18.
2   A conviction can only become spent if the sentence passed was no more than 30 months' imprisonment.

Chapter 13

Fair comment

13.01 Fair comment on a matter of public interest is a defence to an action for defamation. However, it is not a complete defence because the protection of the defence will be lost if the claimant proves that the publication was made with malice[1]. This defence should perhaps be termed honest comment on a matter of public interest since there is no requirement that the comment be 'fair' in the ordinary sense of the word[2]. Since the law presumes the defamatory publication to be false, the defendant must plead and prove[3] that the words complained of were fair comment on a matter of public interest if he is to successfully defend a claim.

This chapter deals with: (a) the CPR requirement for pleading fair comment as a defence, (b) procedural considerations, and (c) the rules about what will or will not amount to fair comment on a matter of public interest.

1   See Chapter 18.
2   *Reynolds v Times Newspapers Ltd* [2001] 2 AC 127, HL, per Lord Nicholls.
3   To the usual civil standard, ie on the balance of probabilities, or, to put it another way, more likely than not.

The requirements for pleading fair comment as a defence

13.02 If a defendant proposes to rely on the defence of fair comment he must plead this in his defence. Upon receipt of the particulars of claim, the rules allow the defendant up to 28 days to serve his defence[1]. CPR Pt 53 PD, para 2.6 provides that where a defendant alleges that the words complained of are fair comment on a matter of public interest, he must (a) specify the defamatory meanings he seeks to defend as fair comment on a matter of public interest, and (b) give details of the matters relied on in support of that allegation[2].

1   See further Chapter 11.
2   Although new to the rules of procedure, this rule stems from the decision in *Control Risks Ltd v New English Library* [1990] 1 WLR 183 and places the requirements for pleading fair comment on a par with those for justification: see Chapter 12.

The defamatory meaning to be defended as fair comment on a matter of public interest

13.03   A defendant pleading fair comment is not required to defend the defamatory meaning which the claimant contends the words bear. If he intends to contend that the words bear a different (usually less serious) defamatory meaning then he must state in his defence what that meaning is. Just as the claimant may plead a natural and ordinary meaning or meanings, and additional or alternative innuendo meanings, so may a defendant plead a natural and ordinary meaning or meanings, and additional or alternative 'reverse' innuendo meanings[1].

At trial, the defendant will seek to defend the words complained of on the meaning or meanings he ascribes to them. It is for the judge to decide whether the words are capable of bearing the meanings contended for by the claimant and defendant[2], but it is for the jury to decide which meaning the words in fact bore[3].

Although it is for the claimant to choose which words in the publication he wishes to complain of, the defendant is entitled to use the whole of the publication as context for the meaning he ascribes to those words[4].

1   See Chapter 3.
2   If either party wishes to challenge the other's pleaded meaning on the basis that the words complained of are not capable of bearing that meaning, or indeed if a party wishes to obtain the court's ruling on his own meaning, he should apply to the court for a ruling on meaning at the earliest opportunity: see CPR Pt 53 PD, para 4 and Chapter 22.
3   *Mapp v News Group Newspapers* [1998] QB 520.
4   But see paragraph 13.08 below.

Details of matters relied on in support of that allegation

13.04   The defendant must always give details of the facts or matters upon which the comment is based. Although the Practice Direction[1] does not appear to require it, the defendant should also specify the matter of public interest relied on. See Volume 25 of *Atkin's Court Forms* for examples of how the particulars should be set out in the defence.

In the past it was imperative that the particulars set out every fact and matter upon which the defendant proposed to rely to establish that the words complained of were fair comment on a matter of public interest, because at trial the ambit of admissible evidence would be determined by the content of those particulars. If the defendant were proposing to adduce at trial evidence of additional facts and matters not set out in the particulars, he would have to apply to amend the defence. However, this rule has softened as a result of *McPhilemy v Times Newspapers Ltd*[2], in which Lord Woolf MR stated that the purpose of pleadings was to make clear the general nature of a case by marking out its parameters. He disapproved of the then current practice of applying to amend the detail of particulars and said that this could be dealt with in witness statements.

Where the words complained of are arguably fact or represent a mixture of fact and comment, it is advisable, and indeed common practice, to plead the defence of fair comment in the alternative to a defence of justification.

Where the words complained of relate to matters published on a privileged occasion, and there is a question as to whether the words are comment or form part of the privileged publication, it is advisable to plead fair comment in the alternative to a defence of absolute, or qualified, privilege, as appropriate.

1   CPR Pt 53 PD, para 2.6 (and see Appendix 4).
2   [1999] 3 All ER 775, [1999] EMLR 751.

Procedural considerations

13.05   In a defamation case once the claimant has established that words were published to a third party which referred to him and are defamatory of him, the burden falls upon the defendant to establish the defence of fair comment. For the defence of fair comment to succeed it is necessary for the jury to find (a) that the words complained of bore the meaning contended for by the defendant, and (b) that they were fair comment on a matter of public interest. The civil standard of proof applies. This means that at trial the defendant must prove on the balance of probabilities (ie that it is more likely than not) that the defence is established.

In the first instance it is for the judge to decide whether the words are fact or comment. If he is satisfied that the words fall into one or other category he should direct the jury to this effect. If, however, he concludes that the ordinary reasonable reader could take either view, the question must be left to the jury[1]. It is for the judge to decide whether the matter commented on is one of public interest. It is for the jury to decide whether the comment is fair, subject to a direction from the judge as to whether on the evidence the comment is capable of satisfying the test[2].

1   *Telnikoff v Matusevitch* [1992] 2 AC 343 at 351, HL, per Lord Keith, citing *Halsbury's Laws of England* (4th edn, 1979), vol 28, p 114, para 228.
2   *McQuire v Western Morning News Co Ltd* [1903] 2 KB 100, CA, approved in *Sutherland v Stopes* [1925] AC 47 at 63, HL, per Viscount Finlay.

Proof of fair comment

13.06   In order to be defended as fair comment on a matter of public interest, the relevant comment must satisfy the following five tests. It must[1]:

(a)   be made on a matter of public interest[2];
(b)   be recognisable as comment, as distinct from an imputation of fact[3];
(c)   be (i) based on facts which are true or (ii) matters protected by privilege[4];
(d)   explicitly or implicitly indicate, at least in general terms, what are the facts or privileged matters on which the comment was made[5]; and
(e)   be a comment which could have been made by an honest person, however prejudiced he might be and however exaggerated or obstinate his views[6].

1   Adopting the five ingredients as identified by Lord Nicholls in *Tse Wai Chun Paul v Cheng* (Ct Final Appeal Hong Kong) FACV No 12 of 2000, [2001] EMLR 777.
2   See paragraph 13.07 below.
3   See paragraph 13.08 below.
4   See paragraph 13.09 below.
5   See paragraph 13.10 below.
6   See paragraph 13.11 below.

Comment made on a matter of public interest

13.07   There is no exhaustive definition of what will amount to a matter of public interest. However, it is clear that the simple fact that the public are interested in it will not pass the public interest test. In *London Artists v Littler*[1], Lord Denning stated that in the modern climate public interest should not be confined within narrow limits[2] and that 'whenever a matter is such as to affect people at large, so that they may be legitimately interested in or concerned at what is going on or what may happen to them or to others; then it is a matter of public interest on which everyone is entitled to make fair comment'. Further, in *Campbell v Spottiswoode*[3], Blackburn J said that 'where a person has done or published anything which may fairly be said to have invited comment . . . everyone has a right to make a fair . . . comment'. Similarly, anything which may fairly be said to 'challenge public attention'[4] will also be a matter of public interest.

Comment on political and state matters[5], the public acts of public persons[6] or bodies with a public role[7], the private acts of such persons or bodies where this has a relevant bearing on their public role[8], the administration of justice[9], religious affairs[10], public performances[11] and performers[12], exhibitions[13], artistic[14], architectural[15] and literary works[16], and advertisements[17] have all been held to be matters of public interest. However, the starting point should always be the tests outlined in paragraph 13.06 above.

1 [1969] 2 QB 375 at 391, per Lord Denning, cited with approval by Lord Nicholls in *Reynolds v Times Newspapers Ltd* [2001] 2 AC 127, HL; and in *Tse Wai Chun Paul v Cheng* (Ct Final Appeal Hong Kong) FACV No 12 of 2000, [2001] EMLR 777.
2 *London Artists Ltd v Littler* [1969] 2 QB 375.
3 (1863) 3 B & S 769 at 781.
4 *Seymour v Butterworth* (1862) 3 F & F 372 at 386, per Cockburn CJ.
5 *Hedley v Barlow* (1865) 4 F & F 224; *Mulkern v Ward* (1872) LR 13 Eq 619. A governmental body (as distinct from the individual members of it) is no longer permitted to sue for defamation: see *Derbyshire County Council v Times Newspapers Ltd* [1993] AC 534, HL.
6 *Silkin v Beaverbrook Newspapers Ltd* [1958] 1 WLR 743.
7 *South Hetton Coal Co v North-Eastern News* [1894] 1 QB 133, CA.
8 *Seymour v Butterworth* (1862) 3 F & F 372.
9 *Hibbins v Lee* (1864) 4 F & F 243.
10 *Kelly v Tinling* (1865) LR 1 QB 699.
11 *Merivale v Carson* (1887) 20 QBD 275, CA.
12 *London Artists Ltd v Littler* [1969] 2 QB 375.
13 *Green v Chapman* (1837) 4 Bing NC 92.
14 *Thompson v Shackell* (1828) 1 Mood & M 187.
15 *Soane v Knight* (1827) Mood & M 74.
16 *Campbell v Spottiswoode* (1863) 3 B & S 769.
17 *Paris v Levy* (1860) 9 CBNS 342.

Comment recognisable as comment, as distinct from an imputation of fact

13.08 In theory the principle as to which statements will be protected as fair comment and which will not is straightforward. The defence of fair comment on a matter of public interest is concerned with the protection of comment, not imputations of fact. If the imputation is one of fact, a ground of defence must be sought elsewhere, for example as justification or privilege. To fall within the defence of fair comment, the comment must be understood by the ordinary reasonable reader as comment, as distinct from an imputation of fact[1].

However, the distinction between comment and fact is rather more difficult to make in practice and perhaps for this reason the case law has made no attempt to provide a comprehensive definition of what will or will not amount to comment. However, the decided cases have highlighted various factors which will point either towards or away from a conclusion that the words amount to comment. Whether a statement is a comment or an imputation of fact is almost entirely dependent upon its context. A simple example was given by Ferguson J in *Myerson v Packer and Smith's Weekly Publishing Co*[2]:

> 'To say that a man's conduct was dishonourable is not comment, it is a statement of fact. To say that he did certain specific things and that his conduct was dishonourable is a statement of fact coupled with a comment.'

If no facts or privileged matters to support the comment are set out or referred to in the words, the words will be treated as a statement of fact. In *Kemsley v Foot*[3], Lord Porter said[4] that 'if a writer chooses to publish an expression of opinion which has no relation by way of criticism to any fact before the reader, then such an expression of opinion depends on nothing but the writer's own authority and stands in the same position as an allegation of fact.'

Whether the words are comment will be determined by reference to the publication complained of alone. The defendant cannot rely upon prior or subsequent publications in order to establish that the words in context were comment and not statements of fact[5].

Prefacing words with statements such as 'in my opinion' or 'in my view' are indicative, but by no means decisive, of comment[6].

It must always be borne in mind that the test is whether the ordinary reasonable reader would understand the words to be comment. Therefore, for example, words appearing in comment pages, leader articles or letters in a newspaper or other publication are more likely to be held to be comment than words appearing in news stories.

1   See the speech of Lord Nicholls in *Reynolds v Times Newspapers Ltd* [2001] 2 AC 127 at 133, HL.
2   (1922) 24 SR NSW 20 at 26, cited with approval by Lord Nicholls in *Tse Wai Chun Paul v Cheng* (Ct Final Appeal Hong Kong) FACV No 12 of 2000, [2001] EMLR 777.
3   [1952] AC 345, HL.
4   [1952] AC 345 at 356, HL.

5   *Telnikoff v Matusevitch* [1992] 2 AC 343, HL.
6   *Turner v Metro-Goldwyn-Meyer Pictures Ltd* [1950] 1 All ER 449 at 505, HL, per Lord Oakey.

Comment (a) based on facts which are true or (b) matters protected by privilege[1]

Based on facts which are true

13.09   Where the defendant contends that the words were fair comment because they are based on facts which are true, these facts must be pleaded in his defence. If the facts themselves are defamatory, he must plead justification in relation to them and must prove them to be substantially true[2]. Even if they are not defamatory they must still be proved to be true.

As with justification, the defence will not fail by reason alone that the truth of every fact relied upon is not established. Section 6 of the DA 1952 provides in such a case that the defence will not fail if it can be shown that the comment was fair comment on the basis of those facts which are shown to be true. If the comment is based upon untrue 'facts' then the comment cannot be fair comment on a matter of public interest and the defence will fail[3]. The fact that the commentator reasonably believed the facts to be true at the time of publication is irrelevant.

A further requirement is that the facts must have been in existence at the time of publication[4].

1   See *London Artists Ltd v Littler* [1969] 2 QB 375 at 395.
2   *Broadway Approvals v Odhams Press Ltd* [1964] 2 QB 683. See also Chapter 12.
3   See *Hunt v Star Newspaper Co Ltd* [1908] 2 KB 309 at 320, CA, per Fletcher Moulton LJ.
4   *Cohen v Daily Telegraph Ltd* [1968] 2 All ER 407, CA.

Based on matters protected by privilege

13.10   Where the defendant contends that the words were fair comment because they are based on matters protected by privilege, these facts and matters must be pleaded in his defence. If the facts and matters themselves are defamatory, he must plead absolute or qualified privilege in relation to them and must prove that they are so protected[1].

Where the comment is made upon facts and matters protected by privilege the defence will succeed even where those facts and matters are untrue[2]. However, the comment must be made on a fair and accurate account of them if the defence is to succeed[3]. The fact that the commentator genuinely believed that the matters were privileged or that the account of them was a fair and accurate one is irrelevant.

1 *Broadway Approvals v Odhams Press Ltd* [1964] 2 QB 683. See also Chapters 14 and 15.
2 However, if the commentator was aware that the statement was untrue this will be evidence of malice: see Chapter 18.
3 See *Brent Walker Group plc v Time Out Ltd* [1991] 2 QB 33, CA.

Comment which explicitly or implicitly indicates, at least in general terms, what are the facts or privileged matters on which the comment was made

13.11 In either case, the facts or matters must be stated or summarised in the publication, or indicated with sufficient clarity to enable the readers to ascertain the facts or matters upon which the comment is based[1]. The reader or hearer should be in a position to judge for himself how far the comment was well founded[2].

1 See the speech of Lord Nicholls in *Reynolds v Times Newspapers Ltd* [2001] 2 AC 127 at 133, HL; and *Kemlsey v Foot* [1952] AC 345, HL.
2 Per Lord Nicholls in *Tse Wai Chun Paul v Cheng* (Ct Final Appeal Hong Kong) FACV No 12 of 2000, [2001] EMLR 777.

Comment is comment which could have been made by an honest person, however prejudiced he might be and however exaggerated or obstinate his views[1]

13.12 The most important point to bear in mind is that to be protected as fair comment, the comment need not be 'fair' in the ordinary sense of the word. The word 'fair' in this context is a misnomer, and has been criticised in the most senior courts on two recent occasions[2]. A more appropriate term would be 'honest comment', since the defence exists to protect even the most prejudiced, exaggerated or unjust comment, provided it is a comment which could be honestly made and germane to the subject matter criticised: 'Dislike of an artist's style would not justify an attack upon his morals or manners. But a critic need not be mealy-mouthed in denouncing what he disagrees with. He is entitled to dip his gall for the purposes of legitimate criticism'[3].

Some of the older case law suggests that where the commentator imputes a dishonest, corrupt or dishonourable motive to the claimant from the facts or matters upon which he relies the defence of fair comment is not available[4]. However, more recent cases suggest that provided the test that the comment is comment which an honest person could have made is satisfied, then the defence of fair comment will apply[5].

1   See Lord Porter in *Turner v Metro-Goldwyn-Meyer Pictures Ltd* [1950] 1 All ER 449 at 461.
2   In *Reynolds v Times Newspapers Ltd* [2001] 2 AC 127, HL; and in *Tse Wai Chun Paul v Cheng* (Ct Final Appeal Hong Kong) FACV No 12 of 2000, [2001] EMLR 777.
3   Per Lord Nicholls in *Tse Wai Chun Paul v Cheng* (Ct Final Appeal Hong Kong) FACV No 12 of 2000, [2001] EMLR 777, referring to Jordan CJ in *Gardiner v Fairfax* (1942) 42 SR NSW 171 at 174.
4   See, eg, *Campbell v Spottiswoode* (1863) 3 B & S 769.
5   *Jeyaretnam v Goh Chok Tong* [1989] 1 WLR 1109, PC.

Chapter 14

Absolute privilege

14.01 The law recognises that on certain occasions the need for uninhibited expression is of such a high order that it will protect statements published on them absolutely, regardless of truth or falsity. This means that once it is established that a statement was published on an occasion which the law will so protect, that statement (and therefore its publisher) is completely protected from an action for defamation and the claimant's claim will fail. It is the occasion or circumstances in which the statement was made which are central to establishing the defence of absolute privilege. Any other consideration, such as whether the statement is true or false, or the motive of the publisher, is irrelevant.

This chapter deals in turn with: (a) the requirements for pleading absolute privilege as a defence, (b) procedural considerations arising when the defence of absolute privilege is pleaded, and (c) the occasions of publication which are protected by absolute privilege.

The requirements for pleading absolute privilege as a defence

14.02 Strictly speaking, a defendant who contends that a statement was published on an occasion of absolute privilege is not utilising a defence at all, but is simply contending that in the given circumstances the words complained of are not actionable as a matter of law because he is immune from suit[1]. For this reason it would in theory be possible for a defendant to strike out the claim or to obtain summary judgment without pleading and serving a defence at all.

However, the invariable practice is for a defendant who proposes to rely on absolute privilege to plead it in his defence[2]. CPR Pt 53 PD, para 2.7 requires a defendant who contends that the words complained of were published on a privileged occasion to specify the circumstances which he relies upon in support of that contention in the defence. For sample pleas of absolute privilege see Volume 25 of *Atkin's Court Forms*.

1 See *Taylor v Director of the Serious Fraud Office* [1999] 2 AC 177, HL.
2 See further Chapter 11.

Procedural considerations

14.03 The burden is upon the defendant to prove on the balance of probabilities all the facts establishing the circumstances which render the statement absolutely privileged.

Whether the privilege exists at all is a question for the judge. The judge is therefore required to determine whether the circumstances in which the publication was made were such as to make the publication privileged. If the facts are in dispute, the jury is called upon to consider the evidence and make findings of fact. It is for the judge, however, to decide whether the facts found by the jury make the publication privileged or to instruct the jury as to what facts they must find in order to hold the publication privileged. Whether those facts, if established, would be such as to render the statement absolutely privileged is a question of law for the judge[1].

1 See the commentary to the summary of functions of judge and jury at section 619 of the American Law Institute, *Restatement of the Law, Torts* (1977), cited with approval by Lord Steyn in *Reynolds v Times Newspapers Ltd* [2001] 2 AC 127 at 154, HL.

Disposal prior to full trial of the action

14.04 In many circumstances it will be appropriate, taking into account the overriding objective[1] and the interest of the client in having the matter dealt with as inexpensively and expeditiously as possible, to take steps to have the question of whether the defence of absolute privilege applies in the circumstances or would apply if the facts relied upon by the defendant are proved.

1 See CPR 1.

Applications to strike out or for summary judgment

14.05 An application to strike out the defence of absolute privilege under CPR 3.4 will be appropriate where it is plain, even on the defendant's case, that the words were not published on an occasion of absolute privilege. Where it is plain that the words complained of were published on an occasion of absolute privilege, an application for summary judgment under CPR 24 or summary disposal under the DeA 1996, ss 8–10[1] will be more appropriate than an application to strike out, since determination of the question will determine the outcome of the action. Such applications should be made at the earliest opportunity in order to avoid incurring unnecessary costs. See Chapter 22 for guidance on applications.

1   See also CPR Pt 53 PD, para 5 (and see Appendix 4).

Trial as a preliminary issue

14.06   However, where the question of the existence of the protection of absolute privilege requires serious argument and careful consideration, the proper course is to raise the point in the defence and thereafter to consider making an application to have the question tried as a preliminary issue[1].

Trial of the question of privilege as a preliminary issue may also be advisable where the defence has been pleaded in the alternative or in addition to a defence of justification and/or fair comment where to do so could determine the outcome of the case and thus avoid the likely length and expense of a trial of those defences. This practice was endorsed by the Court of Appeal in *GKR Karate UK Ltd v Yorkshire Post Newspapers Ltd*[2].

1   See *Waple v Surrey County Council* [1998] 1 WLR 860 at 869, CA, per Brooke LJ, citing *Gatley on Libel and Slander* (9th edn, 1998), para. 26.43.
2   [2000] EMLR 396, CA.

Publications protected by absolute privilege

14.07   Aside from some miscellaneous exceptions[1], publications protected by absolute privilege fall into three broad classes: (a) judicial proceedings, (b) Parliamentary proceedings, and (c) the conduct of affairs of state. Each is considered in turn below.

Any extension of absolute privilege beyond the recognised categories or classes will be resisted by the court until the necessity for it can be demonstrated[2]. A recent illustration of the unwillingness of the courts to extend the doctrine is to be found the decision of the Court of Appeal in *S v Newham London Borough Council*[3]. In this case, a local authority had, pursuant to its statutory duty, communicated its decision that a social worker was not suitable to work with children to the Consultancy Service at the Department of Health. The Consultancy Service advised local authorities and other organisations regarding the suitability of those they proposed to employ in child care posts. It kept an index of those who were deemed unsuitable (arising from either conviction for an offence or dismissal from a child care post in certain circumstances), upon which the social worker's name was placed. She brought an action for libel against the local authority. The local authority contended that its communication was absolutely privileged and immune from suit.

The Court of Appeal recognised that the importance of protecting children from harm of the type against which the index was designed to give protection could not be exaggerated and had no difficulty in accepting that this was a public interest which could qualify for protection from suit if that was necessary and appropriate. However, it did not accept that a local authority would be deterred from providing appropriate information to the Consultancy Service by the threat of litigation and in light of this, among other factors, held that absolute privilege did not apply. However, the publication was protected by qualified privilege[4].

1   As to which, see paragraph 14.27 below.
2   See *Mann v O'Neill* (1997) 71 ALJR 903 at 907, cited with approval by Lord Hoffman in *Taylor v Director of the Serious Fraud Office* [1999] 2 AC 177 at 213–214, HL.
3   [1998] EMLR 583, CA.
4   See Chapter 15.

Judicial proceedings

14.08   The general rule is that statements made by judges, advocates, witnesses, parties or juries during the ordinary course of proceedings before any court or judicial tribunal recognised by law are protected by absolute privilege[1]. The protection of the privilege attaches not just to proceedings at trial, but applies to all stages of proceedings, including statements of case, witness statements, disclosure of documents and even statements made as part of the process of investigating a crime or possible crime.

1   See *Royal Aquarium v Parkinson* [1892] 1 QB 431 at 451, CA, per Lopes LJ.

The tribunals whose proceedings are protected

14.09   In order to be protected by absolute privilege, a statement must be made in or for the purpose of proceedings before a court or tribunal or body exercising the judicial power of the state in the United Kingdom[1]. The protection also extends to statements made in or for the purpose of proceedings before other tribunals recognised by law and acting judicially.

In order to determine whether a particular body or tribunal is to be treated as a judicial one for the purposes of the protection of absolute privilege, the court will scrutinise: (1) the authority under which that tribunal or body acts, (2) the nature of the question into which it is its duty to inquire, (3) the procedure it adopts, and (4) the legal consequences of the conclusion it reaches[2]. Now that the HRA 1998 is in force, there is an additional requirement (5) that the court must be satisfied that any proposed extension of the protection of absolute privilege does not contravene Article 6(1) of the European Convention on Human Rights[3].

In *Trapp v Mackie*[4] the House of Lords considered whether the proceedings of a local inquiry before a commissioner appointed under statute[5] were protected by absolute privilege. In concluding that they were, Lord Diplock identified considerations (1) to (4) above and set out the ten characteristics of the inquiry's proceedings which caused him to take that view:

(1)   It was authorised by law; it was constituted pursuant to an Act of Parliament.

(2)   It was inquiring into an issue in dispute between adverse parties of a kind similar to issues that commonly fall to be decided by courts of justice.

(3)   The inquiry was held in public.

(4)   Decisions as to what oral evidence should be led and what documents should be tendered or their production called for by the adverse party were left to the contending parties.

(5)   Witnesses whom either of the adverse parties wished to call were compellable, under penal sanctions, to give oral evidence or to produce documents, and were entitled to the same privilege to refuse to answer a question or to produce a document as would apply if the inquiry were a proceeding in a court of law.

(6)   The oral evidence was given upon oath; if it were false to the knowledge of the witness he would incur criminal liability for the offence of perjury.

(7)   Witnesses who gave oral testimony were subject to examination-in-chief and re-examination by the party calling them and to cross-examination by the adverse party, in accordance with the normal procedure of courts of law.

(8) The adverse parties were entitled to be, and were in fact, represented by legally qualified advocates or solicitors and these were given the opportunity of addressing the tribunal on the evidence that had been led.

(9) The opinion of the tribunal as reported to the Secretary of State, even though not of itself decisive of the issue in dispute between the adverse parties, would have a major influence upon his decision either to require the education committee to reconsider its resolution to dismiss Dr Trapp, or to let the matter rest.

(10) As a result of the report either of the parties to the inquiry might be ordered by the Secretary of State to pay the whole or part of the expenses of appearing at the inquiry incurred by the adverse party, and such expenses would be recoverable in the same manner as expenses incurred in a civil action in a court of law[6].

1 Since the DeA 1996, s 14 protects reports of such proceedings absolutely, this must follow. See paragraph 14.10 below.
2 See *Trapp v Mackie* [1979] 1 WLR 377, HL, per Lord Diplock.
3 See, eg, *Osman v United Kingdom* [1991] 1 FLR 193. The European Court found that Article 6(1) had been contravened because the rule providing blanket immunity to police from negligence claims was not proportionate to the public policy grounds advanced in its support.
4 [1979] 1 WLR 377, HL.
5 The Education (Scotland) Act 1946, s 81(3).
6 After listing these ten characteristics Lord Diplock stated 'I am far from suggesting either that the presence of any one of these characteristics taken in isolation would suffice to attract absolute privilege for witnesses in respect of testimony given by them before a tribunal or that the absence of any one of these characteristics would be fatal to the existence of such absolute privilege'.

Examples of tribunals or bodies protected

14.10 Absolute privilege has been held to extend to proceedings before the following:

- barrister's disciplinary proceedings[1];
- coroners' courts[2];
- inquiry set up by the Secretary of State under statutory powers[3];
- military courts[4];
- Security Association authorisation tribunals[5];
- solicitors' disciplinary tribunals[6].

However, now that the HRA 1998 is in force it cannot be assumed on the basis of precedent alone that statements made in or for the purpose of these proceedings will be absolutely privileged[7]. All doctrines of immunity from suit are potentially open to challenge under Article 6(1). Those closest to the boundary between the protection of absolute or qualified privilege will be the most vulnerable to challenge.

1   *Lincoln v Daniels* [1962] 1 QB 237, CA; *Marrinan v Vibart* [1963] 1 QB 528, CA.
2   *McCarey v Associated Newspapers Ltd (No 2)* [1965] 2 QB 86.
3   *Trapp v Mackie* [1979] 1 All ER 489, HL.
4   *Dawkins v Lord Rokeby* (1873) LR 8 QB 255.
5   *Mahon v Rahn (No 2)* [2002] 4 All ER 41, CA.
6   *Addis v Crocker* [1961] 1 QB 11, CA.
7   Assuming that conformity with Article 6(1) was not considered in them. Even if it was, they may still be open to challenge given that the Convention is treated as a living instrument to be interpreted in accordance with contemporary mores.

Examples of tribunals or bodies not protected

14.11   The following proceedings have been held not to be protected by absolute privilege:

- conciliation proceedings between employer and employee[1];
- disciplinary proceedings within a local authority[2];
- EC Commission investigations under Article 89 of the EC Treaty[3];
- local authority committee hearing applications for music and dancing licenses[4];
- parole board adjudications[5];
- planning appeal inquiries[6];
- social security adjudications[7].

With the exception of proceedings before the EC Commission, which for reasons of public interest the court will not adjudicate upon in a defamation action[8], all other proceedings referred to above were protected by qualified privilege[9].

1   *Tadd v Eastwood* [1983] IRLR 320.
2   *Gregory v Portsmouth City Council* [2000] 2 WLR 306 at 316, HL, per Lord Steyn.
3   *Hasselblad (GB) Ltd v Orbinson* [1985] QB 475.
4   *Royal Aquarium v Parkinson* [1892] 1 QB 431, CA.
5   *Daniels v Griffiths* [1998] EMLR 489, CA.
6   *Richards v Cresswell* (1987) Times, 24 April.
7   *Purdew v Serres-Smith* [1993] IRLR 77, [1992] 34 LS Gaz R 40.
8   Thus creating the same result as if the proceedings were absolutely privileged: see *Hasselblad (GB) Ltd v Orbinson* [1985] QB 475.
9   See further Chapter 15.

Proceedings outside the United Kingdom

14.12 Since fair and accurate contemporaneous reports of proceedings in the European Court of Justice or any court attached to it, the European Court of Human Rights, any international criminal tribunal established by the Security Council of the United Nations or by an international agreement to which the United Kingdom is a party are protected by absolute privilege, it must logically follow that the proceedings of those tribunals are also protected.

Protection applies to all stages of proceedings

14.13 Absolute privilege attaches not merely to proceedings at the trial, but to all proceedings which are essentially steps in judicial proceedings, such as statements in statements of case, witness statements and communications between solicitor and client which are relevant to the matter.

Statements to solicitors

14.14 The privilege has been held to extend to statements made to solicitors by witnesses or prospective witnesses for the purpose of preparing a statement, proof of evidence or affidavit in court proceedings, or in contemplation for doing so, unless it had no reference at all to the subject matter of the proceedings[1].

1   *Smeaton v Butcher* [2000] EMLR 985, CA.

Investigation of crime

14.15 In *Taylor v Serious Fraud Office*[1] the House of Lords held that the protection of absolute privilege applied to any statement which could fairly be said to be part of the process of investigating a crime or possible crime. However, in *Darker (representative of Docker) v Chief Constable of West Midlands Police*[2] the House of Lords held that the protection did not extend to the fabrication of evidence by the police during the course of their investigations, even though the false testimony and witness statements prepared as a result would be absolutely privileged.

The effect of this decision is that a statement which is part of the process of investigating a crime or a possible crime will be absolutely privileged unless it is alleged to be fabricated. This rather subverts an assumption of general principle in relation to absolute privilege – namely that a statement is protected regardless of truth or falsity or the motivation of the person who publishes it. The apparent illogicality of the decision was expressly acknowledged by Lord Hutton, who excused it by saying that considerations of greater weight applied (namely the right of someone who has suffered a wrong to have access to a remedy).

Absolute privilege has also been held to apply to investigations in proceedings analogous to criminal proceedings. In *Mahon v Rahn (No 2)*[3] the Court of Appeal held that a letter received by the Securities Association, a financial services regulatory body, during an investigation by it into a person's fitness to carry on an investment business was protected by absolute privilege. It was not possible to distinguish between a criminal investigator seeking evidence to support a criminal charge and a financial investigator seeking evidence to put before a tribunal that someone was not a fit and proper person to conduct an investment business. There was a clear public interest in protecting the public from unfit investment advisers, which could be put at risk if informants to regulatory bodies feared they may be harassed by libel proceedings.

It may be the case that statements made in the course of, or having an immediate link with, any type of possible proceedings of a judicial nature will be protected by absolute privilege[4]. This would seem logical given the public policy reasons which cause the proceedings themselves to be protected. It is certainly clear that the corollary of this is true – where the proceedings themselves are not protected by absolute privilege, no steps taken in those proceedings will be protected by absolute privilege[5].

---

1   [1999] 2 AC 177, HL. See also *Mahon v Rahn (No 2)* [2000] EMLR 873, HL. The protection of the immunity is available even if a trial does not take place: *Stanton v Callaghan* [2000] 1 QB 75.

2   [2001] 1 AC 435, HL.

3   [2000] EMLR 873, CA.

4   See *Waple v Surrey County Council* [1998] 1 WLR 860, CA, where communications by council officers acting in Children Act matters were held not to be protected by absolute privilege on the basis that court proceedings were not inevitable and the communication was therefore not a statement made in the course of, or having an immediate link with, possible legal or quasi-legal proceedings.

5   See, eg, *Daniels v Griffiths* [1998] EMLR 489, CA, where it was held that communications to the parole board were not protected by absolute privilege because the proceedings of the parole board were not of a judicial nature.

Statements made in those proceedings which will be protected

14.16 In order to be protected by absolute privilege, the statement must be made for the purpose of the proceedings in which it is made, and must be made by someone who has a duty to make statements in those proceedings. A statement will not be protected if it is not made for the purpose of the proceedings[1] or if it is uttered for the purpose of the proceedings, but by someone who does not have a duty to make statements in the proceedings[2]. However, the test of whether a statement was made for the purpose of proceedings is a very wide one – the simple fact that a statement is irrelevant does not mean that it was not made for the purpose of the proceedings.

1 *Seaman v Netherclift* (1876) 2 CPD 53 at 60, CA.
2 *Delegal v Highley* (1837) 3 Bing NC 950 at 961; *Keenan v Wallace* (1916) 51 ILT 19.

Reports of judicial proceedings

14.17 The DeA 1996, s 14 provides that a fair and accurate report of proceedings in public before certain courts will be absolutely privileged if published contemporaneously with those proceedings.

The section applies to court proceedings before:

(1) any court in the United Kingdom (which includes any tribunal or body exercising the judicial power of the state);
(2) the European Court of Justice or any court attached to it;
(3) the European Court of Human Rights; and
(4) any international criminal tribunal established by the Security Council of the United Nations or by an international agreement to which the United Kingdom is a party[1].

There is no English decision as to the meaning of the word 'contemporaneously' in section 14 or indeed under the previous law. However, section 14(2) provides that a report of proceedings which has had to be postponed because of a court order or as a consequence of any statutory provision shall be treated as published contemporaneously 'if it is published as soon as practicable after publication is permitted'. It would therefore seem to follow from this that a report will be published 'contemporaneously' within the meaning of section 14(1) if it is published as soon as practicable after each day's proceedings or, where only the outcome is intended to be reported, as soon as practicable after the conclusion of the proceedings. The phrase 'as soon as practicable' calls for consideration of the individual circumstances of each publisher. Whether a publication is contemporaneous will therefore depend upon factors such as the frequency of the publication and the time it goes to press.

1   Section 14(3).

Parliamentary proceedings

14.18   Words spoken by a Member of Parliament in Parliament during the course of a Parliamentary debate or proceeding are immune from suit[1]. The DeA 1996, s 13(5) extends the protection to:

(a)   the giving of evidence before either House or a committee;
(b)   the presentation or submission of a document to either House or a committee;
(c)   the preparation of a document for the purposes of or incidental to the transacting of any such business;
(d)   the formulation, making or publication of a document, including a report, by or pursuant to an order of either House or a committee; and
(e)   any communication with the Parliamentary Commissioner for Standards or any person having functions in connection with the registration of Members' interests.

1   Article 9 of the Bill of Rights 1688. See also *Burdett v Abbot* [1811] 14 East 1; *Stockdale v Hansard* [1839] 9 Ad & EL 1; *Bradlaugh v Gossett* (1884) 12 QBD 271; *Pickin v British Railways Board* [1974] AC 765; *Pepper v Hart* [1993] AC 593; *Prebble v Television New Zealand Ltd* [1995] 1 AC 321.

Questioning Parliamentary proceedings in the courts and waiver of privilege

Questioning Parliamentary proceedings

14.19   Freedom of speech and debates or proceedings in Parliament may not be questioned in any court or place outside Parliament[1]. This means that no court in any proceedings can hear or inquire into allegations about issues arising in or concerning the Houses of Parliament, such as whether a Member had misled the House or had acted there from improper motives.

In October 1994 *The Guardian* published allegations that Neil Hamilton MP had received money from Mohammed Al-Fayed in return for asking questions in the House of Commons concerning the battle for the House of Fraser in what became know as the 'cash for questions' scandal. Mr Hamilton brought proceedings for libel which were stayed in July 1995 on the ground that the issues raised could not be fairly tried without infringing Parliamentary privilege[2]. The effect of this was to deny Mr Hamilton the opportunity to vindicate his reputation, even though the allegations made against him were of the utmost seriousness and went to the very core of his integrity in his chosen profession. In light of this, section 13 of the DeA 1996 was enacted.

1   Article 1 of the Bill of Rights 1688.
2   Due to a lack of funds, he subsequently discontinued the proceedings.

Waiver

14.20   Section 13 of the DeA 1996 provides that where the conduct of a person in or in relation to proceedings in Parliament is in issue in defamation proceedings, then so far as concerns him, he may waive the protection of Parliamentary privilege for the purpose of those proceedings which would otherwise prevent proceedings in Parliament being questioned or impeached in any place outside Parliament[1].

1   The DeA 1996, s 13(1) (and see Appendix 2).

Waiver applicable only to person waiving privilege

14.21   Waiver of privilege only applies to the person waiving it and does not affect another person who has not waived the privilege[1]. This means that where, for example, defamatory allegations are made about a Member acting jointly with others, and those others do not waive privilege, it may still be necessary to stay court proceedings on the ground that there cannot be a fair trial of the action.

1   The DeA 1996, s 13(3) (see Appendix 2).

No waiver on liability

14.22   Privilege cannot be waived in order to render those who qualify for the protection of it liable for anything said or done in Parliamentary proceedings[1]. Section 13 of the DeA 1996 does not permit a Member sued for slander for words spoken in the course of a

Parliamentary debate who wishes to defend his words as, for example, justified, to waive privilege in order that he may do so. His publication of those words remains protected by Parliamentary privilege, and cannot be waived.

1   See the DeA 1996, s 13(4) (see Appendix 2).

The effect of the Defamation Act 1996, s 13

14.23   The effect of section 13 of the DeA 1996 was considered by the House of Lords in *Hamilton v Al-Fayed*[1]. After *The Guardian* case, the Parliamentary Commissioner for Standards ('PCS') conducted a detailed inquiry investigating allegations concerning Mr Hamilton and a number of other MPs. In July 1997 he reported his conclusion that Mr Hamilton had received cash payments from Mr Al-Fayed as a reward for lobbying. Meanwhile in January 1997 Channel 4 broadcast *Dispatches*, in which Mr Al-Fayed repeated his cash for questions allegations. In January 1998 Mr Hamilton commenced proceedings for libel against Mr Al-Fayed.

Mr Al-Fayed applied to strike out the action on the grounds that it would infringe Parliamentary privilege as a whole, as opposed to Mr Hamilton's individual privilege, and section 13 of the DeA 1996 did not permit this. Section 13 of the DeA 1996 only permitted Mr Hamilton to waive his individual privilege: apart from situations where section 13 applied, the rule that the courts were precluded from questioning or impeaching Parliamentary proceedings remained extant. The House of Lords held that once a person had waived privilege, then under section 13(2) of the DeA 1996 any questioning of Parliamentary proceedings, and even the challenge of findings made about his conduct, would not be treated as a breach of Parliamentary privilege. Following waiver, it could not be said that the waiver did not operate so as to override any privilege belonging to Parliament as a whole.

1   [2000] EMLR 531, HL.

Reports of Parliamentary proceedings

14.24   All reports, papers, votes and proceedings published by, or by authority of, Parliament are absolutely privileged[1]. The Parliamentary Papers Act 1840 (PPA 1840) makes provision for a summary stay of any proceedings brought in respect of such reports on application by the defendant and with 24 hours' notice to the claimant. Copies and extracts from such reports, command papers and newspaper and other media reports of Parliamentary proceedings are protected by qualified privilege only[2].

1 The PPA 1840, s 1.
2 See Chapter 15.

Affairs of state

14.25 Certain communications made between officers of state acting in their official capacity are protected by absolute privilege. Foreign state communications are similarly privileged[1]. The privilege protects communications made at the highest level of office but lower down the hierarchy the boundaries between what will be protected and what will not are unclear. However, where an officer is not of sufficient seniority the communication will be protected by qualified privilege[2]. Where armed forces communications are concerned it is easier to satisfy the test of sufficient seniority[3].

In *Friend v Civil Aviation Authority*[4], Popplewell J held that communications between a senior civil servant, who was Head of Civil Aviation at the Department of Environment, Transport and the Regions, and the Chairman of the CAA, a government quango, for the purpose of providing the Secretary of State with information to enable him to respond to an inquiry by Paddy Ashdown MP, was protected by absolute privilege. Publication to Mr Ashdown was protected by ancillary privilege[5].

1 See *Fayed v Al-Tajir* [1988] QB 712, CA.
2 See, for example, *S v Newham London Borough Council* [1998] EMLR 583, CA. See further, Chapter 15. In a case where there is a doubt as to whether absolute privilege will apply, the sensible course is to plead qualified privilege in the alternative to absolute privilege.
3 *Dawkins v Lord Paulet* (1869) LR 5 QB 94.
4 (21 December 2000, unreported), QBD.
5 As to which see paragraph 14.27 below.

Official reports

14.26 Absolute privilege has been conferred on certain official reports. Any report by the Parliamentary Commissioner for Administration to Parliament ('PCA') is absolutely privileged as is[1]:

● any matter published by a Member of the House of Commons in communicating with the PCA and his officers or by him or his officers in communicating with the Member;

- any matter published by the PCA in making a report to either House of Parliament;
- publications by a Member of the House of Commons to the person by whom the complaint was made of a report or statement sent to the Member in respect of the complaint; and
- publications by the PCA to the principal officer of the department or authority concerned and to any other person who is alleged in a complaint to have taken or authorised the action complained of, or a report of the results of the investigation.

The reports of Monopolies and Mergers Commission and the Director of Fair Trading are protected under the Competition Act 1980. The reports of the Local Commissioners for Administration in England and Wales and ancillary publications are protected under the Local Government Act 1974.

1   See the Parliamentary Commissioner Act 1967, s 10(5).

Miscellaneous

14.27   Various statutes confer absolute privilege upon reports, statements and findings of a number of persons and bodies performing investigative or regulatory functions. An exhaustive list of these provisions and analysis of the scope of the privilege conferred is beyond the ambit of this book but the reader is advised to check the applicable statutory provisions whenever proceedings are proposed against such a person or body. For example, the Health Services Commissioners Act 1993 and the Pensions Act 1995 confer absolute privilege upon various reports and statements made pursuant to the provisions of those Acts[1].

1   See section 14(5) of the Health Services Commissioners Act 1993 and sections 103(2) and 113(2) of the Pensions Act 1995.

Chapter 15

Qualified privilege

Introduction

15.01 The law recognises that there are certain occasions where the need for uninhibited expression, though not of such a high order that it will protect statements published on them absolutely[1], nevertheless warrants a lesser form of protection which will apply regardless of whether a defamatory statement is in fact untrue. For this reason, certain occasions of publication are protected by the defence of qualified privilege. Once it is established that qualified privilege attaches to a publication then that publication will be protected unless the claimant can prove that the defendant was motivated by malice[2] when he made that publication.

Occasions of publication protected by qualified privilege are defined both by statute and at common law. At common law, qualified privilege attaches to a defamatory statement, irrespective of whether it was true or false, if it was published on an occasion where the maker of the statement has a social, legal or moral duty or interest to make the statement, and the recipient has a corresponding duty or interest to receive it. This chapter deals in turn with: (a) the requirements for pleading qualified privilege as a defence, (b) procedural considerations arising when the defence of qualified privilege is pleaded, and (c) the occasions of publication which are protected by qualified privilege, (i) at common law and (ii) by statute.

1 As to which see Chapter 14.
2 See Chapter 18.

The requirements for pleading qualified privilege as a defence

15.02 Paragraph 2.7 of the Practice Direction to CPR Pt 53 requires a defendant who contends that the words complained of were published on a privileged occasion to specify the circumstances which he relies upon in support of that contention in the defence. For sample pleas of qualified privilege see Volume 25 of *Atkin's Court Forms.*

Procedural considerations

15.03 The burden is upon the defendant to prove on the balance of probabilities all the facts establishing the circumstances which render the statement protected by qualified privilege.

Whether the privilege exists at all is a question for the judge. The judge is therefore required to determine whether the circumstances in which the publication was made were such as to make the publication privileged. If the facts are in dispute, the jury is called upon to consider the evidence and make findings of fact. It is for the judge, however, to decide whether the facts found by the jury made the publication privileged or to instruct the jury as to what facts they must find in order to hold the publication privileged. Whether those facts, if established, would be such as to render the statement protected by qualified privilege is a question of law for the judge[1].

1   See the commentary to the summary of functions of judge and jury at section 619 of American Law Institute, *Restatement of the Law, Torts* (1977), cited with approval by Lord Steyn in Reynolds v Times Newspapers Ltd [2001] 2 AC 127 at 154, HL.

Disposal prior to full trial of the action

15.04 In many circumstances it will be appropriate, taking into account the overriding objective[1] and the interest of the client in having the matter dealt with as inexpensively and expeditiously as possible, to take steps to have the question of whether the defence of qualified privilege applies in the circumstances or would apply if the facts relied upon by the defendant are proved prior to the full trial of the claim.

1   See CPR 1.

Applications to strike out or for summary judgment

15.05 An application to strike out the defence of qualified privilege under CPR 3.4 will be appropriate where it is plain, even on the defendant's case, that the words were not published on an occasion of qualified privilege. Where it is plain that the words complained of were published on an occasion of qualified privilege, an application for summary judgment under CPR 24 or[1] summary disposal under the DeA 1996, ss 8–10[2] will be more appropriate than an application to strike out, since determination of the question could determine the outcome of the action. However, such an application will not be appropriate unless there is no plea of malice on the record or it is also contended that the plea of malice cannot amount to a proper plea as a matter of law. Where the plea of malice is a proper plea, but it is contended that it has no realistic prospect of success on the facts, the application should be made under the DeA 1996, ss 8–10 since CPR 24 does not permit a judge alone to decide questions of fact which Parliament has determined should be decided by a jury unless the question would have been withdrawn from the jury on the basis that the evidence, taken at its highest, was such that no reasonable jury properly directed could have come to the necessary factual conclusion[3]. Any applications should be made at the earliest opportunity in order to avoid incurring unnecessary costs. See Chapter 22 for further guidance on applications.

1   They may not be invoked in tandem: see CPR 53.2(3).
2   See also CPR Pt 53 PD, para 5.
3   *Safeway Stores plc v Tate* [2001] QB 1120; *Alexander v The Arts Council of Wales* [2001] 1 WLR 1840.

Trial as a preliminary issue

15.06   However, where the question of the existence of the protection of qualified privilege requires serious argument and careful consideration, the proper course is to raise the point in the defence and thereafter to apply to have the question tried as a preliminary issue[1].

Trial of the question of privilege as a preliminary issue may also be advisable where the defence has been pleaded in the alternative or in addition to a defence of justification and/or fair comment where to do so could determine the outcome of the case and thus avoid the likely longevity and expense of a trial of those defences. This practice was endorsed by the Court of Appeal in *GKR Karate UK Ltd v Yorkshire Post Newspapers Ltd*[2].

1   See *Waple v Surrey County Council* [1998] 1 WLR 860 at 869, CA, per Brooke LJ, citing *Gatley on Libel and Slander* (9th edn, 1998), para 26.43.
2   [2000] EMLR 396, CA.

Occasions of publication which are protected by qualified privilege: common law

15.07 The foundation on which the defence of qualified privilege rests is 'the common convenience and welfare of society'[1], that is the public interest. Translated into plain English this simply means that the law has recognised that in certain circumstances people should be free (or perhaps 'more free') to speak their minds even though they may publish false and defamatory statements, provided that they do so honestly and are not reckless as to whether what they say is true or not.

The traditional formulation of the circumstances which will give rise to the existence of the privilege is that stated by Lord Atkinson in *Adam v Ward*[2]:

'a privileged occasion is . . . an occasion where the person who makes a communication has an interest or a duty, legal, social, or moral, to make it to the person to whom it is made, and the person to whom it is so made has a corresponding interest or duty to receive it. This reciprocity is essential.'

'Duty' in the sense in which that term is used in this context has been defined as[3]:

'a duty recognised by English people of ordinary intelligence and moral principle, whether civil or criminal . . . Would the great mass of like minded men in the position of the defendant have considered in their duty under the circumstances to make the communications? In considering the question whether the occasion was an occasion of privilege, the court will regard the alleged libel and will examine by whom it was published, to whom it was published, when, why, and in what circumstances it was published, and will see whether these things establish a relation between the parties which give rise to a social or moral right or duty, and the consideration of these things may involve the consideration of questions of public policy.'

1 *Toogood v Spyring* (1834) 1 Cr M&R 181 at 183, per Parke B.
2 [1917] AC 309 at 334.
3 *Stuart v Bell* [1891] 2 QB 341 at 350, per Lindley LJ.

15.08 In *Loutchansky v Times Newspapers Ltd*[1], the judge at first instance had defined the test of duty as whether failure to publish would have given rise to legitimate criticism. The Court of Appeal held that although a publisher's claim to privilege would be indisputable where failure to publish would have given rise to legitimate criticism, the converse was not true. In determining whether qualified privilege attached to a defamatory newspaper publication to the world at large, the court had to ask itself if the test of whether there was a duty to publish the material to the intended recipients and whether they had an interest in receiving it, was satisfied. The interest was that of the public in a modern democracy in free expression and in the promotion of a free and vigorous press to keep the public informed, and the corresponding duty on the newspaper was to behave responsibly. No privilege could arise unless the publisher acted responsibly, and the question to be posed was whether it was in the public interest to publish the article, true or false.

It is important to note that both the absence of malice and/or the presence of a belief on the part of the defendant that the occasion of publication was privileged or that he had a duty to make the communication will not render privileged an occasion that would otherwise not be so protected[2]. However, the belief of the defendant is relevant to the extent that in order for an occasion of publication to be protected, not only must (a) the facts giving rise to the privilege have been in existence at the time of publication but (b) those facts must be known to the defendant at the time of publication since the defendant must honestly believe that he is under a duty to publish[3].

It is also important to note that in order for a publication to be protected the person or persons to whom it is made must also have a corresponding duty to receive it. A publication to persons who do not meet this test will not in general be protected by qualified privilege[4]. Thus it is possible for publication of the same material to be published simultaneously to different persons and for the publication to some of those persons to be protected by qualified privilege whilst the publication to the others is not[5].

1   [2001] EWCA Civ 536, [2002] QB 321.
2   *Stuart v Bell* [1891] 2 QB 341, CA.
3   *Loutchansky v Times Newspapers Ltd* [2001] EWCA Civ 536, [2002] QB 321.
4   See *Williamson v Freer* (1874) LR 9 CP 393.
5   See *Mutch v Robertson* 1981 SLT 217.

Ancillary privilege

15.09   Ancillary or incidental privilege arises when communications are made to persons who have no interest or duty to receive the communication, but the communication was nevertheless published to them reasonably and in the ordinary course of business. So, for example, defamatory but privileged words do not lose their privilege by being dictated to and typed up by a secretary: 'If a business communication is privileged, as being made on a privileged occasion, the privilege covers all the incidents of the transmission and treatment of that communication which are in accordance with the reasonable and usual course of business'[1].

1   *Edmondson v Birch & Co Ltd* [1907] 1 KB 371 at 372, CA, per Fletcher Moulton LJ.

Answers to questions and the presence of third parties

15.10   A statement by the defendant to the claimant, although uttered in the presence of third persons, is a statement made on a privileged occasion if and in so far as it is made in answer to a question put by the claimant[1]. Where a defendant speaks words (in a slander case) to persons in circumstances where qualified privilege attaches, the mere fact that one, or even a number of, persons who had no duty or interest happened to be present and heard what was said will not necessarily prevent the occasion from being a privileged one[2].

1   See *Adam v Ward* [1917] AC 309, HL; *London Artists v Littler* [1969] 2 QB 375.
2   See *Toogood v Spyring* (1834) 1 Cr M&R 181 at 194, per Parke B. Contrast this with the position in libel – publication to interested persons will be privileged whilst simultaneous publication to uninterested persons will not. This protection is also much wider than ancillary or incidental privilege. It seems, however, that such publications are protected for similar reasons – the business of life could not be properly carried on if restraints of absolute and strict privacy were placed upon such conversations.

Inclusion of irrelevant material

15.11   The inclusion of irrelevant material in a publication can affect the question of whether the privilege attaches as well as the later question of whether the publication was made with malice[1]. The extent to which it should affect the very existence of the privilege was considered in *Horrocks v Lowe*[2] and the modern position was set out by Lord Diplock[3]:

'Logically it might be said that such irrelevant matter falls outside the privilege altogether. But if this were so it would involve the application by the court of an objective test of relevance to every part of the defamatory matter published on the privileged occasion; whereas, as everyone knows, ordinary human beings vary in their ability to distinguish that which is logically relevant from that which is not and few, apart from lawyers, have had any training which qualifies them to do so. So the protection afforded by the privilege would be illusory if it were lost in respect of any defamatory matter which upon logical analysis could be shown to be irrelevant to the fulfilment of the duty or the protection of the right upon which the privilege was founded. As Lord Dunedin pointed out in *Adam v Ward* [1917] AC 309 at 326–327 the proper rule as respects irrelevant defamatory matter incorporated in a statement made on a privileged occasion is to treat it as one of the factors to be taken into consideration in deciding whether, in all the circumstances, an inference that the defendant was actuated by express malice can properly be drawn. As regards irrelevant matter the test is not whether it is logically relevant but whether, in all the circumstances, it can be inferred that the defendant either did not believe it to be true or, though believing it to be true, realised that it had nothing to do with the particular duty or interest on which the privilege was based, but nevertheless seized the opportunity to drag in the irrelevant defamatory matter to vent his personal spite, or for some other improper motive. Here . . . judges and juries should be slow to draw this inference.'

In *Cunningham v Essex County Council*[4] Eady J noted that, 'It is true that this passage is not altogether easy to reconcile with some of the words used by their Lordships, including Lord Dunedin, in *Adam v Ward* [1917] AC 309 at 326–327'. He went on to state that, 'Nevertheless, for words to fall outside the protection of privilege altogether, it seems to me that they would have to be so far removed from the subject matter and purpose of the communication as to be obviously and wholly extraneous'. The test would therefore appear to be whether the irrelevant material included in a defamatory publication for which qualified privilege is claimed is so far removed from its subject matter and purpose as to be wholly extraneous. However, the inclusion of such material does not cease to be relevant, because it will then fall to be considered as part of any case on malice[5].

1   See Chapter 18.
2   [1975] AC 135, HL.
3   [1975] AC 135 at 151D–H, HL.
4   (26 June 2000, unreported), QBD.
5   See Chapter 18.

The principal categories of qualified privilege at common law

15.12   The principal categories of qualified privilege are:

(a)   communications to the public at large, or to a section of the public, made pursuant to a legal, social or moral duty to do so or in reply to a public attack;

(b)   limited communications between persons having a common and corresponding duty or interest to make and receive the communication;

(c)   fair and accurate reports, published generally, of the proceedings before certain persons and bodies.

Communications to the general public

15.13   The common law principle that qualified privilege attaches to a publication made between parties who share a common and corresponding interest in the subject matter of the publication, or to a publication made pursuant to a duty to a person having a corresponding interest or duty to receive it, applies as much to mass communications as to publications to a very limited number of persons.

Until very recently the position at common law was that circumstances would rarely arise where a general duty to publish information to the world at large, for example in the columns of a national newspaper, would be recognised. Thus in 1984 Fox LJ said in *Blackshaw v Lord*[1]:

'I think that states the principle rather too widely. It is necessary to a satisfactory law of defamation that there should be privileged occasions. But the existence of privilege involves a balance of conflicting pressures. On the one hand there is the need that the press should be able to publish fearlessly what is necessary for the protection of the public. On the other hand there is a need to protect the individual from falsehoods. I think there are cases where the test of "legitimate and proper interest to English newspaper readers" would tilt the balance to an unacceptable degree against the individual. It would, it seems to me, protect persons who disseminate any untrue defamatory information of apparently legitimate public interest provided only that they honestly believe it and honestly thought that it was information which the public ought to have. See *London Artists Ltd v Littler* [1968] 1 WLR 607 at 615.'

This passage was expressly approved by the Court of Appeal in *Reynolds v Times Newspapers Ltd*[2]. Furthermore, in the same case in the House of Lords[3], Lord Cooke[4] commended *Blackshaw* 'as adopting substantially the right approach'. However, the House of Lords in *Reynolds* recognised that in contemporary conditions appropriate weight needs to be given to the importance of freedom of expression by the media on all matters of public concern, as a result of which it should in future be easier for a publisher to establish qualified privilege than it has been in the past[5].

Although *Reynolds* has enlarged the ambit of qualified privilege, the conceptual foundation for the defence remains the existence of a reciprocity of duty and interest on the part of the publisher and the publishees respectively[6]. Therefore, the mere existence of a legitimate interest on the part of the readership of a newspaper to have the information imparted to them will not of itself suffice to establish the privilege – there must also be established, in the circumstances, a duty on the part of the publisher to publish. Thus, whether a particular publication is protected by qualified privilege depends on the circumstances of the case – 'the concrete facts of the case' are determinative of the privilege.

1   [1984] QB 1 at 42.
2   [1998] 3 All ER 961.
3   [2001] 2 AC 127, HL.
4   [2001] 2 AC 127 at 163, HL.
5   See *McCartan Turkington Breen v Times Newspapers Ltd* [2001] 2 AC 277 at 296, per Lord Cooke.
6   This dual requirement was confirmed by all the members of the House of Lords in *Reynolds* itself.

15.14   As a result of the House of Lords decision in *Reynolds v Times Newspapers Ltd*[1] the process for determining whether such a mass publication will be protected by qualified privilege has been greatly clarified. Lord Nicholls, giving the leading judgment, set out a non-exhaustive list of ten factors to be taken into account in the determination of whether a publication would be so protected[2]. He also stated that 'The weight to be given to these and any other relevant factors will vary from case to case.' The ten factors were[3]:

(1)   The seriousness of the allegation: the more serious the charge the more the public is misinformed and the individual harmed, if the allegation is not true.
(2)   The nature of the information, and the extent to which the subject matter is a matter of public concern.
(3)   The source of the information: some informants have no direct knowledge of events, some have their own axes to grind, or are being paid for their stories.
(4)   The steps taken to verify the information.
(5)   The status of the information: the allegations may have already been the subject of an investigation which commands respect.

(6)   The urgency of the matter: news is often a perishable commodity.

(7)   Whether comment was sought from the claimant: he may have information others do not possess or have not disclosed. An approach to the claimant will not always be necessary.

(8)   Whether the article contained the gist of the claimant's side of the story.

(9)   The tone of the article: a newspaper can raise queries or call for an investigation. It need not adopt allegations as statements of fact.

(10) The circumstances of the publication, including the timing.

1   [2001] 2 AC 127, HL.
2   [2001] 2 AC 127 at 205, HL; intended as a non-exhaustive list.
3   The extent to which these factors will be relevant and applicable in a non-mass publication case is yet to be fully explained by the courts.

Reynolds v Times Newspapers Ltd in practice[1]

Grobbelaar v News Group Newspapers Ltd

15.15   *Reynolds* has been applied or considered by the courts in a number of subsequent cases[2], of which the most useful for the purposes of illustration is the Court of Appeal decision in *Grobbelaar v News Group Newspapers Ltd*[3]. In *Grobbelaar* the claimant, a well-known professional goalkeeper, had brought a claim against the publishers of *The Sun* newspaper over a series of prominent articles which alleged that he was guilty of corruption. The defamatory meaning alleged by the claimant and admitted by the defendant was that he had dishonestly taken bribes and had fixed or attempted to fix the results of games of football in which he had played and had dishonestly taken bribes with a view to fixing the results of games in which he would be playing.

The story as it emerged during the course of the trial was that in November 1992 the claimant was introduced to a Mr Lim by another player, John Fashanu. Between then and spring 1994 the claimant received cash payments from Mr Lim totalling £8,000. The claimant maintained that these payments were initially for forecasting match results (not including his club) and later, because he proved so inept, for information about footballers and clubs. The newspaper's case was that these payments and at least one further and larger payment of £40,000 were for match-fixing and that the

£40,000 was paid to the claimant at John Fashanu's London address in November 1993 following his club's 3-0 defeat by Newcastle two days earlier. The claimant denied receiving any money on this visit and maintained that £20,000 which he admitted handing over to a Mr Vincent for a project on about that date and £5,000 paid into his testimonial fund a few days later came from cash kept in his sock drawer at home.

On 6 September 1994 Mr Vincent went to *The Sun* to sell his story. His version of the story included allegations that the claimant had received £40,000 after his club lost to Newcastle and that he would have been paid £80,000 had they lost another match against Norwich but they drew it accidentally because the claimant accidentally saved a shot with his foot whilst diving the wrong way. *The Sun* then set up a series of covertly recorded meetings between the claimant and Mr Vincent in order to obtain corroboration of Mr Vincent's story. In essence, Mr Vincent was to put a corrupt proposal for future match-fixing to the claimant in the hope of obtaining such admissions as he could of the claimant's past misconduct. He appeared to have succeeded – during those taped conversations the claimant admitted taking money from Mr Lim for losing matches, including the £40,000, and to having missed out on further such payments for failing to do so, and that he took £2,000 in cash from Mr Vincent pursuant to a proposal that he should fix matches in the future. (The claimant later maintained that he had said these things in order to entrap Mr Vincent and that the 'confessions' were therefore false.)

In November 1994 the claimant was due to fly to Zimbabwe to represent that country in an international match. At Gatwick Airport he was confronted by a number of *Sun* reporters and photographers and challenged with 'a series of grave allegations which the paper intends publishing tomorrow'. The claimant denied wrongdoing and then telephoned the editor at the reporters' suggestion and repeated his denials to him. The newspaper duly went to print the next morning despite receipt of a letter before action faxed at 2.15 am that morning asserting the claimant's innocence. Proceedings were commenced in 1994 but the trial of the action was substantially delayed by two criminal trials of the claimant arising from the allegations, both of which resulted in hung juries and/or acquittal on the various counts.

The defendant pleaded qualified privilege and justification[4]. The essence of the defendant's case on qualified privilege was that professional football is both a major sport and a major industry in the UK, that corruption in the Far East has had a devastating effect on the game there (dramatically reducing attendances), and that the evidence obtained by it revealed a serious risk of corruption (financed by Far Eastern betting syndicates) spreading to the UK and damaging the sport here too. The defendant contended that it was accordingly under a duty to inform and warn the general public of this insidious development which it had just uncovered.

1   [2001] 2 AC 127.
2   See, eg, *Loutchanksy v Times Newspapers Ltd* [2001] EWCA Civ 1805, [2002] QB 321; *GKR Karate (UK) Ltd v Yorkshire Post Newspapers Ltd* [2000] 1 WLR 2571; and *Bonnick v Morris* [2002] 3 WLR 820, PC.
3   [2001] EWCA Civ 33, [2001] 2 All ER 437. The case eventually went to the House of Lords, but on the separate question of whether the jury's verdict in the claimant's favour was perverse. A majority of their Lordships held that it was not, but substituted the original award of £85,000 with nominal damages of £1.
4   The plea of justification was ultimately unsuccessful.

15.16   In order to determine whether the publications were protected by qualified privilege, the Court of Appeal applied each of the ten specific considerations listed by Lord Nicholls in *Reynolds*. In the event, the Court of Appeal found that the publications were not protected by qualified privilege. Two of the three members of the Court of Appeal, Lords Justices Simon Brown[1] and Jonathan Parker[2], considered the application of each of the ten *Reynolds* criteria separately as follows[3].

1   At paragraphs 33–47 of the judgment.
2   At paras 200–213.
3   The third judge, Thorpe LJ, dealt with the issue very shortly in one paragraph: see para 108.

Factor 1: the seriousness of the allegations

15.17   Simon Brown LJ stated that the seriousness of the allegations cannot be doubted. They were very grave and, if untrue, hugely damaging to the claimant's reputation. Jonathan Parker LJ also noted that the allegations were 'extremely serious' to the extent that 'This aspect needs no elaboration'[1].

1   At para 200.

Factor 2: the nature of the information and the extent to which the subject matter is a matter of public concern

15.18   Simon Brown LJ stated that though the allegations were serious, it was equally clear that the subject matter was of very substantial public concern. It was imperative that football should not be tainted by corruption and that matches are competitively played rather than their outcome determined or influenced by corrupt payments in the interests of foreign gambling syndicates.

Jonathan Parker LJ agreed that allegations of corruption against a well-known professional football player were plainly a matter of public concern. He stated that *The Sun*'s duty in relation to such allegations was not limited to making them known to the appropriate authorities and appears to have come to this conclusion in acknowledgment of the commercial reality: 'Investigative journalism can be of considerable public benefit, but without the incentive of being in a position to publish an exclusive story on a sensational subject a newspaper will inevitably be less enthusiastic about committing its time and resources to investigating a story. The prospect of the resulting "scoop" seems to me to be part and parcel of the process of investigative journalism'[1].

1   At para 201.

Factor 3: the reliability and motivation of the sources of the information

15.19   The claimant had argued that the 'source' of the information was Mr Vincent, and was therefore clearly very disreputable. The newspaper had argued that the 'source' was the claimant himself, in his taped conversations.

Jonathan Parker LJ accepted the newspaper's argument that the source of the information was the claimant himself. His Lordship did not go on to express any view on this but since he found the source to be the claimant, and the claimant was taped apparently making admissions against his own interest, it is safe to conclude that he considered the source to be a good one.

15.20   Simon Brown LJ considered factors 3 and 4 together 'in order to sidestep the arid debate as to whether the source was Mr Vincent and the taped admissions its verification, or whether the taped admissions themselves were realistically the source for this story'. He stated that there was every reason to doubt the reliability of Mr Vincent because he plainly had an axe to grind on his own admission – he had told another witness that he was destitute and shortly to be bankrupted because the claimant had reneged on an agreement with him to fund a project. The defendant's counsel had himself described him as 'a wholly unreliable witness . . . someone whose evidence we believe may be highly suspect and whose whole character may be deeply flawed'. Against that was the fact that aspects of Mr Vincent's story coincided with the claimant's taped admissions. His Lordship then made reference to the fact that the claimant criticised *The Sun* for failing to investigate the particular matches mentioned in the tapes to see whether the claimant's confession were to be regarded as true and reliable rather than simply up. (The claimant had called powerful and substantially unchallenged expert evidence that the games referred to showed no evidence of anything other than good, and in some cases outstanding, goalkeeping by the claimant.)

Factor 4: the steps taken to verify the information

15.21   Jonathan Parker LJ held that *The Sun* took steps to verify the information provided to it by Mr Vincent by arranging for covert tape recordings of the claimant although he also found the manner in which *The Sun* carried out its investigation to be 'amateurish' – the recording failed on one occasion because the coat worn by Mr Vincent was too thick, and on subsequent occasions much of the conversation was 'indecipherable'. He also noted that *The Sun* took no steps to verify the charges of actual match-fixing by examining recordings of the matches in question with an expert and, 'most surprisingly', did not even seek the assistance in that connection with its own football journalists who had been present at the matches in question[1].

1   At paras 204–205.

Factor 5: the status of the information

15.22   Simon Brown LJ pointed out that there was no question here of the story having already been the subject of some independent investigation which commanded respect. It had no status whatsoever save as an apparently genuine admission by the claimant against his own interests. Jonathan Parker LJ agreed that the information had no 'status' in the sense in which Lord Nicholls had used the word.

Factor 6: the urgency of the matter

15.23   So far as urgency was concerned, Simon Brown LJ recognised that the story was a scoop for *The Sun* and that news was often a perishable commodity. However, he considered it equally obvious that there was no urgency with regard to the public's need to know. Jonathan Parker LJ approached the question differently, stating that the matter was urgent only in the sense that if the information was true it was in the public interest that the guilty parties be exposed sooner rather than later. However, he went on to say, 'On the other hand, the date of initial publication was fixed to suit *The Sun*. So far as *The Sun* was concerned, any urgency lay in the need for it to publish a world exclusive on a sensational subject'[1].

1   Para 207.

Factor 7: whether comment was sought from the claimant

15.24   Simon Brown LJ acknowledged that comment was sought from the claimant in the sense that he was given the opportunity to refute the allegations at Gatwick Airport, first when confronted by the journalists and second in his telephone call to Mr Higgins. The claimant complained that the confrontation by the journalists was no more than an ambush and the defendants had admitted that surprise was a key element. Although his Lordship accepted that undoubtedly the claimant had been put under great pressure, he also stated that if 'qualified privilege is ever to extend to scoops of this nature, it is difficult to see what fuller opportunity for comment could be given'. He also relied upon Lord Nicholl's statement in *Reynolds* that 'an approach to the [claimant] will not always be necessary'.

Jonathan Parker LJ chose not to mince his words and described the 'ambush' of the claimant at Gatwick as 'a thoroughly deplorable way of confronting Mr Grobbelaar with the extremely serious allegations made against him'. The occasion was orchestrated by *The Sun* to achieve maximum publicity and to cause the claimant maximum surprise, embarrassment and distress. An editorial decision had already been taken to publish the story, and most of the articles had been written many days before. The purpose of the ambush was not to enable the claimant to give his side of the story but 'to put him in a position of maximum discomfort and at the greatest possible disadvantage, for the delectation of *The Sun*'s readers'[1]. This had been followed a few moments later but it was unreal to suggest that either afforded the claimant the chance to respond coherently, logically or rationally.

1   At para 208.

Factor 8: whether the article contained the gist of the claimant's side of the story

15.25   Simon Brown LJ concluded that the gist of the claimant's side of the story was included in the articles, given that they were substantially based on the claimant's taped admissions and that his side of the story, as it emerged during the Gatwick confrontation and telephone call, consisted largely of a bald denial of wrongdoing coupled with the assertions that he had never thrown a game in his life and that the £40,000 was part of his testimonial fund. However, they attracted scant attention in the massive overall coverage of the story and were in any event reported in such a way as to indicate *The Sun*'s profound disbelief in their veracity. His Lordship also pointed out that this was all the explanation offered on behalf of the claimant at the time, who did not explain until later his case that he was attempting to entrap Mr Vincent.

Jonathan Parker LJ noted that *The Sun* printed some of the exchanges which occurred during the course of the 'ambush at Gatwick' and in the subsequent telephone conversation.

Factor 9: the tone of the article

15.26   Jonathan Parker LJ was extremely critical of the tone of the article, stating that 'not only were allegations paraded as facts, but the accused was repeatedly held up to public ridicule. It was as if *The Sun* had placed Mr Grobbelaar in the stocks, to be publicly mocked, abused and derided for the amusement of the populace'. He viewed the involvement in one of the articles of the claimant's wife and children as 'particularly distasteful'[1].

Simon Brown LJ considered factors 9 and 10 together and viewed these as 'the critical considerations'. The story was covered not by a single article but massive and relentless coverage over seven days, generally spread across several pages and under prominent headlines. The articles did not raise questions or call for an investigation but asserted the claimant's guilt in the most unequivocal terms. Certain aspects of the coverage went beyond what the claimant had in fact admitted on tape and other features of the coverage calculated to add credence to the central allegation of corrupt match-fixing were unsupported even by Mr Vincent, including inferring that the claimant had gone to Gatwick to evade justice and claiming that Mr Vincent was a close friend who was appalled by the claimant's behaviour and decided to speak out for the sake of the claimant's loyal fans, rather than a paid informant in a vengeful mood against the claimant for having brought him to penury. The language used was emotive in the highest degree. It was a 'sustained and mocking campaign of vilification' and 'there was in addition the lamentable involvement of his family', doorstepping of his wife and asking her questions such as 'How much of what's been happening have you told the children about?' and 'Have they been getting a hard time at school?'. In the view of Simon Brown LJ, the articles were calculated not only to embarrass the claimant but also his wife and children. He concluded, 'There can be no doubt that considered as a whole this newspaper campaign carried the prejudgment of guilt to its uttermost limits. It is difficult to dispute the validity of [counsel for the claimant's] criticism that *The Sun* "took upon themselves the roles of police, prosecuting authority, judge and jury" '.

1   At para 211.

Factor 10: the circumstances of the publication, including the timing

15.27   Jonathan Parker LJ took this aspect very shortly, stating 'I described the circumstances of the publication earlier in this judgment. As to timing, the publication of the material complained of was timed to suit *The Sun*'[1].

1   At para 212.

Grobbelaar: conclusions

15.28   Simon Brown LJ held that in assessing whether a succession of defamatory statements of this nature could attract qualified privilege, the ultimate question is always whether the general public was entitled to receive the information contained in these publications irrespective of whether in the end it turned out to be true or false. Who should bear the risk – the publisher or the person about whom the material is published? His Lordship answered the questions as follows:

> 'To my mind there can only be one answer to these questions. If newspapers choose to publish exposés of this character, unambiguously asserting the criminal guilt of those they investigate, they must do so at their own financial risk. Given the obvious commercial benefits attending this style of journalism – the editor here ordered an increase in *The Sun*'s print run in advance of its Grobbelaar exclusive – and the substantially reduced level of damages awards now recoverable under modern libel law, it seems to me absurd to suggest that *The Sun* will be

discouraged from pursuing its investigatory role unless protected by qualified privilege. On the contrary, the protection of publications of this nature would in my judgment give rise to the altogether greater risk that newspaper investigations would become less thorough, and their exposés more sensational, (even) than at present. As their Lordships' speeches in *Reynolds* – not least that of Lord Hobhouse – made plain, there is no human right to disseminate information which is untrue, no public interest in being misinformed.'[1]

In holding that the publications complained of were not protected by qualified privilege, Simon Brown LJ repeated Lord Nicholls' warning that the courts should be slow to conclude that a publication was not in the public interest and, therefore, that the public had no right to know, and that in the light of this any lingering doubts should be resolved in favour of publication. However, he professed himself to have 'no "lingering doubts" whatsoever'[2]. He stated that the defence would obviously have applied had *The Sun* simply passed on the information to the police. He would also have held it to apply had *The Sun* 'chosen instead to publish a restrained piece couched in the language of suspicion and allegation rather than, as here, an unqualified assertion of guilt'[3].

Jonathan Parker LJ was also unequivocal in concluding that the publication was not protected by qualified privilege, expressing that he had 'no hesitation' in reaching that conclusion. The strength of views expressed in the Court of Appeal on this occasion, including its extremely vocal condemnation of the 'tabloid' approach, is no small indication that it will be a rare case indeed where a tabloid newspaper is able to successfully claim the protection of qualified privilege.

1 At para 40. An 'additional consideration' was the fact that publishing allegations of serious criminality was likely to prejudice any future trial and, in circumstances where such allegations are made, 'it is surely preferable not totally to prejudge, and thereby risk prejudicing, the criminal process in advance' (para 41).
2 Para 46.
3 Para 47.

Reply to attack

15.29 Qualified privilege will attach where a person has been publicly criticised or attacked and responds to that criticism or attack to the same or substantially the same audience[1]. This is because a person whose character or conduct has been attacked in the public press is entitled to have recourse to the press in his defence and vindication

Thus where a person is attacked in *The Times*, he may respond in *The Times*, and where he is attacked in a letter published to two other persons, he may similarly respond and be protected by qualified privilege. However, a person who is attacked in a letter published to two other persons but responds in *The Times* will not be protected by the defence of qualified privilege.

The attack may give rise to a duty upon others to reply on the victim's behalf[2] and to an ancillary privilege in the newspaper or other medium publishing the reply, particularly if it published the original attack[3].

1   *Adam v Ward* [1917] AC 309, HL; *London Artists Ltd v Littler* [1969] 2 QB 375, CA.
2   *Adam v Ward* [1917] AC 309, HL.
3   *Watts v Times Newspapers Ltd* [1997] QB 650, CA.

Communications to a limited audience

15.30   An occasion of publication is privileged where the person who makes a statement has a legal, social or moral duty or interest to make it to the person to whom it is made, who himself has a corresponding duty or interest to receive it. The privilege will only protect the communication of matter upon the subject with respect to which the privilege exists. Below is a non-exhaustive list intended to indicate the sorts of publication which the law has recognised as protected by qualified privilege[1]:

(a)   statements as to employee's characters, ie employment references[2];
(b)   statements as to conduct of candidates for public office[3];
(c)   statements made as to the commercial credit of a person[4];
(d)   communications by a solicitor on his client's behalf[5];
(e)   statements made during the investigation of crime[6];
(f)   statements made at committees and council meetings[7];
(g)   communications on private or family matters[8];
(h)   statements made in the protection of a person's own interests[9];
(i)   statements made for the purpose of redressing a grievance[10];
(j)   statements made in defence of a principal's interests[11];

(k)   complaints about public officers, or persons in authority or with public responsibilities[12].

1   But these are not special categories of protection – in each case the statement must pass the duty and interest test. See *Reynolds v Times Newspapers Ltd* [2001] 2 AC 127, HL.

2   *Pullman v Walter Hill & Co Ltd* [1891] 1 QB 524, CA; *Coxhead v Richards* (1846) 2 CB 569; *Hodgson v Scarlett* (1818) 1 B & Ald 232. But the existence of the privilege does not insulate the defendant from liability for negligence: *Spring v Guardian Assurance plc* [1995] 2 AC 296, HL.

3   *Bruce v Leisk* (1892) 19 R 482; *Bradney v Virtue* (1909) 28 NZLR 828; *Braddock v Bevins* [1948] 1 KB 580, CA.

4   *Waller v Loch* (1881) 7 QBD 619 at 622, CA; *Greenlands v Wilmshurst* [1913] 3 KB 507 at 546; *London Association v Greenlands Ltd* [1916] 2 AC 15. But a credit reference agency operating for profit and with its records open for inspection to those who pay operates at its own risk and without the protection of qualified privilege: see *Macintosh v Dunn* [1908] AC 390, PC.

5   *Baker v Carrick* [1894] 1 QB 838, CA; *Browne v Dunn* (1893) 6 R 67, HL. In *Regan v Taylor* [2000] EMLR 549, CA it was held that where a solicitor makes a statement to the press which falls within the scope of his general instructions to deal with the media on his client's behalf, the occasion is privileged even though the particular statement was made without the client's explicit authority. See also category (j).

6   *Force v Warren* (1864) 15 CBNS 806; *Harrison v Fraser* (1881) 29 WR 652; *Padmore v Lawrence* (1840) 11 Ad & El 380; *Collins v Cooper* (1902) 19 TLR 118, CA; *Stuart v Bell* [1891] 2 QB 341, CA.

7   *Royal Aquarium Society Ltd v Parkinson* [1892] 1 QB 431, CA; *Pittard v Oliver* [1891] 1 QB 474, CA; *Mapey v Barker* (1909) 73 JP 289, CA. Such statements may also be covered by statutory qualified privilege: see paragraphs 15.37 and 15.38 below.

8   *Todd v Hawkins* (1837) 2 Mood & R 20; *Whitely v Adams* (1863) 15 CBNS 392; *Bennett v Deacon* (1846) 2 CB 628; *Stuart v Bell* [1891] 2 QB 341, CA. But see also *Toogood v Spyring* (1834) 1 Cr M&R 181 and *Dickeson v Hilliard* (1874) LR 9 Exch 79.

9   *Coward v Wellington* (1836) 7 C & P 531; Laughton v Bishop of Sodor and Man (1872) LR 4 PC 495; *Towell v Fallon* (1913) 47 ILT 176; *Turner v Metro-Goldwyn-Meyer Pictures Ltd* [1950] 1 All ER 449, HL.

10 *Fairman v Ives* (1822) 5 B & Ald 624; *Waring v M'Caldin* (1873) Ir R 7 CL 282; *Winstanley v Bampton* [1943] KB 319.

11 *Steward v Young* (1870) LR 5 CP 122; *Baker v Carrick* [1894] 1 QB 838; *Watts v Times Newspapers Ltd* [1997] QB 650, CA.

12 *Harrison v Bush* (1855) 5 E & B 344; *Woodward v Lander* (1834) 6 C & P 548; *Mowlds v Fergusson* (1940) 64 CLR 206; *Somerville v Cliff* (1942) 15 LGR 40 (NSW); *Beach v Freeson* [1972] 1 QB 14.

Privileged reports

15.31   Fair and accurate reports of certain types of public proceedings are protected by qualified privilege at common law, although much of the protection has now been rendered otiose by the protection afforded by statute. The privilege will only exist for proceedings for which the public could have admittance. It does not cover material that is not for the public benefit[1]. Fair and accurate reports of judicial proceedings are protected at common law, and the protection has been held to extend to reports of ex parte proceedings before magistrates[2], public proceedings before a judge in chambers[3], a coroner[4] and a registrar in bankruptcy[5].

1 *Steele v Brannan* (1872) LR 7 CP 261.
2 *Usill v Hales* (1878) 3 CPD 319; *Kimber v Press Association Ltd* [1893] 1 QB 65, CA.
3 *Smith v Scott* (1847) 2 Car & Kir 580.
4 *Lynam v Gowing* (1880) 6 LR Ir 259.
5 *Ryalls v Leader* (1866) LR 1 Exch 296.

Occasions of publication which are protected by qualified privilege: statute

15.32 The DeA 1996 provides for certain occasions of publication to be protected by qualified privilege. This means that, once it is established that a publication falls within a definition provided for in the Act, it will be protected by qualified privilege unless and until defeated on proof of malice[1].

1 The DeA 1996, s 15(1).

Two categories of statement

15.33 The DeA 1996 recognises two categories of statement: first, statements having qualified privilege without explanation or contradiction[1]; and, second, statements having qualified privilege subject to explanation or contradiction[2]. The statements defined as falling within each of these categories are listed at paragraphs 15.36 and 15.37 below. A statement falling within the second category will not be protected by statutory qualified privilege if the claimant shows that the defendant (a) was requested by him to publish in a suitable manner a reasonable letter or statement by way of explanation or contradiction, and (b) refused or neglected to do so[3]. 'In a suitable manner' is defined as 'in the same manner as the publication complained of or in a manner that is adequate and reasonable in the circumstances'[4]. There is no requirement of contemporaneity for the protection of qualified privilege to attach[5].

1   The DeA 1996, Sch 1, Pt I.
2   The DeA 1996, Sch 1, Pt II.
3   The DeA 1996, s 15(2).
4   The DeA 1996, s 15(2).
5   Contrast the position with contemporaneity requirements for the protection of absolute privilege: see Chapter 14.

Publication to the public must be of public concern and for the public benefit

15.34   The DeA 1996 further provides that a statement falling within either category of statement will not attract statutory qualified privilege where publication is made to the public, or a section of the public, of matter which is not of public concern and the publication of which is not for the public benefit[1].

1   The DeA 1996, s 15(3).

No protection for publications otherwise prohibited and no limitation on qualified privilege at common law or under any other statute

15.35   Section 15(4) of the DeA 1996 expressly provides that it must not be read so as to give the protection of qualified privilege to the publication of matter which is prohibited by law. It also expressly preserves any pre-existing qualified privilege either at common law, under statute or brought into being elsewhere in the DeA 1996 itself by providing that nothing within it shall be construed as limiting or abridging any privilege subsisting apart from that section.

The Defamation Act 1996, Sch 1, Pt I: Statements having qualified privilege without explanation or contradiction

15.36
1   A fair and accurate report of proceedings in public of a legislature[1] anywhere in the world.

2   A fair and accurate report of proceedings in public before a court[2] anywhere in the world.

3   A fair and accurate report of proceedings in public of a person appointed to hold a public inquiry by a government or legislature[3] anywhere in the world.

4   A fair and accurate report of proceedings in public anywhere in the world of an international organisation[4] or an international conference[5].

5   A fair and accurate copy of or extract from any register or other document required by law to be open to public inspection.

6   A notice or advertisement published by or on the authority of a court[6], or of a judge or officer of a court, anywhere in the world.

7   A fair and accurate copy of or extract from matter published by or on the authority of a government or legislature[7] anywhere in the world.

8   A fair and accurate copy of or extract from matter published anywhere in the world by an international organisation or an international conference.

1   Defined in the DeA 1996, Sch 1, Pt III, para 16(1). For the purposes of paragraphs 1, 3 and 7 'legislature' is further defined in Sch 1, Pt III, para 16(4) to the DeA 1996: see Appendix 2.

2   Defined in the DeA 1996, Sch 1, Pt III, para 16(1). For the purposes of paras 2 and 6 'court' is further defined in Sch 1, Pt III, para 16(3) to the DeA 1996: see Appendix 2.

3   Defined in the DeA 1996, Sch 1, Pt III, para 16(1). For the purposes of paragraphs 1, 3 and 7 'legislature' is further defined in Sch 1, Pt III, para 16(4) to the DeA 1996: see Appendix 2.

4   Defined in the DeA 1996, Sch 1, Pt III, para 16(1): see Appendix 2.

5   Defined in the DeA 1996, Sch 1, Pt III, para 16(1): see Appendix 2.

6   For the purposes of paragraphs 1, 3 and 7 'legislature' is further defined in Sch 1, Pt III, para 16(4) to the DeA 1996: see Appendix 2.

7   Defined in the DeA 1996, Sch 1, Pt III, para 16(1). For the purposes of paragraphs 1, 3 and 7 'legislature' is further defined in Sch 1, Pt III, para 16(4) to the DeA 1996: see Appendix 2.

The Defamation Act 1996, Sch 1, Pt II: Statements privileged subject to explanation or contradiction

15.37

9(1)   A fair and accurate copy of or extract from a notice or other matter issued for the information of the public by or on behalf of—

(a)   a legislature in any member State or the European Parliament;

(b)   the government of any member State[1], or any authority performing governmental functions in any member State or part of a member State, or the European Commission;

(c)   an international organisation or international conference.

(2)   In this paragraph 'governmental functions' includes police functions.

10 A fair and accurate copy of or extract from a document made available by a court in any member State or the European Court of Justice (or any court attached to that court), or by a judge or officer of any such court.

11(1) A fair and accurate report of proceedings at any public meeting or sitting in the United Kingdom of—

    (a)   a local authority or local authority committee;

    (aa) in the case of a local authority which are operating executive arrangements, the executive of that authority or a committee of that executive;

    (b)   a justice or justices of the peace acting otherwise than as a court exercising judicial authority[2];

    (c)   a commission, tribunal, committee or person appointed for the purposes of any inquiry by any statutory provision, by Her Majesty or by a Minister of the Crown a member of the Scottish Executive or a Northern Ireland Department;

    (d)   a person appointed by a local authority to hold a local inquiry in pursuance of any statutory provision;

    (e)   any other tribunal, board, committee or body constituted by or under, and exercising functions under, any statutory provision.

(1A) In the case of a local authority which are operating executive arrangements, a fair and accurate record of any decision made by any member of the executive where that record is required to be made and available for public inspection by virtue of section 22 of the Local Government Act 2000 or of any provision in regulations made under that section.

(2) In sub-paragraphs (1)(a), (1)(aa) and (1A)—

'local authority' means—

    (a)   in relation to England and Wales, a principal council within the meaning of the Local Government Act 1972, any body falling within any paragraph of section 100J(1) of that Act or an authority or body to which the Public Bodies (Admission to Meetings) Act 1960 applies,

    (b)   in relation to Scotland, a council constituted under section 2 of the Local Government etc (Scotland) Act 1994 or an authority or body to which the Public Bodies (Admission to Meetings) Act 1960 applies,

    (c)   in relation to Northern Ireland, any authority or body to which sections 23 to 27 of the Local Government Act (Northern Ireland) 1972 apply; and

'local authority committee' means any committee of a local authority or of local authorities, and includes—

    (a)   any committee or sub-committee in relation to which sections 100A to 100D of the Local Government Act 1972 apply by virtue of section 100E of that Act (whether or not also by virtue of section 100J of that Act), and

(b)   any committee or sub-committee in relation to which sections 50A to 50D of the Local Government (Scotland) Act 1973 apply by virtue of section 50E of that Act.

(2A)   In sub-paragraphs (1) and (1A)—
'executive' and 'executive arrangements' have the same meaning as in Part II of the Local Government Act 2000.

(3)   A fair and accurate report of any corresponding proceedings in any of the Channel Islands or the Isle of Man or in another member State.

12(1)   A fair and accurate report of proceedings at any public meeting[3] held in a member State.

(2)   In this paragraph a 'public meeting' means a meeting bona fide and lawfully held for a lawful purpose and for the furtherance or discussion of a matter of public concern, whether admission to the meeting is general or restricted.

13(1)   A fair and accurate report of proceedings at a general meeting of a UK public company.

(2)   A fair and accurate copy of or extract from any document circulated to members of a UK public company—

(a)   by or with the authority of the board of directors of the company,

(b)   by the auditors of the company, or

(c)   by any member of the company in pursuance of a right conferred by any statutory provision.

(3)   A fair and accurate copy of or extract from any document circulated to members of a UK public company which relates to the appointment, resignation, retirement or dismissal of directors of the company.

(4)   In this paragraph 'UK public company' means—

(a)   a public company within the meaning of section 1(3) of the Companies Act 1985 or Article 12(3) of the Companies (Northern Ireland) Order 1986, or

(b)   a body corporate incorporated by or registered under any other statutory provision, or by Royal Charter, or formed in pursuance of letters patent.

(5)   A fair and accurate report of proceedings at any corresponding meeting of, or copy of or extract from any corresponding document circulated to members of, a public company formed under the law of any of the Channel Islands or the Isle of Man or of another member State.

14   A fair and accurate report of any finding or decision of any of the following descriptions of association, formed in the United Kingdom or another member State, or of any committee or governing body of such an association—

(a)   an association formed for the purpose of promoting or encouraging the exercise of or interest in any art, science, religion or learning, and empowered by its constitution to exercise control over or adjudicate on matters of interest or concern to the association, or the actions or conduct of any person subject to such control or adjudication;

    (b)   an association formed for the purpose of promoting or safeguarding the interests of any trade, business, industry or profession, or of the persons carrying on or engaged in any trade, business, industry or profession, and empowered by its constitution to exercise control over or adjudicate upon matters connected with that trade, business, industry or profession, or the actions or conduct of those persons;

    (c)   an association formed for the purpose of promoting or safeguarding the interests of a game, sport or pastime to the playing or exercise of which members of the public are invited or admitted, and empowered by its constitution to exercise control over or adjudicate upon persons connected with or taking part in the game, sport or pastime;

    (d)   an association formed for the purpose of promoting charitable objects or other objects beneficial to the community and empowered by its constitution to exercise control over or to adjudicate on matters of interest or concern to the association, or the actions or conduct of any person subject to such control or adjudication.

15(1) A fair and accurate report of, or copy of or extract from, any adjudication, report, statement or notice issued by a body, officer or other person designated for the purposes of this paragraph—

    (a)   for England and Wales or Northern Ireland, by order of the Lord Chancellor, and

    (b)   for Scotland, by order of the Secretary of State.

(2)   An order under this paragraph shall be made by statutory instrument which shall be subject to annulment in pursuance of a resolution of either House of Parliament.

1   Defined in the DeA 1996, Sch 1, Pt III, para 16(2).
2   For example, licensing justices.
3   In *McCartan Turkington Breen v Times Newspapers Ltd* [2001] EMLR 1, HL, the House of Lords held that a press conference can be a 'public meeting' because it was a meeting 'bona fide and lawfully held for a lawful purpose and for the furtherance or discussion of any matter of public concern'.

15.38   Paragraph 15 of Sch 1, Pt II to the DeA 1996 provides that a fair and accurate report of, or copy of or extract from, any adjudication, report, statement or notice issued by a body, officer or other person designated for the purposes of this paragraph by order of the Lord Chancellor by statutory instrument shall be protected by statutory qualified privilege subject to explanation or contradiction. The Government issued a consultation paper asking for views on which bodies should be designated under paragraph 15 of Schedule 1[1]. This explained that the power was included because it was recognised that it would not, in practice, be possible to draft Schedule 1 so that it included all the bodies, the reports of whose adjudications, and so on, might appropriately attract qualified privilege. Also, the paper acknowledged, even if the list in the DeA 1996 was successful, that there would be problems with making amendments to that list. There was concern that bodies which were either not in existence at the time or subsequently changed their name would be excluded until Parliamentary time could be found for amending primary legislation. It was therefore decided to include the provision for making a designation by statutory instrument subject to the negative resolution procedure before Parliament. However, despite the fact that the paper asked for responses by 10 November 1999, at the date of writing no designation under paragraph 15 had yet been made.

The consultation paper included a table of bodies which had been recommended for designation at the time it was published. It was acknowledged in the consultation paper that some of the bodies recommended may already fall within one of the other provisions of Schedule 1. In particular, it noted that it had been suggested that both the Press Complaints Commission, the Advertising Standards Authority and other analogous bodies are, as self-regulatory bodies, covered by Sch 1, Pt II, paragraph 14(b) to the DeA 1996. Nevertheless, those bodies were included in the table. The table, which contains generic as well as specific descriptions, is reproduced in full below:

Table A: Bodies which have been recommended for designation by the Lord Chancellor under paragraph 15 of Schedule 1 to the DeA 1996

Advertising Standards Authority	Human Rights Act 'public authorities'
Advisory Committee on Animal Feedingstuffs	Independent Scientific Group on Cattle Tuberculosis Commission
Advisory Committee on Novel Foods and Processes	Independent Television Commission
Armed Forces	Insurance Ombudsman
Banking Ombudsman	Local authorities
Board of Visitors to Penal Establishments	London Regional Transport
British Airports Authority	Millennium Commission
British Board of Film Censors	Monopolies and Mergers Commission

BBC Programme Complaints Unit	National Health Service
BBC Governor's Programme Complaints Appeals Committee	National Trust
Broadcasting Standards Commission	Northern Lighthouse Board
Building Societies Ombudsman	Parliamentary Commissioner for Administration
City Panel on Take-overs and Mergers	Police Complaints Authorities
Commission for Racial Equality	Police Disciplinary Tribunals
Committee of Advertising Practice	Police Discipline Appeals Tribunals
Consumer Panel	Police Forces and Police Authorities
Council of the Stock Exchange	Press Complaints Commission
Criminal Injuries Compensation Board	Prison Service Agency
Data Protection Registrar	Privatised utility companies
District auditors	Public authority contractors (if a UK public company)
The Environment Agency	Radio Authority
Equal Opportunities Commission	Royal Botanic Gardens
Expert Group on Vitamins and Minerals	S4C
Farm Animal Welfare Council	Schools
Food Advisory Committee	Security and intelligence services
Further education colleges	Security Services Tribunal
Health Service Commissioner	Spongiform Encephalopathy Advisory Committee and sub-groups
HM Inspector of Prisons	Statutory Regulatory Bodies (eg OFTEL)
HM Inspector of Schools	UK Atomic Energy Authority

Horticulture Research International	UK Register of Organic Food Standards
Hospital trusts and similar bodies	Universities

1   Accessible on the Internet at www.lcd.gov.uk.

Other statutory provisions

The Broadcasting Standards Commission

15.39   The Broadcasting Act 1996 (BA 1996), s 121 provides that the following matters are protected by qualified privilege[1]:

(a)   publication of any statement in the course of the consideration by the Broadcasting Standards Commission ('BSC') of, and their adjudication on, a fairness complaint[2];

(b)   publication by the BSC of directions under section 119(1)[3] of the BA 1996 relating to a fairness complaint;

(c)   publication of a report of the BSC, so far as the report relates to fairness complaints.

1   Again, the section is expressed not to limit any privilege subsisting apart from it: the BA 1996, s 121(2).
2   A 'fairness complaint' is a complaint to the BSC of unjust or unfair treatment in a BBC programme or programme under a television or radio licensed service; or unwarranted infringement of privacy in, or in connection with, the obtaining of material included in, such a programme: see sections 110(4) and 107(1) of the BA 1996.
3   Section 119(1) of the BA 1996 provides for the BSC to give directions as to the publication of its findings in relation to a fairness complaint.

Parliamentary papers and reports

15.40   Section 3 of the PPA 1840 provides that the publication in print of an extract from, or abstract of, any Parliamentary paper, report, vote or proceedings published by or under the authority of either House of Parliament is privileged, provided that the defendant proves that he published it bona fide and without malice. Note that this reverses the burden of proof of a defendant on the issue of malice. However, given the protection now provided by the DeA 1996, Sch 1, Pt I, para 7, this provision is probably obsolete.

A number of other statutes, beyond the scope of this book, also provide for the issue of certain types of information to the public of official documents to be protected by qualified privilege. See, for example, the Local Government Act 1988, s 8(6) and the Public Bodies (Admissions to Meetings) Act 1960, s 1.

Chapter 16

Other defences

Consent ('leave and license' or 'volenti non fit injuria')

16.01 If an individual consents to the publication of certain statements, he will obviously not be entitled to libel damages because of that publication. Accordingly, there is a defence to a defamation action where the defendant can show that the claimant expressly or impliedly consented to the publication of the defamatory material.

If the claimant has consented to publication, but publication is to a wider audience than that to which the claimant consented, the defence is likely to fail. In *Cook v Ward*[1], the claimant told an anecdote about himself as part of an after-dinner speech at a private function, which was then reported in a newspaper. Consent was not available as a defence for the newspaper because, although the claimant had obviously consented to the limited publication at the private function, this was not the same as consenting to publication in a newspaper with its considerably larger circulation.

Similarly, where an individual gives information to a newspaper in an off the record interview, there has been no consent to its publication. However, it will usually be the case when a newspaper interviews an individual that the interviewee is deemed to have given his implied consent to publication, unless he expressly makes clear that the information is not for publication. Where an interviewer puts to a claimant a defamatory statement, which he then refutes, there will be no consent.

Sometimes an individual may invite another to repeat in front of witnesses something defamatory that person has already said about him in private. In these circumstances, consent is unlikely to be available to the defendant because the invitation by the claimant is a clear indication that the claimant intends to sue if the statement is repeated.

Evidence of consent must be clear and unequivocal and, if oral, should be backed up by a witness.

1   (1830) 6 Bing 409.

Res judicata

16.02   It would not be right if a claimant could keep bringing libel actions in respect of the same publication. Accordingly, it is a complete defence that the claimant has already brought an action against the defendant in respect of the same publication. If the claimant wants recompense for damage suffered by publication, he must sue for all of it in one action – it would not be an efficient use of court time and would be very unfair on the defendant if a number of actions could be brought when one was sufficient. It is no argument for the defendant to say that he has suffered further damage since judgment in the initial action, because when damages are awarded for libel, the lump sum is intended to take into account future damage as well as damage already suffered.

However, where there is fresh publication of the same or similar words, res judicata does not prevent a claimant bringing a new action. This is because each publication of defamatory matter gives a claimant a new cause of action. So, for example, there is nothing to stop a claimant bringing actions against different newspapers for publication of the same or similar allegations.

Accord and satisfaction (or 'release')

16.03   There is a complete defence to a libel action where the defendant can show that the claimant has previously agreed to settle the claim. For the defence to succeed, the agreement must conform to the legal requirements for enforceable contracts. This means that the agreement must have been executed under seal (that is, by deed) or for valid consideration. Valid consideration means there must be benefit to both parties, so in return for dropping the action (the benefit to the defendant), the claimant must have received something (perhaps a sum of money or a written apology).

As with consent, it is sometimes difficult to establish the existence of the agreement. An oral agreement is acceptable, but will be hard to prove unless it was recorded or there are witnesses to the agreement.

Where there is more than one defendant in an action, a claimant must be careful in agreeing to discharge one of the defendants from liability. This is because the liability of multiple defendants is said to be indivisible, so where a claimant settles a claim against one of them, the claimant will be treated as having waived his right to continue against the others – unless he reserves his right to pursue the other defendants in the agreement.

Limitation

16.04   Under section 4A of the LA 1980[1] a claim for defamation or malicious falsehood is barred if an action is not commenced within one year of the date on which the cause of action is accrued. In libel, since damage is presumed, that is one year from the date of publication. An action in respect of an article published in a newspaper on 26 November 2002 will, therefore, become time-barred on 26 November 2003. This is known as the limitation period. It exists to prevent claimants from bringing stale libel claims and to protect defendants from being at continual risk of being sued.

Each sale of a newspaper or magazine constitutes a new publication and correspondingly starts the limitation period running. The fact that a publication was originally published more than one year ago is irrelevant so long as at some point there is a fresh publication. In *Duke of Brunswick v Harmer*[2], the claimant sent an employee to buy a back issue of a newspaper that had originally been published 17 years earlier. The issue of the newspaper contained a libel and the court held that the sale of the newspaper to the employee was a fresh publication upon which the claimant was entitled to sue, so long as he did so within the limitation period.

In slander or malicious falsehood, time will begin to run on the date that damage is suffered. Where a claimant intends to rely on a statutory or common law exception to the requirement to prove damage, it is submitted that, as with libel, time should begin to run on the date of publication.

Where the limitation period for bringing a claim has expired, the court still has a discretion to allow the claim to proceed, under section 32A of the LA 1980[3]. Section 4(1) states that when deciding whether to exercise this discretion, the court should balance the prejudice to the claimant of his not being allowed to proceed with his claim against the prejudice to the defendant of allowing him to do so.

Section 32A(2) states that in considering the balance of prejudice between the parties, the court should have regard to all the circumstances of the case and in particular:

- the length of any delay by the claimant and the reason for that delay;
- where the claimant's reasons for delay include the fact that he did not know within the limitation period any facts relevant to his claim, the court will consider how promptly he acted once he knew these facts;

- the extent to which the delay in bringing the claim has made it likely that relevant evidence will be unavailable or less cogent than it would have been had the claim been brought within the one-year limitation period.

Despite the court's discretion to disapply the limitation period and allow the claimant's claim to proceed, this is unlikely to happen very often. This is partly because the CPR view delay unfavourably. With regard to defamation claims, it is also significant that its supposed purpose is to vindicate the claimant; for vindication to be worth anything, it needs to be prompt, so delay on the part of the claimant will again be viewed critically. In *Steedman v BBC*[4], the court emphasised that it would only be in exceptional circumstances that the limitation period would be disapplied.

1   As amended by s 5 of the DeA 1996 (see Appendix 2).
2   (1849) 14 QB 185.
3   As amended by s 4 of the DeA 1996 (see Appendix 2).
4   [2001] EWCA Civ 1534, [2002] EMLR 318.

Secondary publisher's defence (the Defamation Act 1996, s 1)

16.05   For the purposes of defamation, the meaning of the term 'publisher' is very broad. However, some protection has been given to secondary publishers by section 1 of the DeA 1996. This states that an individual will have a defence to defamation proceedings if he can show that:

- he was not the author, editor or publisher (as defined by the DeA 1996) of the statement complained of;
- he took reasonable care in relation to its publication; and
- he did not know, and had no reason to believe, that what he did caused or contributed to the publication of a defamatory statement[1].

Broadly speaking, the DeA 1996 defines author, editor and publisher as those primarily responsible for publication. Section 1(3) sets out categories of persons who are not considered to be author, editor or publisher. These include printers, live broadcasters and the 'operator of or provider of access to a communications system'. This last category covers Internet service providers in their function as Internet access providers and website hosts. However, they would not be covered in respect of a news service, for example, which would render them publishers for the purposes of the DeA 1996.

In deciding whether a person took reasonable care, or had reason to believe that what he did caused or contributed to the publication of a defamatory statement, the court will have regard to:

- the extent of his responsibility for the content of the statement or the decision to publish it;
- the nature or circumstances of the publication; and
- the previous conduct or character of the author, editor or publisher.

The burden is on the defendant to show that he has acted with the requisite care and responsibility. The fact that a secondary publisher may not have had a chance to read the material complained of before publication[2] will be a relevant factor. With regard to 'conduct or character', if a defendant has received previous complaints, it will be relevant to the consideration of reasonable care and knowledge because he may be deemed to have been aware of the risk of someone being defamed.

This was most recently demonstrated in the case of *Baron v Housman's Bookshop*[3], brought over an anti-Nazi pamphlet which the bookshop had stocked and which defamed the claimant. This was one of a series of cases brought against the radical bookshop and others since 1996. The shop unsuccessfully ran a DeA 1996, s 1 defence which failed because the claimant had sent a letter of claim complaining about the pamphlet before issuing proceedings and the shop did not then remove the material complained about. (However, Mr Baron was ultimately awarded just £14.00 in damages by the jury.)

1   The DeA 1996, s 1(1) (and see Appendix 2).
2   For example, a live TV interview or a message posted directly onto an Internet bulletin board.
3   (2002) unreported.

16.06   As mentioned above, section 1(3)(d) of the DeA 1996 provides that a person shall not be considered the author, editor or publisher of a statement if he is only involved as the broadcaster of a live programme containing the statement in circumstances in which he has no effective control over the maker of the statement. An example of a successful action in a situation of this sort before the DeA 1996 was passed was one in which a vet sued one of the independent television companies over defamatory remarks made by an invited guest during a morning television programme before a studio audience. In that case[1] the action was settled at a comparatively early stage – but it was clear the television company had not known that the guest was going to make the remarks he did. However, the format of the show was designed to whip up controversial discussion. Would the television company succeed in deploying the defence under section 1(3)(d) if it was held to have openly or tacitly encouraged controversy? Should it have used a tape delay mechanism or some other safeguard? It will need case law to establish the guidelines.

1   *Duncan Davidson v Granada Television* (1997) unreported.

16.07   It is the DeA 1996, s 1 which attempts to deal with electronic media as well as the more traditional forms of communication. Section 1(3)(e) provides protection to service providers on the Internet who fall under the definition. Internet service providers who simply provide access to the system in return for a subscription charge would seem to be protected, although once again the sub-section is confined to makers of defamatory statements over whom the service provider has 'no effective control'. This introduces difficulties for service providers, many of whom now seek to attract customers by providing 'value-added services' such as digitally stored versions of conventional print publications and electronic bulletin boards (often dedicated to special interest groups). A responsible service provider might offer in its package of services some sort of monitoring service to its customers. However, by doing so it may take itself outside the protection afforded by the DeA 1996 because it has accepted a measure of responsibility for the publication. On the other hand, a service provider or bulletin board operator who does nothing to monitor its services may also fall outside the DeA 1996 because it has not taken reasonable care.

Until the courts have the opportunity to rule on what constitutes 'effective control', it will be difficult to advise with certainty on what situations are or are not protected by the DeA 1996. One anticipates that the courts will be cautious in generalising and will emphasise that each ruling depends on the facts of the particular case.

One case which attracted a great deal of publicity was the action brought by Dr Laurence Godfrey[1], a nuclear physicist, against Demon Internet Ltd, an Internet service provider, over anonymous postings to a newsgroup (the Internet's global discussion forum) carried by Demon. Mr Justice Morland held at an interlocutory hearing that Demon had no protection under section 1 of the DeA 1996 because they knew the words complained of had a defamatory content – Dr

Godfrey had drawn the posting to Demon's attention and had asked them to remove it, but Demon had not done so. The case continued and Demon ultimately settled the claim shortly before trial. It seems probable that if Demon had responded to Dr Godfrey's complaint by removing the defamatory posting then they would have succeeded in a section 1 defence if Dr Godfrey had then sued them on the defamatory publication. Morland J's ruling seems to send the message to Internet service providers that they should not ignore valid complaints about defamatory material.

1   *Godfrey v Demon Internet Ltd* [1999] 4 All ER 342.

16.08   One can only really say at this stage that while the DeA 1996 retains the old two part test for publishers (that they must have (1) had knowledge and (2) been negligent), it does extend the defence dramatically by including all secondary publishers, ie everyone other than 'the originator of the statement', the 'person having editorial or equivalent responsibility' and/or the 'commercial publisher' (being 'a person whose business is issuing material to the public').

It should mean that claimants will be more reluctant to make tactical claims against those more remotely involved in the publication process. For example, when John Major and Claire Latimer brought their high profile libel actions against *Scallywag* and the *New Statesman*, it was in fact their less well-publicised actions against the distributors and retailers which achieved the most successful and profitable results. One wonders whether those actions against, in particular, the secondary publishers of the *New Statesman* would have been issued in the light of the DeA 1996 (although the defamatory nature of the front cover of the magazine would not have assisted their defence).

As far as the Internet is concerned, the best advice one can offer at present is that operators of bulletin boards and service providers should take steps to make it absolutely clear what they intend to monitor and what they do not intend to monitor. In other words, they must try to establish an industry standard for what represents 'reasonable care'. This proactive step would be more likely to attract the sympathy of the courts, and they must establish procedures to deal with complaints from those who allege they have been defamed.

Offer of amends

16.09   The fact that a defendant did not intend to defame someone is irrelevant to liability. This can be harsh on those who unintentionally defame an individual; for example where a newspaper reports something involving an individual whose name is shared by someone else[1]. The defence of offer of amends[2] exists to give a defendant who innocently defames someone the chance to settle the litigation early on, by offering to make satisfactory amends to the claimant.

1   See, eg *Newstead v London Express* [1940] 1 KB 377.
2   The DeA 1996, ss 2–4.

History

16.10   The 1991 Neill Committee on Defamation suggested that the DA 1952, s4 (the 'unintentional defamation' provisions) be repealed:

> 'and a new "offer of amends" defence enacted for the purpose of enabling defendants where they recognise that the claimant has been defamed, to curtail proceedings by making such an offer which would not have to include the expression of a willingness to pay damages to be assessed by a judge.'

Introduction

16.11   The provisions relating to the 'offer to make amends' defendant are found in the DeA 1996, ss 2–4[1]. They provide a defendant with a procedure to resolve a claim where a mistake has been made. An offer to make amends is effectively an admission of liability since the provisions do not allow the defendant to run another defence as well.

An offer to make amends is an offer in writing[2] by which the defendant indicates it will make a 'suitable correction' of the statement complained of and a 'sufficient apology' to the claimant, that it will publish the correction in a manner that is 'reasonable and practicable', and that it will pay such compensation and costs as may be agreed or determined. It must be emphasised that these components are essential. The defendant cannot cherry pick the ones it likes and ignore the others. Any dispute over terms is resolved by application to the judge alone. Where an offer has been properly made and then rejected by the claimant, then the defence arises.

An offer to make amends can be made before issue of proceedings and so represents another means of resolving a defamation claim without litigation.

The DeA 1996, s 2(3)(c), allows a defendant to make what is termed a 'qualified offer' to make amends. This is designed to cater for a different interpretation of the meaning of the words complained of. For example, a newspaper might be prepared to admit that an article it wrote about a solicitor meant that he had a tendency to drink too much at social occasions. However, the claimant solicitor might contend that in fact it inferred that his drinking affected the service he provided for his clients and his legal competence. The newspaper could make a 'qualified' offer of amends in relation to the lower meaning. If this was not accepted, the litigation could continue with the newspaper relying on the qualified offer as its defence. If the jury decided the article bore the lower meaning, then the claimant would lose. However, if the jury agrees with the solicitor's interpretation of meaning, damages and, inevitably, costs are likely to be much higher as a result of the newspaper's persistence in downplaying the extent to which it defamed the solicitor.

1   See Appendix 2.
2   The DeA 1996, s 2(3).

The offer

16.12   Section 2 of the DeA 1996 states that the offer must be made before the service of the defence, must be in writing and expressly state that it is an offer of amends under section 2 of the DeA 1996. The offer is to:

- make a suitable correction and apology;
- publish the correction and apology in a manner which is reasonable and practicable; and
- pay the aggrieved party such compensation (if any) and such costs as may be agreed or be determined to be payable.

If the offer is accepted[1]

16.13   If the claimant accepts the offer, the proceedings end. If the parties cannot agree on the correction and apology to be published, it may be made by way of a statement in open court, which will be approved by the court. Similarly, where the amount of damage to be paid cannot be agreed, a judge determines the amount.

1   The DeA 1996, s 3.

If an offer is refused or ignored[1]

16.14 Where the claimant does not accept the offer, the defendant will have a defence to the action provided the court holds that he did not know and had no reason to believe that the words complained of were false and defamatory of the claimant. Significantly, it is the claimant who has the burden of showing that the publication was not innocent.

If an offer of amends is not accepted and the defendant then chooses to rely on another defence, the defendant may rely on the offer of amends in mitigation of damages[2].

If an offer of amends is relied on by the defendant as a defence, he cannot rely on any other defences[3]. This does not prevent the defendant from withdrawing the offer of amends before it is accepted and choosing an alternative defence.

1 The DeA 1996, s 4.
2 The DeA 1996, s 4(5).
3 The DeA 1996, s 4(4).

Chapter 17

Reply

17.01 Once the claimant has been served with the defence then, depending upon its contents, he may be required to prepare, file and serve a reply. The purpose of a reply is to allege facts in answer to the defence which were not included in the claim. This is the usually the final[1] document served in the proceedings forming part of the statement of case. This chapter sets out: (a) the general rules which apply to replies, and (b) the rules of specific application to certain defences in defamation proceedings.

1   It is rare to serve any further statement of case and indeed the court's permission is needed to do so: CPR 15.9. Undoubtedly the reply will contain matters with which the defendant takes issue but in a defamation case such matters should and will normally be dealt with in witness statements: see on a related point *McPhilemy v Times Newspapers Ltd* [1999] 3 All ER 775, [1999] EMLR 751.

General rules

17.02 The general rule is that a reply is optional[1]. However, if a claimant is to serve a reply he should file and serve his reply upon all other parties at the same time as the allocation questionnaire is filed[2]. The allocation questionnaire, which is served on all parties by the court following service of the defence, will specify the date upon which it (and therefore the reply) must be filed[3].

Unlike the defendant, who does not deal in his defence with an allegation made against him in the particulars of claim, a claimant who does not file a reply will not be taken to admit the matters in the defence. Where a claimant does file a reply but fails to deal with a matter raised in the defence, he will be taken to require that matter to be proved[4]. The reply must not contradict or be inconsistent with the claim form and particulars of claim. In the event that a claimant does wish to depart from his original case, the proper course is to seek to amend the claim rather than serve a reply[5]. As with all other statements of case, the reply must be verified by a statement of truth[6].

1 But see paragraphs 17.03 and 17.04 below.
2 CPR 15.8. Note that the court will not serve the reply.
3 CPR 26.3(6).
4 CPR 16.7.
5 See CPR Pt 16 PD, para 10.2 and CPR 17 generally (amendments to statements of case).
6 See CPR 16.7 and CPR 22 generally (statements of truth).

Rules of specific application in defamation claims

Defences of truth or fair comment

17.03   The Practice Direction to CPR Pt 53 provides that a reply must be served whenever a defence alleges that the words are true, or are fair comment[1]. In each case, the claimant is required to serve a reply (in accordance with the provisions set out at paragraph 17.02 above), specifically admitting or denying the allegation and setting out the facts upon which he relies. Paragraph 2.8 of the Practice Direction makes no provision for non-admissions, but it is submitted that in the event that the claimant is genuinely in no position to either admit or deny certain facts, it would be nonsensical to prevent him from making a non-admission, provided he states the reason for it. For examples of replies to defences of justification or fair comment, see Volume 25 of *Atkin's Court Forms*.

1 CPR Pt 53 PD, para 2.8 (and see Appendix 4).

Allegations of malice[1]

17.04   A defence of fair comment or qualified privilege can only be defeated by proof of malice on the part of the defendant[2]. CPR Pt 53 PD provides that if the defence contends that any of the words or matters complained of are fair comment or were published on an occasion of qualified privilege, and the claimant intends to allege that the defendant acted with malice, the claimant must serve a reply giving details of the facts and matters relied on[3]. For examples of replies alleging malice, see Volume 25 of *Atkin's Court Forms.*

1   Note that even where malice has been pleaded in aggravation the claimant should file and serve a reply giving particulars of malice where there is a defence of fair comment or qualified privilege as he is relying on those particulars for a different purpose.

2   CPR Pt 53 PD, para 2.9. In fact the wording of the paragraph would appear to cover absolute as well as qualified privilege, but since the defence of absolute privilege cannot be lost on proof of malice, it would serve no practical purpose to serve a reply alleging malice in such a case.

3   See Chapter 18.

Chapter 18

Malice

18.01 The protection of the defences of fair comment on a matter of public interest and qualified privilege will be lost if the claimant can prove on the balance of probabilities that the defendant was, to use the common legal expression, 'actuated by malice' in making the publication.

Any claimant proposing to plead should be warned at the outset that it is exceptionally rare for malice to be proved to the satisfaction of a jury. In *Sugar v Associated Newspapers Ltd*[1], Eady J, a High Court judge who has over 30 years of experience as a defamation practitioner, noted that he personally had only come across one case in which a finding of malice was made against a defendant. This was a qualified privilege case[2]. He had never come across a case where a plea of fair comment was defeated by malice.

'Malice' in the context of the law of defamation is a legal term of art which is much wider than its popular meaning. To confuse matters further, it now seem likely to be the case that the word 'malice' has a different meaning in the context of the defence of qualified privilege to the meaning it bears in the context of the defence of fair comment[3]. Practitioners should also beware of older cases, which often use the word 'malice' to connote publication without lawful excuse, a concept which is no longer of relevance to defamation actions today.

Until the decision of the Hong Kong Court of Final Appeal in *Tse Wai Chun Paul v Cheng*[4] in November 2000, learned textbook writers and practitioners alike had for at least 25 years assumed that the concept of 'malice' was of identical application to both defences. *Cheng* has swept away that assumption. The decision was followed by the High Court in *Sugar v Associated Newspapers Ltd*[5] and in *Branson v Bower*[6], and therefore represents the law unless and until the higher courts decide otherwise[7]. As a result, fair comment 'malice' has a much narrower construction than qualified privilege 'malice'.

This chapter sets out: (a) the CPR requirement for pleading malice, (b) procedural considerations, (c) malice and qualified privilege, (d) malice and fair comment, (e) the evidence from which malice may be inferred and proved, and finally (f) malice and the liability of concurrent tortfeasors.

1 (6 February 2001, unreported), QBD.
2 Following Eady J's decision in *Lillie and Reed v Newcastle City Council* [2002] EWHC 1600, QB, the total is now two.
3 See paragraphs 18.07–18.09 below.
4 (Ct Final Appeal Hong Kong) FACV No 12 of 2000, [2001] EMLR 777.
5 (6 February 2001, unreported), QBD, per Eady J.
6 [2001] EMLR 809, QBD.
7 This would appear to be unlikely, since the leading judgment in *Cheng* was given by Lord Nicholls of *Reynolds* fame: see Chapter 15.

The CPR requirement for pleading malice

18.02 If a defendant has served a defence pleading qualified privilege or fair comment, and the claimant intends to allege that the defendant acted with malice, then he must serve a reply[1] giving details of the facts and matters upon which he relies. If malice is not pleaded and proved by the claimant, it is presumed that the defendant was not malicious. Therefore, in the absence of a successful plea of malice, once the defendant establishes that the words are protected by fair comment or qualified privilege, he will succeed.

The normal practice is to allege that the defendant published the words complained of with 'express malice' and to follow that with particulars of facts which show, or from which it can be inferred, that the defendant acted maliciously. For sample replies to defences of fair comment and qualified privilege see Volume 25 of *Atkin's Court Forms*.

1 Where the defendant has pleaded fair comment the claimant is in any event required to serve a reply specifically admitting or denying the allegation of fair comment and giving the facts upon which he relies: CPR Pt 53 PD, para 2.8. See further Chapter 17 for more detailed information about replies generally.

Procedural considerations

18.03 It is for the judge to decide, as a matter of law, whether there is any evidence of malice to put before the jury. Once the question of malice goes before the jury, it is for them to decide (guided by the judge as to the law) whether the defendant was in fact malicious. The question of malice will go before the jury if the judge is satisfied that the evidence is more consistent with the presence of malice than with its absence[1].

1 *Somerville v Hawkins* (1851) 10 CB 583.

Pre-trial

18.04 If the claimant pleads particulars of malice in his reply which cannot in law amount to a proper plea of malice, then the proper course is for the defendant to apply to strike out the plea under CPR 3.4. In circumstances where the claimant has no reasonable prospect of challenging a defence that the words complained of were published on an occasion of qualified privilege or are fair comment on a matter of public interest, then such an application should include an application for summary judgment under CPR 24.2.

There is some authority to the effect that where, after exchange of witness statements, the defendant contends that there is no reasonable prospect of succeeding in establishing malice (although the plea of malice in the reply is proper on its face) then the defendant may likewise make an application under CPR 24.2[1]. However, it is plain from the decision of the Court of Appeal in *Safeway Stores v Tate*[2] that such an application would not be appropriate because if there is sufficient evidence of malice to go before the jury, then the claimant is entitled to have the jury decide the issue. It is only permissible for the court to enter summary judgment under CPR 24.2 on an issue of fact where the judge would have withdrawn the issue from the jury on the basis that no reasonable jury properly directed could come to that conclusion. This is because Parliament has provided a right to trial by jury[3] which cannot be eroded except by further express Parliamentary provision. For this reason, any application for summary disposal on the question of malice where the plea is proper in law should probably be made under sections 8–10 of the DeA 1996[4].

1 See, eg *S v Newham London Borough Council* (5 November 1999, unreported),QBD, Gray J.
2 [2001] QB 1120, as explained in *Alexander v The Arts Council of Wales* [2001] 1 WLR 1840.
3 The Supreme Court Act 1981, s 69.
4 See Chapter 22.

At trial

18.05 Since the burden is on the claimant to prove that the defendant was malicious, it is open to the defendant to make a submission at the end of the claimant's case to the effect that no reasonable jury could find, on the evidence given for the claimant, that the defendant was malicious. If successful, the issue of malice will be withdrawn from the jury and the defendant's witnesses need not give evidence or be cross-examined about it. More usually, however, the judge will reserve judgment until the end of the defendant's case and may even wait until after the jury's finding on malice. In a case where the judge has reserved judgment and the jury finds the defendant malicious (and therefore finding for the claimant), it remains open to the judge to enter judgment for the defendant notwithstanding the jury's verdict, on the basis that there was no proper evidence on which malice in law could be found.

Directions to the jury

18.06 In *Tse Wai Chun Paul v Cheng*[1], Lord Nicholls recommended that the term 'malice' be avoided when directing juries, who should be told that the defence of fair comment is defeated by proof that the defendant did not genuinely hold the views he expressed. When directing juries on qualified privilege, juries can be directed that the defence is defeated by proof that the defendant used the occasion for some purpose other than that for which the occasion was privileged. This direction can be elaborated in a manner appropriate to the facts and issues in the case.

1   (Ct Final Appeal Hong Kong) FACV No 12 of 2000, [2001] EMLR 777.

Malice and qualified privilege

18.07 The meaning of malice in the context of the defence of qualified privilege was comprehensively analysed by Lord Diplock in the leading case of *Horrocks v Lowe*[1]. He explained that[2] 'in all cases of qualified privilege there is some special reason of public policy why the law accords immunity from suit[3] ... If he uses the occasion for some other reason he loses the protection of the privilege'. He went on[4]:

> ' "Express malice" is the term of art descriptive of such a motive. Broadly speaking, it means malice in the popular sense of a desire to injure the person who is defamed and this is generally the motive which the plaintiff sets out to prove. But to destroy the privilege the desire to injure must be the dominant motive for the defamatory publication;

knowledge that it will have that effect is not enough if the defendant is nevertheless acting in accordance with a sense of duty or in bona fide protection of his own legitimate interests.

The motive with which a person published defamatory matter can only be inferred from what he did or said or knew. If it be proved that he did not believe that what he published was true this is generally conclusive evidence of express malice, for no sense of duty or desire to protect his own legitimate interests can justify a man in telling deliberate and injurious falsehoods about another, save in the exceptional case where a person may be under a duty to pass on, without endorsing, defamatory reports made by some other person.

Apart from those exceptional cases, what is required on the part of the defamer to entitle him to the protection of the privilege is positive belief in the truth of what he published or, as it is generally though tautologously termed, "honest belief". If he publishes untrue defamatory matter recklessly, without considering or caring whether it be true or not, he is in this, as in other branches of the law, treated as if he knew it to be false. But indifference to the truth of what he publishes is not to be equated with carelessness, impulsiveness or irrationality in arriving at a positive belief that it is true. The freedom of speech protected by the law of qualified privilege may be availed of by all sorts and conditions of men in affording to them immunity from suit if they have acted in good faith in compliance with a legal or moral duty or in protection of a legitimate interest the law must take them as it finds them. In ordinary life it is rare indeed for people to form their beliefs by a process of logical deduction from facts ascertained by a rigorous search for all available evidence and a judicious assessment of its probative value. In greater or in less degree according to their temperaments, their training, their intelligence, they are swayed by prejudice, rely on intuition instead of reasoning, leap to conclusions on inadequate evidence and fail to recognise the cogency of material which might cast doubt on the validity of the conclusions they reach. But despite the imperfection of the mental process by which the belief is arrived at it may still be "honest", that is, a positive belief that the conclusions they have reached are true. The law demands no more.

Even a positive belief in the truth of what is published on a privileged occasion – which is presumed unless the contrary is proved – may not be sufficient to negative express malice if it can be proved that the defendant misused the occasion for some purpose other than that for which the privilege is accorded by the law. The commonest case is where the dominant motive which actuates the defendant is not a desire to perform the relevant duty or to protect the relevant interest, but to give vent to his personal spite or ill will towards the person he defames. If this be proved, then even positive belief in the truth of what is published will not enable the defamer to avail himself of the protection of the privilege to which he would otherwise have been entitled. There may be instances of improper motives which destroy the privilege apart from personal spite. A defendant's dominant motive may have been to obtain some private advantage unconnected with the duty or the interest which constitutes the reason for the privilege. If so, he loses the benefit of the privilege despite his positive belief that what he said or wrote was true.

Judges and juries should, however, be very slow to draw the inference that a defendant was so far actuated by improper motives as to deprive him of the protection of the privilege unless they are satisfied that he did not believe that what he said or wrote was true or that he was indifferent to its truth or falsity. The motives with which human beings act are mixed. They find it difficult to hate the sin but love the sinner. Qualified privilege would be illusory, and the public interest that it is meant to serve defeated, if the protection which it affords were lost merely because a person, although acting in compliance with a duty or in protection of a legitimate interest, disliked the person whom he defamed or was indignant at what he believed to be that person's conduct and welcomed the opportunity of exposing it. It is only where his desire to comply with the relevant duty or to protect the relevant interest plays no significant part in his motives for publishing what he believes to be true that "express malice" can properly be found.

There may be evidence of the defendant's conduct upon occasions other than that protected by the privilege which justify the inference that upon the privileged occasion too his dominant motive in publishing what he did was personal spite or some other improper motive, even although he believed it to be true. But where, as in the instant case, conduct extraneous to the privileged occasion itself is not relied on, and the only evidence of improper motive is the content of the defamatory matter itself or the steps taken by the defendant to verify its accuracy, there is only one exception to the rule that in order to succeed the plaintiff must show affirmatively that the defendant did not believe it to be true or was indifferent to its truth or falsity. Juries should be instructed and judges should remind themselves that this burden of affirmative proof is not one that is lightly satisfied.

The exception is where what is published incorporates defamatory matter that is not really necessary to the fulfilment of the particular duty or the protection of the particular interest upon which the privilege is founded. Logically it might be said that such irrelevant matter falls outside the privilege altogether. But if this were so it would involve application by the court of an objective test of relevance to every part of the defamatory matter published on the privileged occasion; whereas, as everyone knows, ordinary human beings vary in their ability to distinguish that which is logically relevant from that which is not and few, apart from lawyers, have had any training which qualifies them to do so. So the protection afforded by the privilege would be illusory if it were lost in respect of any defamatory matter which upon logical analysis could be shown to be irrelevant to the fulfilment of the duty or the protection of the right upon which the privilege was founded. As Lord Dunedin pointed out in *Adam v Ward* [1917] AC 309, 326–327 the proper rule as respects irrelevant defamatory matter incorporated in a statement made on a privileged occasion is to treat it as one of the factors to be taken into consideration in deciding whether, in all the circumstances, an inference that the defendant was actuated by express malice can properly be drawn. As regards irrelevant matter the test is not whether it is logically relevant but whether, in all the circumstances, it can be inferred that the defendant either did not believe it to be true or, though believing it to be true, realised that it had nothing to do with the particular duty or interest on which the privilege was based, but nevertheless seized the opportunity to drag in irrelevant defamatory matter to vent his personal spite, or for some other improper motive. Here, too, judges and juries should be slow to draw this inference.'

1   [1975] AC 135, HL.
2   [1975] AC 135 at 149E–F, HL.
3   See further Chapter 15.
4   [1975] AC 135 at 149F–151H, HL.

18.08   'Malice' for the purposes of the defence of qualified privilege may therefore be summarised as follows:

(a)   The fact that the defendant did not believe the words were true is usually conclusive evidence of malice.

(b)   If the defendant published the words recklessly, without considering whether they were true or not, he will be treated as if he knew they were false; but mere carelessness, impulsiveness or irrationality will not suffice to prove malice.

(c)   Even an honest belief in the truth of the words will not save a defendant who can otherwise be proved to have had some dominant improper motive for publishing them. However, judges and juries should be slow to draw the inference of improper motive in such circumstances and for that reason an honest belief in the truth of the words will usually suffice to negate malice.

Malice and fair comment

18.09   In *Tse Wai Chun Paul v Cheng*[1] Lord Nicholls, with whom the rest of the Hong Kong Court of Final Appeal agreed, stated that the test of malice as applied to qualified privilege is not identical to the test of malice applicable to the defence of fair comment on a matter of public interest. The issue before the Court was whether in a case where the defendant relied on the defence of fair comment, proof of the purpose for which he stated an honestly held opinion could be held to be evidence of malice which would deprive him of the protection of the defence. The

Court had to decide whether stating an honestly held opinion for the purpose of inflicting injury upon the claimant, or simply out of spite, would be sufficient to deprive the defendant of the defence, as it would be in a case where the defendant had relied on qualified privilege.

Lord Nicholls noted that there had been surprisingly little discussion of malice in the context of fair comment over the last 150 years. He observed that most textbooks incline to the view that, as the honest defendant may lose the protection of the defence of qualified privilege if he published the words with an improper motive, so too was the case where an honest defendant relied upon the defence of fair comment.

However, he stated that the purposes for which the law has accorded the defence of qualified privilege and the defence of fair comment are not the same. The rationale of the defence of qualified privilege is the law's recognition that there are circumstances when there is a need, in the public interest, to receive frank and uninhibited communication of particular information from a particular source. The rationale of the defence of fair comment is different. Its basis is the high importance of protecting and promoting the freedom of comment by everyone at all times on matters of public interest, irrespective of their particular motives. Lord Nicholls stated that the purpose and importance of the defence of fair comment are inconsistent with its scope, being restricted to comments made for particular reasons or particular purposes, some being regarded as proper, others not. He stated that[2]:

> 'Commentators, of all shades of opinion, are entitled to "have their own agenda". Politicians, social reformers, busybodies, those with political or other ambitions and those with none, all can grind their axes. The defence of fair comment envisages that everyone is at liberty to conduct social and political campaigns by expressing his own views, subject always . . . to the objective safeguards which mark the limits of the defence.'

Lord Nicholls gave particular and specific consideration to comments made out of spite or ill will, or with a deliberate intention to injure. He considered the problems raised to be more academic than practical, because he doubted whether such comments would satisfy the objective criteria[3] or the test of genuine belief in the truth of the comment. Even where these criteria could be satisfied he was 'far from persuaded that the law should minister a remedy. The spiteful publication of a defamatory statement attracts no remedy if the statement is proved to be true. Why should the position be different for the spiteful publication of a defamatory, genuinely held comment based on true fact . . .?'.

Therefore a defendant will only be acting with malice for the purpose of the defence of fair comment where he 'does not genuinely hold the view he expressed. In other words, when making the defamatory comment the defendant acted dishonestly. He put forward as his view something which, in truth, was not his view. It was a pretence. The law does not protect such statements. . . . [T]he law protects freedom to express opinions, not vituperative make-believe.' A defendant who does not believe his comment to be true, or who was recklessly indifferent to the truth or falsity of his comments, will be acting dishonestly and this will suffice to establish malice.

Malice in the context of the defence of fair comment therefore carries a different and narrower meaning from that it carries in the context of qualified privilege because actuation by spite, animosity, intent to injure, intent to arouse controversy or other motivation, whatever it may be, even if it is the dominant or sole motive, will not of itself defeat the defence of fair comment. Lord Nicholls noted however, that proof of such motivation may be evidence, sometimes compelling evidence, from which a lack of genuine belief in the view expressed may be inferred and that proof of motivation may also be relevant to other issues in the action, such as damages.

1   (Ct Final Appeal Hong Kong) FACV No 12 of 2000, [2001] EMLR 777.
2   See the five criteria set out at Chapter 13, paragraph 13.06.
3   See the five criteria set out at Chapter 13, paragraph 13.06.

The evidence from which malice may be proved

18.10   There are two means by which malice may be proved, and the claimant is entitled to employ either or both of them. The first is by reference to the content of the publication itself ('intrinsic evidence') and the second is by reference to matters outside the content of the publication itself, such as the conduct of the defendant before, at or since the publication ('extrinsic evidence').

Intrinsic evidence

Excessive language

18.11   In the context of qualified privilege, the use of excessive or exaggerated language in the publication complained of may be evidence from which malice can be inferred[1]. However, '[t]o submit the language of privileged communications to a strict scrutiny and hold all excess beyond the exigency of the occasion to be evidence of malice, would in effect greatly limit, if not altogether defeat, that protection which the law throws over privileged communications'[2].

But it would be illogical to permit use of excessive language to defeat the defence of fair comment. Once a jury has found that the words were fair comment in that they reflect views which an honest person could hold, it cannot then go on to find, on the basis of those same words, that they are evidence from which malice, ie dishonesty, can be inferred[3].

1　See, eg *Spill v Maule* (1869) LR 4 Ex Ch 232 at 235, per Lord Cockburn CJ.
2　Per curiam in *Laughton v Bishop of Sodor and Man* (1872) LR 4 PC 495, approved in *Nevill v Fine Arts Co* [1895] 2 QB 156.
3　*Broadway Approvals Ltd v Odhams Press Ltd* [1965] 1 WLR 805, CA.

Irrelevant material

18.12　Where the defence is one of qualified privilege, malice may be inferred from the inclusion of irrelevant defamatory material in the publication complained of. However, 'As regards irrelevant matter the test is not whether it is logically relevant but whether, in all the circumstances, it can be inferred that the defendant either did not believe it to be true or, though believing it to be true, realised that it had nothing to do with the particular duty or interest on which the privilege was based, but nevertheless seized the opportunity to drag in irrelevant defamatory matter to vent his personal spite, or for some other improper motive'[1].

1　Per Lord Diplock in *Horrocks v Lowe* [1975] AC 135 at 151, HL.

Extrinsic evidence

The pre-publication relationship between claimant and defendant

18.13　Malice may be inferred from evidence of a history of animosity between the parties. Thus, evidence of a previous quarrel between the parties may be adduced[1]. In a nutshell, anything that shows that the parties 'lived on bad terms'[2] may be adduced as evidence of malice. Although evidence that shows that the defendant was moved by hatred or dislike, or a desire to injure the claimant, could suffice to establish that the defendant misused an occasion of qualified privilege for that purpose, it will not cause the defendant in a fair comment case to lose the protection of the defence unless it can be inferred from such evidence that the defendant did not honestly believe what he wrote.

1   *Simpson v Robinson* (1848) 12 QB 511.
2   *Simpson v Robinson* (1848) 12 QB 511 at 515, per Lord Denman CJ.

The circumstances of publication itself

18.14   Malice may be inferred from evidence which shows that the defendant deliberately chose to make his publication in circumstances which would increase the damage it would cause to the claimant. In a qualified privilege case, for example, the fact that the defendant shouted the words at the claimant in a place where he should expect others to overhear or spoke them to him in a crowded public could be evidence of malice. The fact that a privileged communication was sent by postcard, when it could have been sent in a sealed envelope, has been held to be evidence of malice[1].

1   *Sadgrove v Hole* [1901] 2 KB 1.

Other publications by the defendant

18.15   The fact that the defendant has on other occasions made defamatory statements about the claimant, whether before or after the publication complained of, may be evidence from which malice can be inferred[1]. It is not necessary that the defamatory statement should have been made to the same publishees or that it is or was actionable[2]. The claimant will also be permitted to adduce evidence of other publications by the defendant about him which, though not defamatory, is evidence from which malice can properly be inferred[3].

In the light of the decision in *Tse Wai Chun Paul v Cheng*[4], evidence of other publications by the defendant where the defence is one of fair comment should only be admissible where they can properly go to establish a lack of honest belief. For example, evidence that the defendant has conducted a campaign against the claimant in which he has repeatedly taken the same line about the claimant's actions should not, of itself, be admissible against him as evidence of malice since far from suggesting a lack of honest belief, it would go to support his case that he did honestly believe what he wrote.

1　See *Camfield v Bird* (1852) 3 Car & Kir 56.
2　*Mead v Daubigny* (1792) Peake 125.
3　For example, previous expressions of spite or ill will: *Wright v Woodgate* (1835) 2 Cr M & R 573 at 577, per Parke B.
4　(Ct Final Appeal Hong Kong) FACV No 12 of 2000, [2001] EMLR 777.

Post-publication conduct

18.16　The way the defendant behaves towards the claimant after the publication of the words complained of may be evidence of malice. In a qualified privilege case a failure to apologise will be evidence of malice where it can be shown that the defendant became aware of the fact that the publication was false. By contrast, the failure to apologise in a fair comment case is unlikely to be evidence of malice, since this is entirely consistent with the defendant's honest belief in the truth of the words stated. If the material facts upon which the comment was based were false, the defendant would not be protected by the defence of fair comment at all, and the question of malice would not therefore arise.

Malice may also be inferred from the actions of the defendant during the course of litigation and the content of and manner in which he gives his evidence at trial. Further, malice may be inferred where the defendant has placed on the record a plea of justification and persists in it (unsuccessfully) to trial.

One step which a defendant can take in order to negate any inference of malice is to offer the claimant an opportunity to reply in the same medium as the publication complained of by him.

Malice and the liability of concurrent tortfeasors

Co-defendants

18.17　Where there is more than one defendant (ie more than one publisher), the defences of fair comment or qualified privilege apply to protect each of them separately in relation to the publication complained of. For this reason it is necessary to prove in relation to each publisher that he was malicious. Therefore, even where three out of four publishers are proved to have been malicious, the fourth will not be liable because he cannot be 'infected' by the malice of the others.

In *Longdon-Griffiths v Smith*[1] four trustees published a report containing a defamatory statement on an occasion of qualified privilege. One trustee was malicious. It was held that each of the four had a separate duty independent of the others to publish the report and in those circumstances the finding of malice against one trustee did not impair the independent privilege enjoyed by each of the other three.

Likewise, in *Egger v Viscount Chelmsford*[2] there was a joint publication on an occasion of qualified privilege by members of a committee, some of whom were malicious. It was held that the non-malicious committee members were not liable to the plaintiff, for each had in relation to the joint publication an independent and individual privilege which could not be defeated by the malice of the others taking part in the joint publication.

1   [1951] 1 KB 295.
2   [1965] 1 QB 248.

Agents and employees

18.18   Where it is alleged that the publication was made by an agent or an employee in the course of his employment, the ordinary principles of tort apply. The principal or employer will accordingly be liable for the malice of his agent or employee as he is vicariously liable for the publication[1]. However, the employee or agent must have been responsible for the publication in the sense that he has something to do with the composition of the libel or the approval of its contents. The principal or employer will not be liable for the malice of a 'mere instrument through whose hands the libel passed for publication'[2]. In *Hay v Australasian Institute of Marine Engineers*[3] a privileged report was published by a trade union. The report recorded resolutions made at a conference which were defamatory of the claimant. The secretary of the union, who had had nothing to do with the preparation of the report, simply handed it out to members as he was duty-bound to do. Malice could be proved against the secretary but there was no other evidence of malice. The union was held not to be liable.

1   *Egger v Viscount Chelmsford* [1965] 1 QB 248 and *Gros v Crook* (1969) 113 Sol Jo 408.
2   *Adam v Ward* [1917] AC 309 at 340, HL, per Lord Atkinson.
3   (1906) 3 CLR 1002.

Non-human defendants

18.19   Many types of non-human entity have a legal personality and may be sued for defamation[1]. Such entities can be liable in their own right, irrespective of considerations of vicarious liability or agency. However, they obviously have no 'state of mind' of their own. The question therefore arises as to how the state of mind of such an entity is to be assessed for the purposes of establishing a case on malice. It may be, for example, that a company is comprised of ten individuals, none of whom individually has a state of mind which could be said to be malicious. Is it permissible in such circumstances to 'add together' the states of mind of those ten people to establish a case of malice against the company?

In *Broadway Approvals Ltd v Odhams Press Ltd*[2] the claimant's plea of malice was partly based on the premise that through its advertising department the defendant had formerly encouraged the very trade practice which it condemned in the words complained of. It was held by Sellers LJ[3] that '[t]he advertising was a separate department and it is no evidence of malice that one department did not know what the other was doing. It might be said to show inconsistency within the company but a company's mind is not to be assessed on the totality of knowledge of its servants'.

By contrast, in *Riddick v Thames Board Mills*[4], Waller LJ indicated[5] that in an action concerning the publication of a libel outside a company, it may well be possible to examine the conduct of all its employees and, if any of them were malicious, to say that would defeat a defence of qualified privilege. However, in the same case Stephenson LJ stated that[6] the company must answer only for the malice of those who were the publishers and it was on this basis that he decided the case.

It is submitted that the correct approach in order to establish malice against a non-human entity is to demonstrate malice on the part of the humans within it who were responsible for the publication. Indeed, such an approach was adopted by Eady J on an application to strike out in *S v Newham London Borough Council*[7].

1   See Chapter 4.
2   [1965] 1 WLR 805, CA.
3   [1965] 1 WLR 805 at 813G, CA.
4   [1977] QB 881, CA.
5   [1977] QB 881 at 908G, CA.
6   [1977] QB 881 at 900A, CA.
7   (5 November 1999, unreported), QBD. See also the Australian authorities *Musgrave v Commonwealth* (1937) 57 CLR 514 at 536, per Lord Latham CJ; *Pinniger v John*

Fairfax & Sons (1979) 26 ALR 55 at 58, per Lord Barwick CJ; *Waterhouse v Broadcasting Station* [1985] 1 NSWLR 58 at 72F; *Bruton v Estate Agents Licensing Authority* [1996] 2 VR 274 at 279, per Batt J.

Chapter 19

Case management hearings

19.01 This chapter deals with the case management conference ('CMC') that the parties will be required to attend before a defamation trial. As May LJ stated in *McPhilemy v Times Newspapers Ltd*[1]:

'... Libel actions should by proper case management be confined within manageable and economic bounds. They should not descend into uncontrolled and wide-ranging investigations akin to public inquiries, where that is not necessary to determine the real issues between the parties. The Court will ... strive to manage the case so as to minimise the burden on litigants of slender means. This includes excluding all peripheral material which is not essential to the just determination of the real issues between the parties, and whose examination would be disproportionate to its importance to those issues.'

1   [1999] 3 All ER 775.

The case management conference

19.02 Every step in a defamation claim or defence, from the opening exchange of correspondence in compliance with the pre-action protocol, should be taken with the knowledge that at the end of what can be a long and twisting road may be the ultimate determination of the issues – the trial.

However, the parties' minds will really start to focus on the prospect of a trial at the CMC. This will take place when the statement of case has been completed and the allocation questionnaire has been filed. Its purpose is to enable a timetable to be set before costs have become too significant – although in a fully defended defamation action, the costs are already likely to be substantial by the time a reply has been filed and served.

A CMC will normally take place following the filing of an allocation questionnaire and at the close of the parties' statements of case. It is an appropriate time for the parties and the court to take stock and consider how the case should proceed from then on until trial.

In a defamation action, which will generally be proceeding in the Royal Courts of Justice in the Strand, it is likely the parties will prefer the CMC to be listed before one of the specialist defamation judges, but it can equally well be heard by the designated Master (who may decide not to release it to the judge in any event). In district registries, the CMC will be dealt with by the district judge.

The civil procedure reforms were meant to give the judge an enhanced role in litigation as a case manager, and a CMC gives him that opportunity. Indeed, the judge will dictate the timetable unless a fully completed allocation questionnaire has been prepared and the parties have proposed some directions which they can justify at the hearing.

What follows are some of the matters which the parties should consider in advance of the CMC, and in respect of which directions may need to be made. It is not intended to be comprehensive because every case is different and may throw up the need for a direction outside the norm.

Issues in the action

19.03
● What issues are in dispute?
● What are the agreed issues of fact?
● What are the disputed issues of fact?
● What evidence will be needed to determine the issues?

The court's understanding of the case may be assisted if the claimant prepares a case summary. CPR Pt 29 PD, para 5.7 stipulates that this should set out a brief chronology, the issues of fact which are agreed or in dispute and the evidence needed to determine them. The other parties should be invited to agree a case summary before the CMC.

Preliminary issues

19.04   Is there scope to determine any issues as preliminary issues – either at a pre-trial hearing or at the start of the trial itself?[1]

1   See Chapter 22 for more detail about possible pre-trial applications for court orders.

Order of issues

19.05 It might be appropriate to determine the order in which the issues are tried.

Amendments

19.06 If either party wishes to make amendments to its statement of case it would be appropriate to seek to obtain permission at this hearing. The court might be significantly less sympathetic to any application to amend at a later stage and the costs consequences would almost certainly be more severe since one's opponent will have prepared his disclosure and witness evidence on the basis of the pleaded case, and it will be expensive to revisit these to deal with a later amendment.

Requests for information

19.07 Now that statements of case have closed, either party may wish to request further information about his opponent's case if it has not been pleaded with sufficient detail. CPR 18.1 provides that the court may order a party *at any time* (so one need not wait until the CMC) to:

(a) clarify any matter which is in dispute in the proceedings; or
(b) give additional information in relation to any such matter whether or not it is contained or referred to in the statement of case. Such requests should, if possible, be made in one document rather than as a series of separate requests[1]. The CMC provides an opportunity to obtain an order in respect of any request compelling a response.

1   CPR Pt 18 PD, para 1.3.

Admissions

19.08 It is prudent with a view to saving costs to consider whether it is worthwhile admitting any facts – the judge as case manager will not be impressed if facts over which there is no dispute are denied and contested for the sake of it. A sensible approach to possible admissions complies with the overriding objective to save expense[1]. If your client thinks it is a sign of weakness to concede anything, explain the potential costs consequences of forcing the issue to trial and he may see the virtue of condensing the action to the real issues in dispute.

1   CPR 1.1(2)(b).

Alternative dispute resolution

19.09   The CMC is a sensible time to consider whether the case or any issue in it might sensibly be submitted to ADR. The judges or Master may express a strong view about this and it is not unusual these days for a direction to be made staying a case for a period (for example, one month) to allow the parties to consider ADR – and this is something which has occurred in defamation cases as well as elsewhere.

Disclosure

19.10   Disclosure and inspection of documents in the parties' possession, custody or control relevant to the issues in the action will be ordered at the CMC.

Where the case involves a large amount of documentation the judge will try to tailor the disclosure order to the case. The judge will consider whether to:

(a)   dispense with or limit standard disclosure[1];
(b)   order standard disclosure[2];
(c)   order specific disclosure[3].

In a document-heavy case there may be an application for trial by judge alone – as occurred in Jonathan Aitken's libel action against *The Guardian*.

1   CPR 31.5(2).
2   CPR 31.5(1).
3   CPR 31.2.

Witnesses of fact

19.11   Statements will have to be prepared and exchanged.

Expert evidence

19.12   Will there be a need for expert evidence? If so, directions will be needed about the appointment of either one agreed expert or the instruction of an expert for each party whose reports will then have to be prepared, filed and served. A meeting of experts to narrow the issues will be needed in advance of the trial.

Pre-trial checklists

19.13   The court should send out a pre-trial checklist to be completed and returned by a date no more than eight weeks before trial. The objectives are to:

(a)   fix a date for trial or to confirm the date already given;
(b)   confirm the estimated length of trial;
(c)   set a trial timetable;
(d)   decide whether to hold a pre-trial review.

Further hearings

19.14   Will a further CMC or a pre-trial review be needed? In a defamation action it is a safe bet that it will.

Length of trial

19.15   How long will the trial last? Counsel and their instructing solicitors will need to discuss and agree their estimate.

Costs

19.16   The court may also want to know what the costs position is to date and perhaps also the estimated costs to trial. The costs order on a CMC is likely to be costs in the case unless either party makes applications of the sort discussed in Chapter 22.

Chapter 20

Disclosure and inspection of documents

20.01 This chapter deals with the process of disclosure in a typical defamation action, setting out: (a) what is meant by disclosure of documents, (b) the process by which disclosure is effected, (c) the process of inspection of documents, (d) applications for specific disclosure and inspection, and (e) the purposes for which disclosed documents may be used. Finally, this chapter sets out the process for obtaining disclosure of documents (f) against potential parties before proceedings are issued and (g) against non-parties prior to and during proceedings.

In a defamation action, as with all other civil litigation, the parties 'play with an open hand' in the sense that each knows, through advance exchange of documents and witness statements, as much as possible about the state of the evidence prior to the trial. Any claimant proposing to bring an action for defamation should be warned that they cannot pick and choose what they want to show the other side because there are rules dictating what must be shown. Solicitors owe a duty to the court to ensure that their clients preserve all relevant documents in anticipation of disclosure and later, to ensure that their clients have disclosed all relevant documents[1].

Disclosure of documents is governed by CPR 31. At the case management conference, the court will, amongst other things[2], have made orders directing when each party should give 'disclosure' and allow 'inspection' of their documents to the other party or parties in the case.

---

1   *Rockwell Machine Tool Co Ltd v EP Barrus (Concessionaires) Ltd* [1968] 2 All ER 98; *Woods v Martins Bank Ltd* [1959] 1 QB 55 at 60.
2   See Chapter 19.

What is meant by disclosure of documents

'Documents'

20.02 The meaning of the word 'document' for the purposes of what must be disclosed in a defamation (or indeed any civil) action is much broader than the ordinary, everyday sense of the word. It applies not just to paper materials, but 'anything in which information of any description is recorded'[1]. 'Document' is therefore defined widely enough to cover tape recordings[2], word processing files[3] and computer databases[4] as well as paper.

1 CPR 31.4.
2 *Grant v Southwestern and County Properties Ltd* [1975] Ch 185.
3 *Alliance and Leicester Building Society v Ghahremani* [1992] RVR 198.
4 *Derby & Co Ltd v Weldon (No 9)* [1991] 1 WLR 652.

'Disclosure'

20.03 A document is disclosed when a statement is made by a party to the effect that the document exists or has existed[1]. A party need only disclose documents which are or have been in his control. If a party has or has had physical possession of a document then clearly it is or has been in his control. However, the rules go further than this and state that a document which is or has been in a party's control extends to documents to which he has or has had a right to possession of and documents which he has or has had a right to inspect or take copies of[2]. Unless the court directs otherwise, a court order to give 'disclosure' will be to give 'standard disclosure'. This means that in relation to each and every document which is or has been in control of a party:

(a)   on which that party relies; and/or
(b)   which:
    (i)   adversely affects that party's case;
    (ii)   adversely affects another party's case;
    (iii)   supports another party's case;
(c)   which he is required to disclose by a relevant practice direction,

that party must state whether or not the document exists or has existed. Once he has done so in accordance with the procedure prescribed by the Civil Procedure Rules, he will have complied with his duty of disclosure.

The rules make provision for a person to apply to the court, without giving notice to the other party or parties, for an order permitting him to withhold disclosure of a document on the ground that disclosure would damage the public interest[3]. For the purpose of deciding an application to withhold disclosure of a document, the court may require the person seeking to withhold it to produce it to the court and can invite any person, whether or not a party, to make representations[4]. The application should be made in accordance with CPR 23 and must be supported by evidence[5]. CPR 23.4(2) allows the making of an application under CPR 23 without notice. If such an order is granted, the usual result is that the other party or parties will never know about it or the application, and will therefore never know about the existence of the document or documents in question, since an order under CPR 31.19(1) must not be served on any other person or be open to inspection by any person unless the court orders otherwise[6].

1 CPR 31.2.
2 CPR 31.8.
3 CPR 31.19(1). For further information on this subject, the reader should refer to specialist publications on disclosure.
4 CPR 31.10(6).
5 CPR 31.19(7).
6 CPR 31.19(2).

The process of disclosure[1]

20.04 Each party must make a list all of the documents which fall within the definitions at paragraph 20.03 above on Form N265[2]. This list must then be served on every other party to the case. Before making the list, a party is duty-bound by the rules to make a reasonable search[3] for all documents which fall within categories (b) and (c) at paragraph 20.03 above[4]. The parties should bear in mind the overriding principle of proportionality[5]. It may, for example, be reasonable to decide not to search for documents coming into existence before some particular date, to limit the search to documents in some particular place or places, or to documents falling into particular categories[6].

The list must identify the documents in a convenient order and manner and as concisely as possible[7]. Paragraph 3.2 of the Practice Direction to CPR Pt 31 states that in order to comply with this requirement it will normally be necessary to list the documents in date order, number them consecutively and to give each a concise description (eg 'letter, claimant to defendant'). Where there is a large number of documents all falling into a particular category the disclosing party may list those documents as a category rather than individually (eg '50 bank statements relating to account number 12345 at Bloggins Bank').

The list must also indicate those documents in respect of which the party claims a right or duty to withhold inspection[8]. Where a party makes such a claim, he must state in writing that he has such a right or duty and must also state the grounds on which he claims that right or duty. This statement must be made in the list in which the document is disclosed[9]. One very common circumstance in which a claim to a right to withhold from inspection will arise is where documents are protected by legal professional privilege. Broadly speaking, communications between a solicitor and his client for the purposes of obtaining legal advice and assistance are privileged whether or not litigation was contemplated at the time. Communications between solicitors and third parties or clients/parties and third parties may be privileged if they came into existence for the purposes of existing or anticipated proceedings. Where privilege is claimed for a document it need not be listed in the same detail as other documents. It is not required that the dates of documents be specified nor that the names of their makers be given. For example 'correspondence between the claimant and his solicitors for the purposes of obtaining legal advice' is sufficient[10].

The list must also include those documents which are no longer in the party's control, together with an explanation as to what has happened to those documents.

1 CPR 31.10.
2 CPR Pt 31 PD, para 3.1.
3 The reasonableness of the search is determined, for example, by the number of documents involved, the nature and complexity of the proceedings, the ease and expense of retrieval of any particular document and the significance of any document which is likely to be located during the search: CPR 31.7(2).
4 CPR 31.7.
5 CPR 1.1(2)(c) and see footnote 3 to paragraph 20.05 below.
6 CPR Pt 31 PD, para 2.
7 CPR 31.10(3).
8 That is, examination or sight of the document in question. The necessarily detailed consideration of the circumstances in which a party will have a right or duty to withhold inspection are beyond the remit of this book but the reader should refer to specialist texts available on this subject.
9 CPR 31.19(3).
10 See *Gardner v Irvin* (1878) LR 4 Ex D 49, CA.

20.05 Finally, the list must include a disclosure statement, which is a statement made by the party disclosing the documents setting out the extent of the search that has been made to locate documents, certifying that he understands the duty to disclose documents and that, to the best of his knowledge, he has carried out that duty[1]. Where a party has not searched for a category or class of document on the grounds that to do so would be unreasonable, he must state this in his disclosure statement and identify the category or class of document[2]. Where the party giving disclosure considers that it would be disproportionate[3] to the issues in the case to permit inspection of documents within a category or class of document disclosed under CPR 31.6(b)[4], he must state in his disclosure statement that inspection will not be permitted on the grounds that to do so would be disproportionate[5].

Where the party making the disclosure statement is a company, firm, association or other organisation, the statement must also identify the person making the statement and explain why he is considered an appropriate person to make it[6]. Very often this will be a member of an in-house legal team or the solicitor instructed in the case.

The form of disclosure statement is set out in the Annex to the Practice Direction to CPR Pt 31 and reads as follows:

'**Disclosure statement**

I, the above named claimant [or defendant] [if party making disclosure is a company, firm or other organisation identify here who the person making the disclosure statement is and why he is the appropriate person to make it] state that I have carried out a reasonable and proportionate search to locate all the documents which I am required to disclose under the order made by the court on [   ] day of [   ]. I did not search:
(1)   for documents predating . . . .,
(2)   for documents located elsewhere than,
(3)   for documents in categories other than.
I certify that I understand the duty of disclosure and to the best of my knowledge I have carried out that duty. I certify that the list above is a complete list of all documents which are or have been in my control and which I am obliged under the said order to disclose.'

It is worth noting that the rules make specific provision for proceedings for contempt of court to be brought against a person who makes or causes to be made a false disclosure statement, without an honest belief in its truth[7].

The obligations of disclosure are continuing, in that they do not cease once a list has been prepared and served but continue until the proceedings have come to an end. If, after a list of documents has been prepared and served, the existence of further documents to which the order applies comes to the attention of the party giving disclosure, that party must immediately notify every other party and prepare and serve a supplemental list of documents[8].

1   CPR 31.10.
2   Which may be challenged by the party seeking inspection on application to the court: CPR 31.7. See paragraph 20.08 below.
3   As to the meaning of 'disproportionate' in this context, see the overriding objective at CPR 1.1 of dealing with cases justly and in particular CPR 1.1(2)(c) where the relevant considerations for proportionality are the amount of money involved, the importance of the case, the complexity of the issues and the financial position of each party. See also CPR 31.7(2) where the reasonableness of a search for documents includes consideration of the following factors: the number of documents involved, the nature and complexity of the proceedings, the ease and expense of retrieval of any particular document and the significance of any document which is likely to be located during the search.
4   That is, where a party has disclosed documents which adversely affect his own or another party's case, or the documents which support another party's case.
5   CPR 31.3(2)(b).
6   CPR 31.10(7).
7   CPR 31.23.
8   CPR 31.11 and CPR Pt 31 PD, para 3.3.

Disclosure of copies of documents

20.06   A 'copy' of a document is defined as 'anything onto which information recorded in the document has been copied, by whatever means and whether directly or indirectly'[1]. The definition will therefore cover, for example, scanned and manually copied documents, or parts of them, as well as straightforward photocopies. A party is not required to disclose more than one copy of a document, except to the extent that the copy or copies contain a marking, modification, obliteration or feature on which a party intends to rely or which adversely affects his own or another party's case or supports another party's case, in which case that copy document is treated as a separate document, and therefore becomes disclosable as such[2].

1   CPR 31.4.
2   CPR 31.9.

Inspection

20.07 'Inspection' is the process by which the parties actually get to see the documents disclosed by each other. The court order made at the case management conference will usually state the date and time by which this should have taken place, usually a week or more after disclosure (depending upon the anticipated number of documents involved). 'Inspection' extends to examining electronic, audio or visual recordings with appropriate equipment.

A party to whom a document has been disclosed has a right to inspect that document – except in three circumstances[1]. The first is where the document is no longer in the control[2] of the party who disclosed it. The second is where the party disclosing the document has a right or duty to withhold inspection of it[3]. The third is where a party considers that it would be disproportionate to the issues in the case to permit inspection of documents within a category or class of document disclosed under CPR 31.6(b)[4]. The party giving disclosure is not required to permit inspection of the documents within that category or class but he must state in his disclosure statement that inspection will not be permitted on the grounds that to do so would be disproportionate. A party who therefore waits until inspection is requested before making a statement to the effect that to allow it would be disproportionate has left it too late – if he is to make the claim, he should do so in his disclosure statement.

Where a claim to withhold inspection is made, it is up to the other party to challenge this claim by application to the court if he so desires[5]. For the purpose of deciding such an application, the court may require the person seeking to withhold inspection to produce that document to the court and can invite any person, whether or not a party, to make representations[6]. The application should be made in accordance with CPR 23 and must be supported by evidence[7].

Although one might infer from the term 'inspection' that one party or his legal representatives will visit the other party's premises and physically inspect the documents disclosed, this rarely happens in practice[8]. The process usually adopted is that solicitors for the claimant will write to the solicitors for the defendant, asking to be supplied with copies of all documents disclosed, or such documents as they have identified as relevant from the lists, undertaking to pay the reasonable costs of the same (ie photocopying, postage/courier, etc). Where a party has a right to inspect a document he must give the disclosing party written notice of his wish to inspect it. The disclosing party must then permit inspection not more than seven days after the date on which he received the notice. Where a party requests a copy of a document and also undertakes to pay reasonable photocopying costs, the disclosing party must supply a copy of that document not more than seven days after receipt of the request[9].

1   CPR 31.3.
2   That is, he no longer has it in his physical possession (and he cannot obtain it) and/or he no longer has a right to possession of it and/or he no longer has a right to inspect or take copies of it: CPR 31.8(2).
3   Which may be challenged by the party seeking inspection on application to the court: see paragraph 20.08 below.
4   That is, where a party has disclosed documents which adversely affect his own or another party's case or documents which support another party's case.
5   CPR 31.19(5) and CPR Pt 31 PD, para 6.
6   CPR 31.10(6).
7   CPR 31.19(7). For further consideration of CPR 23 see Chapter 22.
8   CPR 31.15.
9   CPR 31.15.

Applications for specific disclosure and specific inspection

20.08   An application for an order for specific disclosure or specific inspection may be made at any time during the proceedings. An order for specific disclosure is an order that a party must do one or more of the following:

(a)   disclose documents or classes of documents specified in the order;
(b)   carry out a search to the extent stated in the order;
(c)   disclose any documents located as a result of that search[1].

An order for specific inspection is an order that a party permit inspection of a document which he has claimed it would be disproportionate to allow inspection of.

Following standard disclosure, an application for specific disclosure may be appropriate. The Practice Direction to CPR Pt 31 makes specific reference to a party making an application for specific disclosure where he 'believes that the disclosure of documents given by a disclosing party is inadequate'[2]. For example, an application for specific disclosure may be appropriate where the disclosing party has referred to a document in its statement of case, witness statement/summary or affidavit which has not been disclosed (whether or not it would have been required to be disclosed through the process of

standard disclosure)[3], relevant documents not caught by the requirement for standard disclosure (ie documents which do not obviously
support or undermine a party's case but are part of the 'story' of the
case) and documents which may lead to a train of inquiry enabling a
party to advance his own case or damage that of another[4].

An application for specific disclosure (or inspection) should be
made in accordance with CPR 23. The application should state what
order is sought and must be supported by evidence. The grounds on
which the order is sought must either be set out in the application
notice itself or in evidence filed in support of the application[5].

In determining whether it is appropriate to make an order for
specific disclosure (or inspection) the court will take into account all
the circumstances of the case and in particular the overriding objective
set out in CPR 1. However, the court will usually make such order as is
necessary to ensure that the obligations of disclosure imposed by a
previous order are complied with[6]. In deciding whether or not to make
an order for specific disclosure, the court must also take into account
the European Convention on Human Rights, balancing the Article
6(1) right to a fair hearing for the party seeking disclosure with the
Article 8 right to respect for private life for the party resisting
disclosure[7].

1   CPR 31.12(2).
2   CPR Pt 31 PD, para 5.1.
3   See CPR 31.14.
4   See *Compagnie Financiere et Commercial du Pacifique v Peruvian Guano Co* (1882)
    LR 11 QBD 55, CA.
5   CPR Pt 31 PD, paras 5.2–5.3.
6   CPR Pt 31 PD, para 5.4.
7   *Nayler v Beard* [2001] EWCA Civ 1201, [2001] 3 FCR 61.

The purposes for which disclosed documents may be used

20.09   The general rule is that a party to whom a document has been
disclosed is only allowed to use that document for the purpose of the
proceedings in which that document was disclosed, ie he is not allowed
to use it in any other proceedings or for any other purpose or reason.
The three exceptions to the rule are:

(a)   where the document has been read to or by the court, or has
      been referred to at a hearing which has been held in public;
(b)   where the court has given permission; or

(c)   where the party who disclosed the document and the person to whom the document belongs agree[1].

From time to time would-be libel claimants have attempted to bring proceedings for libel based on documents disclosed in other proceedings. CPR 31.22(2) expressly provides that the court may make an order restricting or prohibiting the use of a document which has been disclosed, even where the document has been read to or by the court, or referred to at a hearing held in public. An application for such an order may be made by a party or by any person to whom the document belongs.

1   CPR 31.22(1).

Pre-action disclosure against a potential party or parties

20.10   This section deals only with pre-action disclosure against a potential party or parties. For pre-action disclosure against a person or entity who is not the envisaged defendant, see paragraphs 20.11–20.13 below.

An application for disclosure before proceedings have started is governed by CPR 31.16. The application should be made in accordance with CPR 23 and must be supported by evidence[1]. Because there are no proceedings underway at the time of the application, the person making the application is the 'applicant' (not the 'claimant') and the person against whom it is made is the 'respondent' (not the 'defendant').

The applicant's prospect of success will be an important factor in the court's determination of whether to grant an order for disclosure[2].

The court may make an order for pre-action disclosure only where (a) the respondent is likely to be a party to subsequent proceedings, (b) the applicant is also likely to be a party to those proceedings, (c) if proceedings had started, the respondent would have been duty-bound to disclose the document(s) under the rules of standard disclosure[3], and (d) disclosure before proceedings have started is desirable in order to dispose fairly of the anticipated proceedings, and/or assist in the dispute to be resolved without proceedings, and/or save costs[4]. In the defamation context, an application for pre-action disclosure may be appropriate, for example where a would-be claimant knows or has good reason to believe that he has been libelled by an identified individual or entity but has not seen, or has been unable to ascertain the precise content of, the offending publication.

CPR 31.16 further provides that any resulting order for pre-action disclosure must specify the document or the classes of document which the respondent must disclose. It also requires him, when making disclosure, to specify any of those documents which are no longer in his control or in respect of which he claims a right or duty to withhold inspection[5]. The order may require the respondent to indicate what has happened to any document which is no longer in his control and specify the time and date for disclosure and inspection.

1   CPR 31.16(2).
2   See *K v Secretary of State for the Home Office* (28 July 2000, unreported); *Nabina v CC for Greater Manchester* (8 December 2000, unreported).
3   See paragraph 20.03 above.
4   CPR 31.16(3).
5   See paragraph 20.07 above.

Disclosure against non-parties

20.11   This section deals with (a) orders for disclosure against non-parties during proceedings and (b) orders for pre-action disclosure against persons who are not likely to become party to any subsequent proceedings.

Orders for disclosure against non-parties during proceedings

20.12   Orders for disclosure against non-parties during proceedings are governed by CPR 31.17. The application should be made in accordance with CPR 23 and must be supported by evidence[1]. As with pre-action applications, the person making the application is the 'applicant' and the person against whom it is made is the 'respondent'.

The court may make an order for disclosure against a non-party during proceedings only where (a) the documents of which disclosure is sought are likely to support the case of the applicant or adversely affect the case of one of the other parties to the proceedings, and (b) disclosure is necessary in order to dispose fairly of the claim or to save costs[2].

CPR 31.17 further provides that any resulting order for disclosure must specify the document(s) which the respondent must disclose and requires the respondent, when making disclosure, to specify any of those documents which are no longer in his control or in respect of which he claims a right or duty to withhold inspection. The order may require the respondent to indicate what has happened to any documents which are no longer in his control and specify the time and place for disclosure and inspection.

1 CPR 31.17(2).
2 CPR 31.17(3).

Orders for pre-action disclosure against persons who are not likely to become party to any subsequent proceedings

20.13 An order for pre-action disclosure against a person who is not likely to become a party is not dealt with by the CPR, although CPR 31.18 expressly preserves the court's power to make such orders. Therefore orders against such persons prior to the commencement of proceedings are governed by the common law and are achieved by making a claim for disclosure and production, formerly known as an action for discovery.

The starting point in terms of case law on pre-action disclosure against non-parties remains *Norwich Pharmacal Co v Customs and Excise Comrs*[1]. In that case the House of Lords endorsed the principle stated in an earlier case that 'if through no fault of his own a person gets mixed up in the tortious acts of others so as to facilitate their wrongdoing he may incur no personal liability but he comes under a duty to assist the person who has been wronged by him giving him full information and disclosing the identity of the wrongdoers'[2]. It is therefore possible to obtain an order for disclosure as to the identity of a wrongdoer prior to the issue of proceedings, but only where the respondent themselves has somehow facilitated or assisted, however innocently, in the commission of the tort in question which in the present context would be the publication of a libel or slander. It is important to note that it is not possible to obtain an order for the disclosure of the identity of a wrongdoer from someone who just happens to know his identity, but who neither committed nor facilitated in the committal of a tort[3].

In a defamation context, perhaps the most common use of *Norwich Pharmacal* orders, as they are known, is in relation to Internet service providers ('ISPs') who have removed defamatory material published on a website hosted by them upon notification by the would-be claimant (and are therefore likely to be protected from liability under section 1 of the DeA 1996)[4] but who routinely refuse to provide details of the identity of the person who posted the offending material in the absence of a court order for data protection reasons. A reported example is that of *Totalise v Motley Fool*[5] where an ISP which operated a website containing discussion boards was ordered to disclose the identity of an anonymous contributor who was posting messages defamatory of the claimant.

The would-be claimant should also be warned that where a claim for disclosure and production is brought against a mere facilitator, it is likely that he will be expected to pay the facilitator's expenses in providing the information sought. Where the facilitator has doubts about disclosure which properly require determination by the court, the claimant is likely also to be required to pay the facilitator's costs of the proceedings[6]. However, these costs may be recoverable as damages in subsequent proceedings against the wrongdoer[7].

1   [1974] AC 133. See also *P v T Ltd* [1997] 1 WLR 1309.
2   *Upmann v Elkan* (1871) LR 12 Eq 140, per Lord Romilly MR.
3   *Ricci v Chow* [1987] 1 WLR 1658, CA.
4   See Chapter 16.
5   [2001] EMLR 750.
6   *Handmade v Express Newspapers* [1986] FSR 463.
7   *Morton Norwich Products Inc v Intercen Ltd (No 2)* [1981] FSR 337.

Chapter 21

Witness statements

21.01 The Civil Procedure Rules set out in considerable detail various requirements for the form and content of witness statements, much of which is common sense and almost all of which is very dull to read! This chapter attempts to condense the relevant Parts of the CPR, setting out: (a) how a witness statement should look and what it should contain, (b) the circumstances in which it will be necessary to prepare and serve witness statements in support of applications made at hearings prior to trial of the action and (c) for the purposes of the trial. The use of witness statements during the actual course of the trial is dealt with in Chapter 24.

The form and content of a witness statement

Format

21.02 The CPR provide that a witness statement should be headed with the title of proceedings. At the top right-hand corner of the first page there should be clearly written:

(a)   the party on whose behalf it was made;
(b)   the initials and surname of the witness;
(c)   the number of the statement in relation to that witness;
(d)   the identifying initials and number of each exhibit referred to; and
(e)   the date the statement was made[1].

A witness statement should:

(a)   be produced on durable quality A4 paper with a 3.5 cm margin;

(b)   be fully legible and should normally be typed on one side of the paper only;

(c)   where possible, be bound securely in a manner which would not hamper filing, or otherwise each page should be endorsed with the case number and bear the initials of the witness;

(d)   have the pages numbered consecutively as a separate statement (or as one of several statements contained in a file);

(e)   be divided into numbered paragraphs;

(f)   have all numbers, including dates, expressed in figures; and

(g)   give the reference to any document or documents mentioned either in the margin or in bold text in the body of the statement[2].

1   CPR Pt 32 PD, para 17.
2   CPR Pt 32 PD, para 19.2.

Content

21.03   A witness statement is a written statement signed by a person which contains the evidence, and only that evidence, which a person would be allowed to give orally[1]. It should not, therefore, discuss legal propositions or comment on documents. A witness statement is, in effect, a full proof of evidence – it should contain everything that the witness will say in his evidence in support of the issue or matter upon which his evidence is being tendered. Usually a witness statement will follow the chronological sequence of events or matters dealt with; each paragraph of a witness statement should as far as possible be confined to a distinct portion of the subject[2].

A rule more honoured in the breach than the observance – since the vast majority of witness statements are drafted by legal representatives – is that a witness statement should be in the witness's own words[3]. It should be expressed in the first person and should also state:

(a)   the full name of the witness;

(b)   his place of residence or, if he is making the statement in his professional capacity, the address at which he works, the position he holds and the name of his firm or employer;

(c)   his occupation, or, if he has none, his description; and

(d)   the fact that he is a party to the proceedings or is the employee of such a party if that be the case[4].

As hearsay evidence is now generally admissible, a witness statement may include hearsay evidence. However, it must draw attention to any hearsay evidence in it by making clear:

(a)   which of the statements in it are made from the witness's own knowledge and which are information or belief; and

(b)   the source of any matters of information or belief[5].

1   CPR 32.4(1).
2   CPR Pt 32 PD, para 19.2.
3   *Alex Lawrie Factors Ltd v Morgan* (1999) Times, 18 August, CA; CPR Pt 32 PD, para 18.1.
4   CPR Pt 32 PD, para 18.1.
5   CPR Pt 32 PD, para 18.2. The detailed procedural requirements in relation to hearsay evidence, which are beyond the scope of this book, are set out in CPR 33.

Exhibits

21.04   An exhibit used in conjunction with a witness statement should be verified and identified by the witness separately from the witness statement[1]. The usual procedure is to gather all exhibits together and verify them as a bundle. Where a witness refers to an exhibit or exhibits in his witness statement, he should state 'I refer to the (description of exhibit) marked "XX1" '[2].

On the first page of each exhibit should be written:

(a)   the party on whose behalf it is exhibited;
(b)   the initials and surname of the witness;
(c)   the number of the witness statement in relation to that witness;
(d)   the identifying initials and number of that exhibit; and
(e)   the date on which the exhibit was verified.

Letters should be collected together and exhibited in a bundle or bundles, arranged chronologically with the earliest at the top, and firmly secured. The bundle should have a front page attached stating what the bundle consists of. It is perhaps a little known requirement that when photocopies are exhibited instead of original documents the original must be made available for inspection by the other parties prior to the hearing and by the judge at the hearing. Court documents should not be exhibited as they prove themselves. Where an exhibit contains more than one document, a front page should be attached setting out a list of the documents contained in the exhibit. This list should also give the dates of the documents. Items other than paper documents should be clearly marked with an exhibit number or letter in a manner which cannot become detached from the item. Small items may be placed in a container and the container appropriately marked. Where an exhibit contains more than one document the bundle should not be stapled but should be securely fastened in a way that does not hinder the reading of the document and the pages should be numbered consecutively at the bottom centre. Where on account of their bulk the service or exhibits would be difficult or impracticable directions should be sought from the court[3]. Where a witness makes more than one witness statement to which there are exhibits in the same proceedings, the numbering on the exhibits should run consecutively throughout and not start again with each witness statement[4].

1 CPR Pt 32 PD, para 18.3.
2 CPR Pt 32 PD, para 18.4.
3 CPR Pt 32 PD, para 18.5.
4 CPR Pt 32 PD, para 18.6.

Statement of truth

21.05 A witness statement must be signed and verified by a statement of truth[1] because it is the equivalent of the oral evidence which that witness would, if called, give in evidence. The statement must be made by the intended witness – it cannot be signed on his behalf. The witness simply states that he believes the facts in the witness statement are true[2]. The statement of truth comes at the end of the witness statement and should read 'I believe that the facts stated in this witness statement are true'[3]. It should then be signed and dated. The CPR remind us that proceedings for contempt of court may be brought against a person who makes or causes to be made a false statement in a document verified by a statement of truth without an honest belief in its truth[4]. If a witness statement is not verified by a statement of truth the court may direct that it shall not be admissible as evidence[5].

1 CPR 32.8.
2 CPR Pt 32 PD, para 20.1.
3 CPR Pt 32 PD, para 20.2.
4 CPR 32.14.
5 CPR 22.3.

When witness cannot read/sign the statement

21.06 Where a witness statement is made by a person who is unable to read or sign the witness statement, it must contain a certificate made by a person able to administer oaths and take affidavits but need not be independent of the parties or their representatives. That person (known as the 'authorised person') must certify:

(a)   that the witness statement has been read to the witness;
(b)   that the witness appeared to understand it and approved its content as accurate;
(c)   that the declaration of truth has been read to the witness;
(d)   that the witness appeared to understand the declaration and the consequences of making a false witness statement; and
(e)   that the witness signed or made his mark in the presence of the authorised person[1].

The certificate should read as follows[2]:

> 'I certify that I [name and address of authorised person] have read over the contents of this witness statement and the declaration of truth to the witness [if there are exhibits add "and explained the nature and effect of the exhibits referred to in it"] who appeared to understand (a) the statement and approved its content as accurate and (b) the declaration of truth and the consequences of making a false witness statement, and made his mark in my presence.'

1   CPR Pt 32 PD, para 21.
2   CPR Pt 32 PD, Annex 2.

Evidence on applications prior to trial

21.07   It may be necessary to produce a witness statement in support of any application made prior to trial. The circumstances in which such interim applications are commonly made in defamation proceedings and the basic procedure applicable to each is dealt with in Chapter 22. So far as witness statements on interim applications are concerned, the basic principle is that a witness statement will be necessary whenever the submissions to be made to the court on the application contain anything other than pure law, and it is a rare application which depends upon submissions of law alone. Almost inevitably, reference will need to be made to some alleged factual state of affairs and a witness statement will be required for this because the CPR provide that evidence at hearings other than trial is to be by witness statement[1]. A witness statement may not be necessary if the factual matters relied upon are set out in a statement of case or the application notice duly verified by a statement of truth. Provided that the document has been so verified, it may be relied upon in addition to, or instead of, a witness statement (unless required under the rules)[2]. Evidence may be given by affidavit if a witness so wishes[3] but if a witness statement would have sufficed the party placing reliance upon the affidavit places himself at risk of not recovering the additional costs of it[4].

1   Unless the court, a Practice Direction or any other enactment requires otherwise:
    CPR 32.6(1). See also CPR 32(1)(b).
2   CPR 32.6(2), CPR Pt 32 PD, para 1.3.
3   CPR Pt 32 PD, para 1.2. Para 1.4 of the Practice Direction sets out the circumstances in which affidavit evidence must be used. The formal requirements for the content of an affidavit are set out at paragraphs 3–16 of the Practice Direction to CPR Pt 32.
4   CPR 32.15(2).

Witness statements for trial

21.08   Traditionally evidence during trial is given orally by witnesses under oath or affirmation in the witness box. However, the Civil Procedure Rules provide that where a witness is called to give oral evidence his witness statement 'shall stand as his evidence in chief unless the court orders otherwise'[1]. Under this procedure the witness would be sworn, asked to identify his witness statement and agree to its contents and then, perhaps after being asked a few preliminary questions in order to allow the witness to become acclimatised, he would be tendered for cross-examination. Defamation claims are usually tried by jury and, perhaps because juries are perceived to absorb information more readily when it is given orally, the traditional method is still the norm in defamation proceedings. This does not, however, mean that witness statements of the evidence that a witness will give at trial are not required. In accordance with the principle that the parties will 'play with an open hand' in the sense that each knows in advance as much as possible about the state of the evidence prior to the trial, an order will be made at the case management conference to serve on all other parties any witness statement of the oral evidence which he intends to rely on in relation to any issues of fact to be decided at the trial[2]. The usual order is for witness statements to be exchanged simultaneously although occasionally an order for sequential service may be appropriate.

Where a party wishes to rely upon the evidence of a certain witness at trial but is unable to obtain a witness statement for exchange as ordered by the court he may apply to the court for permission to serve a witness summary instead. A witness summary is either a summary of the evidence which would otherwise be included in a witness statement, or, where the nature of the evidence that a witness would give is not known, the matters about which the party serving the witness summary proposes to question the witness[3]. The summary must include the name and address of the intended witness and must be served within the time limits set for exchange of witness statements unless the court orders otherwise[4]. A witness summary should be as close to the witness statement it would have been as possible. If a witness statement or summary for use at trial is not served within the time specified by the court, the witness may not be called to give his evidence unless the court gives permission[5].

A witness giving oral evidence at trial may, with the permission of the court, amplify his witness statement and give evidence in relation to new matters arisen since the witness statement was served on the other parties[6]. The court will only give such permission if it considers that there is good reason not to confine the evidence of the witness to the contents of his witness statement[7].

1   CPR 32.5(2).
2   CPR 32.4(2).
3   CPR 32.9(1) and (2).
4   CPR 32.9(3) and (4).
5   CPR 32.10.
6   CPR 32.5(3).
7   CPR 32.5(4).

Chapter 22

Pre-trial applications for court orders

Introduction

22.01 It will have become clear by now that any claim for defamation must pass through a number of procedural stages prior to the actual trial of the claim before a judge and jury, namely the preparation and service of statements of case, the case management conference, disclosure and inspection, exchange of witness statements and so on. In addition to these standard stages which occur at broadly predictable points it is likely that there will be at least one, if not more, court hearings before a Master[1] or judge as a result of an application made by one or other of the parties, or, exceptionally, as a result of the court's own determination to hold a hearing on some issue or matter[2].

Very broadly, an application to the court may be appropriate whenever one party believes that there is something in the case which requires clarification or 'tidying up' either because there is a defect in the other party's case, or indeed because the other party does not have a case at all. Or it may be that one party wishes to apply for an extension of time in respect of the date set by the CPR or the court for service of a document or documents, or wishes to call to account another party who has failed to respect time limits. The aim of an application is to obtain a court order in the applicant's favour[3]. This chapter deals with: (a) the general rules of how to go about applying for a court order, (b) the specific rules which apply to particular types of application common in defamation claims, (c) the relevant costs considerations, and (d) the broad procedural requirements on appeal.

---

1   Or a district judge if the claim is proceeding in a district registry.
2   Though the CPR make provision for this, it is still rare in practice for the court to take the initiative in a case.
3   The hearing is simply the means by which the order is achieved (or not!) and some applications may be dealt with by the court without a hearing, although in all but the very simplest of cases this is unlikely.

General rules on applying for court orders: CPR 23

22.02 The general rules about applying for court orders are to be found in CPR 23. However, they are 'default provisions' in the sense that they apply unless express provision is made elsewhere in the rules governing a specific type of application.

Stage 1: deciding to make an application

22.03 Every application should be made as soon as it becomes apparent that it is necessary or desirable to make it[1]. Some applications must be made within a specified time; for example, an application made under CPR 11 disputing the court's jurisdiction to try a claim must be made within 14 days after filing the acknowledgment of service[2]. Where this is the case, the application will have been made within time if it is received by the court within the stipulated time period[3]. Wherever possible, applications should be made so that they can be considered at any other hearing for which a date has already been fixed or for which a date is about to be fixed[4].

1 CPR Pt 23 PD, para 2.7.
2 CPR 11(4)(a).
3 CPR 23.5.
4 CPR Pt 23 PD, para 2.8.

Stage 2: completing the form

22.04 The general rule is that an application to the court should be made in an application notice. CPR 23 and the accompanying Practice Direction contain various requirements which must be satisfied in order for a document to be an application notice, though by far the simplest route is to use Form N244 which is available from the court office or can be downloaded from the Court Service website[1]. This form contains various boxes for completion and therefore 'prompts' a party to include all the required information.

The party making the application is known as the 'applicant' and the person against whom it is made is the 'respondent'. Once the applicant has obtained Form N244 (the application notice), he should complete it stating (a) what order he is seeking and (b) the reason(s) why that order is sought. Where the applicant wishes to rely on matters set out in his application notice as evidence, the notice must be verified by a statement of truth[2]. The applicant may, in addition to, or instead of, his application notice seek to rely on his statement of case as evidence (if verified by a statement of truth) or may prepare and include with the application notice a witness statement[3]. If the applicant does rely upon any of these documents in support of his application, he should so indicate by ticking the relevant box(es) on the application notice. Any evidence relied upon in support of the application should be given in one of these three forms, or, exceptionally, by affidavit. Oral evidence is not generally permitted[4].

1   See www.courtservice.gov.uk (forms and leaflets).
2   CPR 23.6, CPR Pt 23 PD, para 9.7. See also CPR 22 (Statements of Truth).
3   See Chapter 21.
4   See CPR 32.6.

Stage 3: filing the form at court

22.05   Once the applicant has completed the notice, he must file it with the appropriate court[1]. CPR 23.2 provides that this must be the court where the claim was started unless it has been transferred, or if notice of trial in another court has been given. An application made before a claim has been started must be made to the court in which it is likely that the prospective claim to which it relates will be started unless there is good reason to make the application in a different court[2]. In a defamation claim in the High Court, the application should be made either to a judge or to a Master[3] (or district judge in the district registry) and this should be indicated on the face of the application notice at section 5 ('Level of Judge'). *Practice Direction (Allocation of Cases to Levels of Judiciary)* and the Queen's Bench Guide both contain information about the types of applications which may be dealt with by Masters or judges. Some types of applications should be dealt with by a judge because of their complexity, whereas others, such as an application for judgment in default where the claimant is seeking in addition to damages an injunction against the defendant prohibiting him from repeating the defamatory statement complained of, must be made to a judge because a Master does not have the power to grant injunctions.

1   CPR 23.3.
2   An example of a claim made before proceedings are started is an application for disclosure of the identity of the publisher made against a third party 'facilitator' of the defamatory publication: see Chapter 20, paragraph 20.13. See also paragraph 20.10.
3   An application notice for a hearing by a Master should be issued in the Master's Support Unit Room (E16). An application notice for a hearing by a judge should be issued in the Listing Office Room (WG5).

Stage 4: consideration of the application notice by the court

22.06   Where an application has been made to a Master or, in the district registry, to a district judge who thinks the application should properly be decided by a judge, he may refer it to a judge, who may either dispose of the matter or refer it back to the Master or district judge[1].

Section 1 of Form N244 asks the applicant to indicate by ticking the relevant box whether he wants his application to be dealt with (a) at a hearing, (b) at a telephone conference or (c) without a hearing. Section 3 asks whether this is agreed by all parties.

Upon receipt of the application the court will notify the applicant of the time and date of the hearing if there is to be one[2]. The applicant must then serve a copy of the application on each person against whom the order is sought[3] as soon as practicable but in any event at least three days before the application is due to be heard[4]. The applicant must serve with the application notice a copy of any written evidence in support of the application (if it has not already been served) and any draft order attached to the notice[5]. A draft order should be included or at the very least brought to the hearing in all but the most simple and straightforward of applications[6].

1   CPR Pt 23 PD, para 1.
2   CPR Pt 23 PD, para 2.2.
3   CPR 23.4(1).
4   CPR 23.7(1); CPR Pt 23 PD, para 4.1.
5   CPR 27(3) and (5).
6   See CPR Pt 23 PD, para 12.1, which further provides that if the case is proceeding in the Royal Courts of Justice and the order is unusually long or complex it should also be supplied on disk by the court office.

Evidence[1]

22.07   The requirement for evidence in certain types of application is set out in various rules and practice directions of the CPR. Where there is no specific requirement to provide evidence it should be borne in mind that the court will often need to be satisfied, by evidence, of the facts that are relied on in support of or in order to oppose, the application[2]. The court may give directions for the filing of evidence in support of or in opposing any application. It may also give directions for filing evidence when it fixes a hearing of its own initiative. The directions may specify the form the evidence is to take and when it is to be served[3]. Where it is intended to rely on evidence which is not contained in the application itself, then that evidence, if not already served, should be served with the application[4]. Where a respondent wishes to rely on evidence which has not yet been served it should be served 'as soon as possible' and in any event in accordance with any directions the court may have given[5]. The same applies to any evidence the applicant may then want to serve in reply[6]. The evidence should be filed with the court as well as served on the parties but exhibits should not be filed unless the court so directs[7].

1   See, generally, Chapter 21 (witness statements).
2   CPR Pt 23 PD, para 9.1.
3   CPR Pt 23 PD, para 9.2.
4   CPR Pt 23 PD, para 9.3.
5   CPR Pt 23 PD, para 9.4.
6   CPR Pt 23 PD, para 9.5.
7   CPR Pt 23 PD, para 9.6.

Stage 5, option (a): application dealt with at a hearing

22.08   The vast majority of applications are dealt with at a hearing. At the hearing, the parties should not only be prepared to deal with the application itself but, so say the rules, should anticipate that the court may wish to review the conduct of the case as a whole and give any necessary case management directions. Parties should be ready to assist the court in doing so and to answer questions the court may ask for this purpose[1]. If legal representatives were to abide by the letter of this provision the costs implications would be huge – for example, a party attending simply to ask for an application for extension of time for service of some document in the case is apparently required to be familiar with the whole history of the case to date and be prepared to assist the court in any review of the case that it may decide to undertake. Though this would not necessarily increase costs where a party was represented by the lawyer who has had conduct of the case throughout, the costs implications could be rather different if another lawyer was sent along in their place, either because that representative is not available, or (ironically) in attempt to keep costs down. Should that legal representative be expected to familiarise himself with the whole of the case on the off chance that the court may decide to 'review' some aspect of it? Surely this would not be proportionate? So far, and to the great relief of all practitioners, the courts do not appear to be making any real use of this facility.

1   CPR Pt 23 PD, para 2.10. Presumably this would also apply to any telephone hearing of the application.

Stage 5, option (b): application dealt with at a telephone conference

22.09   It does not yet seem to be court practice to order hearings by way of telephone conference. The Practice Direction to CPR 23 provides that an order for an application or part of an application to be dealt with by telephone hearing will not normally be made unless every party entitled to be given notice of the application and to be heard at the hearing has consented to the order[1]. Where a court does order a telephone hearing, it will also give any directions necessary for that hearing[2]. Paragraph 6.5 of the Practice Direction sets out the various directions that will apply unless the court directs otherwise[3]. Where a telephone hearing is held, no one at that hearing may attend the judge in person during it unless the other party to the application has agreed to it[4]. Where a party acting in person is one of the parties to the application, or is otherwise entitled to be heard on the application, the court will not make an order for a telephone conference unless arrangements are made for that person's identity to be confirmed by a 'responsible person'[5] at the telephone hearing[6].

1   CPR Pt 23 PD, para 6.2.
2   CPR Pt 23 PD, para 6.3(3).
3   The Civil Procedure Rules are available on the Internet at www.lcd.gov.uk.
4   CPR Pt 23 PD, para 6.4.
5   Defined as 'a barrister, solicitor, legal executive, doctor, clergyman, police officer, prison officer or other person of comparable status': CPR Pt 23 PD, para 6.3(2).
6   CPR Pt 23 PD, para 6.3.

Stage 5, option (c): application dealt with without a hearing

22.10   CPR 23.8 provides that an application may be dealt with without a hearing if the parties agree as to the terms of the order sought, if the parties agree that the court should dispose of the application without a hearing, or if the court does not consider that a hearing would be appropriate. Where an application notice contains a request for an application to be dealt with without a hearing, it will be sent to a Master or district judge who will decide whether the application is suitable for consideration without a hearing[1]. Where the reason for this is the fact that the parties agree that the application can be dealt with without a hearing, each should inform the court in writing and confirm that all the evidence and other material on which he relies has been disclosed to the other parties to the application[2].

Where the court considers that the application is suitable for consideration without a hearing, it will inform the applicant and respondent and may give directions for the filing of evidence[3]. Where the court does not consider that a hearing would be appropriate it will treat the application as if it were proposing to make the order of its own initiative[4]. Where it considers a hearing is necessary, it will notify the applicant and respondent of this and the time, date and place for the hearing, and may also give directions as to the filing of evidence[5].

1 CPR Pt 23 PD, para 2.3.
2 CPR Pt 23 PD, para 11.1.
3 CPR Pt 23 PD, para 2.4.
4 CPR Pt 23 PD, para 11.2.
5 CPR Pt 23 PD, para 2.5.

Applications without notice

22.11 The Practice Direction to CPR Pt 23 provides that an application may be made without serving an application notice only (a) where there is 'exceptional urgency', (b) where the overriding objective is best furthered by doing so[1], (c) where the parties consent, (d) with the permission of the court, (e) where paragraph 2.10 of the Practice Direction applies[2] or (f) where a court order, rule or practice direction permits[3]. For example, CPR 12.11 allows an application for judgment in default to be made without notice in certain circumstances where a claim has been served on a defendant outside the jurisdiction who has failed to acknowledge service. CPR 25.3 provides that the court may grant an interim remedy on an application made without notice if it appears to the court that there are good reasons for not giving notice.

CPR 23.9 provides that where the court disposes of an application which it permitted to be made without service of a copy of the application notice, a copy of the application notice and any evidence relied upon in support must, unless the court orders otherwise, be served with the order on any party or other person against whom the order was made or against whom the order was sought. The order must contain a statement of the right to make an application to set aside or vary the order under CPR 23.10. An application to set aside or vary any order so made must be made within seven days after the date on which the order was served on the person who wishes to make that application[4].

1   See CPR 1.
2   CPR Pt 23 PD, para 2.10 provides that where a date for the hearing has been fixed and a party wishes to make an application at that hearing but he does not have sufficient time to serve an application notice he should inform the other party and the court (if possible in writing) as soon as he can of the nature of the application and the reason for it. He should then make the application orally at the hearing.
3   See also CPR 23.4(2).
4   CPR 23.10.

Specific rules which apply to particular types of application common in defamation claims

22.12   The circumstances in which a party to a defamation action may wish to apply for a court order prior to the trial of the hearing are many and various. Whatever the nature of the application, it will usually be necessary to issue an application notice asking the court to make a certain order. The rules applicable to specific types of application tend to apply in addition to, as opposed to in place of, the general rules of CPR 23 about making applications for court orders[1].

The most common application (excepting simple applications for extension of time) is perhaps the application to strike out under CPR 3.4. An application under CPR 3.4 is not a defamation-specific application, but is considered below because it is often an invaluable weapon which is used not just on its own, but in tandem with or in the alternative on many other types of application. The defamation-specific applications considered below are applications for rulings on meaning and applications for summary disposal under section 8 of the DeA 1996. Applications for summary judgment under CPR 24 also merit brief consideration.

Other common applications which are beyond the scope of this book but worth highlighting are applications for further information about the other party's statement of case[2], 'unless orders' where a party has failed to comply with a court order or a provision of the

CPR, applications for specific disclosure[3], applications to amend a statement of case[4] and applications to disapply the one-year limitation period[5].

1   See, for example, CPR Pt 18 PD, paras 5.1–5.5 in relation to applications for further information, CPR Pt 53 PD, para 4 in relation to applications for rulings on meaning, CPR Pt 53 PD, para 5 in relation to applications for summary disposal and so on.
2   CPR 18.1.
3   See CPR 31.
4   See CPR 17.
5   The LA 1980, s 32A, as amended. See also Chapter 16.

Application to strike out

22.13   CPR 3.4 provides the court with the power to strike out a statement of case or any part thereof if it appears to the court:

(a)   that the statement of case discloses no reasonable grounds for bringing or defending the claim;

(b)   that the statement of case is an abuse of the court's process or is otherwise likely to obstruct the just disposal of the proceedings; or

(c)   that there has been a failure to comply with a rule, practice direction or court order.

The court may strike out a statement of case of its own initiative or following application by any party to the proceedings. Applications to strike out are commonly run in tandem with applications for rulings on meaning, summary judgment and so on.

So far as (a) is concerned, these include claims which set out no facts indicating what the claim is about, those which are incoherent and make no sense, and those which contain a coherent set of facts which, even if true, do not disclose any legally recognisable claim against the defendant[1]. In a defamation claim, a claim which does not set out facts or is incoherent is likely also to be in breach of the pleading requirements set out in CPR 53, and may therefore fall within ground (c) as well. A defence which discloses no reasonable grounds for defending the claim may consist of a bare denial, or set out no coherent statement of facts, or set out a coherent set of facts which, even if true, do not disclose any matter that would amount in law to a defence to the claim[2].

So far as (b) is concerned, this is said to include claims which are 'vexatious, scurrilous or obviously ill-founded'[3]. In *Wallis v Valentine*[4], the Court of Appeal upheld the judge's decision to strike out as an abuse of process, having regard to the overriding objective, a claim for libel where the only publication that could be proved was to the claimant's partner, who had been living with the claimant throughout the period in question and was fully aware of all that had transpired between the parties. This case is interesting because, as a matter of pure law, the claimant had an actionable claim for libel.

So far as (c) is concerned, the courts are likely to be cautious about making any strike out order if the effect of it is to deprive the claimant of his claim or the defendant of his defence because of Article 6 of the European Convention of Human Rights considerations.

1   See CPR Pt 3 PD, para 1.4.
2   See CPR Pt 3 PD, para 1.6.
3   See CPR Pt 3 PD, para 1.5.
4   [2002] EWCA Civ 1034, [2002] All ER (D) 275 (Jul).

22.14 Applications under CPR 3.4 should be made as soon as possible, ideally before allocation[1]. They should be made in the standard form of application notice and be compliant with CPR 23. Many applications under CPR 3.4 can be made without evidence, as the applicant will often be relying upon defects apparent on the face of the statement of case. However, the applicant should consider whether evidence is necessary and, if it is, should prepare and serve it in accordance with CPR 23. Where the application is made by the defendant in respect of the claimant's statement of case, and the defendant has not, at the time of the application, acknowledged service and/or filed and served a defence, the claimant is debarred from obtaining judgment in default until that application has been disposed of[2].

In order to decide an application to strike out, the court should approach the application making all assumptions in favour of the party against whom the application is made so far as pleadings of fact are concerned. The court must also assume that all those pleaded facts would be established in due course at trial[3].

Where a judge at a hearing strikes out all or part of a party's statement of case he may enter such judgment for the other party as that party appears entitled to[4].

1   CPR Pt 3 PD, para 5.1.
2   CPR 23.3(3)(a).
3   See *De Veronique Bataille v Newland* (4 September 2002, unreported), QBD. Presumably this would not be the case where pleadings of fact are themselves obviously ill-founded.
4   CPR Pt 3 PD, para 4(2).

Application for a ruling on meaning

22.15 The CPR require a claimant in a defamation action to specify in his particulars of claim the defamatory meaning which he alleges that the words or other matter complained of conveyed[1]. Likewise, a defendant who alleges that the words were true or fair comment on a matter of public interest is required to specify the meanings he attributes to the words or other matter complained of[2]. Once the defendant has received and reviewed the particulars of claim stating what the claimant alleges the meaning to be, or the claimant has received and reviewed the defendant's version of the meaning, an application to the court for a ruling on meaning should be considered.

An application for a ruling on meaning will usually be in an application to the court to determine whether (a) a statement complained of is capable of having any meaning attributed to it in a statement of case, and/or (b) whether the statement is capable of being defamatory of the claimant. The court may also decide (c) whether the statement is capable of bearing any other meaning defamatory of the claimant[3].

Any party may make an application for a ruling on meaning at any time after service of the particulars of claim and any application should be made promptly[4]. The application should be made to the judge in charge of the jury list but not to a Master or district judge. The reason for this is that the trial judge will be bound by the decision. The application should be made in the standard form of application notice[5]. The notice must state that it is an application for a ruling on meaning made in accordance with the Practice Direction to CPR 52[6]. Either the application notice or the evidence contained or referred to in it, or served with it, must identify precisely the statement, and the meaning attributed to it, that the court is being asked to consider[7].

Where an application is made for a ruling on meaning, it is common practice for skeleton arguments to be exchanged since the argument will be in essence legal and of some complexity. The leading cases on meaning are: *Skuse v Granada Television*[8]; *Mapp v News Group Newspapers*[9]; *Cruise v Express Newspapers*[10]; *Gillick v BBC*[11] and *Berkoff v Burchill*[12]. A recent example of a case in which a ruling on meaning was sought is that of *McCutcheon v CAN International*[13]. The well-known ex-*EastEnders* actress Martine McCutcheon brought proceedings over the publication of an article in *The Mirror* which she alleged meant she had sought to avoid paying a debt lawfully due to her former managers by cynically and dishonestly claiming it was in fact they who owed her money. The defendants sought to justify a less

223

serious meaning. The claimant applied for a ruling on meaning and the court ruled that the article was only capable of bearing a meaning that she had acted dishonestly and knew her assertion that her managers owed her money was untrue. The article was therefore not capable of bearing the meaning relied upon by the defendants. Note that the test on an application for a ruling on meaning is whether the words are *capable* of bearing any given meaning, not what they *actually* mean. The actual meaning of the words is for the jury to decide.

Following a ruling on meaning, the court may exercise its powers to strike out under CPR 3.4.

1 CPR Pt 53 PD, para 2.3.
2 CPR Pt 53 PD, paras 2.5 and 2.6.
3 See CPR Pt 53 PD, para 4.1.
4 CPR Pt 53 PD, para 4.2.
5 Form N244.
6 CPR Pt 53 PD, para 4.3.
7 CPR Pt 53 PD, para 4.4.
8 [1996] EMLR 278.
9 [1998] QB 520.
10 [1999] QB 931.
11 [1996] EMLR 267.
12 [1997] EMLR 139.
13 (19 December 2001, unreported).

Application for summary disposal or summary judgment

22.16 An application for summary disposal or summary judgment is an application to the court which, if successful, will finally determine either the claim or any issue within it which has no real prospect of succeeding at trial, but without a trial. Summary *disposal* is provided for by the DeA 1996 and is specific to claims for defamation. Summary *judgment* is provided for by CPR 24 and is of general application to all civil claims.

In both procedures, the court applies the identical test of whether there is any real prospect of success on the issue or claim which is the subject of the application[1]. If there is not, and there is no other reason for a trial, the issue or claim will be summarily adjudicated. In *Swain v Hillman*[2] Lord Woolf explained the test as follows: 'The words "no real prospect of succeeding" do not need any amplification, they speak for themselves. The word "real" distinguishes fanciful prospects of success or . . . they direct the court to the need to see whether there is a "realistic" as opposed to a "fanciful" prospect of success.'[3]

Since the summary disposal provisions of the DeA 1996 introduced a statutory procedure which removes the right to jury trial enshrined in section 69 of the Supreme Court Act 1981, it can be used to determine questions which section 69 provides should be decided by a jury. By contrast, CPR 24 cannot be so used[4]. An application for summary judgment under CPR 24 should only be made where the question is one which would be decided by the judge as opposed to the jury, that is either (a) a question of law or (b) where on the facts the judge would be entitled to withdraw an issue from consideration by a jury (namely where he concludes that on the evidence, taken at it highest, no reasonable jury properly directed could reach a certain conclusion).

An application for summary judgment or summary disposal will not be appropriate where the court can only determine whether there is any real prospect of success after conducting a 'mini trial'[5]. In *De Veronique Bataille v Newland*[6] one of the defendants made an application to the court to strike out and give summary judgment on the claimant's case on publication against him. The claimant claimed he had participated in the publication of a defamatory letter. The defendant maintained he had not. This was an application under CPR 24, and therefore the court could only give summary judgment against the claimant if it would be perverse for a jury to draw the inference that the defendant *had* participated in the publication of the defamatory letter. The court ruled that since it was impossible to determine this without conducting a 'mini trial' the matter should properly be left to the jury.

It is only on a section 8 (of the DeA 1996) application for summary disposal that a claimant may obtain an order for the publication of an apology. However, damages are limited to £10,000. By contrast, on a CPR 24 application the court has no power to order publication of an apology, but there is no statutory limit on the amount of damages that may be awarded and, once liability is established, damages may be assessed by the jury in the normal way. The applicable procedure and evidence on applications for (a) summary disposal and (b) summary judgment are considered below.

1   See *James Gilbert v MGN* [2000] EMLR 680 at 690–1.
2   [2001] 1 All ER 91.
3   [2001] 1 All ER 91 at 92J.
4   See *Safeway Stores v Tate* [2001] QB 1120, CA and *Alexander v Arts Council of Wales* [2001] EWCA Civ 514, [2001] 4 All ER 205.
5   *Swain v Hillman* [2001] 1 All ER 91 at 95, per Lord Woolf.
6   (4 September 2002, unreported), QBD.

Application for summary disposal under the Defamation Act 1996, ss 8 and 9

22.17   The DeA 1996, ss 8 and 9 provide that the court may dispose summarily of a claim for defamation in the following ways:

(a)   it may dismiss the claimant's claim if it appears to the court that it has no realistic prospect of success and there is no reason why it should be tried[1];

(b)   it may give judgment for the claimant and grant him summary relief if it appears to the court that there is no defence to the claim which has a realistic prospect of success and that there is no other reason why the claim should be tried[2].

In granting 'summary relief' the court may (i) give a declaration that the statement was false and defamatory of the claimant, (ii) order that the defendant publish or cause to be published a suitable correction or apology, (iii) award damages not exceeding £10,000, and/or (iv) make an order restraining the defendant from publishing or further publishing the matter complained of[3]. It should be noted that a court order ordering the publication of a correction or apology can only be obtained on summary disposal – there is no other judicial mechanism for obtaining such an outcome.

An application for summary disposal may be made at any time after the service of particulars of claim[4]. The application should be made to a judge because neither the Master nor the district judge has the power to grant a mandatory injunction.

An application notice for summary disposal should be made in the standard form of application notice[5] in that it should be compliant with the requirements of CPR 23. The applicant must state[6]:

(a)   on the application notice that it is an application for summary disposal made in accordance with the DeA 1996, s 8;

(b)   either in the application notice or the evidence contained or referred to in it or served with it must (i) identify concisely any point of law or provision in a document on which the applicant relies, and/or (ii) state that it is made because the applicant believes that on the evidence the respondent has no real prospect of succeeding on the claim or issue or (as the case may be) of successfully defending the claim or issue to which the application relates and in either case that the applicant knows of no other reason why the disposal of the claim or issue should await trial; and

(c)   in the application notice state whether or not the defendant has made an offer to make amends under section 2 of the DeA 1996 and whether or not it has been withdrawn[7].

1   The DeA 1996, s 8(2).
2   The DeA 1996, s 8(3).
3   The DeA 1996, s 9(1).
4   CPR Pt 53 PD, para 5.2.
5   Form N244.
6   CPR Pt 53 PD, para 5.1.
7   For further information on offer of amends, see Chapter 16.

22.18   As to other requirements, CPR 53.4(2) provides that CPR 24.4, CPR 24.5 and CPR 24. 6 (which govern procedure, evidence and directions on CPR 24 applications for summary judgment) apply also to applications for summary disposal under the DeA 1996, ss 8 and 9. Therefore, where a claimant applies for summary disposal against a defendant who has not yet filed a defence, he need not file a defence before the hearing[1]. Where a hearing date is fixed, either the respondent, or the parties if the hearing is fixed of the court's own initiative, must be given at least 14 days' notice of the date fixed for the hearing and the issues which it is proposed the court will decide at the hearing[2]. Where an application has been made, the respondent who wishes to rely on written evidence at the hearing must file and serve the witness statement at least seven days before the hearing. If the applicant then wishes to rely on any evidence in reply he must file and serve that evidence at least three days before the hearing[3]. Where the hearing has been fixed by the court of its own initiative any party who wishes to rely on evidence at the hearing must file and serve copies of his evidence on every other party at least seven days before the hearing, unless the court orders otherwise. Any party then wishing to rely on written evidence in reply to any other party's evidence must file and serve it on every other party at least three days before the hearing[4]. Evidence need not be filed if it has been filed already, or served if it has been served already[5].

On any application for summary disposal the court may direct the defendant to elect whether or not to make an offer of amends[6], and in doing so will specify the time by which and the manner in which the election is to be made, and notification of it is to be given to the court and the other parties[7].

The court will not act under section 8 of the DeA 1996 unless it is satisfied that summary relief will adequately compensate the claimant for the wrong he has suffered (ie that the claim is worth £10,000 or less), unless the claimant himself asks for summary relief[8]. In *Sir Alex*

Ferguson v Associated Newspapers Ltd[9] the defendant applied for summary disposal of the claim under sections 8 and 9 of the DeA 1996. The claimant had brought a claim for defamation, pleading two defamatory meanings, and a claim for malicious falsehood over the publication of a newspaper article. The second meaning and the malicious falsehood claim had been struck out and the defendant then brought a further application asking for summary disposal on the remaining meaning. The court expressed itself satisfied that summary relief under the section 8 procedure would adequately compensate the claimant even though the claimant had not sought summary disposal. It determined that the remaining meaning, namely that the claimant was 'so greedy and mercenary' that he was only happy to give extensive mid-match and post-match interviews if he was paid a substantial sum of money for doing so, was defamatory. However, it also concluded that the libel was not a grave one and in the light of the fact that the newspaper had published a correction, the court assessed damages at £7,500.

It should be noted that when the court determines a summary disposal application it may give directions as to the filing and service of a defence and/or give further directions about the management of the case.

1   CPR 24.4(2).
2   CPR 24.4(3).
3   CPR 24.5(1) and (2).
4   CPR 24.5(3).
5   CPR 24.5(4).
6   CPR 53.2(4) and see Chapter 16.
7   CPR 53.2(5).
8   The DeA 1996, s 8(3).
9   (15 March 2002, unreported), QBD.

CPR Pt 24 application for summary judgment

22.19   An application for summary judgment under CPR 24 may not be made if either an application for summary disposal has been made and not disposed of, or summary relief has been granted on an application for summary disposal. In contrast to an application for summary disposal under the DeA 1996, s 8, an application for summary judgment may only be made by a claimant once the defendant against whom the application is made has filed an acknowledgment of service or a defence[1]. Whereas a claimant must wait until an acknowledgment of service or defence has been filed, a defendant may apply for summary judgment at any time after the commencement of proceedings. For a DeA 1996, s 8 application for summary disposal, a defendant must wait until service of the particulars of claim. In practice, however, the most appropriate time for any summary judgment or disposal application is likely to be after service of the defence, since that is likely to be the earliest stage at which both parties will have fully stated their relative positions.

The application should be made in the standard form of application notice[2] in that it should be compliant with the requirements of CPR 23. It must also include a statement that it is an application for summary judgment made under CPR 24. The application notice or the evidence contained or referred to in it or served with it must (a) identify concisely any point of law or provision in a document on which the applicant relies, and/or (b) state that it is made because the applicant believes that on the evidence the respondent has no real prospect of succeeding on the claim or issue or (as the case may be) of successfully defending the claim or issue to which the application relates, and in either case that the applicant knows of no other reason why the disposal of the claim or issue should await trial. The application notice should also draw the attention of the respondent to CPR 24.5(1)[3]. Where the respondent is a litigant in person, it is advisable actually to set out the words of CPR 24.5(1), namely that if the respondent wishes to rely upon written evidence at the hearing, he must file the witness statement and serve copies of it on every other party at least seven days before the summary judgment hearing.

Although the CPR envisage that the hearing of the application will normally take place before a Master or a district judge[4], it is likely that the most appropriate forum in all but the most simple and straightforward defamation claims will be a judge. Whenever the application for summary judgment could involve the court ordering an injunction, the application must certainly be made to a judge since neither a Master nor district judge has jurisdiction to make such an order. Whenever the application may involve a ruling on meaning, it will also be advisable to make the application to the judge although the CPR (probably through oversight) does not prohibit such an application being made to a Master or district judge. Even where an application is made to a Master or district judge, he may direct that a judge should hear it[5].

1   Unless the court gives permission or a practice direction provides otherwise: CPR 24.1(i) and (ii).
2   Form N244.
3   CPR Pt 24 PD, para 2.
4   CPR Pt 24 PD, para 3(1).
5   CPR Pt 24 PD, para 3(2).

22.20 Where a hearing date is fixed, either the respondent, or the parties if the hearing is fixed of the court's own initiative, must be given at least 14 days' notice of the date fixed for the hearing and the issues which it is proposed the court will decide at the hearing[1]. Where an application has been made, the respondent who wishes to rely on written evidence at the hearing must file and serve the witness statement at least seven days before the hearing. If the applicant then wishes to rely on any evidence in reply he must file and serve that evidence at least three days before the hearing[2]. Where the hearing has been fixed by the court of its own initiative any party who wishes to rely on evidence at the hearing must file and serve copies of his evidence on every other party at least seven days before the hearing, unless the court orders otherwise. Any party then wishing to rely on written evidence in reply to any other party's evidence must file and serve it on every other party at least three days before the hearing[3]. Evidence need not be filed if it has been filed already, or served if it has been served already[4].

In *Blake v Associated Newspapers Ltd*[5] the defendant applied for summary judgment under CPR 24 on the basis that the claimant had no real prospect at trial of establishing malice, and thereby defeating a defence of qualified privilege. An article published by the defendant had asserted that the claimant was not a real bishop. The claimant had pleaded malice on the basis that he had gone through a valid ordination ceremony but that the defendant had deliberately closed its eyes to this fact when writing the article complained of. The defendant did not dispute the claimant's participation in the ceremony but contended that mere participation did not of itself establish the doctrinal validity and efficacy of ordination. The court held that there was nothing in the case pleaded by the claimant which was capable of supporting the inference that by publishing the words the defendant had acted dishonestly, because nothing the claimant had pleaded went to the root of the defendant's opinion that the claimant was not a real bishop. The court accordingly gave summary judgment for the defendant.

When the court determines a summary judgment application it may give directions as to the filing and service of a defence if one has not yet been served, and/or give further directions about the management of the case. Paragraph 5.1 of the Practice Direction to CPR 24 provides that the orders which a court may make on an application under CPR 24 include (a) judgment on the claim (or an issue therein), (b) the striking out or dismissal of the claim, (c) the dismissal of the application, or (d) a conditional order[6]. The court may also make an order dealing with costs. Where the court dismisses the application or makes an order that does not completely dispose of the claim, the court will give case management directions as to the future conduct of the case[7].

1   CPR 24.4(3).
2   CPR 24.5(1) and (2).
3   CPR 24.5(3).
4   CPR 24.5(4).
5   [2002] EWHC 677 (QB), [2002] All ER (D) 04 (Mar).
6   A conditional order will be made if it appears to the court that in respect of the claim or defence or some issue, it is possible that it may succeed but it is improbable. The order will require the party relying upon the improbable claim, defence or issue to pay a sum of money into court or to take a specified step in relation to his claim/defence or issue and which also provides that that party's claim will be dismissed or his statement of case struck out if he does not comply: CPR Pt 24 PD, para 5.2.
7   CPR Pt 24 PD, para 10.

Costs of applications

22.21   The general rule is that the court will make a summary assessment of costs at the conclusion of any application which has lasted less than one day[1], which means that it will assess them on the spot at the end of the hearing. The CPR place parties and their legal representatives under a duty to assist the court in making a summary assessment of costs by adhering to the following. Each party who intends to claim costs must prepare a schedule of the costs he intends to claim[2] which should follow Form N260[3] as closely as possible and should be filed with the court and served on any party against whom the costs order is sought as soon as possible and in any event not less than 24 hours before the hearing[4]. Where a party fails without reasonable excuse to comply with these requirements, this will be taken into account by the court in deciding what order to make about costs at the hearing, ie he is likely to be penalised on costs. The court may order that the costs assessed should be paid by some specified date or by instalments. If it does not do so the costs become 'automatically' payable under the rules within 14 days[5]. Where an order makes no mention of costs, none are payable in respect of the hearing to which it relates[6].

Costs considerations are dealt with in detail in Chapter 7.

Where it is not practicable to make a summary assessment of costs, the court will order detailed assessment of costs by a costs officer unless any rule, practice direction or other enactment provides otherwise[7].

1   CPR 44 13.2(2).
2   See CPR Pt 44 PD, para 13.5(2) for the detail – available on the Internet at www.lcd.gov.uk.
3   Available from www.courtservice.gov.uk.

4   CPR Pt 44 PD, para 13.5.
5   CPR 44.8.
6   CPR Pt 23 PD, para 13.2 and CPR 44.13(i).
7   See CPR 44.7(b).

Appeals

22.22 A party should consider appealing a ruling of the court whenever he is advised that the decision of the court on any application is wrong or is unjust because of a serious procedural or other irregularity. That party should also bear in mind the substantial increase in costs that will be incurred by the preparation for, and appearance at, any appeal hearing (which must of course be added to the costs of the original hearing) in determining whether it is advisable to appeal. What follows is a very broad and very brief overview of the applicable procedural rules in preparation for an appeal, but the reader is referred to the text of CPR 52 for the detail[1].

The general rules about appeals are found in CPR 52. The general principle is that an appeal lies to the next level of judge in the hierarchy, so an appeal from a decision of the Master or district judge will be to a High Court Judge, and an appeal from a High Court Judge will be to the Court of Appeal, and so on.

1   The CPR are available on the Internet at www.lcd.gov.uk.

Permission: CPR 52.3

22.23 Permission to appeal will be required and the application may be made to the lower court (that is, the court at which the decision to be appealed against was made) at which the decision to be appealed was made, or the appeal court in an appeal notice. Where the lower court refuses permission, a second application to the appeal court in an appeal notice is permitted, thus giving would-be appellants two bites at the cherry. Where the appeal court refuses permission to appeal without a hearing, the person seeking permission may request that the application for permission be dealt with at a hearing, but must file this request with the court within seven days of service of the notice that permission has been refused. Permission to appeal will only be given where the court considers that the appeal would have a real prospect of success or there is some other compelling reason why the appeal should be heard. The order giving permission may limit the issues to be heard and may be subject to conditions.

Appellant's notice: CPR 52.4

22.24 Whether or not permission has been granted, the person seeking to appeal (the 'appellant') must make his application to the appeal court in an appellant's notice. The notice must be in Form N161[1]. There is space on this form to set out the grounds of appeal. These should set out clearly why it is said (a) that the decision of the lower court is wrong, or (b) that the decision of the lower court is unjust because of a serious procedural or other irregularity. Where permission is sought the appellant's notice must also include an application for permission. The lower court may direct the period within such a notice must be filed or, if it does not, the notice must be filed 14 days after the date of the decision of the lower court sought to be appealed. When filing the notice, the appellant must lodge with the appeal court a bundle of relevant documents. Unless the appeal court directs otherwise, the appeal notice should be served on each party in whose favour the decision sought to be appealed was made (the 'respondent') as soon as practicable and in any event not later than seven days after filing.

Every represented appellant is required to prepare a skeleton argument which may either be inserted into section 8 of the appellant's notice, or otherwise provided as a separate document accompanying the appellant's notice. If that is not practicable it must be lodged with the court and served on the respondent within 14 days after filing the appellant's notice. All skeleton arguments for the appeal court should contain a numbered list of points stated in no more than a few sentences which should both define and confine the areas of controversy. Each point should be followed by references to any documentation on which the appellant proposes to rely[2]. The appellant should also consider what other information the court may need, which may include such matters as a list of persons featured in the case[3] and/or explanations of technical terms. A chronology of events will almost always be necessary. Where points of law are concerned, the cases relied upon should be cited with reference to the particular page(s) where the principle concerned is set out[4]. The appellant's notice should also be accompanied by an approved copy of the judgment of the lower court, where available, or a note of the judgment agreed between advocates, where it is not. Where one party is represented and the other is not, the representative must make his note of the judgment available promptly and free of charge to the unrepresented party[5].

1   CPR Pt 52 PD, para 5.1.
2   CPR Pt 52 PD, para 5.10.

3 The 'dramatis personae'.
4 CPR Pt 52 PD, para 5.11.
5 CPR Pt 52 PD, para 5.12.

Respondent's notice: CPR 52.5

22.25 A respondent *may* file a respondent's notice, but he *must* file one if he is either seeking permission to appeal from the appeal court, or if he wishes to ask the appeal court to uphold the order of the lower court for reasons different from, or additional to those given by the lower court. The notice should be in Form N162 and the different/additional grounds relied upon should be entered in section 6 of that notice. Where he is seeking permission he must state this in the respondent's notice. Where the respondent seeks only to uphold the judgment of the court below for the reasons given by that court, he is not required to file a respondent's notice. However, in practice, it is a rare case where no such notice is filed since it affords the respondent the opportunity to argue his case prior to any oral hearing.

The respondent must provide a skeleton argument in all cases where he proposes to address arguments to the court[1]. This may be inserted into section 7 of the appellant's notice or provided as a separate document either accompanying the notice or lodged and served within 21 days after filing of the notice[2]. The skeleton should conform with the requirements of CPR Pt 52 PD, paras 5.10 and 5.11 and should, where appropriate, answer the arguments set out in the appellant's skeleton argument[3].

The lower court may have directed the date by which the notice must be filed. If it does not, the notice must be filed 14 days after either (a) the date the respondent is served with the appellant's notice where permission to appeal was given by the lower court, (b) the date the respondent is served with notification that the appeal court has given the appellant permission to appeal, or (c) the date the respondent is served with notification that the application for permission and the appeal itself are to be heard together. As with the appellant's notice, the respondent's notice must be served on the appellant and any other respondent as soon as practicable and in any event not later than seven days after it is filed.

1 CPR Pt 52 PD, para 7.6.
2 CPR Pt 52 PD, para 7.7.
3 CPR Pt 52 PD, para 7.9.

Chapter 23

Preparations for the trial

General

23.01 Time spent in preparation for trial is never time wasted! Invariably events take on a momentum of their own in the run up to trial; an organised and methodical approach to pre-trial preparations is therefore essential. Anticipation, organisation and preparation are the key factors. To a large extent preparations are dictated by the CPR. However, there are further considerations to bear in mind.

Defamation actions are subject to the multi-track rules[1]. In the allocation questionnaire, parties will have indicated that the claim is one in defamation and, as such, must be tried in the High Court[2]. Preparations for trial will therefore be focused on trial by jury at the Royal Courts of Justice (or occasionally a district registry).

In the usual course of events, an order will have been made at the case management conference containing directions for the progress of the case, including directions allocating a trial date or window trial, and, in an appropriate case, fixing a date for a pre-trial review.

1 CPR Pt 29 PD, para 2.
2 By virtue of the CCA 1984, s 15(2)(c) – unless the parties have agreed to trial in the county court.

Pre-trial checklists (CPR 29.6 and CPR Pt 29 PD)

23.02 At the case management conference, the court will probably have specified a date for completed pre-trial checklists to be lodged. These will be served on the parties 14 days prior to the date they must be filed. When the court receives completed checklists from all parties to the action (usually not later than eight weeks before trial), it will assess what directions have been complied with, consider any outstanding issues and will probably direct that there should be a pre-trial review. It is advisable that parties exchange copies of their pre-trial checklists. The checklist is Form N170.

This should be served and filed not later than eight weeks before the trial or the start of the trial period. The objectives of the pre-trial checklists are to:

(a) fix the trial date;
(b) confirm the estimated length of the trial;
(c) set a timetable for the trial;
(d) decide whether or not to have a pre-trial review.

The form is divided into five parts (see paragraphs 23.03–23.07).

Directions complied with

23.03 If directions remain outstanding, the parties must explain why, and how they will be complied with. A draft order should be filed if any specific further directions are sought. Preferably, these should be agreed with the other party in advance. Otherwise, the court is likely to give directions in relation to any expert evidence, the trial bundle (see paragraphs 23.11–23.15 below) and the trial timetable/time estimate.

Experts

23.04 Written reports or oral evidence? If the latter, that must be justified and details of the experts provided. The availability of the expert witnesses should be provided.

Other witnesses

23.05 The number, names and addresses of the witnesses of fact who the parties are planning to call must be given. If any statements are agreed, that should be noted. Problems with availability or with witnesses requiring special facilities should be raised.

Legal representation

23.06 Litigant in person or representation by lawyers? Again, availability problems should be raised.

Other matters

23.07   For example, a time estimate for the duration of the trial or
whether it will be necessary to have electronic equipment in court for
the trial, perhaps to show the jury a video of a programme complained
of by the claimant.

Pre-trial review (CPR 29.8)

23.08   The CPR envisage that pre-trial review will take place eight to
ten weeks prior to trial, but in practice it can be as little as three or
four days before the trial is due to begin. The pre-trial review will be
heard by the judge allocated to the action and serves as a useful means
of 'housekeeping' – identifying outstanding procedures and evidential
matters, dealing with preliminary applications and any amendments to
pleadings. Additionally, the judge may choose to make directions in
relation to the conduct of the trial itself.

Typical matters to be dealt with at the pre-trial review are:

- whether disclosure of all documentary evidence is complete;
- whether there are any further applications to be made in relation
  to either witness or documentary evidence;
- the time estimate for the trial;
- the preparation and organisation of jury (and any other)
  bundles;
- the fixing of the date/week/place of trial;
- any unique direction (or directions) for the conduct of the trial.

Communication between the parties in advance of the pre-trial review
is always beneficial. If, for example, an order or part of an order
sought can be agreed by the parties in advance, court time will be
saved, and costs thereby kept to a minimum. Any remaining issues will
have been clearly identified in correspondence and can therefore be
canvassed before the trial judge with concision.

Statement of issues

23.09   At the pre-trial review, the court may direct that a statement of
issues between the parties at trial should be prepared. The purpose of
a statement of issues is to assist the court (and the parties) in

identifying the areas of contention between the parties on which the judge or the jury will be required to make a decision. This may be incorporated into the skeleton argument lodged by counsel.

Skeleton arguments

23.10 The date for exchange and lodging of skeleton arguments will either be the subject of a court order (probably at the pre-trial review, if not before) or will be agreed between counsel for the parties. Exchange is normally simultaneous. The preparation of a skeleton argument is the responsibility of counsel, and he may or may not choose to forward a draft to his instructing solicitor prior to lodging it with the judge and exchanging it with his opponent. Where time permits, many barristers will send a draft copy of the skeleton argument to instructing solicitors for comments from them and/or the client prior to lodging and exchange. This practice has the obvious benefit of ensuring that all persons involved in the case are content with the way that counsel proposes to run the argument at trial, and should be encouraged. At the very least, counsel should, as a matter of courtesy, ensure that a copy of the skeleton argument is provided to instructing solicitors at the time of exchange and lodging. Responsibility for lodging the skeleton argument with the court and exchange with opposing counsel prior to the pre-trial review and/or trial also lies with counsel, and the skeleton will be lodged by counsel's clerk together with the bundle of authorities to be relied on.

The skeleton argument is intended to provide a concise summary of the party's submission/case and should be as brief as possible. It is a useful opportunity to familiarise the judge with the factual background of the case, which may be complex. It is good practice for the skeleton to include a chronology of key events – perhaps instructing solicitors could offer to assist in the preparation of this.

Jury bundles

23.11 The trial bundle in a defamation case is of particular importance because of the presence of a jury. What this means is that almost inevitably one will in fact need two bundles – one for the jury and one for the judge.

It is essential that the jury bundle is as user-friendly as possible. One must fight against the lawyer's natural tendency to include everything plus the metaphorical kitchen sink (an instinct which is generally encouraged by one's client who is convinced that once the jury is taken through the four lever arch files of accounts documents, the trial will be as good as won!). User-friendly means slender, and so considerable thought must be applied to which documents really need to be before the jury. During the course of the trial, the bundle will almost inevitably be swelled by the addition of further documents, the relevance and importance of which emerges as the trial unfolds.

What the jury will not have in its bundle is the statement of case and copies of the witness statements. What it will need is a copy of the words complained of and the key documents relevant to that publication, along with the letter of claim and response. Indeed, the importance of the letter of claim is never better demonstrated than by the position it assumes in a defamation trial bundle. The tone and content of that letter can form an impression about the relative merits of the parties and their cases in the jury's mind, which is hard to change.

23.12 Ideally the contents of the jury bundle should be agreed between the parties. However, this is not always the reality. Each party may have different and equally strongly held views about documents which should be included and excluded.

If agreement is not possible, it is common for the parties' counsel to attempt to introduce documentary evidence during evidence given by live witnesses and for the trial judge then to make decisions on their relevance and admissibility. Using this method, documents are added to the bundle 'on the hoof' once the trial has started. However, this can result in interrupted evidence and frequent arguments between counsel for the parties in the absence of the jury, to the detriment of the smooth conduct of the trial before the jury.

The jury bundle should contain only those documents which each party believes are necessary for the jury to make an informed decision. Keep it simple and straightforward – remember the jury is comprised of ordinary men and women who will not be interested in and do not need to know every nuance of the case. They are not lawyers. A case which may have commanded a lawyer's attention for a number of years must be reduced to a form digestible to the lay person – and a concise jury bundle is a good starting point. A voluminous bundle could actually do more harm than good: the jury may be side-tracked from the main issues and a perverse verdict (with all the attendant costs on appeal) could result.

Jury bundles are usually shared one between two jurors. They must be paginated and, where appropriate, the documents be divided. Their contents should be presented in a clear and logical order. Copies should be available for the judge, jury, witness box, counsel for the claimant and defendant and solicitors and, of course, the parties themselves. Occasionally, juries are asked to consider two or more separate bundles, eg claimant's and defendant's bundles.

Parties should begin the process of agreeing the contents of the jury bundle as early as possible because the process is often contentious, and therefore time-consuming, and even more so because input from counsel is required. Preparation will usually be dealt with by the claimant's solicitors, so the impetus should come from them if they want to avoid preparing bundles in the small hours before the trial commences.

Lodging bundles

23.13 Directions at the case management conference/pre-trial review may provide for lodging of bundles. In any event, CPR 39.5(2) provides that the claimant should lodge his bundle not less than three and no more than seven days before the trial.

Reading list and time estimate

23.14 When bundles are lodged for the trial judge, the claimant should also lodge at the same time:

- the reading list for trial judge;
- the estimated length of reading time; and
- the estimated length of the hearing/trial.

Practice Direction (RCJ: Reading List Time Estimates) (1999)[1] provides that this list should be signed by all advocates together with their name, business address and telephone number.

1   [2002] 1 All ER 640.

Other bundles for the judge

23.15 It is inevitable that the judge will be required to consider the statements of case and witness evidence either at pre-trial review applications or at the commencement of or during the trial. Paginated and clearly labelled bundles of the statements of case and witness evidence of all the parties should therefore be prepared – perhaps before the pre-trial review – and lodged for the judge. Copy bundles should be prepared for all other parties to ensure that everyone is working from the same paginated texts, making reference easy for counsel and for the judge. Responsibility for the preparation of such bundles again usually falls upon the claimant's solicitors, unless they do not have adequate facilities for mass reproduction of documents, in which case the defendant's solicitors should perform the task if better equipped.

The trial bundle which one prepares and files for the judge pursuant to CPR PD 39A will include the documents which would expect to find in any civil action, namely:

(a)   the claim form and all statements of case;
(b)   a case summary/chronology where appropriate;
(c)   requests for further information and responses to those requests;
(d)   witness statements and any witness summaries;
(e)   notices of intention to rely on hearsay evidence under CPR 32.2 and any notices of intention to rely on evidence such as plans, photographs or models pursuant to CPR 33.6;
(f)   any experts' reports and responses to them;
(g)   any order giving directions as to the conduct of the trial; and
(h)   any other relevant documents.

The trial bundle must be paginated continuously and indexed with a description of each document in the bundle. One would normally expect the use of dividers to assist the easy location of documents in the bundle if there are more than 100 pages.

Try to agree the contents of the trial bundle with the other parties. However, it is a rare defamation trial which does not feature a 'battle of the bundles' at its outset.

Witness evidence

23.16   Mutual exchange of witness statements of fact should have taken place pursuant to the directions provided at the case management conference. However, there may be reasons why witness statement exchange has not taken place, or a party may wish to adduce additional witness evidence or serve a supplemental witness statement. If a witness statement is not served within the time provided, the rules provide that the witness cannot be called to give oral evidence without the permission of the court. These are matters which should be dealt with at the pre-trial review, having put all relevant parties on notice. It will be necessary to prepare a witness statement in support of any such application, outlining the reason(s) for the late application to the court.

Witness summonses

23.17 A party may have served a signed witness statement of fact or perhaps a summary of the evidence it is hoped/anticipated that a witness will be able to give at trial. For a number of reasons, the witness may require service of a witness summons compelling him to attend trial and give evidence (eg employment circumstances may require this), or service of a summons may be necessary to compel a reluctant witness to attend.

Similarly, a witness summons may be required to compel a witness to attend court and produce specified documents[1].

1   CPR 34.2(1).

Procedure

23.18 The format of the witness summons is Form N20[1]. One witness summons is required per witness/document.

Two copies of the witness summons should be filed with the court to be sealed – one summons will be retained on the court file and one served by the court or returned for service. It may be advisable to consider personal service (by process server) in some circumstances. Also, keep copies of all sealed witness summonses issued and served for reference.

The summons will require the witness to attend and give evidence and/or produce the documents at trial or on a date specified by the court. This can be indicated on the form. Parties may wish to consider inviting the witness producing documents to attend at court at a date earlier than trial pursuant to the provisions laid down in *Khanna v Lovell White Durrant*[2]. This will avoid contested hearings taking place at the outset of a trial. The witness may even agree to produce documents voluntarily once a witness summons has been served. This would avoid any attendance at court. On occasions, production of documents may be resisted, in which case, the trial judge must hear an application for the production of the documents and the arguments opposing production, and give judgment accordingly.

1   This form is available from the court office or may be downloaded from www.courtservice.gov.uk.
2   [1994] 4 All ER 267, ChD.

Conduct money

23.19 It is usual to provide witnesses with conduct money at the time of service of the witness summons to cover out of pocket expenses. The witness should be advised that receipts and invoices must be produced to verify any claims for additional expenses, loss of earnings, etc[1].

1   CPR 34.7 and CPR Pt 34 PD, paras 3.1–3.3.

Permission of the court

23.20 In a number of instances, the court's permission is required prior to the issue of a witness summons, otherwise the procedure is straightforward. Issue and service of witness summonses should not be left until the last minute – both for this reason and because it may cause a witness unnecessary difficulty in attending.

Circumstances where the permission of the court is required are provided in CPR 34.3(2) and include where a party intends to issue a summons:

(a)   less than seven days before trial;
(b)   for a witness to attend court to give evidence or produce documents on any date except the date fixed for trial, ie at an interim hearing;
(c)   for a witness to attend court to give evidence or produce documents at any hearing except the trial.

The court will serve the summons unless a written request is made on issue for the issuing party to effect service. It may be a wise precaution to arrange for service yourself if the attendance of the witness is vital.

Formal admissions of fact (CPR 32.18)

23.21 You should consider, together with counsel and your client, whether it would be prudent and cost-effective prior to trial:

(a)   to make any formal admissions of fact; and/or
(b)   to invite your opponent(s) to make any admissions of fact.

243

This will avoid the necessity (and attendant cost) of either side proving facts at trial.

A fact can be admitted in correspondence, in pleadings or in a response to a notice to admit (Form N266)[1]. A fact can be admitted wholly or in part. A notice to admit must be served no later than 21 days before trial.

1   This form is available from the court office or may be downloaded from www.courtservice.gov.uk.

Proving documents (CPR 32.19)

23.22   Pursuant to CPR 32.19, a party is deemed to admit the authenticity of a document disclosed under CPR 31 unless a notice is served specifying that the document should be proved at trial. Such notices must have been served:

(a)   by the latest date for mutual exchange of witness statements; or
(b)   within seven days of disclosure,

whichever is the latest[1]. You should check your files therefore to ensure whether:

(a)   there are documents which you are required to prove at trial, and make the necessary arrangements to do so; or
(b)   there are documents in connection with which you need to serve or have served notice on your opponent(s) to prove at trial.

1   The correct form is Form N268 – Notice to Prove Documents at Trial. This form is available from the court office or may be downloaded from www.courtservice.gov.uk.

Conferences with counsel

23.23   Without doubt, any trial will be preceded by at least one and probably several conferences with either junior and/or leading counsel. As with other matters, it will assist the client and counsel if these can be arranged with adequate notice to all concerned. Invariably, there will be further tasks to be undertaken after a pre-trial conference with counsel. The earlier the first of these conferences takes place, therefore, the better.

Conferences with counsel should not be used as an opportunity to 'coach' witnesses; this is precluded by Code of Conduct for the Bar of England and Wales, which states at paragraph 705:

'a barrister must not (a) rehearse practice or coach a witness in relation to his evidence or the way in which he should give it; (b) place a witness under any pressure to provide other than a truthful account of his evidence'.

Brief to counsel

23.24 Counsel's brief fee and daily refresher should be agreed with counsel's clerk. It is usual practice that once the trial brief is delivered to counsel, the brief fee becomes payable. Ensure therefore that all settlement opportunities are exhausted prior to incurring what will be a considerable disbursement.

Counsel's brief should include a summary of the case to date, the evidence and the issues between the parties. Counsel will, however, be fully familiar with the case by now. You should include copies of all relevant documents, bundles and any relevant documents/ correspondence. Always keep counsel copied in on relevant party/ party correspondence.

Party/party correspondence

23.25 It is good practice to maintain a paginated bundle of relevant party/party correspondence, and to have copies available at court hearings and at trial. This may have been included in the pre-trial review bundles but should be kept updated. The trial judge can be directed to this during any applications which may arise and the exchanged correspondence may be useful in support of any costs applications made. The bundle should be prepared in chronological order from front to back with the earliest letter first and the most recent last.

Practical considerations

23.26 There are a number of procedural requirements which will tax you in the pre-trial period. However, the practical considerations which can make a huge difference to the smooth running of a trial should not be ignored.

The following is a list of suggestions which may be relevant.

Client

- Accommodation and travel for duration of the trial to be arranged.
- Familiarise the client with the court room if possible, and the layout of the court building.
- Advise the client of the conduct of the trial (ie what will happen and when, where he will sit, where and when he will give evidence).
- How evidence should be given (ie addressed to the judge/jury and at an audible volume).
- Refresh the client's memory with key documents and witness statements.

Witnesses

- Keep witnesses informed of date(s) required to attend trial as far as possible.
- Keep communication lines open with witnesses at all times; their co-operation is essential, so keep them informed of any developments. Maintaining the good will of witnesses is important.
- Ensure the witness has a signed copy of his witness statement and key documents prior to giving evidence.
- Make arrangements to meet with the witness at court on the day he is required to attend.
- Arrange accommodation and travel for witnesses if necessary.
- As with the client, it is a good idea to familiarise the witness with such matters as the court room if at all possible, as well as how to give evidence and so on. A good way of acclimatising is for a witness to turn up slightly early and watch the witness before him or her give evidence.

Electronic equipment

- Arrange delivery and installation of any electronic equipment required for trial with the appropriate company, and in liaison with your opponent and the court staff.

Settlement

23.27   If settlement is agreed between the parties, obviously the court (including the trial judge and the listing clerk) should be notified at the earliest opportunity. Equally, all witnesses should be notified – do not underestimate the inconvenience to witnesses of arranging to attend a trial and give evidence unnecessarily.

Chapter 24

Trial and post-trial

Introduction

24.01 No potential defamation claimant should start proceedings without being prepared to contest his action all the way to trial if necessary. Indeed, he would be well advised to sit in on a day or two of a libel trial at Court 12 or 13 at the Royal Courts of Justice in the Strand (the usual venue) in order to experience, at second hand at least, the peculiar drama and pressure that these occasions inevitably present. Most defamation claims are settled or abandoned long before trial – perhaps only 1% or 2% of the actions which are issued actually end up going all the way. However, every step and every aspect of the preparations carried out by solicitors and counsel should be taken with an eye very firmly on how 'it will play' at trial.

There is a notional structure to the procedure of a defamation trial but, as with a jazz tune, there can be many variations on the theme and scope for improvisation. Generally, the trial should take place within the 'window' which will have been specified by the trial judge many months earlier at the case management conference[1]. At the same time, a time estimate for the trial will have been set by the judge following submissions from the parties' representatives based principally on the number of witnesses who are likely to be called and the complexity of the issues and the documentation.

1   CPR 29.2(2).

Trial bundles

24.02 Before the trial begins, agree and finalise the bundles of documents to be used by the court. There will generally be two separate bundles – the 'jury' bundle which will be used by the jury members, judge, advocates, solicitors and the witnesses, and a second 'legal' bundle which will be used just by the advocates, solicitors and judge. The latter will contain documents such as the statements of case and witness statements which might confuse, mislead or prejudice the jury if they saw them. There are two inevitables about the court bundles[1]: first, that despite the requirement that they be agreed and filed at court not less than three and no more than seven days before the trial, the arguments about their contents will persist not only to the start of the trial but often throughout its duration. Second, despite the urging of the court and the unanimous agreement of the parties that the bundles should be kept as slender as possible, they will grow as alarmingly as a politician's election promises. The sheer volume of paperwork at a defamation trial can be daunting. A minimum of 20 copies of the 'jury' bundle will be needed, and a minimum of seven copies of the 'legal' bundle. In reality, caution, and the Bermuda Triangle qualities of a courtroom, mean many more copies will be stashed in plastic crates between the double doors that lead into Courts 12 and 13.

1   See Chapter 23.

Legal argument

24.03   A trial will often begin with legal argument on a variety of potential issues before the jury is empanelled. These submissions may relate to such matters as the admissibility of certain documents, the evidence of certain witnesses or the order in which the issues between the parties are to be tried. Sometimes these matters will take several days to resolve, although the judge will be unimpressed if they could and should have been dealt with at an earlier case management conference or pre-trial review hearing.

Empanelling the jury

24.04   As mentioned previously, defamation actions are generally tried at the Royal Courts of Justice in the Strand, and the jury courts are normally Courts 12 and 13. The 12 jury members will usually be drawn from the group which has been assembled for criminal trials at the Old Bailey and they in turn will have come from the south east of London and/or Essex. The jury of 12 is drawn by lots from 16 potential members who are ushered into court. Each jury member then enters the jury box and reads the jury oath or affirmation. They may well in addition be asked one or more questions to determine whether there is a risk they may be inherently in favour of one party or the other. For example, where the claimant is a police officer, they may each be asked whether they have a close association with serving or retired police officers or with the newspaper which is defendant in the case[1]. The jury members themselves may raise an objection to being empanelled, something which tends to relate to the length rather than the nature of the case. The trial judge decides whether they may be excused but tends to give short shrift to such requests. An example of where a jury member might be excused is if he runs a small business which would be put in jeopardy if he was absent for three weeks or so[2]. Once they have been empanelled, the jury will be scrutinised with the intensity of horses in a parade ring by the lawyers and the parties for the duration of the trial – every facial expression and fidget being interpreted and discussed. Despite all this attention, juries tend to be notoriously inscrutable – a fact which adds to the drama and tension of a defamation trial.

1 *Bennett v Guardian Newspapers Ltd* (1997) Times, 27 February.
2 *Gladding v Channel Four Television Corpn* [1999] EMLR 475.

Preliminary issues

24.05 If the judge decides, or is persuaded, that the determination of a particular issue at the outset of the trial might save costs and time then he has the power to order it. Since the coming into force of the CPR, judges are of course actively encouraged to take a more hands-on approach to case management. In defamation, the issue most likely determined as a preliminary issue is meaning. An example which pre-dated the CPR occurred in *Marks & Spencer plc v Granada Television*[1] when a *World in Action* documentary alleged goods marked 'made in the UK' were in fact being produced by child labour in Morocco. Marks & Spencer said the programme meant that they knew about this mis-description and the child labour, the defendant said it meant no more than that Marks & Spencer had shown a lack of responsible care in these matters. The trial judge decided meaning should be determined as a preliminary issue and, as he no doubt anticipated, once the issue was determined in the claimant's favour, the defendant settled the action without attempting to justify the higher meaning in a lengthy trial. A more recent example occurred in *Gregson v Channel Four Television Corpn*[2] when the judge ordered that the jury rule on the parties' different submissions as to the meaning of a *Trial and Error* documentary. In that case, the jury decided the programme meant there were strong grounds to suspect the claimant had planted a vital piece of evidence at a crime scene and there were strong grounds to suspect that he had thereby knowingly assisted in bringing about the wrongful conviction of a husband for the murder of his wife, but did not find other meanings claimed for the programme by the claimant. An additional point of interest in that case was that the jury was not told that a decision had already been made to try the case before a judge alone after the determination of meaning had been made. The jury was therefore discharged once they had given their decision on the preliminary issue. Although the trial continued after the meaning ruling, it was only a matter of days before the parties reached a negotiated settlement of the claim.

1   (11 February 1998, unreported).
2   [2002] EWCA Civ 941, [2002] All ER (D) 66 (Jul).

The claimant's case

24.06   The claimant's counsel will generally open the trial before the judge and jury by making his opening speech. It is of course a critical part of the advocacy: after all the preamble of the trial preliminaries, let alone the many months which have probably passed since the proceedings were issued, it is the first time that the jury which will decide the case is introduced to the words complained of by the claimant, the claimant himself, why the case has been brought, and the themes of the action from the claimant's point of view. The speech must accurately reflect the case being brought and must not overstate the pleaded meaning or inaccurately pre-empt the witness evidence to follow. The opportunity will be taken to introduce the jury to the bundle of documents sitting in front of each of its members. If the action concerns a television or radio programme, then the technology to enable the court to view or hear the programme must have been installed in the court room in advance. Defamation claimants tend to be most successful when their case is simply understood and the trial never departs too far from the words complained of. The clarity of the opening speech sets the tone for the trial.

Although the defendant's opening speech sometimes follows the claimant's (and indeed sometimes the whole running order is reversed to allow the defendant's case to come first, as in the *Hamilton v Al Fayed* action[1]), generally once the claimant's opening speech has finished, the claimant's witnesses are called to give evidence. This almost invariably means the claimant himself is first in the witness box. Each witness is examined-in-chief by the other party's advocate and then (if necessary) re-examined by his own advocate. The witnesses who are called will all either have provided witness statements which have been exchanged during the case, or witness summaries will have been served on their behalf if, for whatever reason, they did not or could not provide a statement. If they are unable to attend court for a reason under the Civil Evidence Act 1995, then their statement may be read out[2] . Copies of the witness statements/witness summaries will be included in the 'legal' bundle. One hopes one's witnesses will attend voluntarily, but sometimes, particularly if a witness is giving evidence principally because of the job or office he holds, then it will be necessary to compel their attendance by means of a witness summons[3].

Examination-in-chief should exclude leading questions but should elicit the witness's evidence on all issues on which he can give admissible evidence. It is clearly important that in a defamation case, the injury to the claimant's reputation and the hurt caused to him should be drawn out by the claimant's counsel since the jury will in part be compensating the claimant for those elements should it find in his favour. The evidence from the witnesses must deal with the rebuttal of the matters where the burden of proof lies with the defendant (notably justification) as well as the areas where the burden is with the claimant (for example, identification).

1   [2001] 1 AC 395.
2   CPR 33.2(2). Where a party intends to rely on hearsay evidence at trial that is contained in a witness statement of a person who is *not* being called to give oral evidence, the party must, when serving that statement, inform the other parties (in the covering letter) that the witness is not being called to give evidence and give the reason why the witness will not be called.
3   CPR 34.3; Form N20.

Cross-examination

24.07   Cross-examination does permit leading questions, and a skilled advocate deploys the cross-examination of the claimant in particular to try to raise doubts in the jury about his case and his reputation. The defendant has to put forward his case when cross-examining a witness, so if its counsel is arguing the claimant is a liar or a crook, then questions to this effect must be put to the claimant. In a defamation action, a claimant is presumed to be of good reputation, and if the defendant disputes that, then its counsel will cross-examine the claimant as to credit. In determining the parameters of cross-examination as to credit, the trial judge has a key role. In *Bennett v Guardian Newspapers*[1], the late George Carman QC's cross-examination of a police officer was deemed to have gone too far by Mr Justice French, a ruling upheld by a hastily constituted Court of Appeal. That led to the trial restarting with a newly empanelled jury. Generally, however, the defendant's counsel will be given some leeway in attacking a claimant and his witnesses in cross-examination and will know that the claimant's counsel will be reluctant to demonstrate an over-protective attitude towards his client in front of the jury in the face of hostile questioning.

1   (1997) Times, 27 February.

Re-examination

24.08   Once the defendant's counsel has completed his cross-examination of the claimant (and each of his subsequent witnesses), the claimant's counsel is entitled to re-examine. The general purpose of this is to clarify matters raised in cross-examination and also to draw the jury's attention to the additional distress and damage which may have been caused to the claimant by a particularly brutal cross-examination. It will normally be fairly brief.

The defendant's case

24.09   The pattern established by the claimant's case is repeated in relation to the defendant. Each witness is called, examined-in-chief and then cross-examined. Since the defendant will usually be a media organisation, a key tactical decision will be whether or not to put the journalist and/or editor in the witness box. A jury will always be surprised, and perhaps somewhat cynical, if a journalist who is prepared to dish it out in the article complained of is not prepared to take it in the witness box.

Submission of no case to answer

24.10   At the conclusion of either the claimant's or the defendant's case, the other party's counsel may make a submission that there is no case to put to the jury. In relation to the defendant's case, the claimant's counsel may argue that the evidence presented to the court has been insufficient to support one aspect or another of the pleaded case and it should be withdrawn from the jury. Alternatively, the defendant's counsel may submit the claimant has not made out malice (to defeat a defence of fair comment[1] or qualified privilege[2]).

1 See Chapter 13.
2 See Chapter 15.

Closing speeches

24.11 The defendant's counsel will generally make the first closing speech and the claimant's counsel will follow him. In *Anglesea v HTV, Independent Newspapers and Pressdram*[1], the defendants had been represented by two QCs (and their juniors) and successfully argued that they should each be allowed closing speeches which were made consecutively before the claimant's leading counsel made his speech. The fact that the claimant gets the last word is undoubtedly an advantage on the face of it. Although closing speeches will be more forceful affairs than the opening speeches, they must still be confined to the boundaries of the pleaded cases and should not distort or reinterpret evidence given during the trial (or not given[2]). Counsel can, however, make submissions to the jury on the appropriate level of damages they should award if the claimant is successful. For obvious reasons, the defendant's counsel will be reluctant to make such a submission.

1 (22 November 1994, unreported).
2 *Gladding v Channel Four Television Corpn* [1999] EMLR 475.

Judge's summing up

24.12 Once the closing speeches have been delivered, the judge sums up the case for the jury by précising the evidence which has been presented to them and also directing them on the relevant law. He may also give some guidance on the possible level of damages should they find for the claimant – which may be by reference to personal injury awards. The summing up should be (but rarely is) neutral and without bias to one party or the other. If either party believes the judge has misdirected the jury on the law or has summed up incorrectly, then it should be raised by their counsel at the conclusion of the summing up before the jury retires to enable the judge to correct the error if it is possible to do so. The Court of Appeal is reluctant to order a re-trial at any time and that is particularly the case when the appeal is based on objections to a judge's summing up, although occasionally such appeals are successful[1].

1 *Reynolds v Times Newspapers Ltd* [201] 2 AC 127.

Jury retires to consider verdict

24.13   The jury will retire at the end of the judge's summing up to consider its verdict – but not before it has been given the questions it has to answer. Normally there will be two questions:

(a)   Do you find for the claimant or the defendant?
(b)   If you find for the claimant, then what sum do you award in damages?

However, there are circumstances in which the jury might be asked a series of questions. The decision about what questions should be put to the jury lies with the trial judge following any submissions from counsel. If the parties' counsel agree on the questions then the judge will normally allow them to go to the jury. The emphasis should always be on simplicity and clarity and there is an understandable reluctance to confront the jury with a long, complicated list of questions. However, this may be unavoidable in, say, a qualified privilege case in the post-*Reynolds* era where the judge has to know what the jury's finding is on various questions of fact in order to determine whether the defence can apply as a matter of law on the facts as found.

Frequently, the jury will raise questions during their deliberations. These will be relayed to the judge, who will pass them on to the parties' counsel (in the absence of the jury) and, after hearing their views, the judge will communicate his response.

The verdict and the judgment

24.14   It is always hoped that a verdict will be unanimous, but if the jury has been unable to agree, the judge can allow a majority verdict of 11:1 or 10:2. It is a matter of judgment for him as to when he gives such a direction to the jury. Experience suggests the jury will be allowed to deliberate for about a day before the judge will give a majority direction. If the parties agree, any majority verdict could be returned up to 7:5. If there is a hung jury, then a re-trial will be ordered. Once the jury has delivered its verdict, the judge will enter judgment accordingly. The legal arguments at this stage tend to focus on whether a final injunction is appropriate (it will inevitably have formed part of the claimant's statement of case) and on the issue of costs. The latter will certainly be a matter for argument when, for example, there has been a CPR Pt 36 payment which the claimant has failed to beat. If the losing party wishes to appeal the judgment, then he must seek permission from the trial judge and may also request a stay on the execution of the judgment pending the outcome of any appeal.

Post-trial

24.15 Defamation trials frequently attract considerable media interest and, at the conclusion of the trial, the parties may well be approached for quotes, interviews or reaction – whether you are the claimant, defendant or their respective lawyers. Win or lose, it is not always easy to think as clearly as one would like at the end of a contested trial and immediately following the emotionally draining wait for the jury's verdict. Therefore, it is prudent to prepare two statements – one to be used if you win and one to be used if you lose – in advance of the end of the trial. It goes without saying that these must be discussed and agreed with the client and a decision made about who deals with any media. As the television news confirms almost every night, the client is normally happy to leave this duty to his lawyer. It is certain that the media local to the home of one's client will be very interested in the outcome of a defamation trial involving a local man, but they may not all have the resources to send a journalist to London to cover the trial. In that event, since it is likely a successful claimant in particular will want to let people who live in his area know that his reputation has been vindicated by the court, it is worth identifying all the local media organisations and faxing them details of the result together with your prepared statement.

Chapter 25

Damages

25.01 The main remedy for defamation is damages, that is a payment of money by the defendant to the claimant. The broad purpose of damages is to compensate the claimant for the harm done to his reputation by the defamatory publication. On top of this, the claimant may also recover 'special damages', where he has suffered actual financial loss as a result of publication. In certain circumstances, damages that are intended to punish the defendant ('exemplary damages') can also be awarded.

Actions for defamation are usually tried by a judge and jury, in which case the jury will assess damages. They are faced with the unenviable task of putting a monetary value on the claimant's loss of reputation. Unlike actions for personal injury, damages are 'at large' – there is no official scale or table of damages which can be referred to, and (with minimal restriction[1]) damages will be assessed by the jury entirely subjectively.

This chapter sets out:

(a) procedural requirements for pleading damages;
(b) general damages:
   • the purpose of general damages;
   • factors relevant to assessment of the size of the award;
   • aggravated damages;
   • mitigation of damages;
(c) special damages;
(d) exemplary damages;
(e) damages when there are multiple defendants;
(f) limits on awards of damages.

1 The uppermost limit for the worst type of defamation is generally accepted to be no greater than the maximum award in personal injury – currently £200,000. It is now common practice for the judge and counsel for the claimant to give indications to the jury as to suitable levels of award. Prior to this, numbers will have been canvassed before the judge by all parties in the absence of the jury. The defendant's counsel may not want to address the jury on this point for obvious reasons.

Procedural requirements for pleading damages

25.02 Paragraph 2.10 of the Practice Direction to CPR Pt 53 sets out the general requirements when pleading damages.

The claimant should give full details of the facts and matters upon which he seeks to rely in support of his claim in damages[1].

Similarly, a claim for aggravated or exemplary damages must be specifically pleaded, with the facts relied on[2]. In relation to aggravated damages, it may be that conduct of the defendant after the issue of the particulars of claim gives rise to a claim for aggravated damages. In this case, an amendment of the particulars of claim should be sought.

Special damages must also be fully pleaded[3], identifying the specific loss the claimant claims to have suffered. Interest on the special damage should be pleaded in the body of the particulars of claim and also in the 'prayer' at the end of the particulars of claim[4].

The claimant is not allowed to give evidence at trial of any damage suffered that has not been pleaded, so it is important to ensure that every aspect of the claimant's claim in damages is fully particularised. However, the claimant should also take into consideration the requirement that statements of case are set out 'concisely and in a manner proportionate to the subject matter of the claim'[5].

1 CPR Pt 53 PD, para 2.10(1).
2 CPR Pt 53 PD, para 2.10(2).
3 *Ratcliffe v Evans* [1892] 2 QB 524.
4 CPR 16.4(1)(c).
5 CPR Pt 53 PD, para 2.1.

General damages

The purpose of general damages

25.03 Although an award of general damages is not subdivided, it serves three main purposes: first, to compensate the claimant for injury to his reputation; second, to compensate for hurt to the claimant's feelings; and finally, to vindicate the claimant to the public.

Factors relevant to assessment of the size of the award

25.04 A number of factors will be relevant in assessing the lump sum to be awarded.

The seriousness of the libel

25.05 This will naturally always be an important consideration. It was said in *John v MGN Ltd*[1] that the most serious defamations are those that touch 'the [claimant's] integrity, professional reputation, honour, courage, loyalty and the core attributes of his personality.' It should be remembered that a statement may be defamatory by exposing the claimant to ridicule or causing people to shun him and need not go to any of the above qualities. However, damages are likely to be considerably smaller in these cases.

1   [1997] QB 586.

Publication: to what extent and to whom

25.06 Generally speaking, the greater the circulation of a libel or the greater the number of persons in whose presence a slander was spoken, the greater the award of damages. If, for instance, publication has been in a national newspaper or on television, the award is likely to be considerably greater than if only published to one or two individuals. However, other factors, such as the seriousness or gravity of the defamation statement, also play an important part. An allegation of murder made to an employer, for example, is likely to cause much greater damage to reputation than an allegation made to all the world that X has a conviction for speeding.

Where an innuendo meaning requiring special knowledge is pleaded, or where only persons with special knowledge would identify the claimant, the jury will be directed by the judge that damages should only be assessed in relation to publication to these individuals.

The effect of the publication

25.07 Damages may be increased where the claimant introduces evidence that shows specific damage to his reputation or injury to his feelings resulting from the libel. For example, the claimant may have been subjected to abuse or discrimination by a third party. So long as any distress caused was as a consequence of the libel[1], the jury can take account of it in the assessment of damages[2].

Hurt caused to third parties, for example the claimant's family, is only relevant to the assessment of damages where the claimant has been distressed by the hurt caused to those people.

Some claimants are expected to be more resilient than others to the hurt caused by a libel and this will be reflected in the award of damages. For example, in an action brought by Teresa Gorman, a Conservative MP, the judge observed that her status as a politician meant that she was 'not entitled to be presented to the jury as a particularly vulnerable or sensitive litigant.'[3]

1　Subject to questions of remoteness of general applicability to the law of tort, which are beyond the scope of this book. The reader should refer to specialist texts.
2　*Slipper v BBC* [1991] 1 QB 283.
3　*Gorman v Mudd* (15 October 1992, unreported), CA.

Aggravated damages

25.08　General damages may be increased if 'aggravating' factors are present. This may be any behaviour by the defendant that has somehow added to the hurt and injury suffered by the claimant. In *Cassell & Co Ltd v Broome*[1], Lord Reid said that any 'high-handed, malicious, insulting or oppressive' behaviour by the defendant may give rise to aggravated damages. Again, it is important to note that aggravated damages, which may form part of a single sum awarded, are intended to compensate the claimant, not punish the defendant.

If a claimant wishes to claim aggravated damages, they must be pleaded[2]. The following are commonly pleaded in aggravation.

1　[1972] AC 1027.
2　CPR Pt 53 PD, para 2.10(2).

Defendant's conduct in relation to the publication

25.09　The publication in the media of an article or sequence of articles, which make it look like the claimant has been targeted for a campaign of disparagement, is likely to aggravate damages, as will unnecessarily lurid or sensational treatment of a story. Similarly, failing to publish a claimant's denial or explanation of the allegations, failing to properly verify the allegations, or engaging in deception in order to acquire material for a story may all give rise to an award of aggravated damages. Furthermore, where a code of conduct (such as the PCC Guidelines) governs the publisher, any breaches of the code can be relied upon in aggravation.

Failure to apologise

25.10   Failing to make any or any sufficient apology or withdrawal of the libel may aggravate damages[1], extending as it does the duration of the libel and exacerbating the injury to the claimant's feelings.

1   *Horrocks v Lowe* [1975] AC 135 at 154.

Defendant's conduct during the litigation

25.11   Pre-trial delaying tactics by the defendant or dismissive treatment of the claimant in correspondence is likely to aggravate damages. During the trial itself, common examples of aggravating factors include overly hostile cross-examination of the claimant, sensationalist or unpleasant coverage of the trial in the defendant's publication and any conduct calculated to discourage the claimant from proceeding with the litigation.

Justification

25.12   Maintaining the truth of a libel by pleading justification will extend the duration of the libel and heighten the injury to the claimant's reputation and feelings. Accordingly, in the event that the plea of justification fails and the court finds for the claimant, it may properly be relied upon in aggravation of damages.

Malice

25.13   Malice[1] is usually considered where the claimant hopes to defeat a defence of qualified privilege or fair comment. However, express malice can also be relied upon in aggravation of damages.

1   See Chapter 18.

Further publication of defamatory material

25.14   Where a libel is repeated after the initial publication complained of, the claimant could of course bring additional separate proceedings. The alternative is to plead the subsequent publication or publications in aggravation of damages. Where the defendant publishes derogatory material during the trial, with the apparent intention of deterring the claimant from proceeding, damages are likely to be considerably aggravated[1].

1   See Chapter 18; *A-G v Hislop* [1991] 1 QB 514.

Mitigation of damages

25.15   There are a number of matters commonly relied upon by the defendant which the jury may take into account by reducing damages. These are called mitigating factors.

The reputation of the claimant

25.16   It would not be right if a claimant could get damages in respect of damage to a reputation which he does not have. Accordingly, the defendant may introduce evidence that goes to show that the claimant has a bad reputation, which, if proved, will reduce damages.

However, there are strict rules about what evidence may or may not be admissible on bad reputation in mitigation of damage. The rules are known because of the leading case in this area as 'the rule in *Scott v Sampson*'[1]. In *Scott v Sampson* the publication complained of was to the effect that the claimant, a theatrical critic, had tried to extort money by threatening to publish defamatory matter concerning a deceased actress. There was a defence of justification. The claimant himself did not give evidence in support of his own case. The defendant wanted to cross-examine witnesses, including the claimant (whom the defendant himself called for that purpose), to show that the claimant's general conduct of his magazine was discreditable. The questions were objected to and the trial judge upheld those objections. The defendant also wanted to adduce evidence about the character of the claimant and evidence of rumours about him circulating before the publication of the libel to the same effect as the matters complained of. The judge refused to admit this evidence. The defendant appealed against these decisions which in summary related to: (a) the admissibility of evidence of reputation, (b) rumours of and suspicions to the same effect as the defamatory matter complained of, and (c) particular facts tending to show the character and disposition of the claimant.

On appeal the court upheld the judge's ruling, and until recently the position on the admissibility of evidence of reputation in mitigation of damage was always summarised thus: to be admissible the evidence must be of general bad reputation in the same sector of the claimant's life as that to which the libel is directed. Evidence of rumours that the claimant has done what was charged in the libel, and evidence of particular acts of misconduct on the part of the claimant which discredit him, is not admissible.

The rule in *Scott v Sampson* has been strictly applied ever since but was given a more relaxed interpretation by the Court of Appeal in *Burstein v Times Newspapers Ltd*[2]. In *Burstein* the claimant brought libel proceedings in respect of an article published in the diary column of *The Times* which alleged that he had organised hecklers to wreck performances of modern atonal music. In its defence the newspaper pleaded fair comment and alleged among other matters that three years before the article had been published the claimant had associated with a group called 'The Hecklers' to oppose modernist, atonal music, that the group had encouraged the public to boo at the end of the performance of an opera and that the claimant had been present at that performance and had booed. The judge struck out the defence of fair comment. The newspaper then sought to rely on the matters formerly pleaded in support of its defence of fair comment in mitigation of damage. The judge ruled that the facts related to the claimant's alleged bad conduct and were inadmissible evidence in mitigation of damage because they contravened the rule in *Scott v Sampson*.

On appeal the Court of Appeal held that newspaper was entitled to adduce evidence in mitigation of damage of particular facts which were directly relevant to the background context in which the defamatory publication came to be made. It explained the rule in *Scott v Sampson* which excluded particular evidence of the claimant's general reputation, character or disposition (item (c) above) as limited to that which was not directly connected with the subject matter of the publication. The Court of Appeal noted that in *Scott v Sampson*, the particular facts sought to be adduced did not specifically relate to the defamatory publication that the claimant had tried to extort money from by threatening to publish a defamatory matter concerning the deceased actress. Generally speaking, it would normally be unfair and irrelevant if a claimant complaining of a specific defamatory publication was subjected to a roving inquiry into his life unconnected with the subject matter of the defamatory publication. It was also in accordance with the overriding objective that evidence should be properly confined, both in its subject matter and its duration, to that which was directly relevant to the subject matter of the publication. In the present case the part of the particulars which set out the directly relevant background context of the publication should have been admitted and should have been put before the jury. The relevant confined direct background context to this publication would have been that there was in 1994 a group who called themselves 'The Hecklers'; that the claimant was associated with the group and that he subsequently claimed to have been its co-founder; that he disassociated himself from The Hecklers' boorish tactics of shouting down the opposition in a letter to *The Times* dated 7 April 1994; that Frederick Stocken, under the name of The Hecklers, encouraged people to join him at the performance of *Gawain* at the Royal Opera House on 14 April 1994 when they would be booing at the end; that there was no interruption of *Gawain* that evening during its performance but that there was some booing at the end; and that the claimant was in the audience and joined in the booing. This would have provided the background to the publication. To keep that away from the jury was to put them in blinkers.

1   *Scott v Sampson* (1882) 8 QBD 491.
2   [2001] 1 WLR 579, CA.

Previous convictions

25.17   A long-standing and important exception to the old rule that evidence relating to a claimant's reputation must be general rather than specific is in relation to criminal convictions, which are admissible so long as they also relate to the sector of the claimant's life relevant to the libel.

The conduct of the claimant

25.18   The behaviour of the claimant is also relevant to the question of damages. In *Cassell & Co Ltd v Broome*[1], Lord Hailsham said that the conduct of both defendant and claimant was relevant to the assessment of damages and where the claimant had behaved badly, for instance by provoking the libel or by defaming the defendant in return, damages could be reduced[2].

Delay by the claimant in bringing a complaint can also reduce damages, suggesting as it does that vindication was not a matter of great urgency to the claimant. However, the fact that the defamatory material has been published previously and the claimant has not complained or taken any action is not to be taken into account[3].

In *Campbell v News Group Newspapers*[4], the Court of Appeal reduced a jury award of damages of £350,000 to £30,000 partly because of the conduct of the claimant. *The News of the World* had accused the claimant of active paedophilia. In particular, it had alleged that the claimant had: (a) sexually abused children whom he had lured into his house with the promise of money, (b) made videos of the abuse and marketed those videos, (c) demanded money for the return of a video, (d) admitted enjoying watching teenagers through peep-holes in public lavatories, and (e) generally had a perverted interest in children.

The award of £350,000 exceeded the current top limit of £200,000 in any event but the Court of Appeal found that the newspaper had established significant partial justification in relation to the allegation that the claimant had a perverted interest in boys. In the circumstances an award not exceeding £100,000 would be the most a jury could award. However, during the litigation the claimant had engaged 'in an elaborate and long lasting attempt to pervert the course of justice' such as justified a further reduction in damages to just £30,000.

1   [1972] AC 1027 at 1071.
2   Note that where a libel is or forms part of a response to an attack by another, the defence of 'reply to an attack' qualified privilege may be available to the defendant.
3   *Associated Newspapers v Dingle* [1964] AC 371.
4   [2002] EWCA Civ 1143, [2002] All ER (D) 513 (Jul).

An apology by the defendant

25.19   A genuine and proper apology that is not made at too late a stage will be a significant mitigating factor. This is because an apology shortens the life of the libel and reduces the injury to the claimant's reputation and feelings.

Defendant's honest belief

25.20   Where the defendant had an honest belief in the truth of what he published, perhaps relying on what he considered to be a reliable source, damages may be reduced.

Damages received by the claimant in respect of similar publications

25.21   Where a claimant has already received or agreed to receive damages for libel in respect of words to the same effect, damages may be reduced[1]. This rule is to prevent a claimant recovering more than once in respect of the same libel, for instance where several newspapers have alleged the same or similar things against a claimant, who then sues them all separately. Any settlements or awards of damages could be relied upon by the remaining defendants in mitigation of damages, particularly where the claimant has specifically claimed in aggravation against each that the publication complained of was picked up and published by other newspapers.

1   The DA 1952, s 12.

Special damages

25.22   Unlike an award of general damages, which are incapable of precise estimation, special damages are those that relate to some actual (or 'specific') loss. This damage must be financial, or capable of being estimated in money.

Examples of special damage include the loss of a specific business contract or customer, or the loss of employment. A general loss of business profits may also be recovered as special damages, so long as they are capable of being estimated in financial terms.

A claim for special damages must be expressly pleaded and qualified by the claimant. At trial, the actual loss must be proved so risk of possible future loss is not sufficient. The claimant must also demonstrate that the loss is the result of the defamatory publication and that the loss is a foreseeable consequence of publication in accordance with the principles of general application in the law of tort.

Unlike an award of general damages, the claimant is entitled to make a claim for interest on the amount claimed in special damages. This must also be pleaded.

Exemplary damages

25.23   In certain circumstances the jury is entitled to make an award of exemplary (or punitive) damages as punishment for wrongdoing by the defendant. In *Rookes v Barnard*[1], Lord Devlin explained the basis for an award of exemplary damages:

> 'one man should not be allowed to sell another man's reputation for profit. Where a defendant with a cynical disregard for a claimant's rights has calculated that the money to be made out of his wrongdoing will probably exceed the damages at risk, it is necessary for the law to show that it cannot be broken with impunity ... Exemplary damages can properly be awarded whenever it is necessary to teach a wrongdoer that tort does not pay.'

To establish a right to exemplary damages, the claimant must show that:

(a) the defendant at the time of publication knew, or was reckless as to whether, the defamatory statement was untrue; and

(b) the defendant published the libel having calculated that the financial gain from publication outweighed the potential penalty in damages he might have to pay for it.

1 [1964] AC 1129 at 1226.

Knowledge or recklessness

25.24 The defendant must have published the material complained of knowing it was untrue or without an honest belief in its truth (see Chapter 18). Mere knowledge that the material is defamatory will not be sufficient, nor will an award of exemplary damages be made where the publisher knew it was defamatory but reasonably believed he had a defence.

Calculation

25.25 The fact that a libel is published in the course of business is not by itself enough to show that publication involved the calculation that the financial gain of publication outweighed its risk. Instead, the calculation must relate to the specific publication. So, for example, the defendant could have placed the article on the front page with a sensational headline clearly designed to generate sales.

Exemplary damages may also be awarded where the defendant is a government servant and publication amounts to an oppressive, arbitrary or unconstitutional act[1].

A claim for exemplary damages must be specifically pleaded, together with the facts which the claimant relies upon to found his claim.

1 See *Rookes v Barnard* [1964] AC 1129.

Damages when there are multiple defendants

25.26 A claimant is only entitled to a single award of damages in respect of any single publication of a libel. So where there is more than one defendant, the court does not divide up damages between defendants – each defendant is liable to the claimant for the total amount. If the claimant has only recovered part of the amount awarded, he can seek the remaining amount from another defendant.

Where there are multiple defendants, the single award of damages is assessed on the basis of the least culpable defendant[1]. Consequently, an award of aggravated or exemplary damages will only be made where all defendants are liable for them. Accordingly, where a claimant is aware of different levels of responsibility for a publication, he should be careful to only sue the most blameworthy or to bring separate proceedings.

1   *Cassell & Co Ltd v Broome* [1972] AC 1027 at 1063.

Limits on awards of damages

25.27   The entirely subjective nature of putting a monetary value on injury to an individual's reputation and the lack of assistance available to juries when assessing damages has meant in the past that juries have tended to err on the side of generosity. Perhaps this is also due to a natural sympathy juries feel towards claimants or an antipathy they feel towards corporate media defendants.

However, several recent developments in the law have reduced awards of damages and gone some way to assisting juries in achieving a more consistent approach. First, section 8 of the Courts and Legal Services Act 1990 gave the Court of Appeal the power to substitute its own award of damages for that made by the jury at trial. Then, in *John v MGN Ltd*[1], the Court of Appeal decided that a jury should be informed of damages in previous defamation actions and should be also be told of the maximum amount of awards in personal injury cases for comparison purposes.

In *Campbell v News Group Newspapers plc*[2], the Court of Appeal substituted for an award of £350,000 made by a jury an award of £30,000, where the defendants had established 'significant partial justification' of the serious allegation of sexual abuse of boys.

It seems that the limit for an award of general damages is £200,000, in line with the maximum award of damages for personal injury. This was the amount awarded recently in *Lillie and Reed v Newcastle City Council*[3], where the allegation against two nursery school workers was of child abuse. The judge commented that 'with the possible exception of murder' he found it 'difficult to think of any charge more calculated to lead to the revulsion and condemnation of a person's fellow citizens than that of the systematic and sadistic abuse of children.' Consequently the 'effective ceiling' for an award of damages in libel was deemed appropriate.

1   [1997] QB 586.
2   [2002] EWCA Civ 1373, [2002] 42 LS Gaz R 38.
3   [2002] EWHC 1600 (QB), [2002] All ER (D) 465 (Jul).

Chapter 26

Settlement of defamation claims and CPR 36

26.01 This chapter considers the ways in which both the claimant and the defendant can seek to settle a defamation claim either before proceedings or following issue of proceedings but before trial. See also the 'offer of amends' procedure outlined in Chapter 16.

Introduction

26.02 Most defamation claims settle – trite but true. It may be obvious, but it is important, because while this book may outline the procedures from letter of claim through issue of proceedings to trial and beyond, in the majority of cases they will not, for the most part, be needed.

Parties have always undertaken an assessment of the risks of pursuing or defending a defamation claim at an early stage. However, the importance of that exercise is now paramount because of the introduction of conditional fee arrangements legislation giving the power to recover success fees and insurance premiums from the defendant, and the impetus of the CPR and the pre-action protocol. 'Front loading' of cases used to be a term of complaint and criticism but now, when early settlement is encouraged by the relevant legislation and reinforced by the civil litigation culture, the term has been dignified. What is not yet clear is the extent to which the courts are prepared to bolster the system by making punitive costs orders against those who litigate when they could and should have settled.

There is evidence that even the tabloid press is beginning to realise that their apparent reluctance in the past to apologise when they have got it wrong has actually had the effect of alienating their readers. In the *Press Gazette* on 12 January 2001, the launch of *The Mirror*'s corrections column was reported (following a similar initiative by its unlikely bedfellow *The Guardian* a little earlier) and its editor, Piers Morgan, was quoted as follows:

'There's a lot of cynicism among the public towards tabloid journalism. We're big enough to admit we make mistakes and errors . . . Rather than avoid the issue, we decided to embrace it and make a virtue of it. It'll develop a better bond with our readership and may dilute legal problems.

People usually don't want to take legal action, and if there are genuine mistakes that can be corrected quickly, we can be up front about it and avoid legal wrangles where we might dig our heels in.'

Simple commercial imperative or conversion on the road to Damascus? Time will tell – and it will be seen whether this attitude moves even further back towards the source of the tabloid food chain to the point of 'prevention being better than cure'.

Factors encouraging settlement

Claimant

26.03 A claimant almost invariably brings a defamation claim as a genuine attempt to restore as far as possible a reputation damaged by defamatory allegations. If he sues the defendant, then the only remedies he can actually claim are damages and an injunction. However, what most claimants will actually want is an apology in some form and an assurance that the allegations will not be published again. The recovery of compensation and the legal costs they have incurred are clearly important financial considerations, but they do not have the same impact in restoring a damaged reputation.

This means that the settlement terms either proposed by, or acceptable to, a claimant are likely to include requirements which will not actually be available from the judge and jury (although the summary disposal provisions under the DeA 1996, ss 8–10 do give wider powers to the judge alone)[1].

It is also the case that each element of a settlement package has a value to the claimant. Put bluntly, if a defendant is not prepared to apologise in an acceptable way for defamatory allegations it has published, it is likely to be required to pay for that reluctance.

An early proposal of terms of settlement is always going to appeal to a claimant who is likely to be apprehensive about the prospect of going to head to head with a well-resourced media defendant. The apprehension is more evenly apportioned where the parties do not include media organisations.

1 See Chapter 22.

Defendant

26.04 Receipt of a defamation claim causes understandable concern to a defendant. It can raise important issues of principle and freedom of speech in certain situations. Ultimately, however, a media defendant is likely (in all except cases involving an important matter of principle to it) to adopt a commercial view, particularly if insurers are involved. At its heart will be the simple unavoidable question along the lines: 'Yes, yes, I appreciate all that – but on the balance of probabilities, are we going to successfully defend this claim?'.

The defendant will consider the evidence it already has which supports the publication and the truth of the allegations in it, and the evidence it might reasonably expect to be able to get. It will consider the applicability of the more technical defences of qualified or absolute privilege and fair comment. Above all, it will form a view about what the publication actually means in relation to the claimant (this may well differ from the claimant's own interpretation).

Even if the merits of the defence and its prospects of success are finely balanced, a defendant might wish to contest a claim because it goes to the heart of what the defendant is about. An example might be the approach adopted by a television company to a claim brought in relation to allegations contained in one of its flagship investigative journalism programmes – a *Panorama* or *World in Action*.

Financial considerations will play an important part in the decision-making process. 'Can we afford to fight the case' is not a question which can be avoided by either the defendant or the claimant. There is something to be said for living to fight another day even if a portion of humble pie has to be consumed in consequence.

CPR 36

26.05 CPR 36 encourages parties to assess the strength of their case at all stages of the claim from notification to trial and then to make a proposal fairly representing either what as a claimant you would be prepared to accept, or as a defendant what you would be prepared to offer, by way of terms of settlement. The offer is treated as 'without prejudice save as to costs'. In other words, the offer will remain confidential as between the parties and will not be disclosed to the court until after the verdict has been delivered and the question of the parties' liability for costs has to be determined by the judge. Inevitably, if a claim proceeds to trial, either the claimant or defendant is going to succeed ultimately so there is an unimpeachable logic in seeking to protect your position at an earlier stage by making proposals to your opponent.

How does CPR 36 work and what is the nature of the 'protection' offered?

Defendant

26.06   If a defendant decides to make a CPR Pt 36 offer (or payment into court if proceedings have commenced) then in defamation it will almost certainly include an offer of a sum of damages and probably also an offer of some form of apology, and perhaps an undertaking not to repeat the allegations.

If the claimant rejects the offer and the case proceeds to trial at which he recovers less from the court than was on offer from the defendant then the offer will be brought to the attention of the judge who will almost certainly make two orders for costs. The claimant will be treated as having 'won' the case up to the date he received noticed of the CPR Pt 36 offer or payment. He will get his costs up to that date. However, the defendant will be regarded as having won the case from that date and will be awarded its costs accordingly from the claimant. Since these costs will include the trial costs (depending on when the CPR Pt 36 offer or payment was made), the costs liability to the defendant is likely to obliterate anything the claimant may have gained from the litigation.

The most famous example of the pitfalls which can face a claimant who gambles on the prospect of recovering a higher sum in damages from a jury than the defendant has posted in court remains the experience of William Roache in his 1991 libel action against *The Sun*[1]. The case has (a little unfairly) been labelled the 'Boring Ken Barlow' action; in fact the allegation that the veteran *Coronation Street* actor was boring was only one of a number of allegations made against him. *The Sun* paid a total paid a total of £50,000 into court; the jury awarded Roache precisely that sum. Initially, a sympathetic Mr Justice Waterhouse, exercising his discretion, awarded Roache all his costs despite his failure to beat the payment in. The Court of Appeal disagreed with the judge's view that the claimant should be treated as having 'beaten' the payment in because part of the claim was for an injunction also and the newspaper had given no indication it would not repeat the allegations. It ordered Roache to pay the newspaper's costs from the date of the payment in. Roache found himself facing a bill of more than £115,000, comprising his own and his opponent's costs. He went on to sue his solicitors for negligence – unsuccessfully. Ultimately he had to declare himself bankrupt.

1   *Roache v News Group Newspapers Ltd* [1998] EMLR 161.

Claimant

26.07   A claimant can make a CPR Pt 36 offer to a defendant indicating the terms which he is prepared to accept by way of settlement. This has particular validity in defamation, where a claimant may be prepared to accept a modest sum by way of damages if the defendant is prepared to apologise. A CPR Pt 36 offer can make that position clear while at the same time presenting a defendant with a stark choice: how much is an apology worth? If the claim proceeds to trial and the claimant recovers more from the defendant than he had indicated in his CPR Pt 36 offer he was prepared to accept, then the defendant is likely to suffer additional financial penalties from the court in terms of both costs and interest. The court is entitled to order that the defendant should pay the claimant's costs on the indemnity basis from the latest date when it could have accepted the claimant's CPR Pt 36 offer without the court's consent plus interest on those costs at a rate not exceeding 10% above base rate from the same date. It can also order that the defendant pay interest on the whole or part of any damages sum awarded to him at a rate not exceeding 10% above the base rate; again, from the date when the defendant could have accepted the offer without the court's permission. CPR 36.21(4) stipulates that the court will make an order in these terms unless it is unjust to do so after taking into account all the circumstances of the case.

Circumstances the court might take into account include:

(a)   the terms of the offer, for example its reasonableness;
(b)   when the offer was made;
(c)   at what stage could the defendant make a proper assessment of the offer? (In other words, when was all the relevant material and information in its possession to allow it to take an informed view?);
(d)   the conduct of the parties in providing the information and material to allow an assessment of the offer to be made.

If a claimant fails to beat his own CPR Pt 36 offer at trial there are no adverse consequences. The onus is on the defendant to have made its own offer to exert pressure on the claimant.

Procedural requirements

26.08   The following are requirements of a CPR Pt 36 offer:

(a)   it must be in writing;

(b)   it must state whether it relates to the whole of the claim, whether it is confined to a particular part of it, or only a specific issue within the case;

(c)   it must state whether it takes into account any counterclaim;

(d)   if not inclusive of interest, it must state whether interest is offered and, if so, the amount, the rate and the periods. If you say nothing, then CPR 36.22 means it is assumed to be inclusive of interest up to the last date it could be accepted without the court's consent[1];

(e)   it must state if it takes into account any earlier voluntary interim payment (unlikely to be a factor in defamation);

(f)   it must state that it remains open for acceptance for (at least) 21 days from the date it is made, which means the date it is received;

(g)   it must state that after that 21-day limit, it can only be accepted if the parties agree liability for costs or the court gives its permission;

(h)   if the offer is made less than 21 days before the trial begins, the same terms for acceptance have to be given. Substantial costs are incurred in the weeks leading up to trial and at trial itself so a CPR Pt 36 offer (or payment) made shortly before trial (which still gives the opponent 21 days to consider whether to accept it) eliminates most of the tactical and potential costs benefits of the procedure.

Common sense dictates you should ask the recipient of your CPR Pt 36 offer to acknowledge receipt since the rules do not oblige them to do so.

1   Interest is only likely to be relevant in a defamation claim which includes a claim for special (ie quantified) damage.

Acceptance

Defendant's offer: CPR 36.11

26.09 CPR 36.11 provides that:

(a) the claimant can accept an offer by giving written notice to the defendant within the 21-day time limit from the date the offer was received by him;

(b) if the offer was made less than 21 days before the trial starts or the 21-day limit has expired, then the claimant needs the court's permission to accept unless the parties can agree the costs order between themselves;

(c) if the court's permission is needed, the court will determine the costs order at the hearing at which it gives its permission.

Claimant's offer: CPR 36.12

26.10 CPR 36.12 provides that:

(a) the defendant can accept an offer by giving written notice to the claimant within the 21-day time limit from the date the offer was received;

(b) if the offer was made less than 21 days before the trial starts or the 21-day limit has expired, then, once again, the court's permission will be needed to accept unless the costs order can be agreed between the parties;

(c) where a defendant accepts a claimant's offer (without requiring the court's permission) then it will have to agree to pay the claimant's costs up to the date it serves its notice of acceptance[1].

1   CPR 36.14.

Timing and payments into court

26.11 A CPR Pt 36 offer can be made before proceedings and the court will take it into account when determining its costs order in the same way as an offer made after litigation has started. Having said that, the court is obliged under the CPR to pay regard to any admissible offer to settle which has been made when deciding the costs issues[1] – whether made pursuant to CPR 36 or not.

Once proceedings have started, a defendant who has made an earlier pre-action CPR Pt 36 offer including an offer of damages needs to pay into court a sum at least equal to the earlier offer within 14 days of service of the claim form to secure the potential costs benefits from the date the original offer was made.

In defamation, a CPR Pt 36 offer is likely to consist of non-financial remedies as well as an offer of damages. To make sure it benefits from the potentially advantageous costs consequences of the rules, a defendant should make an offer in relation to the whole of the claimant's claim.

The defendant's CPR Pt 36 payment notice[2] should identify the document setting out the terms of the offer and should state that if the claimant accepts the payment he will also be treated as accepting the offer in relation to the non-financial remedies.

A defendant makes a CPR Pt 36 payment by filing the payment notice, Form N242A, the payment (cheque made payable to HM Paymaster General) and (if it is an action proceeding in the Royal Courts of Justice) a sealed copy of the claim form and Court Funds Office Form 100[3].

A claimant, who accepts a CPR Pt 36 payment by giving the required notice to the defendant, extracts payment from the court by requesting payment in Form N243 and (if it is an action proceeding in the Royal Courts of Justice) by filing Form 201 at the Court Funds Office[4].

A defendant can withdraw or reduce a CPR Pt 36 payment only with the court's permission, following an application with supporting reasons[5].

1   CPR 44.3(4)(c).
2   Form N242A. The form has to be filed at court stating the amount of the payment and how much of the claim and/or the issues within it it relates to.
3   CPR Pt 36 PD, para 4.1.
4   CPR 36.16. Both forms are available from the court office.
5   CPR 36.6(5).

Chapter 27

Statements in open court

Introduction

27.01 One unsatisfactory aspect of defamation law is that while the main reason for bringing a claim is generally to obtain vindication of the claimant's reputation which has been damaged by the words complained of, one is restricted in the claim form and particulars of claim to suing only for damages and an injunction. The claimant cannot include a claim for an apology in his defamation proceedings despite the fact that it may well be the remedy to which he attaches the most importance.

However, there is a device which enables a public apology to be made to the claimant through the court and then reported in the media. This is the statement in open court and it can arise in the following ways:

(a)   under an offer to make amends[1];
(b)   under an order for summary relief made in favour of the claimant[2];
(c)   by agreement as one of the terms of a negotiated settlement;
(d)   following acceptance by the claimant of moneys paid into court. In this situation, the claimant is entitled to a unilateral statement.

1   The DeA 1996, ss 2–4.
2   The DeA 1996, ss 8–10.

Format and advantages of a statement in open court

27.02 A statement in open court is, as its name suggests, a procedure which involves a court hearing. Where it is a joint statement (for unilateral statements see paragraph 27.08 below), the parties agree its terms, which are then approved by the judge[1], which will generally consist of a section for each of the parties' advocates to read out in court. The claimant's section will come first and will summarise the nature of the libel or slander, explain why the words were untrue and defamatory, and that they caused the claimant distress and damage. It will then explain that the defendant now accepts its liability and has agreed to withdraw the allegations and to apologise to the claimant. It will probably also mention the fact (but not the amount of) damages and costs have been paid by the defendant to the claimant.

The defendant's section, to be read by its advocate, will endorse what the claimant's advocate has said, and confirm both the retraction of the allegations and the apology.

The statement will conclude with the claimant's advocate asking for leave for the record to be withdrawn and, if relevant, for the payment out of any moneys in court.

Where a statement is to be read in open court, it has to be listed for hearing by means of an application to the clerk of the lists. There does not appear to be any set procedure for the listing and reading of a statement in open court where proceedings have not been issued. However, it has been permitted where an application was made to the court in Form N244 (£50 fee) but with no claim number, attaching a copy of the statement to be read in open court along with a further copy of the statement signed by all the parties. The application needs to be referred first to the Practice Master in order for it to be released to the judge in charge of the jury list for approval and reading. If the court insists on a claim form being issued one could use a CPR Pt 8 claim form, for which the issue fee is £120. Normally, the reading of the statement will be listed to take place before the court's main business of the day gets underway which means they tend to take place at 10:30 am in Courts 12 or 13 at the Royal Courts of Justice and will usually take no more than ten minutes to deal with.

1   CPR Sch 1, RSC Ord 82 r5.

27.03   It is now commonplace for statements to be read by the parties' solicitors rather than their counsel, even though the hearing is in open court. This means that the solicitor must not forget to wear his court robes.

A statement in open court involving high profile celebrity parties will attract considerable journalistic interest. It is essential to have a ready supply of copies of the statement to distribute to members of the media who are in court. One might also wish to issue the text of the statement to the media by means of a press release if the claimant wants to garner as much publicity as possible for the defendant's public climb down. Even when statements are read in claims involving non-celebrities, there will be a couple of court reporters in court to hear it and they will want copies of the statement to put on the wire to, for example, the claimant's local newspapers and radio stations.

It is following the reading of a statement in open court that a solicitor is most likely to be collared by a journalist for a comment or reaction. This could be a press or a TV or radio journalist and to have a radio microphone thrust into one's face or a camera waiting for you on emerging from court is an experience which certainly teaches you the validity of the old army adage 'time spent in reconnaissance is never wasted'! It is definitely a sensible precaution to prepare (and agree with one's client) what you will say to the media if approached after the reading of a statement in open court.

A statement read in open court does of course attract privilege, so the fact that the actionable libel or slander is generally read out or paraphrased within the statement does not expose you to a potential further claim from your own client! Similarly, fair and accurate reports of the statement published or broadcast in the media also attract privilege so the statement can be reported with impunity. This means maximum publicity can be obtained from a statement if the media is interested enough to co-operate. This is why the procedure of a statement in open court is a device which assists a claimant in achieving publicity for his vindication.

27.04 One important point to note regarding statements in open court is that they should not defame third parties who are not parties to the action. In that event, one might find those third parties intervening to amend the terms of the statement. This occurred in the unreported case of *Williamson v Metropolitan Police Comr*[1], where six police officers successfully intervened to amend the terms of a statement to be read in a case which had been settled where the claimant had sued the Police Commissioner for wrongful arrest, false imprisonment, malicious prosecution and assault. The statement set out in graphic detail the alleged wrongdoing of the officers who had dealt with Mr Williamson. It did not say the officers strongly denied the allegations and that is what they intervened to try and achieve. They were successful at first instance at the Central London County Court in obtaining an order adding a sentence to the statement which made it clear they denied the claimant's account of events and that they had not been parties to the action or the terms of settlement. They also obtained an order for their costs against Mr Williamson. The matter went to the Court of Appeal where the County Court Judge's decision was upheld. Judge LJ gave a judgment which provides helpful guidance about statements in open court generally. He said that a judge:

'... must first decide whether it was appropriate to permit a statement to be made, and if so, whether the statement should be made in the terms proposed. When the parties are agreed about the terms of the statement, the judge will not readily interfere with what they have agreed, but he nevertheless remains entitled, and if he thinks appropriate, obliged to require the proposed statement to be amended, or to refuse to approve it. Among the many considerations to which he should attend, there will on occasions be the interests of those who are not parties to the litigation, or the settlement, who may nevertheless be damaged, possibly beyond remedy, by the terms of a statement made under the protection of absolute privilege. In the context of all the relevant circumstances, therefore, the judge must balance the proper protection of their interests against the interests of the plaintiff who wishes to be vindicated. The judge's decision to approve the statement, whether in the terms proposed by the parties, or in an amended form, represents the exercise of his discretion in the particular circumstances of an individual case and this court will only interfere on well-known principles.'

1   Noted at (1996) 140 *Solicitors Journal* 1179 and (1997) 141 *Solicitors Journal* 1024 and 1025.

Circumstances when a statement in open court may arise in a defamation claim

Offer to make amends

27.05   When a defendant chooses to defend a libel action by deploying an offer to make amends pursuant to section 2 of the DeA 1996, one of the elements must be an offer 'to make a suitable correction of the statement complained of and a sufficient apology to the aggrieved party'[1]. Section 3(4) of the DeA 1996 states that 'If the parties do not agree on the steps to be taken by way of correction, apology and publication, the party who made the offer may take such steps as he thinks appropriate, and may in particular—(a) make the correction and apology by a statement in open court in terms approved by the court, and (b) give an undertaking to the court as to the manner of their publication.'

1   The DeA 1996, s 2(4)(a).

Summary disposal of claim

27.06 Sections 8–10 of the DeA 1996 set out the provisions whereby the court can either dismiss the claimant's claim on the defendant's application[1] or give judgment for the claimant on his application and grant him summary relief[2]. The summary relief ordered by the court can include an order that the defendant publish or cause to be published a suitable correction and apology[3]. If the parties cannot agree on the content, the court may direct the defendant to publish or cause to be published a summary by the court's judgment agreed by the parties or settled by the court[4]. Clearly, there might be circumstances (if, for example, the defendant is not a media publisher or broadcaster with the means to publish an apology to the recipients of the words complained of) in which a statement in open court would be the most effective way of publishing a suitable correction and apology.

1 The DeA 1996, s 8(2).
2 The DeA 1996, s 8(3).
3 The DeA 1996, s 9(1)(b).
4 The DeA 1996, s 9(2).

Statement in open court as a term of settlement

27.07 Often where a negotiated settlement of a defamation claim has been achieved, the parties agree to read a joint statement in open court as one of the terms of settlement. This may be in addition, or as an alternative, to a published apology. A statement in open court is very often sought as one of the claimant's requirements in his letter of claim.

The draft statement will pass back and forward between the parties before it is agreed and the extent to which its terms vary between an overwhelming vindication of the claimant and a more neutral concession of the defendant's wrongdoing will usually be dictated by the seriousness of the defamation and the viability or otherwise of the defendant's potential defences.

Unilateral statement in open court

27.08 The Civil Procedure Rules[1] provide that where a claimant wishes to accept a CPR Pt 36 offer or a CPR Pt 36 payment or other offer of settlement in a defamation claim, he may apply for permission to make a statement in open court either before or after accepting the offer of payment[2]. The statement has to be submitted for the approval of the court and must accompany the notice of application[3] (made in accordance with CPR 23). The time for making the statement can be postponed if other claims relating to the subject matter of the statement are still proceeding[4].

When drafting the statement, clearly the extent to which the vindication of the claimant can be emphasised will depend on the seriousness of the words complained of and the extent of the defendant's capitulation demonstrated by the generosity of the offer or payment which is to be, or has been, accepted by the claimant. Put simply, in terms of figures, accepting damages of, for example, £100,000 would warrant a comprehensive and conclusive statement in favour of the claimant, while accepting damages of £1,000 would warrant only a lukewarm statement of vindication. The court will heed Gilbert and Sullivan when approving the terms of a draft statement and make sure 'the punishment fits the crime'.

Inevitably, a unilateral statement in open court has less impact and a lower level of satisfaction for a claimant because the defendant does not join with it and endorse the contents, so demonstrating its contrition for the defamatory allegations.

1   CPR Pt 53 PD, paras 6.1–6.4.
2   CPR Pt 53 PD, para 6.2.
3   CPR Pt 53 PD, para 6.3.
4   CPR Pt 53 PD, para 6.4.

Chapter 28

Alternative dispute resolution

28.01 Legal disputes often revolve around complex issues and with the passage of time parties become bitter and entrenched in their stance, making an agreement difficult to achieve. Alternative dispute resolution ('ADR') refers to problem-solving procedures which do not require litigation.

There are various types of ADR.

Executive or mini trial

28.02 This is the most formal means of ADR, where representations are made by each party to a panel of senior executives from both parties and usually a mediator.

Early mutual evaluation

28.03 This method of ADR requires the appointment of a mutual evaluator who either reads or hears each party's submissions and delivers a non-binding view of the merits of each party's case.

Adjudication

28.04 This requires the appointment of a mutual expert or adjudicator who hears submissions and delivers a legally binding decision.

Mediation[1]

28.05 This is the most popular method of ADR and requires the appointment of an independent, experienced mediator. The mediator's job is to listen to each party's case and identify sources of real dispute. It is not the mediator's job to find fault or apportion blame but to work towards a solution.

1   See further, Chapter 29.

Procedure

28.06 Organisations such as CEDR (the Centre for Dispute Resolution) or the ADR Group can find an appropriate mediator from their panel of accredited members and can usually arrange a venue. For a mediation to take place three rooms are required: one main room for all parties to be present together and then each party has 'a break out room' where they can talk confidentially to colleagues and the mediator. The idea is that the mediator will carry out shuttle diplomacy and encourage the parties to reach common ground. All parties must agree to mediation and the results are not binding unless settlement terms are agreed by both parties and a formal contract is signed.

Both sides are usually responsible for their own costs, but parties can agree something different between themselves. The costs of mediation are on a sliding scale dependent on the quantum of the claim. For example, claims under £20,000 attract a fee per party per day of £450. If a claim is worth between £50,000–£100,000 the fee per party per day is £750 and claims between £500,000–£1m attract a fee of £1,500 per party per day. Legal aid is not available for mediation.

Research and various pilot studies have shown that recourse to mediation results in 80–90% of cases settling. ADR offers skilled intervention allowing identification of real sources of dispute and the channelling of energies into a form of resolution. The mediators offer confidentiality and neutrality and can address any area of law or business. Parties remain in control of the proceedings rather than the court assuming power, the results are very quick and significant costs can be saved.

It is also important to be aware of the importance attributed to ADR by the Civil Procedure Rules. CPR 1.4(2) states that the court should 'encourag[e] the parties to use an alternative dispute resolution procedure, if the court considers that appropriate and facilitat[e] the use of such procedure'. Similarly, under CPR 26.4(1), 'a party may, when filing the completed allocation questionnaire, make a written request for the proceedings to be stayed while the parties try to settle the case by alternative dispute resolution or other means'. Further, the defamation pre-action protocol[1] expects parties to produce evidence to the court that alternative means of resolving their dispute were considered.

The greater significance attributed to ADR as a result of the CPR means that ADR might be seriously considered before litigation is embarked upon, and continue to be assessed throughout the duration of the litigation.

1   See Chapter 8 and Appendix 3.

Chapter 29

Mediation

29.01 This chapter provides guidance on one of the key ways in which parties to a defamation action may be able to avoid the cost and trauma of litigating a dispute to trial, namely mediation.

Background

29.02 Lord Woolf's examination of the civil justice system which led to the Civil Procedure Rules was entitled 'Access to Justice' and that title encapsulated a prime concern about the way in which the civil system had developed. It was clear that a vast number of ordinary people felt disenfranchised from the legal process as a way of resolving civil disputes because it cost too much, was too complicated and took too long.

The Civil Procedure Rules, particularly through the pre-action protocols[1], encourage parties to consider alternative means of resolving disputes to the blunt instrument of litigation. Perhaps the highest hope was held out in this regard for mediation.

1   See Chapter 8.

Definition

29.03 Mediation involves the parties to a dispute (whether before or after proceedings have been issued) endeavouring, through the assistance of a mediator, to negotiate a consensual resolution of the issues between them. That resolution (if achieved) is then embodied in an agreement between the parties, usually drawn up and signed at the conclusion of the mediation.

Applicability to defamation

29.04 On the face of it, defamation seems a promising area for the mediation of disputes: in a defamation action a claimant can only seek damages, an injunction and costs when what he will often really want is an apology and vindication from the defendant. Frequently, financial compensation is a secondary consideration – although it tends to acquire importance as litigation progresses. Surely the opportunity to negotiate a resolution where there are no restrictions on what can be agreed between the parties is something that would be attractive to a claimant or a defendant?

Similarly, save where matters of principle are concerned or where an opportunity presents itself to nudge the law in a helpful way, a media defendant will generally favour a swift and relatively inexpensive negotiated resolution over protracted and expensive litigation when a meritorious claim against it has been initiated.

The defamation pre-action protocol requires the parties to consider ADR[1] and that requirement is now being supplemented by a greater willingness among the judiciary to suggest (even if they cannot yet require) that parties mediate defamation disputes. This is particularly the case where, at an interlocutory hearing, they see huge legal costs looming on the horizon – perhaps in the disclosure and witness statement stages. Lord Woolf continues to voice his support for mediation and his frustration that it is not being adopted by the legal profession. The *Law Society Gazette*'s front page headline on 17 February 2002 was 'Woolf rails against lack of mediation' and the article proclaimed that 'Lord Woolf has made an impassioned plea to lawyers to mediate more and litigate less . . .'.

1 See Chapter 28.

Procedure

29.05 There is no procedure for mediation. However, before that bald statement has litigation lawyers reaching for the smelling salts as they sense a security blanket being snatched away, a format for the conduct of defamation mediations has evolved and it is safe to suggest that this is likely to be followed in most cases. Remember – the process is without prejudice.

Once the parties have decided to try mediation, they should jointly agree on a mediator. A number of bodies now offer a mediation service[1] and they will have on their books the CVs of various mediators who will have received training and will have acquired experience in conducting mediations. These 'dispute resolution' bodies will gladly organise the mediation and the mediator – but there will be a price to pay for their assistance. Alternatively, there is no reason why the parties should not identify a mediator they are happy with and approach him direct. Anyone can be appointed – there is no requirement to be a trained mediator – but when you consider the qualities a mediator will need to possess (see paragraphs 29.07 and 29.08 below) you may decide an experienced mediator would be preferable.

Once the mediator has been appointed, a date and venue for the mediation should be agreed. The venue needs to have at least three rooms of sufficient comfort for a number of people to occupy for what may be many hours. Refreshments will be needed throughout what is likely to be a long and demanding day.

The mediator is likely to ask that at least a week before the mediation hearing he is provided with a case summary by each party, together with any documents in support. This is where one must try to suppress one's litigation instincts – or at least control them. The claimant's case summary should set out succinctly such matters as the factual background, the publication(s) complained of, the meanings attributed, the damage caused by that publication, relevant reference evidence if necessary, and the steps that have been taken to date to try and restore the damaged reputation through letters of claim, proceedings and any negotiations. However, there is no set format. What the case summary should not be is the equivalent of a counsel's closing speech at trial since that is likely only to have the effect of entrenching the defendant's position and resistance, rendering a successful mediation less likely. The case summary should be clear, concise, calm and convincing. The documents in support should be kept to a minimum – do not include 30 witness statements when one will make the point. Do include any statements of case, but do not duplicate their contents in the summary.

1   For example, CEDR and the ADR Group.

29.06   Similarly, the defendant's case summary should identify the defences to the claim and set out any alternative meanings attributed to the words complained of. If there are extenuating circumstances surrounding the publication consider including them. If there are valid points to be made about delay in the claimant's pursuit of his claim or the damage caused to him, by all means make them, but in an even, factual way. This is not the time to be raising the claimant's blood pressure any further. Again, relevant documents should be provided, as long as these do not duplicate the claimant's.

The case summaries and documents should be served on the mediator and will normally also be exchanged by the parties.

At the mediation itself, the mediator will normally keep the two camps separate at the outset while he introduces himself and 'breaks the ice'. The parties are then likely to be brought together. The mediator will lay down the ground rules for the day and invite each party to make any opening submissions. It will have been emphasised in advance of the mediation that these should not consist of a mere repetition of the case summaries – it can be assumed these have been read and understood. Instead this gives a valuable opportunity for the parties to size each other up and quite often the first opportunity for the defamer and the defamed to look each other in the eye. Normally one would expect the solicitors respectively representing the claimant and the defendant to each make an opening submission (the cost of deploying counsel for this purpose could rarely be justified, quite apart from the impression it conveys of importing advocacy skills into the mediation as a means of achieving one's end). It is also an extremely valuable opportunity for the claimant to say something about why he is bringing the claim and how the publications have damaged and upset him. It turns him from a mere name in a letter into a person and the impact can be dramatic. In the same way, the editor or journalist may want to say something and this may demonstrate that they were not cynically out to damage the claimant but were genuinely trying to publish an honest piece of journalism. If the parties can be turned from demons into people in the other's eyes at the outset of the mediation then it will assist the prospect of a positive outcome.

After this opening session, the mediator is likely to return the parties to their separate rooms, and then a round of shuttle diplomacy will commence, with the mediator spending time alone with one group then with the other. How the process evolves after that point will differ in every case. There may be further joint sessions; there may be individual meetings between the parties or their solicitors; an acceptable compromise may emerge purely from the to-ing and fro-ing of the mediator.

If consensual terms of agreement are reached then the lawyers for each party will get together to prepare an (often handwritten) agreement. This will be signed and dated and hopefully the day will finish with handshakes and contentment all round.

If mediation successfully resolves ongoing proceedings then the terms of agreement will best be embodied in a draft consent order.

Choosing a mediator

29.07 No qualifications are required to be allowed to mediate a defamation dispute (or indeed any other) but parties will generally prefer to appoint someone who has:

(a) been trained in mediation skills by a recognised body;
(b) has some experience of mediating disputes – this should be evident from the mediator's CV;
(c) has some defamation experience as a lawyer. Ignorance is not a total bar but a lack of understanding of such principles as reference, meaning, privilege and malice could slow the process and frustrate the parties.

29.08 The ability to mediate a dispute is a notable skill and a combination of the right personality and the judgment to know when to use your training as a mediator and when to jettison your inclinations as a lawyer (most mediators are lawyers) is required. The ideal mediator should at least possess the following qualities:

(a) Accessibility, approachability and affordability – he has got to be able to establish a connection and working relationship with a variety of people in a short space of time. Awkwardness of manner or conversation will stall the process at first base.
(b) Trustworthiness – the parties will be tense and will need to feel they can trust the mediator.
(c) Sufficient gravitas and leadership – the mediator has to impose his approach on a situation which can get heated and emotional. The parties must respect the mediator and listen to and abide by his suggestions.
(d) The ability to express himself clearly, in other words to say precisely what he means – the function of a mediator involves shuttling back and forwards between two or more parties who will unburden themselves often in an extreme and passionate way. The mediator must extract something positive from what he is told, frame it in a manner which is agreed by the party who he has been with, and then go to the other party and communicate that positive message with the correct weight and emphasis, staying strictly within the parameters set by the other party. The importance of this in the mediation process cannot be over

291

emphasised: a mediator could easily derail a mediation by communicating what one party wishes to say to the other in a clumsy or inaccurate manner.

(e) The ability not to take sides – for obvious reasons.

(f) The stoic ability to sit there while a party unburdens himself of all the anger and frustration he feels about his opponent and not only not take it personally but to listen out for the pieces of information which can move the mediation forward.

(g) Empathy – the parties need to believe that the mediator understands their feelings about their case and genuinely cares about facilitating a fair and just outcome.

(h) Patience.

(i) Stamina.

Who should attend the mediation?

29.09 For the claimant:

(a) the claimant himself;

(b) the claimant's solicitor or legal representative;

(c) if relevant, the person who has responsibility for making financial decisions about the costs of the dispute;

(d) if the claimant wishes, a friend or colleague whose judgment he trusts, or a union representative who has been supporting him in his case.

For the defendant (assuming a media defendant):

(a) ideally, the editor;

(b) the journalist who wrote the words complained of;

(c) the defendant's solicitor;

(d) the insurer or representative of the publishing or broadcasting company who can make financial decisions about costs.

Just as judges may be ill-suited to become mediators because they are trained to determine rather than negotiate disputes, so counsel can find the mediation process somewhat alien because they are trained to advocate for a particular cause. Solicitors are more familiar with negotiation and compromise and find the concept of mediation easier to take on board. This is a generalisation, but it is broadly true and one must be certain that you will not turn a mediation into a trial if you decide to instruct your counsel to prepare your case summary, present your opening submissions and act as the party's spokesperson in a mediation.

Advantages of mediation

29.10 Mediation offers a number of advantages:

- Speed – if properly organised, from deciding to mediate to mediation should not take more than a month and could take much less.
- Cost – the costs associated with preparing for and attending a mediation are insignificant compared to those related to a defamation trial.
- Privacy – a mediation is without prejudice and conducted in private without any publicity, unlike a defamation trial which tends to attract considerable publicity.
- Communication – at a mediation the alleged defamer and defamed get the chance to meet face to face. The claimant can express the hurt and anger which the words complained of have caused, and the defendant can explain how and why those words were published. These encounters can be cathartic and assist settlement. The initial joint session at which opening submissions are made is often followed at some point during the mediation by a meeting between the defamer and defamed without their lawyers present.
- Informality – the legal process can seem alien and remote to lay parties, who can feel marginalised by litigation as they end up fulfilling a function like chess pieces manipulated by clever lawyers playing an incomprehensible game. Mediation is much more informal, much less 'legal' and engages the parties directly in the dispute resolution process.
- Innovation – there are no rules governing what can be agreed on mediation. This means there is scope for innovative and non-legal solutions not achievable by litigation.

EXAMPLE: A libel claim was brought by a teacher and rugby coach over remarks made to the press by the president of the local referees' society to the effect that he had sworn at match officials in front of school children and so was unfit to teach and coach. It was resolved at mediation on terms which included establishing a working party (with both the teacher and the referees' president as members) to devise a proper complaints system and to provide education and training about the special considerations of schools rugby to the referees' society. This sort of outcome is not possible through the courts, but was welcomed by both parties in this dispute.

Disadvantages of mediation

29.11 On the other side of the coin, there can also be disadvantages to the mediation process:

- Defamation is an area of law in which the claimant often feels very strongly that he should achieve total vindication by means of an apology, compensation and the payment of legal costs. Mediation relies on the preparedness of both parties to compromise, and if the claimant believes his initial demands were modest and just or the defendant refuses to budge on an important aspect, the mediation process can stall in a frustrating impasse. It is by its nature difficult for a party to achieve conclusive victory in mediation. Not every case is appropriate for mediation.
- Financial imbalance between the status of the parties can introduce complications. If one party knows it can outspend and outlast the other party in litigation, then it may adopt a more entrenched position at a mediation. For mediation to work, both parties must start the process with an open mind and a willingness to explore all settlement possibilities seriously.
- If the claimant is being represented on a conditional fee agreement ('CFA') then it makes mediation difficult because the claimant's lawyer cannot realistically contemplate any resolution which does not involve payment of their client's costs. It could lead to a conflict of interest between the claimant and his lawyers if, for example, at a mediation the defendant offered the claimant adequate compensation and a fulsome apology but proposed that each side bear their own costs.
- It takes two to tango! Unless all parties are committed and open to the mediation process it is bound to fail. There is the danger a cynical litigant might propose mediation merely as a delaying tactic within the litigation.
- The informality of the mediation process and the lack of emphasis on documentary and witness evidence can mean important issues are sidelined or do not emerge as they should. The

advantage of the litigation process is that it does tend to shine a light into the murky corners. One wonders what the outcome of a mediation of Jonathan Aitken's infamous libel action against *The Guardian* would have been?

- If a mediation comes down to a situation where the defendant is going to pay damages, then it runs the risk of descending into a Dutch auction, with the mediator scurrying back and forward between the rooms with offers and counter-offers. That is not really the intended spirit of ADR.

The future

29.12   Mediation is here to stay, however unappealing it may be to some lawyers who feel it smacks of 'touchy-feeliness' and compromises the icy precision of the legal process with its checks and balances evolved over the centuries. If clients decide they like it then it will gather pace. Certainly there are media defendants who favour establishing a form of ADR as a first way of trying to resolve defamation claims[1]. Lord Woolf will continue to press for the legal profession to adopt mediation at a faster pace and if it does not, then expect more powers to be given to the judiciary to order mediation as part of their case management function.

Shakespeare advised that 'If it were done when 'tis done, then 'twere well it were done quickly'[2] and that is sound advice in relation to mediation. In defamation, costs can quickly become a very significant issue in the claim and this can provide a barrier to a successful mediation. The successful future of mediation in defamation claims will probably be linked to how early mediation is canvassed and deployed. The requirement to consider ADR stipulated in the pre-action protocol should not be regarded as just a box to tick.

The Government's civil and legal aid reforms have led to the active encouragement of both mediation and CFAs, yet the two seem incompatible. CFAs are best suited to the brutal certainty of the litigation process. Practitioners are going to need clearer direction and assurance about how CFAs and mediation can work together if the latter process, with its many advantages and attractions, is going to secure a foothold as a realistic means of resolving defamation disputes.

1   For example, Times Newspapers Ltd developed 'Fast track arbitration rules for the resolution of "meaning" or "quantum" disputes in libel actions'.
2   *Macbeth*, Act I, scene VI.

Chapter 30

Other possible causes of action arising from the publication of statements

30.01 This chapter sets out the essential ingredients of the other main causes of action available through which it may be possible to seek redress for the publication of statements. These are: (a) malicious falsehood, (b) negligent misstatement, (c) breach of confidence/invasion of privacy, and (d) passing off. Each is dealt with briefly, and in outline only, and compared for its advantages and disadvantages with an action for defamation.

The aim of this chapter is to draw to the attention of the reader the other possible *legal* avenues through which redress may be sought where all the necessary ingredients for defamation are lacking or questionable. The reader should then refer to specialist texts on these causes of action before embarking on, or seeking to defend, any such claim. For non-legal redress, for example through complaint to the Press Complaints Commission, the Broadcasting Standards Commission or the Advertising Standards Authority, the reader is referred to Chapters 31–33.

Malicious falsehood

30.02 A claimant will have an actionable claim for malicious falsehood[1] if he can establish the following:

(a)   the defendant published words to third parties;
(b)   which are false;
(c)   that refer to the claimant or his property or business;
(d)   that were published maliciously; and
(e)   that special damage has resulted or that the words are likely to cause pecuniary damage to the claimant (in a case falling within the DA 1952, s 3(1))[2].

1   Malicious falsehood is also known as injurious falsehood or an action on the case. It is a generic name given to the malicious publication of false statements which cause damage to the claimant. It incorporates such torts as slander of title and slander of goods, which are not discussed separately here as distinctions are archaic. A claimant may now simply bring an action for malicious falsehood and need not identify the 'class' of malicious falsehood alleged.

2   See Appendix 1 and paragraph 30.07 below.

Publication

30.03   As with defamation, the offending publication must be made to a third party or parties. Publication to the claimant alone reveals no cause of action.

Falsity

30.04   The claimant must prove that the words complained of are false. In order to determine whether a statement is false, it is necessary to decide what it means. The meaning of a statement is derived in the same way as it is in defamation.

Reference

30.05   The claimant must prove that the words in question referred to himself or his property or business. It does not appear to be the case that a claimant who has proved reference to his property or business must then go on to prove that the words were understood to refer to himself.

Malice

30.06   Malice in a malicious falsehood action has the same meaning as malice in a defamation action[1].

1   See *Spring v Guardian Assurance plc* [1993] 2 All ER 273, CA. The decision was reversed in the House of Lords but malicious falsehood was not in issue. However, following *Tse Wai Chun Paul v Cheng* (Ct Final Appeal Hong Kong) FACV No 12 of 2000, [2001] EMLR 777, malice in the context of fair comment and qualified privilege now has two separate meanings. Which of these will be applied to malicious falsehood is unclear. See also Chapter 18.

Special damage

30.07 Originally a claimant would have to plead and prove special damage, that is the actual financial loss suffered as a result of the publication. Section 3(1) of the DA 1952 provides an exception in certain cases:

> 'In an action for . . . malicious falsehood, it shall not be necessary to allege or prove special damage:
> (1)   if the words upon which the action is founded are calculated to cause pecuniary damage to the plaintiff[1] and are published in writing or some other permanent form; or
> (2)   if the said words are calculated to cause pecuniary damage to the plaintiff in respect of any office, profession, calling, trade or business held or carried on by him at the time of publication.'

The references in this section to 'words' have been taken by the courts without argument to include pictures or any other representation and it is submitted that this must be correct[2]. 'Calculated' does not imply a requirement to prove any intention on the part of the publisher but simply means 'likely'[3]. The reference to 'permanent form' includes broadcasting and material published during the course of a performance of a play[4].

Once the claimant has established that he has suffered special damage or that he falls within the section 3(1) exceptions, aggravated damages can be awarded for injury to feelings caused by the defendant's conduct[5]. If the claimant fails to prove either special damage, or that he comes within section 3(1), he will get nothing. An award of damages for injury to feelings in an action for malicious falsehood is parasitic upon the special damage or section 3(1) award.

1   Now called the claimant.
2   See *Khodaparast v Shad* [2000] 1 WLR 618, CA.
3   *Customglass Boats v Salthouse Boats* [1976] RPC 589 (dealing with the New Zealand equivalent); *Stewart-Brady v Express Newspapers plc* [1997] EMLR 192.
4   The Broadcasting Act 1990, s 166(2) and the Theatres Act 1968, s 4(1) and (2).
5   *Khodaparast v Shad* [2000] 1 WLR 618, CA.

Malicious falsehood and defamation compared

30.08 Malicious falsehood is very much the poor relation of defamation. A claimant will only ever be advised to bring a claim for malicious falsehood when the circumstances of his claim do not fit a claim for defamation[1].

Malicious falsehood has five advantages over defamation for the potential claimant:

(a)   It provides a remedy for the publication of non-defamatory, as well as defamatory statements, provided they are false and published maliciously.

(b)   It is not necessary for the claimant to prove reference to himself, provided he can show that the statement referred to his property or his business[2].

(c)   Unlike proceedings for defamation, an action for malicious falsehood may be brought in the county court without the consent of the defendant, which saves the expense of a high court action.

(d)   If a party dies during the course of proceedings for malicious falsehood, the action does not die with him: his right or liability vests in his estate. For this reason, an elderly or seriously ill claimant should consider bringing a claim for malicious falsehood as an alternative in addition to his defamation claim.

(e)   Although a political party[3] or an organ of local government would no longer permitted to bring an action for defamation, it apparently can do so for malicious falsehood[4].

The disadvantages, however, will in most cases far outweigh the advantages.

(a)   The claimant must prove that the statement is false, whereas in a defamation action, the offending publication is presumed false until the defendant proves otherwise.

(b)   The claimant must prove that the words were published maliciously. There is no such requirement in a defamation action unless the defendant pleads and proves qualified privilege or fair comment.

(c)   Because the origins of malicious falsehood lie in the defence of property rights rather than in vindication of reputation, the claimant has to prove that the publication has caused him actual financial damage ('special' damage) or that it was likely to cause him such damage (in a case falling within the DA 1952, s 3(1))[5]. In an action for libel and certain slanders, damage to reputation is presumed and damages are awarded accordingly. Until recently, it was unclear whether a claimant in an action for malicious falsehood could recover damages for injury to feelings.

It has now been established that they can, but damages which are awarded are still likely to be far lower than those awarded in a comparable defamation case[6].

1 Until fairly recently, legal aid was available for malicious falsehood, so many claims which could and should have been framed as defamation, for which legal aid is not available, were brought as malicious falsehood.
2 *Alcott v Millar's Karri Ltd* (1904) 91 LT 722.
3 *Goldsmith v Bhoyrul* [1998] QB 459.
4 The Court of Appeal, in *Derbyshire County Council v Times Newspapers Ltd* [1992] QB 770, observed that a claim for malicious falsehood would still be available, and the House of Lords referred to this without disapproval: [1993] AC 534 at 551.
5 See paragraph 30.07 above.
6 See, for example, *Khodaparast v Shad* [2000] 1 WLR 618.

Main use: trade disputes

30.09 Actions for malicious falsehood most commonly arise from disputes between businesses over advertisements criticising the products of others and exaggerating the virtues of their own. However, an action for malicious falsehood will provide no remedy for B, no matter what the damage caused, where A has made no false representation about B's goods. Additionally, the law provides no protection against what are known as 'mere puffs', that is statements to the effect that one's own goods are better than another's. To do so would mean that 'the courts of law would be turned into a machinery for advertising rival productions by obtaining a judicial determination which of the two was better'[1].

1 *White v Mellin* [1895] AC 154 at 165, per Lord Herschell.

Negligent misstatement

30.10 Liability in negligence can arise where A has relied on a statement by B and has acted on it to his detriment. What is considered below is not this, but liability arising from statements in a scenario akin to defamation, namely where A suffers loss as a result of a statement made about him by B to a third party, C. A claimant will have an actionable claim for negligent misstatement if he can establish the following:

(a) the existence of a 'special relationship'[1] between the claimant and defendant such that in law a duty of care is owed by the

defendant to the claimant in respect of a statement it made which the claimant claims caused him loss;
(b) breach of that duty of care by the defendant in failing to reach the standard of care imposed by law in making a misstatement;
(c) a causal connection between the defendant's careless conduct and the damage caused to the claimant;
(d) that the particular kind of damage caused to the claimant is not so unforeseeable as to be too remote.

The leading case on negligent misstatement is *Spring v Guardian Assurance plc*[2]. In that case the claimant had been an employee/independent contractor of the defendant until his dismissal. He sought new employment and in accordance with certain regulatory rules of a body set up under statute, his new employer sought a reference from the defendant. The defendant provided a reference which stated that the claimant was 'of little or no integrity and could not be regarded as honest'. This statement was untrue. However, the reference was supplied on an occasion which was protected by qualified privilege and there was a finding of no malice. The claim for libel therefore failed, but the court held that the defendant owed the claimant a duty of care and had failed to exercise reasonable care in making the statement, and, on appeal, a majority of the House of Lords held that if causation could be established, the claimant had a cause of action in negligence.

1 *Hedley Byrne & Co Ltd v Heller & Partners Ltd* [1964] AC 465, HL.
2 [1995] 2 AC 296, HL.

Negligent misstatement and defamation compared

30.11   There are three advantages of a claim in negligence over a claim in defamation:

(a) The limitation period is longer, being either three or six years depending upon the nature of the loss caused by the statement[1].
(b) Provided that the statement is a misstatement, there is no requirement that it be defamatory.
(c) As in *Spring v Guardian Assurance plc*[2], a claim arising from a negligent misstatement may succeed where a defamation claim would fail, since there is no defence of qualified privilege available.

The disadvantages, however, are manifold. Not only does a claimant have to establish a sufficient nexus between himself and the defendant for there to be a duty of care, he must also prove breach, causation and damage. In a defamation action there is no requirement that there be any connection between the claimant and defendant *at all*, and all the claimant has to prove is publication, reference and defamatory meaning. In libel, and many types of slander case, damage is presumed and the burden falls to the defendant to establish a defence if he has one. It would seem that an action for negligent misstatement should only even be considered in a defamation-type case where there is a fairly strong claim to qualified privilege and no evidence of malice.

1   Three years if the claim is for personal injury, six years otherwise.
2   [1995] 2 AC 296, HL.

Breach of confidence/invasion of privacy

30.12   Until the enactment of the HRA 1998[1], there was no recognition of a right to privacy as such in English law. For this reason, the claimant who wished to seek redress for what in essence was an invasion of his privacy would frequently resort to alternative claims such as trespass, harassment or action under the Data Protection Acts. Traditionally the most frequently used cause of action for what was in fact an invasion of privacy was a claim for breach of confidence.

The HRA 1998 was ratified by the UK and became part of domestic law on 2 October 2000. This Act represents a shift in the traditional way of thinking with a move towards a positive 'rights-based' culture. The HRA 1998 requires public bodies to pay proper attention to individuals' rights when making certain decisions and should ensure that the rights of individuals are not ridden over rough-shod.

There are 14 Articles to the HRA 1998 which set out the various rights to be protected. From a media perspective, the two most important Articles are Articles 8 (right to privacy) and 10 (right of freedom of expression.)

Article 8 states that:

(a)   Everyone has the right to respect for his private and family life, his home and his correspondence.
(b)   There shall be no interference by a public authority with the exercise of this right except such as is in accordance with the law and is necessary in the democratic society in the interests of national security, public safety or the economic wellbeing of the

country, for the prevention of disorder or crime, for the protection of health or morals or for the protection of the rights and freedoms of others.

Article 10 states that:

'1. Everyone has the right to freedom of expression. This right shall include freedom to hold opinions and to receive and impart information and ideas without interference by public authority and regardless of frontiers. This Article shall not prevent States from requiring the licensing of broadcasting, television or cinema enterprises.

2. The exercise of these freedoms, since it carries with it duties and responsibilities, may be subject to such formalities, conditions, restrictions or penalties as are prescribed by law and are necessary in a democratic society, in the interests of national security, territorial integrity or public safety, for the prevention of disorder or crime, for the protection of health or morals, for the protection of the reputation or rights of others, for preventing the disclosure of information received in confidence, or for maintaining the authority and impartiality of the judiciary.'

The provisions of the HRA 1998 are only directly enforceable against public bodies. The Act is not directly enforceable against private bodies and therefore is not directly enforceable against, for example, the companies that own newspapers. At the time the HRA 1998 first came into force, however, some practitioners envisaged that a right to privacy actionable against public and private bodies alike would emerge in the following way. Section 6(1) of the HRA 1998 provides that it is unlawful for a public authority to act in a way which is incompatible with a Convention right. Section 6(3) provides that a court is included in the definition of a public authority; therefore if a court was asked to adjudicate a claim for invasion of privacy, it would be required to act in a way compatible with the Article 8 right to privacy and provide a remedy for the breach, even where both parties to the action were private persons.

1   Which adopts the European Convention on Human Rights Article 8 into English law.

30.13   The enactment of the HRA 1998 has not, however, necessitated the establishment of a common law tort of invasion of privacy, although initially it looked as if the courts were on the brink of developing it.

In *Douglas v Hello! Ltd*[1], the Court of Appeal indicated that the time had apparently come to extend a claim in breach of confidence to the protection of a distinct right to privacy. This case concerned the unauthorised publication of photographs of the wedding of Michael Douglas and Catherine Zeta Jones by *Hello!* Magazine. The claimants had signed an exclusive deal with *OK!* Magazine in relation to publication of their wedding photos. It became apparent that *Hello!* planned to publish unauthorised photos which the claimants claimed represented an invasion of their privacy. The Court of Appeal, whilst recognising the rights to privacy conferred by the HRA 1998, did not decide the case on privacy issues but rather sought to balance the commercial interests of all parties by refusing to impose an injunction.

In *H (A Healthcare Worker) v Associated Newspapers Ltd*[2] Lord Phillips MR made reference to 'the development of the law of privacy under the stimulus of the Human Rights Act, as a result of which the possibility of a new civil law right to privacy is being recognised as one that can legitimately be protected by the grant of an injunction'.

However, in *Wainwright v Home Office*[3] the Court of Appeal held that there was no common law tort of invasion of privacy, and Lord Woolf CJ stated that the HRA 1998 'certainly cannot be relied on to change the substantive law by introducing a retrospective right to privacy which did not exist at common law'. Mummery LJ stated that it was for Parliament, not judges, to change the substantive law to recognise a cause of action of infringement of privacy[4]. Buxton LJ took a different view but with the same end result, namely that the Court of Appeal decision in *Kaye v Robertson*[5] was binding authority to the effect that there was no tort of infringement of privacy which precluded its development by the courts[6].

1   [2001] 1 QB 967, CA.
2   [2002] EWCA Civ 195, [2002] EMLR 425.
3   [2001] EWCA Civ 2081, [2002] 3 WLR 405.
4   [2001] EWCA Civ 2081 at paras 108 and 111.
5   [1991] FSR 62. That case concerned Gorden Kaye, the well-known star of *'Allo 'Allo*, who was photographed and allegedly interviewed by a tabloid newspaper after he had undergone extensive surgery and was recovering in hospital following a road accident. He had relied on causes of action in trespass to the person, malicious falsehood, passing off and libel, though, perhaps curiously, not breach of confidence.
6   [2001] EWCA Civ 2081 at paras 97–101.

30.14 Nonetheless, the whole concept of confidence and privacy remains under the spotlight, following a plethora of cases involving celebrities alleging that the British press have gone too far in reporting details of their private lives.

In July 2001, *The Daily Mail* and *OK!* published photos of the newsreader Anna Ford clad in a bikini on a Majorcan beach. She did not bring an action for breach of confidence/invasion of privacy, but instead complained to the Press Complaints Commission[1]. The PCC held that she could not have any reasonable expectation of privacy whilst on a public beach at the height of the holiday season. She later failed in her attempt to get a judicial review of the PCC's decision as the court declined to intervene in recognition of the discretion which the PCC had. Nonetheless, this gives an insight into how the case may have been decided had it been brought before the courts and therefore acts as a guide as to what constitutes an invasion of privacy.

By contrast, in December 2001, actress Amanda Holden was photographed topless at a private villa in Tuscany. She and her husband Les Dennis took proceedings against Express Newspapers and recovered approximately £40,000 in an out of court settlement, plus payment of their legal fees which were rumoured to be in the region of £120,000. This case demonstrates how fact-sensitive the issue of privacy is and that the real test, if a tort were to be developed, in ascertaining whether there is a right to be protected, would focus upon the expectation of privacy the complainant should have had in the situation they found themselves in. Clearly, whilst on private property it was fair to assume that Ms Holden was entitled to her privacy, unlike Ms Ford who was on a six-mile long beach at the height of the summer season.

In 2002, the TV presenter Jamie Theakston sought to obtain an injunction restraining an alleged threatened breach of confidence, in that he sought to prevent the publication by *The Sunday People* of photos and 'kiss and tell' stories arising from his visit to a Mayfair brothel before Christmas 2001[2]. The court did not allow publication of the photos on the basis that this would constitute an intrusion into his personal and private life in a damaging and humiliating way. But *The Sunday People were* allowed to publish the prostitutes' accounts of the incident, which had the captions 'TV Jamie in Bondage Brothel Shame' and 'Jamie had Sex with 3 Hookers in Torture Chamber Brothel'.

It was held that Mr Theakston had eroded any rights to privacy, or more accurately to confidentiality, by giving interviews about his relationships with well-known personalities. The Judge stated, 'The claimant cannot complain if the publicity given to his sexual activities is less favourable in this instance'. Additionally the Judge found no relationship of confidentiality between Mr Theakston and the prostitute.

The issue of sexual conduct came under the spotlight again soon after the *Theakston* case in *A v B plc (sub nom Flitcroft v MGN Ltd)*[3].

This case was concerned with the Premiership footballer Gary Flitcroft's extra-marital affairs. In April 2001 he became aware that *The Sunday People* were going to publish articles about his 'sleazy affairs' and comment that he had tricked two women into commencing the liaisons and that he was therefore a sexual predator. A temporary injunction was granted on the basis that sexual acts that occur privately were covered by the law of confidence. Clearly the grant of the injunction, which was challenged in March 2002, did not sit well with the judgment in the *Theakston* case. Unsurprisingly the injunction was set aside.

In making its decision, the court noted that Mr Flitcroft's liaisons were found not to be distinguished by commitment, discretion or moral scruple (which accords with the *Theakston* judgment). The court continued that public figures who put their private lives into the public domain have weaker grounds upon which to make a later objection to intrusion, particularly when they seek to keep their own misconduct secret. Importantly, the court also recognised another HRA 1998 freedom, namely the Article 10 freedom of expression, and concluded that the press have more freedom in relation to a public person than a private individual, and that suppression of press freedom was undesirable.

1 See further, Chapter 31.
2 [2002] EWCA Civ 337, [2002] 2 All ER 545.
3 [2002] 3 WLR 542.

30.15 The most recent high profile case to make the news is that of Naomi Campbell, who brought a claim against Associated Newspapers Ltd[1] over the publication of details of her attendance at Narcotics Anonymous in Chelsea, London, including photographs of her leaving an NA meeting. Ms Campbell brought claims alleging data protection breaches, breach of confidence and infringement of privacy[2].

Through her lawyers, Ms Campbell conceded that she had falsely held herself up, on a television appearance in America, to be one of the few models who had not succumbed to drug use and therefore that the newspapers were entitled to 'set the record straight'. Consequently, the matters which Ms Campbell complained of at trial were not that she had a drug problem for which she sought treatment, but rather over the publication of a photo of her outside Narcotics Anonymous and details pertaining to her treatment. It is this question of degree which makes the case an interesting one as, but for her assertion that she did not take drugs, Ms Campbell would undoubtedly have benefited from the protection of the law of confidence[3].

In the first instance, the court addressed the issue of confidence and found that a breach had occurred on the basis that the information bore the 'badge of confidentiality' and that there was similarly a breach of data protection legislation. Despite this, Ms Campbell was awarded just £2,500 general damages and £1,000 aggravated damages. The newspaper appealed and in a judgment handed down on 14 October 2002, the appeal was allowed. The court found that:

(a)   The published information of which Ms Campbell complained was not of a confidential nature. An ordinary person, on reading that Ms Campbell was a drug addict, would not find it offensive to know that she was attending Narcotics Anonymous meetings. (Reference was made to the case of *ABC v Lenah Game Meats Pty Ltd*[4], which gave guidance on what test could be applied as to what amounted to an invasion of privacy, namely what is 'highly offensive to a reasonable person of ordinary sensibilities'.) The details published were not sufficiently significant to amount to a breach of confidence.

(b)   The primary information to be conveyed was that Ms Campbell was attending Narcotics Anonymous and therefore the inescapable secondary inference was that she was a drug addict. The court found that it was unrealistic to say that *The Mirror* should have published the secondary inference without publishing the primary fact from which the inference is drawn. The detail and photographs were a legitimate part of the journalistic package designed to demonstrate that the claimant had deceived the public and the publication was justified in the public interest.

(c)   The court was asked to rule on whether a publisher can only be liable for a breach of confidence if he knows it represents an unjustifiable breach, ie the publisher will only be liable if he has acted dishonestly. The court rejected this argument: the media should be able to recognise confidential material which would be offensive for publication without good reason. The media must accept responsibility for their decisions.

1   [2002] EWHC 499 (QB), [2002] EMLR 30, Morland J.
2   The claim for infringement of privacy was not pursued at trial.
3   It is a basic principle of the law of confidence that there is no confidence in iniquity.
4   (2001) HCA 63.

30.16   Though the enactment of the Article 8 right to privacy has clearly provided claimant practitioners with another weapon for the litigation armoury, it would be foolhardy to bring proceedings for invasion of privacy in isolation. If such a claim is to be pursued at all, it should be in the alternative to an established cause of action, such as breach of confidence (and the client should be given a health warning!)[1].

A claimant will have a claim in breach of confidence for an invasion of his privacy if he can establish that:

(a) the information which is the subject matter of the claim was of a confidential nature;
(b) the information was communicated in circumstances importing an obligation of confidence; and
(c) there was some misuse of the information.

It should be noted that a threatened breach of confidence can be restrained by injunction. However, as a number of celebrities have discovered to their cost, the law of confidence does not afford protection to acts of iniquity, or where publication was in the public interest, and the wrongdoer will not therefore be protected simply because the information he does not want published was confidential.

1 The real test will come when a claim for breach of privacy is brought in factual circumstances which cannot be comfortably squeezed into any established cause of action.

Breach of confidence and defamation compared

30.17 A claim for breach of confidence has four main advantages over a claim for defamation, although it may be argued that each is more apparent than real.

(a) It does not matter whether the information published or threatened to be published is true or not. Provided that the material is confidential, a claimant may seek to restrain, or bring a claim in respect of, the publication of the information. However, in order to restrain publication or make any award in respect of it, the court must be satisfied that there was no public interest in the publication of the material in question.
(b) An injunction is much more readily granted to restrain a threatened breach of confidence than a threatened libel or slander, where injunctions are extremely rare. However, a court will not grant an injunction to restrain a threatened breach of confidence which appears to be a defamation claim 'disguised' in an attempt to get an injunction.

(c) Since a claim for breach of confidence is a claim for equitable relief, there is no statutory limitation period. However, a court will refuse such relief if a claimant fails to act with reasonable promptness.

(d) The application of the public interest defence is applied more leniently in cases of breach of confidence. In the case of *A v B plc (sub nom Flitcroft v MGN Ltd)*[1], salacious sexual details were awarded public interest rating: the court adopted the rationale that to protect such information may lead to an undesirable drop in newspaper sales. By contrast, in the case of *Grobbelaar v News Group Newspapers Ltd*[2], the defendant's public interest defence (qualified privilege) was rejected on the basis that the presentation of the material was designed to serve the newspaper's private commercial interests rather than public interest.

The obvious disadvantages of a claim for breach of confidence when compared with a claim for defamation are that it is a defence to a claim to establish that the information was already in the public domain, or that the confidentiality of the information did not impress itself upon the defendant. By contrast, every publication of a defamatory statement can give rise to a cause of action in defamation, and the number and extent of previous publications is irrelevant for the purposes of establishing liability. Likewise, the publisher's knowledge in relation to the statement is completely irrelevant.

1   [2002] 3 WLR 542.
2   [2001] EWCA Civ 33, [2001] 2 All ER 437.

Passing off

30.18   The tort of passing off was first developed to meet the principle that nobody has a right to represent his goods as the goods of somebody else[1]. It is designed to ensure a degree of honesty and fairness in the way trade is conducted. As such, it is closely connected to, and dependent upon, what is happening in the market place and has been developed over time in line with prevailing mores. As such it is recognised for its flexibility in application. The traditional statement of the law of passing off is that the claimant must establish the following[2]:

(a) that the claimant's goods or services have acquired a goodwill or reputation in the market and are known by some distinguishing feature;

(b) that there has been a misrepresentation by the defendant (whether or not intentional) leading or likely to lead the public to believe that the goods or services offered by the defendant are goods or services of the claimant; and

(c) that the claimant has suffered or is likely to suffer damage as a result of the erroneous belief engendered by the defendant's misrepresentation.

1   *Reddaway v Banham* [1896] AC 199 at 204, per Lord Halsbury.
2   *Reckitt & Colman Products Ltd v Borden Inc* [1990] 1 All ER 873 at 880, HL.

30.19   Passing off is included in this chapter because of its recent application in a false product endorsement case, *Irvine v Talksport Ltd*[1], where the image of Formula 1 racing driver Eddie Irvine was used without his consent or authorisation for the promotion of the defendant's services. In *Irvine*, Talksport Radio had embarked on a promotional campaign using a brochure which featured on its front a photograph of Mr Irvine. In the photograph Mr Irvine was holding a radio bearing the name 'Talk Radio' to his ear. The photograph was in fact doctored from an original in which Mr Irvine had been holding a mobile telephone to his ear. The use of the photograph had not been authorised by the claimant but the right to use it had been legitimately acquired by the defendant. Mr Justice Laddie in the High Court held, adapting the traditional statement of the ingredients set out at points (a) and (b) in paragraph 30.18 above, that liability could be established if the claimant proved:

(a) at the time of the acts complained of he had significant reputation or goodwill; and

(b) that the actions of the defendant gave rise to a false message which would be understood by a not insignificant section of his market that his goods had been endorsed, recommended or were approved of by the claimant.

Previously, a person complaining of a false product endorsement may have had to resort to a claim in defamation, treading a fairly tortuous route in order to establish liability. In *Tolley v J S Fry and Sons Ltd*[2] the claimant was a prominent amateur golfer. The defendant was a firm of chocolate manufacturers which issued an advertisement consisting of a caricature of the golfer with a packet of their chocolate protruding from his pocket, likening the excellence of his drive to that of the chocolate. The advertisement was published without the knowledge or consent of the golfer. Since a statement to the effect that the claimant liked the defendant's chocolate and was happy to promote it could not on its face have lowered the claimant in the estimation of right thinking people generally, the claimant pleaded an innuendo meaning. In essence his case on defamatory meaning was that people would think that he had consented to the use of his image for financial reward and that therefore, those who knew of his amateur status would conclude that he was not maintaining his amateur status as he purported to. Before rushing to issue any claim for passing off, however, it should be noted that *Irvine* has been appealed on liability[3] and it is expected that the Court of Appeal will hear the appeal in March 2003.

1   [2002] EWHC 367 (Ch), [2002] EMLR 679, Laddie J.
2   [1931] AC 333, HL.
3   In fact, both an appeal on damages and a cross-appeal on liability are awaiting determination.

Passing off and defamation compared

30.20   Assuming that *Irvine v Talksport Ltd*[1] remains good law, pursuing a claim in passing off in a false product endorsement case has three main advantages over a claim for defamation. First, it is not necessary to establish any denigration to the claimant caused by the publication complained of. Given that in a false product endorsement case the defendant will usually be seeking to take advantage of a positive perception of a person's character or reputation in order to promote his products, a claimant will not have to resort to pleading and proving a somewhat tortuous innuendo meaning in order to succeed. Related to this is the second advantage[2], in that a false product endorsement claim framed as passing off is likely to be available to a much wider pool of potential claimants than defamation because of the fact that no denigration need be proved. In *Tolley v J S Fry and Sons Ltd*[3], the claimant was able to rely on an innuendo meaning based on the fact that he was a professional masquerading as an amateur. This option was not available to Mr Irvine, a recognised professional. The third advantage for the potential claimant is that the limitation period is six years. A claim for defamation must be brought within one year.

The big disadvantage of a claim for passing off compared with defamation is that (if indeed it is properly possible to compare the two) it would appear that the level of damages likely to be awarded is much lower, in particular because there is no equivalent of an award of damage to reputation. Damages awarded are in essence for financial loss. In *Irvine* the court's approach to the assessment of damages was that: (a) if it could be shown that the claimant had suffered direct loss then such losses might be recoverable; (b) if the claimant had a habit of endorsing such products then it might be that the standard fee would have been correct measure of loss; and (c) (as was the case) in the absence of those types of circumstances the court should adopt the reasonable endorsement fee approach which was the equivalent of a reasonable royalty in patent cases. In the event, the court awarded Mr Irvine just £2,000[4]. He had claimed for damages of £50,000 and the defendants had argued for damages of £500.

1   [2001] EWHC 367 (Ch), [2002] EMLR 679, Laddie J.
2   At least so far as potential claimants are concerned!
3   [1931] AC 333, HL.
4   The award is under appeal and is expected to be heard in March 2003.

Chapter 31

The Press Complaints Commission

What is the Press Complaints Commission?

31.01   The Press Complaints Commission ('PCC') is a private body funded by newspaper proprietors (to the tune of £1.423m in 2001) to which complaints about newspapers and journals may be made. Those complaints are adjudicated by reference to the 16 clause PCC Code of Practice. The full text of the Code appears at Appendix 17.

The PCC has no legal powers but the adjudications which its Complaints Committee makes in relation to upheld complaints will be published in the newspaper or magazine which has been the subject of the complaint. However, the PCC has no power to dictate the position given to the publication of its adjudications, which means that they tend to be tucked out of harm's way by editors – even though they are supposed to be published with 'due prominence'.

The PCC was formed in January 1991 following the recommendations of the *Report of the Committee on Privacy and Related Matters* chaired by David Calcutt in June 1990, and the subsequent demise of the Press Council. The Calcutt Report had recommended that the press be given a final chance to demonstrate that voluntary self-regulation could work, that a PCC be established and that it should concentrate on providing an effective means of redress for complaints against the press. The reason the PCC exists, therefore, is because the print media is anxious to persuade the Government (and the public to a lesser extent) that it can regulate itself, and so avoid the imposition of legislation to achieve that effect. It is interesting to contrast the acres of editorial space which newspapers devote to criticisms of the systems and procedures whereby, for example, the police service, Members of Parliament and lawyers investigate wrongdoing within their ranks with the warm approval generally extended to the operation of the PCC. In fact, arguably, the principal beneficiaries of the PCC in the last decade have been members of the Royal Family; a regular flow of prompt and positive adjudications have emanated in their favour. The experience of ordinary individuals complaining about breaches of the PCC Code tends to be less satisfactory.

The PCC has its offices at 1 Salisbury Square, London, EC4 where its full-time Director (currently Guy Black) and his small full-time staff operate. The current Acting Chairman is Professor Robert Pinker of the London School of Economics. He chairs the four-man Appointments Committee which chooses the public members of the Complaints Committee (which he also chairs). The Complaints Committee currently consists of 14 members (with one vacancy), of which seven are newspaper and magazine editors and seven are 'members of the public'. In addition to the Appointments and Complaints Committees there is also a Code Committee, consisting entirely of senior members of press organisations or newspapers, which is responsible for formulating and reviewing the PCC Code.

Dealing with complaints

31.02 Although the PCC receives several thousand complaints a year it only adjudicates in a small number of cases. In 2001, 3,033 complaints were made, of which 41 were adjudicated and only 19 upheld. A further 935 were either resolved or not pursued – but the PCC's Annual Report does not give the split between those resolved and those not pursued. The Complaints Committee meets for half a day a month to consider the rulings prepared by the Chairman and staff and these are then issued in a quarterly bulletin. All cases are decided on written submissions and the Committee will not entertain oral hearings. The PCC rejects any complaint which it decides is outside its remit and any complaint made by a third party (rather than the person or organisation directly affected). Complaints should be made within a month of the publication complained of although the PCC will extend that time in special circumstances (for example, if a legal remedy is being pursued and provided the complainant notifies them what is going on). A complaint is forwarded to the relevant editor, who should then contact the complainant direct to seek an amicable settlement. If this does not occur then the editor produces a written response on which the complainant is invited to comment. Correspondence shuttles back and forth until the issues have emerged and each party has dealt with what the other has to say. The PCC Chairman and staff then produce a draft ruling on the basis of what has emerged from the exchanges and this is forwarded the Complaints Committee members for comment and, hopefully, agreement. Where there is disagreement, the adjudications are debated at the monthly half-day meetings. Finalised adjudications appear in the quarterly bulletin and on the PCC website at www.pcc.org.uk. The PCC Code states that, 'If the Commission upholds your complaint the publication concerned will be obliged to publish our criticism of them in full and with due prominence'.

PCC adjudications are not appealable. One or two individuals have sought judicial reviews of PCC decisions, notably Anna Ford, the newsreader, following the PCC's ruling that a newspaper which published photos of her in a bikini on a beach while on holiday had not invaded her privacy in breach of the Code because the beach was a public one. The lack of basic legal entitlements in the complaints procedure (for example, no oral hearing, no disclosure of documents, no right to cross-examine) certainly makes it appear susceptible to judicial review in the right case. The underwhelming rewards of a favourable adjudication may be what has deterred dissatisfied complainants from turning to the courts to put right what they see as a wrong adjudication against them.

31.03   A possible cloud on the horizon for the press may be found in the HRA 1998. To date, the press has been able to shelter behind a PCC Code which on its face seems reasonably fair and stringent while taking comfort in the knowledge that the PCC itself will rarely produce an unfavourable adjudication (the 'public interest' exception attached to most clauses of the Code is extremely elastic), and even where an adjudication against a newspaper is made, it can be tucked away in small print next to the greyhound results without any danger of censure.

However, section 12(4)(b)[1] of the HRA 1998 requires the courts to pay attention to 'any relevant privacy code' when considering whether to grant relief which, if granted, might affect the exercise of the Convention right to freedom of expression. The PCC Code (and even more so, the National Union of Journalists Code of Conduct) set the ethical bar fairly high and the courts might well take a different view about what is acceptable under these Codes than the PCC Complaints Committee. If so, then a judicial view of how the PCC Code should operate might gradually emerge[2].

1   See Appendix 5.
2   Privacy and breach of confidence are considered at Chapter 30, paragraphs 30.12–30.17.

When should a complaint be made?

31.04 The short answer to this question is when there is no viable legal remedy, when there has been a clear breach of the PCC Code and where one's client is determined that some sort of action should be taken over the words of which he complains. A PCC complaint rarely achieves a satisfactory outcome because the process tends to be relatively long-winded with no impetus on the newspaper to sort things out promptly. If the matter ends up before the PCC Complaints Committee even a favourable adjudication is most unlikely to contain the condemnatory language which your client hopes for, and it is most unlikely to be published by the newspaper in as prominent a position as the article or photo complained about. The exercise can sometimes create more frustration and anger than doing nothing. It is a sad reflection on the general view of the PCC outside the newspaper world that a complaint can only be recommended as the last resort of a disgruntled client and even then it must come with a health warning. Where is it viable, a defamation claim made directly to the newspaper is far more likely to achieve the outcome a complainant desires that a complaint to the PCC.

The final point to note, of course, is that even a successful complaint to the PCC does not entitle the complainant to recover any compensation, let alone the costs associated with pursuing the complaint. The PCC has no power to award damages or costs.

Chapter 32

The Broadcasting Standards Commission

Introduction

32.01 The Broadcasting Standards Commission ('BSC') was created on 1 April 1997 following the passing of the BA 1996 and the subsequent merger of the Broadcasting Standards Council and the Broadcasting Complaints Commission.

The BSC is an independent body, with members appointed by the Secretary of State for Culture, Media and Sport. The members must not be 'concerned with or have an interest in the preparation or provision of radio or television programmes.'

The functions of the BSC are set out in the BA 1996, which requires that the BSC:

(a) produces codes of guidance in relation to standards and fairness (to include privacy) for the industry to follow[1];
(b) considers and adjudicates complaints; and
(c) monitors and reports on matters of standards and fairness in broadcasting. Standards assessment is a subjective matter which clearly requires a great deal of research, to monitor, identify and focus on trends.

The BSC covers all broadcasting within the UK including radio and television (terrestrial, satellite, digital and cable).

1   See Appendix 18.

Complaints

32.02 In 2000/2001 there were 7,183 standards complaints and 358 fairness complaints made to the BSC. Of these:

- 1,059 standards complaints and 244 fairness complaints were outside the remit of the BSC.
- 4,229 standards complaints and 63 fairness complaints were the subject of a signed adjudication.
- 9% of the total standards complaints and 12.5% of the fairness complaints were upheld in their entirety.

Fairness complaints stem mostly from consumer programmes such as *Watchdog* or from individuals complaining of invasion of privacy. Complaints with regard to standards mainly stem from soaps and can be identified by certain scenes depicting sex, violence or bad language.

Standards complaints must be lodged within two months of the television programme complained of or within three weeks of a radio broadcast.

Fairness complaints must be made within 'a reasonable time'. This can extend up to five years following the death of a complainant.

A standards complaint can be made by anyone but a fairness complaint can only be made by 'persons affected' – namely an individual, members of his family, etc.

The BSC has no remit in relation to licensing issues and is not permitted to consider complaints if subject to legal proceedings or if capable of appropriate remedy through legal channels.

Complaints procedure

32.03 If a complaint is received and it is deemed outside of the remit of the BSC the complainant is duly notified. If the complaint is something that can be dealt with by the BSC it is referred to the Commission. A copy of the complaint must be sent to the broadcasting body responsible and they are under a duty to provide a written response and may have to provide a copy of the programme, a transcript and correspondence, if applicable. Thereafter the complainant is invited to make comment to which the broadcaster is allowed to respond.

The Commission has discretion to decide the complaint without a hearing. Usually complaints in relation to a fall in standards are decided without a hearing. Fairness complaints (and particularly privacy issues) can be decided by a hearing, attended by the complainant, the broadcaster and potentially a representative of the Independent Television Commission.

Sanctions

32.04 The BSC can only offer one sanction, namely the publication of adjudications. The publication appears in digest form in the Commission's monthly bulleting. The BSC also has the power to direct a broadcasting body to publish an approved summary of the complaint and the findings in a manner specified by the Commission.

The Fairness Code

32.05 Broadcasters are held to be responsible for avoiding unfairness to anyone featured in a programme. Unfairness can arise as a result of inaccurate information or distortion of the facts, leading to misleading conclusions.

When dealing with contributors to a programme, broadcasters should make their intentions clear and ensure that individuals know what the programme is about and what contribution will be sought from them. Information or pictures may not be obtained by misrepresentation or deception.

Broadcasters should take all reasonable steps to ensure factual accuracy and be wary of unsubstantiated allegations being made in the course of discussion programmes or 'phone-ins'.

If a programme makes criticisms of individuals or organisations, those concerned should be allowed the right of reply in respect of the allegations.

If a broadcast has been unfair the person affected can request an apology and prompt correction which should be given with due prominence, unless there are legal reasons to prevent this.

The Privacy Code

32.06 The Commission recognises that individuals have a general right to privacy but its Code also sets out guidelines as to when any infringement is warranted, in the overriding public interest.

When broadcasters are covering events in public places they should seek to ensure that images are clearly in the public domain to justify broadcasting without consent. The right to privacy of people in the public eye is recognised to be different to private individuals. Yet the Code recognises that they do not wholly forfeit their right to privacy but must accept that where their private behaviour raises broader public issues, there may be justification in broadcasting.

The use of equipment for secret recording should only be used when necessary to add credibility or authenticity to a story. Unattended recording devices should not be left on private property without consent of the occupiers and nor should cameras or recording devices be operated in a public area where the subject is on private property.

In relation to telephone calls, broadcasters should identify themselves from the outset and seek consent to broadcast a recording of the conversation. When a broadcaster seeks to question and record a person in the news in a public place, the questions should be fair and broadcasters should be aware that repeated attempts to obtain an interview when consent has not been provided can amount to an infringement of an individual's privacy.

Broadcasters are asked to take into consideration vulnerable individuals such as children and those involved in a personal tragedy or emergency situation.

The Code on Standards

32.07 The Code requests that care is given to the scheduling of programmes to ensure that the content is appropriate for the audience. In relation to television the 'watershed' recognises that programmes televised between 9.00 pm and 5.30 am are intended for adult viewing. The Code advises broadcasters to consider such issues also in relation to advertisements, trailers and programme repeats.

The Code gives guidance as to what could be considered an affront to taste and decency, bearing in mind issues such as use of language, portrayal of drugs, alcohol, smoking, religion, mental health, race and crime.

Special attention is given to the portrayal of violence and sexual conduct.

The Independent Television Commission

32.08 The Independent Television Commission ('ITC') was established by the Broadcasting Act 1990 to govern the licensing and regulation of independent television, teletext, cable and satellite (save for the BBC and the Welsh Authority).

The ITC has extensive statutory powers and has established and enforces codes of practice designed to maintain proper standards in respect of taste, decency, portrayal of sex and violence and politically sensitive material. The ITC monitors the content of programmes, advertising and sponsorship and technical performance.

The codes only apply to broadcasters who hold an ITC licence and therefore do not cover any satellite services broadcast into the UK.

The penalties that can be imposed are:

- broadcasters can be directed to provide an apology or correction on the offending channel;
- a demand that there be no repeat of the offensive programme;
- a formal warning can be issued for breach of a licence;
- a licence can be shortened or even revoked;
- a fine of up to 3% of a broadcaster's advertising revenue for a first offence and 5% for further offences.

There is clearly a confusing overlap between the BSC and the ITC in relation to complaints. The reality is that the ITC tends to deal with matters relating to issues of taste and decency and refers privacy and fairness complaints directly to the BSC. In fact the ITC is always informed of complaints that are being investigated by the BSC and is invited to attend upon the hearing of the complaints. If a BSC complaint is upheld, the ITC can be asked to require its licensee to publish its findings or a summary of the decision.

The main differences between the ITC and the BSC are:

- the ITC cannot adjudicate on BBC broadcasts; and
- the ITC cannot adjudicate on radio broadcasts.

With the inception of OFCOM[1], all confusion between the scope of the regulators' work should be removed.

1   See paragraph 32.10 below.

The Radio Authority

32.09   The Radio Authority was set up by the Broadcasting Act 1990 and in essence performs the same function as the ITC but in respect of commercial radio services as opposed to television. The Authority licenses and regulates all national, local and cable stations and will eventually licence national and local digital services. The Authority does not cover hospital radio, student radio or freely radiating services.

Licences are granted for eight years to 'fit and proper' people. The Authority publishes codes of guidance in relation to programming, advertising, sponsorship and engineering. The Authority has the same enforcement powers as the ITC.

Future regulation

32.10 In 2003, all of the above regulators will cease to exist. A new body will be created called the Office of Communications ('OFCOM'). OFCOM will then carry out the work previously conducted by the following regulators:

* the BSC;
* the ITC;
* the Radio Authority;
* the Office of Telecommunications ('OFTEL'); and
* the Radio Communications Agency.

There has always been a degree of overlap between the BSC and the ITC and this has led to a situation of double jeopardy, where broadcasters may get one adjudication from one regulator and the opposite from another. Clearly, there was a good argument to reduce the multiplicity of regulators.

At the time of print, key policy decisions are still being debated. One issue of concern is whether the BBC should come within OFCOM's remit. Additionally, concern has been expressed as to a danger of centralising too much power in one body and chairman. It is hoped that the Communications Bill will ensure sufficient accountability in the system. There has additionally been discussion as to the possibility of the creation of a Communications Select Committee in the Houses of Parliament. Nonetheless, what is certain is that it is hoped that OFCOM will have a clear focus and a cutting edge approach, and will establish a flexible regulator, who builds on the expertise of the existing bodies.

Chapter 33

The Advertising Standards Authority

Introduction

33.01 The Advertising Standards Authority ('ASA') was established in 1962 and is an independent, self-regulatory body, which aims to ensure that everybody who commissions, prepares and publishes adverts in non-broadcast media within the UK observes British codes of advertising and sales promotion. The ASA covers all adverts except for radio and television. The codes are devised to require adverts to be 'legal, decent, honest and truthful and in line with principles of fair competition'.

Complaints procedure

33.02 When the ASA receives a complaint it will send an acknowledgment card to the complainant and then assess the allegations raised. The ASA then must make a decision as to the whether the case needs investigation, or whether the complainant should be advised that there is no case to answer under the codes. Should investigation be required, the ASA will seek the advertiser's comments on the complaint and the advertisement must then be assessed in the light of the advertiser's response. A draft adjudication is then sent to the ASA Council, who are required to make the final decision. The Council's decision is notified to the complainant and the advertisers. Where the complaint is upheld, the ASA requires the advertisement to be amended or withdrawn. If the advertiser refuses to take such action, the ASA will inform media organisations on the Committee of Advertising Practice, which may result in financial penalties to the advertiser. The ASA will also publish the outcome of the investigations in its monthly report, which is circulated to journalists, members of the industry, government bodies and other relevant bodies. The ASA will then finally check that all advertisements have been changed or withdrawn.

In 1998 a total of 12,217 complaints were made, and of this sum 3,385 were investigated. The main sources of complaint stemmed from health and beauty advertisements, religion, financial advertisements, animal advertisements and weight loss and slimming. 13.5% of all complaints related to just ten adverts, of which six were found to break the code. Interestingly, the most complained about advert was for the soft drink 'Irn-Bru'. The advert showed a picture of a cow with the caption stating 'When I am a burger, I want to be washed down with Irn-Bru'. This advert was found not to break the codes of practice.

Appendix I

Defamation Act 1952

1952 CHAPTER 66

An Act to amend the law relating to libel and slander and other malicious falsehoods

[30th October 1952]

1 . . .

. . .

NOTES
Amendment
Repealed by the Broadcasting Act 1990, s 203(3), Sch 21.

2   Slander affecting official, professional or business reputation
In an action for slander in respect of words calculated to disparage the plaintiff in any office, profession, calling, trade or business held or carried on by him at the time of the publication, it shall not be necessary to allege or prove special damage, whether or not the words are spoken of the plaintiff in the way of his office, profession, calling, trade or business.

NOTES
Initial Commencement
Specified date: 30 November 1952: see s 18(1).

3   Slander of title, etc
(1)   In an action for slander of title, slander of goods or other malicious falsehood, it shall not be necessary to allege or prove special damage—
    (a)   if the words upon which the action is founded are calculated to cause pecuniary damage to the plaintiff and are published in writing or other permanent form; or
    (b)   if the said words are calculated to cause pecuniary damage to the plaintiff in respect of any office, profession, calling, trade or business held or carried on by him at the time of the publication.
(2)   Section one of this Act shall apply for the purposes of this section as it applies for the purposes of the law of libel and slander.

NOTES
Initial Commencement
Specified date: 30 November 1952: see s 18(1).

See Further
See further, in relation to programme services: the Broadcasting Act 1990, s 166(1), (2).

4 ...
...

NOTES
Amendment
Repealed by the Defamation Act 1996, s 16, Sch 2.

5   Justification
In an action for libel or slander in respect of words containing two or more distinct charges against the plaintiff, a defence of justification shall not fail by reason only that the truth of every charge is not proved if the words not proved to be true do not materially injure the plaintiff's reputation having regard to the truth of the remaining charges.

NOTES
Initial Commencement
Specified date: 30 November 1952: see s 18(1).

6   Fair comment
In an action for libel or slander in respect of words consisting partly of allegations of fact and partly of expression of opinion, a defence of fair comment shall not fail by reason only that the truth of every allegation of fact is not proved if the expression of opinion is fair comment having regard to such of the facts alleged or referred to in the words complained of as are proved.

NOTES
Initial Commencement
Specified date: 30 November 1952: see s 18(1).

7 ...
...

NOTES
Amendment
Repealed by the Defamation Act 1996, s 16, Sch 2.

8 ...
...

NOTES
Amendment
Repealed by the Defamation Act 1996, s 16, Sch 2.

9   Extension of certain defences to broadcasting

(1)   Section three of the Parliamentary Papers Act 1840 (which confers protection in respect of proceedings for printing extracts from or abstracts of parliamentary papers) shall have effect as if the reference to printing included a reference to broadcasting by means of wireless telegraphy.

(2), (3) . . .

NOTES
Initial Commencement
   Specified date: 30 November 1952: see s 18(1).
Amendment
   Sub-ss (2), (3): repealed by the Defamation Act 1996, s 16, Sch 2.

10   Limitation on privilege at elections

A defamatory statement published by or on behalf of a candidate in any election to a local government authority [to the Scottish Parliament] or to Parliament shall not be deemed to be published on a privileged occasion on the ground that it is material to a question in issue in the election, whether or not the person by whom it is published is qualified to vote at the election.

NOTES
Initial Commencement
   Specified date: 30 November 1952: see s 18(1).
Amendment
   Words "to the Scottish Parliament" in square brackets inserted by the Scotland Act 1998, s 125, Sch 8, para 10.
   Date in force: 19 November 1998: (no specific commencement provision).

11   Agreements for indemnity

An agreement for indemnifying any person against civil liability for libel in respect of the publication of any matter shall not be unlawful unless at the time of the publication that person knows that the matter is defamatory, and does not reasonably believe there is a good defence to any action brought upon it.

NOTES
Initial Commencement
   Specified date: 30 November 1952: see s 18(1).

12   Evidence of other damages recovered by plaintiff

In any action for libel or slander the defendant may give evidence in mitigation of damages that the plaintiff has recovered damages, or has brought actions for damages, for libel or slander in respect of the publication of words to the same effect as the words on which the action is founded, or has received or agreed to receive compensation in respect of any such publication.

NOTES
Initial Commencement
Specified date: 30 November 1952: see s 18(1).

13   Consolidation of actions for slander, etc
Section five of the Law of Libel Amendment Act 1888 (which provides for the consolidation, on the application of the defendants, of two or more actions for libel by the same plaintiff) shall apply to actions for slander and to actions for slander of title, slander of goods or other malicious falsehood as it applies to actions for libel; and references in that section to the same, or substantially the same, libel shall be construed accordingly.

NOTES
Initial Commencement
Specified date: 30 November 1952: see s 18(1).

14   Application of Act to Scotland
This Act shall apply to Scotland subject to the following modifications, that is to say:—

    (a)   sections one, two, eight and thirteen shall be omitted;

    (b)   for section three there shall be substituted the following section—

"3   Actions for verbal injury
In any action for verbal injury it shall not be necessary for the pursuer to aver or prove special damage if the words on which the action is founded are calculated to cause pecuniary damage to the pursuer.";

    (c)   subsection (2) of section four shall have effect as if at the end thereof there were added the words "Nothing in this subsection shall be held to entitle a defender to lead evidence of any fact specified in the declaration unless notice of his intention so to do has been given in the defences."; and

    (d)   for any reference to libel, or to libel or slander, there shall be substituted a reference to defamation; the expression "plaintiff" means pursuer; the expression "defendant" means defender; for any reference to an affadavit made by any person there shall be substituted a reference to a written declaration signed by that person; for any reference to the High Court there shall be substituted a reference to the Court of Session or, if an action of defamation is depending in the sheriff court in respect of the publication in question, the sheriff; the expression "costs" means expenses; and for any reference to a defence of justification there shall be substituted a reference to a defence of *veritas*.

NOTES
Initial Commencement
Specified date: 30 November 1952: see s 18(1).

15 ...

...

NOTES
Amendment
Repealed by the Northern Ireland Constitution Act 1973, s 41(1), Sch 6, Pt I.

16 Interpretation
(1) Any reference in this Act to words shall be construed as including a reference to pictures, visual images, gestures and other methods of signifying meaning.
(2) ...
(3) ...
(4) ...

NOTES
Initial Commencement
Specified date: 30 November 1952: see s 18(1).
Amendment
Sub-s (2): repealed by the Defamation Act 1996, s 16, Sch 2.
Sub-s (3): repealed by the Defamation Act 1996, s 16, Sch 2.
Date in force (in relation to England and Wales): 28 February 2000: see SI 2000/222, art 3(b)(i)–(vi).
Date in force (in relation to Scotland): 31 March 2001: see SSI 2001/98, art 3(b)(i).
Sub-s (4): repealed by the Cable and Broadcasting Act 1984, s 57(2), Sch 6.

17 Proceedings affected and saving
(1) This Act applies for the purposes of any proceedings begun after the commencement of this Act, whenever the cause of action arose, but does not affect any proceedings begun before the commencement of this Act.
(2) Nothing in this Act affects the law relating to criminal libel.

NOTES
Initial Commencement
Specified date: 30 November 1952: see s 18(1).

18 Short title, commencement, extent and repeals
(1) This Act may be cited as the Defamation Act 1952 and shall come into operation one month after the passing of this Act.
(2) This Act . . . shall not extend to Northern Ireland.
(3) ...

NOTES
Initial Commencement
Specified date: 30 November 1952: see sub-s (1) above.
Amendment
Sub-s (2): words omitted repealed by the Northern Ireland Constitution Act 1973, s 41(1), Sch 6, Part I.
Sub-s (3): repealed by the Statute Law (Repeals) Act 1974.

SCHEDULE

. . .

. . .

Part I

. . .

. . .

NOTES
Amendment
    Repealed by the Defamation Act 1996, s 16, Sch 2.

Part II

. . .

. . .

NOTES
Amendment
    Repealed by the Defamation Act 1996, s 16, Sch 2.

Part III

. . .

. . .

NOTES
Amendment
    Repealed by the Defamation Act 1996, s 16, Sch 2.

Appendix 2

Defamation Act 1996

1996 CHAPTER 31

An Act to amend the law of defamation and to amend the law of limitation with respect to actions for defamation or malicious falsehood

[4th July 1996]

BE IT ENACTED by the Queen's most Excellent Majesty, by and with the advice and consent of the Lords Spiritual and Temporal, and Commons, in this present Parliament assembled, and by the authority of the same, as follows:—

Responsibility for publication

1 Responsibility for publication

(1) In defamation proceedings a person has a defence if he shows that—
   (a) he was not the author, editor or publisher of the statement complained of,
   (b) he took reasonable care in relation to its publication, and
   (c) he did not know, and had no reason to believe, that what he did caused or contributed to the publication of a defamatory statement.

(2) For this purpose "author", "editor" and "publisher" have the following meanings, which are further explained in subsection (3)—
   "author" means the originator of the statement, but does not include a person who did not intend that his statement be published at all;
   "editor" means a person having editorial or equivalent responsibility for the content of the statement or the decision to publish it; and
   "publisher" means a commercial publisher, that is, a person whose business is issuing material to the public, or a section of the public, who issues material containing the statement in the course of that business.

(3) A person shall not be considered the author, editor or publisher of a statement if he is only involved—
   (a) in printing, producing, distributing or selling printed material containing the statement;
   (b) in processing, making copies of, distributing, exhibiting or selling a film or sound recording (as defined in Part I of the Copyright, Designs and Patents Act 1988) containing the statement;
   (c) in processing, making copies of, distributing or selling any electronic medium in or on which the statement is recorded, or in

operating or providing any equipment, system or service by means of which the statement is retrieved, copied, distributed or made available in electronic form;

(d)   as the broadcaster of a live programme containing the statement in circumstances in which he has no effective control over the maker of the statement;

(e)   as the operator of or provider of access to a communications system by means of which the statement is transmitted, or made available, by a person over whom he has no effective control.

In a case not within paragraphs (a) to (e) the court may have regard to those provisions by way of analogy in deciding whether a person is to be considered the author, editor or publisher of a statement.

(4)   Employees or agents of an author, editor or publisher are in the same position as their employer or principal to the extent that they are responsible for the content of the statement or the decision to publish it.

(5)   In determining for the purposes of this section whether a person took reasonable care, or had reason to believe that what he did caused or contributed to the publication of a defamatory statement, regard shall be had to—

(a)   the extent of his responsibility for the content of the statement or the decision to publish it,

(b)   the nature or circumstances of the publication, and

(c)   the previous conduct or character of the author, editor or publisher.

(6)   This section does not apply to any cause of action which arose before the section came into force.

NOTES
Initial Commencement
Specified date: 4 September 1996: see s 19(2).

Offer to make amends

2   Offer to make amends

(1)   A person who has published a statement alleged to be defamatory of another may offer to make amends under this section.

(2)   The offer may be in relation to the statement generally or in relation to a specific defamatory meaning which the person making the offer accepts that the statement conveys ("a qualified offer").

(3)   An offer to make amends—

(a)   must be in writing,

(b)   must be expressed to be an offer to make amends under section 2 of the Defamation Act 1996, and

(c)   must state whether it is a qualified offer and, if so, set out the defamatory meaning in relation to which it is made.

(4)   An offer to make amends under this section is an offer—

(a) to make a suitable correction of the statement complained of and a sufficient apology to the aggrieved party,

(b) to publish the correction and apology in a manner that is reasonable and practicable in the circumstances, and

(c) to pay to the aggrieved party such compensation (if any), and such costs, as may be agreed or determined to be payable.

The fact that the offer is accompanied by an offer to take specific steps does not affect the fact that an offer to make amends under this section is an offer to do all the things mentioned in paragraphs (a) to (c).

(5) An offer to make amends under this section may not be made by a person after serving a defence in defamation proceedings brought against him by the aggrieved party in respect of the publication in question.

(6) An offer to make amends under this section may be withdrawn before it is accepted; and a renewal of an offer which has been withdrawn shall be treated as a new offer.

NOTES
Initial Commencement
  To be appointed: see s 19(3).
Appointment
  Appointment (in relation to England and Wales): 28 February 2000: see SI 2000/222, arts 2, 3(a).
  Appointment (in relation to Scotland): 31 March 2001: see SSI 2001/98, art 3(a).

3 Accepting an offer to make amends

(1) If an offer to make amends under section 2 is accepted by the aggrieved party, the following provisions apply.

(2) The party accepting the offer may not bring or continue defamation proceedings in respect of the publication concerned against the person making the offer, but he is entitled to enforce the offer to make amends, as follows.

(3) If the parties agree on the steps to be taken in fulfilment of the offer, the aggrieved party may apply to the court for an order that the other party fulfil his offer by taking the steps agreed.

(4) If the parties do not agree on the steps to be taken by way of correction, apology and publication, the party who made the offer may take such steps as he thinks appropriate, and may in particular—

(a) make the correction and apology by a statement in open court in terms approved by the court, and

(b) give an undertaking to the court as to the manner of their publication.

(5) If the parties do not agree on the amount to be paid by way of compensation, it shall be determined by the court on the same principles as damages in defamation proceedings.

The court shall take account of any steps taken in fulfilment of the offer and (so far as not agreed between the parties) of the suitability of the correction, the sufficiency of the apology and whether the manner of their publication was reasonable in the circumstances, and may reduce or increase the amount of compensation accordingly.

(6) If the parties do not agree on the amount to be paid by way of costs, it shall be determined by the court on the same principles as costs awarded in court proceedings.

(7) The acceptance of an offer by one person to make amends does not affect any cause of action against another person in respect of the same publication, subject as follows.

(8) In England and Wales or Northern Ireland, for the purposes of the Civil Liability (Contribution) Act 1978—

    (a) the amount of compensation paid under the offer shall be treated as paid in bona fide settlement or compromise of the claim; and

    (b) where another person is liable in respect of the same damage (whether jointly or otherwise), the person whose offer to make amends was accepted is not required to pay by virtue of any contribution under section 1 of that Act a greater amount than the amount of the compensation payable in pursuance of the offer.

(9) In Scotland—

    (a) subsection (2) of section 3 of the Law Reform (Miscellaneous Provisions) (Scotland) Act 1940 (right of one joint wrongdoer as respects another to recover contribution towards damages) applies in relation to compensation paid under an offer to make amends as it applies in relation to damages in an action to which that section applies; and

    (b) where another person is liable in respect of the same damage (whether jointly or otherwise), the person whose offer to make amends was accepted is not required to pay by virtue of any contribution under section 3(2) of that Act a greater amount than the amount of compensation payable in pursuance of the offer.

(10) Proceedings under this section shall be heard and determined without a jury.

NOTES

Initial Commencement

To be appointed: see s 19(3).

Appointment

Appointment (for the purposes of sub-ss (1)–(8), (10)) (in relation to England and Wales): 28 February 2000: see SI 2000/222, arts 2, 3(a).

Appointment (for the purposes of sub-ss (1)–(7), (9), (10)) (in relation to Scotland): 31 March 2001: see SSI 2001/98, art 3(a).

Extent

Extent: sub-s (8) does not extend to Scotland; sub-s (9) applies to Scotland only.

4   Failure to accept offer to make amends

(1) If an offer to make amends under section 2, duly made and not withdrawn, is not accepted by the aggrieved party, the following provisions apply.

(2) The fact that the offer was made is a defence (subject to subsection (3)) to defamation proceedings in respect of the publication in question by that party against the person making the offer.

A qualified offer is only a defence in respect of the meaning to which the offer related.

(3) There is no such defence if the person by whom the offer was made knew or had reason to believe that the statement complained of—

(a) referred to the aggrieved party or was likely to be understood as referring to him, and

(b) was both false and defamatory of that party;

but it shall be presumed until the contrary is shown that he did not know and had no reason to believe that was the case.

(4) The person who made the offer need not rely on it by way of defence, but if he does he may not rely on any other defence.

If the offer was a qualified offer, this applies only in respect of the meaning to which the offer related.

(5) The offer may be relied on in mitigation of damages whether or not it was relied on as a defence.

NOTES

Initial Commencement

To be appointed: see s 19(3).

Appointment

Appointment (in relation to England and Wales): 28 February 2000: see SI 2000/222, arts 2, 3(a).

Appointment (in relation to Scotland): 31 March 2001: see SSI 2001/98, art 3(a).

Limitation

5   Limitation of actions: England and Wales

(1)–(5) . . .

(6) The amendments made by this section apply only to causes of action arising after the section comes into force.

NOTES

Initial Commencement

Specified date: 4 September 1996: see s 19(2).

Amendment

Sub-ss (1)–(5): substitute the Limitation Act 1980, ss 4A, 32A and amend ss 28, 36.

Extent

This section does not extend to Scotland.

6   Limitation of actions: Northern Ireland

(1)–(4) . . .

(5) The amendments made by this section apply only to causes of action arising after the section comes into force.

NOTES
Initial Commencement
 Specified date: 4 September 1996: see s 19(2).
Amendment
 Sub-ss (1)–(4): amend the Limitation (Northern Ireland) Order 1989, SI 1989/1339, arts 6, 48, 51
Extent
 This section applies to Northern Ireland only.

The meaning of a statement

7   Ruling on the meaning of a statement
In defamation proceedings the court shall not be asked to rule whether a statement is arguably capable, as opposed to capable, of bearing a particular meaning or meanings attributed to it.

NOTES
Initial Commencement
 To be appointed: see s 19(3).
Appointment
 Appointment (in relation to England and Wales): 28 February 2000: see SI 2000/222, art 3(a).
Extent
 This section does not extend to Scotland.

Summary disposal of claim

8   Summary disposal of claim
(1)   In defamation proceedings the court may dispose summarily of the plaintiff's claim in accordance with the following provisions.

(2)   The court may dismiss the plaintiff's claim if it appears to the court that it has no realistic prospect of success and there is no reason why it should be tried.

(3)   The court may give judgment for the plaintiff and grant him summary relief (see section 9) if it appears to the court that there is no defence to the claim which has a realistic prospect of success, and that there is no other reason why the claim should be tried.
       Unless the plaintiff asks for summary relief, the court shall not act under this subsection unless it is satisfied that summary relief will adequately compensate him for the wrong he has suffered.

(4)   In considering whether a claim should be tried the court shall have regard to—
       (a)   whether all the persons who are or might be defendants in respect of the publication complained of are before the court;
       (b)   whether summary disposal of the claim against another defendant would be inappropriate;
       (c)   the extent to which there is a conflict of evidence;

(d)   the seriousness of the alleged wrong (as regards the content of the statement and the extent of publication); and

(e)   whether it is justifiable in the circumstances to proceed to a full trial.

(5)   Proceedings under this section shall be heard and determined without a jury.

NOTES
Initial Commencement
To be appointed: see s 19(3).
Appointment
Appointment (in relation to England and Wales): 28 February 2000: see SI 2000/222, art 3(a).
Extent
This section does not extend to Scotland.

9   Meaning of summary relief

(1)   For the purposes of section 8 (summary disposal of claim) "summary relief" means such of the following as may be appropriate—

(a)   a declaration that the statement was false and defamatory of the plaintiff;

(b)   an order that the defendant publish or cause to be published a suitable correction and apology;

(c)   damages not exceeding £10,000 or such other amount as may be prescribed by order of the Lord Chancellor;

(d)   an order restraining the defendant from publishing or further publishing the matter complained of.

(2)   The content of any correction and apology, and the time, manner, form and place of publication, shall be for the parties to agree.

If they cannot agree on the content, the court may direct the defendant to publish or cause to be published a summary of the court's judgment agreed by the parties or settled by the court in accordance with rules of court.

If they cannot agree on the time, manner, form or place of publication, the court may direct the defendant to take such reasonable and practicable steps as the court considers appropriate.

(3)   Any order under subsection (1)(c) shall be made by statutory instrument which shall be subject to annulment in pursuance of a resolution of either House of Parliament.

NOTES
Initial Commencement
To be appointed: see s 19(3).
Appointment
Appointment (in relation to England and Wales): 28 February 2000: see SI 2000/222, art 3(a).
Extent
This section does not extend to Scotland.

10   Summary disposal: rules of court
(1)   Provision may be made by rules of court as to the summary disposal of the plaintiff's claim in defamation proceedings.
(2)   Without prejudice to the generality of that power, provision may be made—
    (a)   authorising a party to apply for summary disposal at any stage of the proceedings;
    (b)   authorising the court at any stage of the proceedings—
        (i)   to treat any application, pleading or other step in the proceedings as an application for summary disposal, or
        (ii)   to make an order for summary disposal without any such application;
    (c)   as to the time for serving pleadings or taking any other step in the proceedings in a case where there are proceedings for summary disposal;
    (d)   requiring the parties to identify any question of law or construction which the court is to be asked to determine in the proceedings;
    (e)   as to the nature of any hearing on the question of summary disposal, and in particular—
        (i)   authorising the court to order affidavits or witness statements to be prepared for use as evidence at the hearing, and
        (ii)   requiring the leave of the court for the calling of oral evidence, or the introduction of new evidence, at the hearing;
    (f)   authorising the court to require a defendant to elect, at or before the hearing, whether or not to make an offer to make amends under section 2.

NOTES
Initial Commencement
    To be appointed: see s 19(3).
Appointment
    Appointment (in relation to England and Wales): 28 February 2000: see SI 2000/222, art 3(a).
Extent
    This section does not extend to Scotland.

11   Summary disposal: application to Northern Ireland
In their application to Northern Ireland the provisions of sections 8 to 10 (summary disposal of claim) apply only to proceedings in the High Court.

NOTES
Initial Commencement
    To be appointed: see s 19(3).
Extent
    This section applies to Northern Ireland only.

Evidence of convictions

12 Evidence of convictions

(1) . . .

The amendments made by this subsection apply only where the trial of the action begins after this section comes into force.

(2) . . .

The amendments made by this subsection apply only for the purposes of an action begun after this section comes into force, whenever the cause of action arose.

(3) . . .

The amendments made by this subsection apply only where the trial of the action begins after this section comes into force.

NOTES

Initial Commencement

Specified date: 4 September 1996: see s 19(2).

Amendment

Sub-s (1): words omitted amend the Civil Evidence Act 1968, s 13.

Sub-s (2): words omitted amend the Law Reform (Miscellaneous Provisions) (Scotland) Act 1968, s 12.

Sub-s (3): words omitted amend the Civil Evidence Act (Northern Ireland) 1971, s 9.

Extent

Extent: sub-s (1) does not extend to Scotland; sub-s (2) applies to Scotland only; sub-s (3) applies to Northern Ireland only.

Evidence concerning proceedings in Parliament

13 Evidence concerning proceedings in Parliament

(1) Where the conduct of a person in or in relation to proceedings in Parliament is in issue in defamation proceedings, he may waive for the purposes of those proceedings, so far as concerns him, the protection of any enactment or rule of law which prevents proceedings in Parliament being impeached or questioned in any court or place out of Parliament.

(2) Where a person waives that protection—

    (a) any such enactment or rule of law shall not apply to prevent evidence being given, questions being asked or statements, submissions, comments or findings being made about his conduct, and

    (b) none of those things shall be regarded as infringing the privilege of either House of Parliament.

(3) The waiver by one person of that protection does not affect its operation in relation to another person who has not waived it.

(4) Nothing in this section affects any enactment or rule of law so far as it protects a person (including a person who has waived the protection

referred to above) from legal liability for words spoken or things done in the course of, or for the purposes of or incidental to, any proceedings in Parliament.

(5) Without prejudice to the generality of subsection (4), that subsection applies to—

    (a)   the giving of evidence before either House or a committee;

    (b)   the presentation or submission of a document to either House or a committee;

    (c)   the preparation of a document for the purposes of or incidental to the transacting of any such business;

    (d)   the formulation, making or publication of a document, including a report, by or pursuant to an order of either House or a committee; and

    (e)   any communication with the Parliamentary Commissioner for Standards or any person having functions in connection with the registration of members' interests.

In this subsection "a committee" means a committee of either House or a joint committee of both Houses of Parliament.

NOTES
Initial Commencement
    Specified date: 4 September 1996: see s 19(2).

Statutory privilege

14   Reports of court proceedings absolutely privileged

(1) A fair and accurate report of proceedings in public before a court to which this section applies, if published contemporaneously with proceedings, is absolutely privileged.

(2) A report of proceedings which by an order of the court, or as a consequence of any statutory provision, is required to be postponed shall be treated as published contemporaneously if it is published as soon as practicable after publication is permitted.

(3) This section applies to—

    (a)   any court in the United Kingdom,

    (b)   the European Court of Justice or any court attached to that court,

    (c)   the European Court of Human Rights, and

    (d)   any international criminal tribunal established by the Security Council of the United Nations or by an international agreement to which the United Kingdom is a party.

In paragraph (a) "court" includes any tribunal or body exercising the judicial power of the State.

(4)   . . .

NOTES
Initial Commencement
    To be appointed: see s 19(3).

Appointment
Appointment: 1 April 1999: see SI 1999/817, art 2(a).
Amendment
Sub-s (4): amends the Rehabilitation of Offenders Act 1974, s 8(6) and the Rehabilitation of Offenders (Northern Ireland) Order 1978, SI 1978/1908, art 9(6).

15   Reports, &c protected by qualified privilege
(1)   The publication of any report or other statement mentioned in Schedule 1 to this Act is privileged unless the publication is shown to be made with malice, subject as follows.
(2)   In defamation proceedings in respect of the publication of a report or other statement mentioned in Part II of that Schedule, there is no defence under this section if the plaintiff shows that the defendant—
(a)   was requested by him to publish in a suitable manner a reasonable letter or statement by way of explanation or contradiction, and
(b)   refused or neglected to do so.
For this purpose "in a suitable manner" means in the same manner as the publication complained of or in a manner that is adequate and reasonable in the circumstances.
(3)   This section does not apply to the publication to the public, or a section of the public, of matter which is not of public concern and the publication of which is not for the public benefit.
(4)   Nothing in this section shall be construed—
(a)   as protecting the publication of matter the publication of which is prohibited by law, or
(b)   as limiting or abridging any privilege subsisting apart from this section.

NOTES
Initial Commencement
To be appointed: see s 19(3).
Appointment
Appointment: 1 April 1999: see SI 1999/817, art 2(a).

Supplementary provisions

16   Repeals
The enactments specified in Schedule 2 are repealed to the extent specified.

NOTES
Initial Commencement
Specified date (for certain purposes): 4 September 1996: see s 19(2).
To be appointed (for remaining purposes): see s 19(3).
Appointment
Appointment (for certain purposes): 1 April 1999: see SI 1999/817, art 2(b).
Appointment (for certain purposes) (in relation to England and Wales): 28 February 2000: see SI 2000/222, arts 2, 3(b).

Appointment (for remaining purposes) (in relation to Scotland): 31 March 2001: see SSI 2001/98, art 3(b)(i).

17 Interpretation

(1) In this Act—

"publication" and "publish", in relation to a statement, have the meaning they have for the purposes of the law of defamation generally, but "publisher" is specially defined for the purposes of section 1;

"statement" means words, pictures, visual images, gestures or any other method of signifying meaning; and

"statutory provision" means—

    (a)   a provision contained in an Act or in subordinate legislation within the meaning of the Interpretation Act 1978,

    [(aa)   a provision contained in an Act of the Scottish Parliament or in an instrument made under such an Act,] or

    (b)   a statutory provision within the meaning given by section 1(f) of the Interpretation Act (Northern Ireland) 1954.

(2) In this Act as it applies to proceedings in Scotland—

"costs" means expenses; and

"plaintiff" and "defendant" mean pursuer and defender.

NOTES

Initial Commencement

Specified date (so far as this section applies to ss 1, 5, 6, 12, 13 and to s 16 and Sch 2 so far as consequential on those provisions): 4 September 1996: see s 19(2).

To be appointed (remaining purposes): see s 19(3).

Appointment

Appointment (so far as this section applies to ss 14, 15, Sch 1): 1 April 1999: see SI 1999/817, art 2(a).

Sub-s (1): Appointment (for remaining purposes) (in relation to England and Wales): 28 February 2000: see SI 2000/222, arts 2, 3(b).

Appointment (for remaining purposes) (in relation to Scotland): 31 March 2001: see SSI 2001/98, art 3(b)(ii).

Amendment

Sub-s (1): in definition "statutory provision" para (aa) inserted by the Scotland Act 1998, s 125, Sch 8, para 33(2).

Date in force: 6 May 1999: see SI 1998/3178, art 2(2), Sch 3.

Extent

Extent: sub-s (2) applies to Scotland only.

General provisions

18 Extent

(1) The following provisions of this Act extend to England and Wales—

section 1 (responsibility for publication),

sections 2 to 4 (offer to make amends), except section 3(9),

section 5 (time limit for actions for defamation or malicious falsehood),

section 7 (ruling on the meaning of a statement),
sections 8 to 10 (summary disposal of claim),
section 12(1) (evidence of convictions),
section 13 (evidence concerning proceedings in Parliament),
sections 14 and 15 and Schedule 1 (statutory privilege),
section 16 and Schedule 2 (repeals) so far as relating to enactments
extending to England and Wales,
section 17 (interpretation),
this subsection,
section 19 (commencement) so far as relating to provisions which extend
to England and Wales, and
section 20 (short title and saving).

(2) The following provisions of this Act extend to Scotland—
section 1 (responsibility for publication),
sections 2 to 4 (offer to make amends), except section 3(8),
section 12(2) (evidence of convictions),
section 13 (evidence concerning proceedings in Parliament),
sections 14 and 15 and Schedule 1 (statutory privilege),
section 16 and Schedule 2 (repeals) so far as relating to enactments
extending to Scotland,
section 17 (interpretation),
this subsection,
section 19 (commencement) so far as relating to provisions which extend
to Scotland, and
section 20 (short title and saving).

(3) The following provisions of this Act extend to Northern Ireland—
section 1 (responsibility for publication),
sections 2 to 4 (offer to make amends), except section 3(9),
section 6 (time limit for actions for defamation or malicious falsehood),
section 7 (ruling on the meaning of a statement),
sections 8 to 11 (summary disposal of claim),
section 12(3) (evidence of convictions),
section 13 (evidence concerning proceedings in Parliament),
sections 14 and 15 and Schedule 1 (statutory privilege),
section 16 and Schedule 2 (repeals) so far as relating to enactments
extending to Northern Ireland,
section 17(1) (interpretation),
this subsection,
section 19 (commencement) so far as relating to provisions which extend
to Northern Ireland, and
section 20 (short title and saving).

NOTES
Initial Commencement
Royal Assent: 4 July 1996: see s 19(1).

19   Commencement

(1)   Sections 18 to 20 (extent, commencement and other general provisions) come into force on Royal Assent.

(2)   The following provisions of this Act come into force at the end of the period of two months beginning with the day on which this Act is passed—

section 1 (responsibility for publication),

sections 5 and 6 (time limit for actions for defamation or malicious falsehood),

section 12 (evidence of convictions),

section 13 (evidence concerning proceedings in Parliament),

section 16 and the repeals in Schedule 2, so far as consequential on the above provisions, and

section 17 (interpretation), so far as relating to the above provisions.

(3)   The provisions of this Act otherwise come into force on such day as may be appointed—

(a)   for England and Wales or Northern Ireland, by order of the Lord Chancellor, or

(b)   for Scotland, by order of the Secretary of State,

and different days may be appointed for different purposes.

(4)   Any such order shall be made by statutory instrument and may contain such transitional provisions as appear to the Lord Chancellor or Secretary of State to be appropriate.

NOTES

Initial Commencement

Royal Assent: 4 July 1996: see s 19(1).

Subordinate Legislation

UK

Defamation Act 1996 (Commencement No 1) Order 1999, SI 1999/817 (made under sub-s (3)).

Defamation Act 1996 (Commencement No 2) Order 2000, SI 2000/222 (made under sub-ss (3), (4)).

Scotland

Defamation Act 1996 (Commencement No 3 and Transitional Provision) (Scotland) Order 2001, SSI 2001/98 (made under sub-ss (3)(b), (4)).

20   Short title and saving

(1)   This Act may be cited as the Defamation Act 1996.

(2)   Nothing in this Act affects the law relating to criminal libel.

NOTES

Initial Commencement

Royal Assent: 4 July 1996: see s 19(1).

SCHEDULE 1
Qualified Privilege

Section 15

Part I
Statements Having Qualified Privilege Without Explanation or
Contradiction

1   A fair and accurate report of proceedings in public of a legislature anywhere in the world.

2   A fair and accurate report of proceedings in public before a court anywhere in the world.

3   A fair and accurate report of proceedings in public of a person appointed to hold a public inquiry by a government or legislature anywhere in the world.

4   A fair and accurate report of proceedings in public anywhere in the world of an international organisation or an international conference.

5   A fair and accurate copy of or extract from any register or other document required by law to be open to public inspection.

6   A notice or advertisement published by or on the authority of a court, or of a judge or officer of a court, anywhere in the world.

7   A fair and accurate copy of or extract from matter published by or on the authority of a government or legislature anywhere in the world.

8   A fair and accurate copy of or extract from matter published anywhere in the world by an international organisation or an international conference.

NOTES
Initial Commencement
    To be appointed: see s 19(3).
Appointment
    Appointment: 1 April 1999: see SI 1999/817, art 2(a).

Part II
Statements Privileged Subject to Explanation or Contradiction

9   (1)   A fair and accurate copy of or extract from a notice or other matter issued for the information of the public by or on behalf of—

(a)   a legislature in any member State or the European Parliament;

(b)   the government of any member State, or any authority performing governmental functions in any member State or part of a member State, or the European Commission;

(c)   an international organisation or international conference.

(2)   In this paragraph "governmental functions" includes police functions.

10   A fair and accurate copy of or extract from a document made available by a court in any member State or the European Court of Justice (or any court attached to that court), or by a judge or officer of any such court.

11   (1)   A fair and accurate report of proceedings at any public meeting or sitting in the United Kingdom of—

(a)   a local authority or local authority committee;

[(aa)   in the case of a local authority which are operating executive arrangements, the executive of that authority or a committee of that executive;]

(b)   a justice or justices of the peace acting otherwise than as a court exercising judicial authority;

(c)   a commission, tribunal, committee or person appointed for the purposes of any inquiry by any statutory provision, by Her Majesty or by a Minister of the Crown [a member of the Scottish Executive] or a Northern Ireland Department;

(d)   a person appointed by a local authority to hold a local inquiry in pursuance of any statutory provision;

(e)   any other tribunal, board, committee or body constituted by or under, and exercising functions under, any statutory provision.

[(1A)   In the case of a local authority which are operating executive arrangements, a fair and accurate record of any decision made by any member of the executive where that record is required to be made and available for public inspection by virtue of section 22 of the Local Government Act 2000 or of any provision in regulations made under that section.]

(2)   *In sub-paragraph (1)(a)—* [In sub-paragraphs (1)(a)[, (1)(aa)] and (1A)—
. . .]

"local authority" means—

(a)   in relation to England and Wales, a principal council within the meaning of the Local Government Act 1972, any body falling within any paragraph of section 100J(1) of that Act or an authority or body to which the Public Bodies (Admission to Meetings) Act 1960 applies,

(b)   in relation to Scotland, a council constituted under section 2 of the Local Government etc (Scotland) Act 1994 or an authority or body to which the Public Bodies (Admission to Meetings) Act 1960 applies,

(c) in relation to Northern Ireland, any authority or body to which sections 23 to 27 of the Local Government Act (Northern Ireland) 1972 apply; and

"local authority committee" means any committee of a local authority or of local authorities, and includes—

    (a) any committee or sub-committee in relation to which sections 100A to 100D of the Local Government Act 1972 apply by virtue of section 100E of that Act (whether or not also by virtue of section 100J of that Act), and

    (b) any committee or sub-committee in relation to which sections 50A to 50D of the Local Government (Scotland) Act 1973 apply by virtue of section 50E of that Act.

[(2A) In sub-paragraphs (1) and (1A)—

"executive" and "executive arrangements" have the same meaning as in Part II of the Local Government Act 2000.]

(3) A fair and accurate report of any corresponding proceedings in any of the Channel Islands or the Isle of Man or in another member State.

12 (1) A fair and accurate report of proceedings at any public meeting held in a member State.

(2) In this paragraph a "public meeting" means a meeting bona fide and lawfully held for a lawful purpose and for the furtherance or discussion of a matter of public concern, whether admission to the meeting is general or restricted.

13 (1) A fair and accurate report of proceedings at a general meeting of a UK public company.

(2) A fair and accurate copy of or extract from any document circulated to members of a UK public company—

    (a) by or with the authority of the board of directors of the company,

    (b) by the auditors of the company, or

    (c) by any member of the company in pursuance of a right conferred by any statutory provision.

(3) A fair and accurate copy of or extract from any document circulated to members of a UK public company which relates to the appointment, resignation, retirement or dismissal of directors of the company.

(4) In this paragraph "UK public company" means—

    (a) a public company within the meaning of section 1(3) of the Companies Act 1985 or Article 12(3) of the Companies (Northern Ireland) Order 1986, or

    (b) a body corporate incorporated by or registered under any other statutory provision, or by Royal Charter, or formed in pursuance of letters patent.

(5) A fair and accurate report of proceedings at any corresponding meeting of, or copy of or extract from any corresponding document circulated to

members of, a public company formed under the law of any of the Channel Islands or the Isle of Man or of another member State.

14 A fair and accurate report of any finding or decision of any of the following descriptions of association, formed in the United Kingdom or another member State, or of any committee or governing body of such an association—

(a) an association formed for the purpose of promoting or encouraging the exercise of or interest in any art, science, religion or learning, and empowered by its constitution to exercise control over or adjudicate on matters of interest or concern to the association, or the actions or conduct of any person subject to such control or adjudication;

(b) an association formed for the purpose of promoting or safeguarding the interests of any trade, business, industry or profession, or of the persons carrying on or engaged in any trade, business, industry or profession, and empowered by its constitution to exercise control over or adjudicate upon matters connected with that trade, business, industry or profession, or the actions or conduct of those persons;

(c) an association formed for the purpose of promoting or safeguarding the interests of a game, sport or pastime to the playing or exercise of which members of the public are invited or admitted, and empowered by its constitution to exercise control over or adjudicate upon persons connected with or taking part in the game, sport or pastime;

(d) an association formed for the purpose of promoting charitable objects or other objects beneficial to the community and empowered by its constitution to exercise control over or to adjudicate on matters of interest or concern to the association, or the actions or conduct of any person subject to such control or adjudication.

15 (1) A fair and accurate report of, or copy of or extract from, any adjudication, report, statement or notice issued by a body, officer or other person designated for the purposes of this paragraph—

(a) for England and Wales or Northern Ireland, by order of the Lord Chancellor, and

(b) for Scotland, by order of the Secretary of State.

(2) An order under this paragraph shall be made by statutory instrument which shall be subject to annulment in pursuance of a resolution of either House of Parliament.

NOTES
Initial Commencement
To be appointed: see s 19(3).
Appointment
Appointment: 1 April 1999: see SI 1999/817, art 2(a).

Amendment

Para 11: sub-para (1)(aa) inserted in relation to England by SI 2002/1057, arts 2(h), 12(b); a corresponding amendment has been made in relation to Wales by SI 2002/808, arts 2(p), 30(a), (see Miscellaneous note below).

Date in force (in relation to England): 6 May 2002: see SI 2002/1057, art 1(1).

Para 11: in sub-para (1)(c) words "a member of the Scottish Executive" in square brackets inserted by the Scotland Act 1998, s 125, Sch 8, para 33(3).

Date in force: 6 May 1999: see SI 1998/3178, art 2(2), Sch 3.

Para 11: sub-para (1A) inserted in relation to England by SI 2001/2237, arts 1(2), 2(q), 31(b), and in relation to Wales by SI 2002/808, arts 2(p), 30(b).

Date in force (in relation to England): 11 July 2001: see SI 2001/2237, art 1(1).

Date in force (in relation to Wales): 1 April 2002: see SI 2002/808, art 1(1).

Para 11: in sub-para (2) words "In sub-paragraph (1)(a)—" in italics repealed and subsequent words in square brackets substituted in relation to England by SI 2001/2237, arts 1(2), 2(q), 31(c), and in relation to Wales by SI 2002/808, arts 2(p), 30(c).

Date in force (in relation to England): 11 July 2001: see SI 2001/2237, art 1(1).

Date in force (in relation to Wales): 1 April 2002: see SI 2002/808, art 1(1).

Para 11: in sub-para (2) reference to ", (1)(aa)" in square brackets inserted, in relation to England, by SI 2002/1057, arts 2(h), 12(c)(i).

Date in force: 6 May 2002: see SI 2002/1057, art 1(1).

Para 11: in sub-para (2) definition "executive" and "executive arrangements" (omitted) repealed, in relation to England, by SI 2002/1057, arts 2(h), 12(c)(ii).

Date in force: 6 May 2002: see SI 2002/1057, art 1(1).

Para 11: sub-para (2A) inserted, in relation to England, by SI 2002/1057, arts 2(h), 12(d).

Date in force: 6 May 2002: see SI 2002/1057, art 1(1).

Miscellaneous

SI 2002/1057, arts 2(h), 12(a) amended para 11(1)(a) above, in relation to England. This negated the previous amendment made, in relation to England, by SI 2001/2237. Para 11(1)(a) now reads as originally enacted.

Part III
Supplementary Provisions

16 (1) In this Schedule—

"court" includes any tribunal or body exercising the judicial power of the State;

"international conference" means a conference attended by representatives of two or more governments;

"international organisation" means an organisation of which two or more governments are members, and includes any committee or other subordinate body of such an organisation; and

"legislature" includes a local legislature.

(2) References in this Schedule to a member State include any European dependent territory of a member State.

(3) In paragraphs 2 and 6 "court" includes—

(a) the European Court of Justice (or any court attached to that court) and the Court of Auditors of the European Communities,

(b)   the European Court of Human Rights,

(c)   any international criminal tribunal established by the Security Council of the United Nations or by an international agreement to which the United Kingdom is a party, and

(d)   the International Court of Justice and any other judicial or arbitral tribunal deciding matters in dispute between States.

(4)   In paragraphs 1, 3 and 7 "legislature" includes the European Parliament.

17   (1)   Provision may be made by order identifying—

(a)   for the purposes of paragraph 11, the corresponding proceedings referred to in sub-paragraph (3);

(b)   for the purposes of paragraph 13, the corresponding meetings and documents referred to in sub-paragraph (5).

(2)   An order under this paragraph may be made—

(a)   for England and Wales or Northern Ireland, by the Lord Chancellor, and

(b)   for Scotland, by the Secretary of State.

(3)   An order under this paragraph shall be made by statutory instrument which shall be subject to annulment in pursuance of a resolution of either House of Parliament.

NOTES
Initial Commencement
To be appointed: see s 19(3).
Appointment
Appointment: 1 April 1999: see SI 1999/817, art 2(a).

SCHEDULE 2
Repeals

Section 16

Chapter	Short title	Extent of repeal
1888 c 64	Law of Libel Amendment Act 1888	Section 3
1952 c 66	Defamation Act 1952	Section 4
		Sections 7, 8 and 9(2) and (3).
		Section 16(2) and (3)
		The Schedule
1955 c 20	Revision of the Army and Air Force Acts (Transitional Provisions) Act 1955	In Schedule 2, the entry relating to the Defamation Act 1952

Chapter	Short title	Extent of repeal
1955 c 11 (NI)	Defamation Act (Northern Ireland) 1955	Section 4
		Sections 7, 8 and 9(2) and (3)
		Section 14(2)
		The Schedule
1972 c 9 (NI)	Local Government Act (Northern Ireland) 1972	In Schedule 8, paragraph 12
1981 c 49	Contempt of Court Act 1981	In section 4(3), the words "and of section 3 of the Law of Libel Amendment Act 1888 (privilege)"
1981 c 61	British Nationality Act 1981	In Schedule 7, the entries relating to the Defamation Act 1952 and the Defamation Act (Northern Ireland) 1955
1985 c 43	Local Government (Access to Information) Act 1985	In Schedule 2, paragraphs 2 and 3
1985 c 61	Administration of Justice Act 1985	Section 57
SI 1986/594 (NI 3)	Education and Libraries (Northern Ireland) Order 1986	Article 97(2)
1990 c 42	Broadcasting Act 1990	Section 166(3)
		In Schedule 20, paragraphs 2 and 3.

NOTES
Initial Commencement
Specified date (in part): 4 September 1996: see s 19(2).
To be appointed (remainder): see s 19(3).
Appointment
Appointment (in part): 1 April 1999: see SI 1999/817, art 2(b).
Appointment (in part) (in relation to England and Wales): 28 February 2000: see SI 2000/222, arts 2, 3(b)(i)–(vi).
Appointment (remainder) (in relation to Scotland): 31 March 2001: see SSI 2001/98, art 3(b)(i).

Appendix 3

Pre-action protocol for defamation

Contents

1   Introduction

2   Aims of the Protocol

3   Pre-action Protocol

1   Introduction

1.1   Lord Irvine of Lairg, in his foreword to the Pre-Action Protocol for Personal Injury Claims identified the value of creating Pre-Action Protocols as a key part of the Civil Justice Reforms. He hoped that Pre-Action Protocols would set effective and enforceable standards for the efficient conduct of pre-action litigation.

1.2   Lord Irvine went on to state that:

'The protocol aims to improve pre-action communication between the parties by establishing a timetable for the exchange of information relevant to the dispute and by setting standards for the content of correspondence. Compliance with the protocol will enable parties to make an informed judgment on the merits of their cases earlier than tends to happen today, because they will have earlier access to the information they need. This will provide every opportunity for improved communications between the parties designed to lead to an increase in the number of pre-action settlements.'

1.3   It is against this background that a Pre-Action Protocol for Claims in Defamation is submitted. This Protocol is intended to encourage exchange of information between parties at an early stage and to provide a clear framework within which parties to a claim in defamation, acting in good faith, can explore the early and appropriate resolution of that claim.

1.4   There are important features which distinguish defamation claims from other areas of civil litigation, and these must be borne in mind when both applying, and reviewing the application of, the Pre-Action Protocol. In particular, time is always 'of the essence' in defamation claims; the limitation period is (uniquely) only 1 year, and almost invariably, a Claimant will be seeking an immediate correction and/or apology as part of the process of restoring his/ her reputation.

1.5   This Pre-Action Protocol embraces the spirit of the reforms to the Civil Justice system envisaged by Lord Woolf, and now enacted in the Civil

Procedure Rules. It aims to incorporate the concept of the overriding objective, as provided by the Rules at Part 1, before the commencement of any Court proceedings, namely:
dealing with a case justly includes, so far as is practicable:-
*   ensuring that the parties are on an equal footing;
*   saving expense;
dealing with the case in ways which are proportionate:-
*   to the amount of money involved;
*   to the importance of the case;
*   to the complexity of the issues; and
*   to the financial position of each party;
*   ensuring that it is dealt with expeditiously and fairly; and
*   allotting to it an appropriate share of the Court's resources, while taking into account the need to allot resources to other cases.

2   Aims of the protocol

2.

*   This protocol aims to set out a code of good practice which parties should follow when litigation is being considered.
*   It encourages early communication of a claim.
*   It aims to encourage both parties to disclose sufficient information to enable each to understand the other's case and to promote the prospect of early resolution.
*   It sets a timetable for the exchange of information relevant to the dispute.
*   It sets standards for the content of correspondence.
*   It identifies options which either party might adopt to encourage settlement of the claim.
*   Should a claim proceed to litigation, the extent to which the protocol has been followed both in practice and in spirit by the parties will assist the Court in dealing with liability for costs and making other Orders.
*   Letters of claim and responses sent pursuant to this Protocol are not intended to have the same status as a Statement of Case in proceedings.
*   It aims to keep the costs of resolving disputes subject to this protocol proportionate.

3   Pre-action protocol

Letter of claim
3.1   The Claimant should notify the Defendant of his/her claim in writing at the earliest reasonable opportunity.
3.2   The Letter of Claim should include the following information:
*   name of Claimant;

353

- sufficient details to identify the publication or broadcast which contained the words complained of;
- the words complained of and, if known, the date of publication; where possible, a copy or transcript of the words complained of should be enclosed;
- factual inaccuracies or unsupportable comment within the words complained of; the Claimant should give a sufficient explanation to enable the Defendant to appreciate why the words are inaccurate or unsupportable;
- the nature of the remedies sought by the Claimant.
- Where relevant, the Letter of Claim should also include:-
  - any facts or matters which make the Claimant identifiable from the words complained of;
  - details of any special facts relevant to the interpretation of the words complained of and/or any particular damage caused by the words complained of.

3.3   It is desirable for the Claimant to identify in the Letter of Claim the meaning(s) he/she attributes to the words complained of.

Defendant's response to letter of claim

3.4   The Defendant should provide a full response to the Letter of Claim as soon as reasonably possible. If the Defendant believes that he/she will be unable to respond within 14 days (or such shorter time limit as specified in the Letter of Claim), then he/she should specify the date by which he/she intends to respond.

3.5   The Response should include the following:
- whether or to what extent the Claimant's claim is accepted, whether more information is required or whether it is rejected;
- if the claim is accepted in whole or in part, the Defendant should indicate which remedies it is willing to offer;
- if more information is required, then the Defendant should specify precisely what information is needed to enable the claim to be dealt with and why;
- if the claim is rejected, then the Defendant should explain the reasons why it is rejected, including a sufficient indication of any facts on which the Defendant is likely to rely in support of any substantive defence;
- It is desirable for the Defendant to include in the Response to the Letter of Claim the meaning(s) he/she attributes to the words complained of.

Proportionality of costs

3.6   In formulating both the Letter of Claim and Response and in taking any subsequent steps, the parties should act reasonably to keep costs proportionate to the nature and gravity of the case and the stage the complaint has reached.

Alternative dispute resolution

3.7 Both the Claimant and Defendant will be expected by the Court to provide evidence that alternative means of resolving their dispute were considered. It is not practical in this protocol to address in detail how the parties might decide which method to adopt to resolve their particular dispute. However, summarised below are some of the options for resolving disputes without litigation.

- Determination by an independent third party (for example, a lawyer experienced in the field of defamation or an individual experienced in the subject matter of the claim) whose name and fees, along with the precise issues which are to be determined, will have been agreed by the parties in advance.

- Mediation or any other form of Alternative Dispute Resolution.

- Arbitration (which does of course carry statutory implications).

Appendix 4

CPR Part 53
Defamation Claims

Scope of this Part	Rule 53.1
Summary disposal under the Defamation Act 1996	Rule 53.2
Sources of information	Rule 53.3

Scope of this Part

53.1 This Part contains rules about defamation claims.

Summary disposal under the Defamation Act 1996

53.2 (1) This rule provides for summary disposal in accordance with the Defamation Act 1996 ('the Act').

(2) In proceedings for summary disposal under sections 8 and 9 of the Act, rules 24.4 (procedure), 24.5 (evidence) and 24.6 (directions) apply.

(3) An application for summary judgment under Part 24 may not be made if—

    (a) an application has been made for summary disposal in accordance with the Act, and that application has not been disposed of; or

    (b) summary relief has been granted on an application for summary disposal under the Act.

(4) The court may on any application for summary disposal direct the defendant to elect whether or not to make an offer to make amends under section 2 of the Act.

(5) When it makes a direction under paragraph (4), the court will specify the time by which and the manner in which—

    (a) the election is to be made; and

    (b) notification of it is to be given to the court and the other parties.

Sources of information

53.3 Unless the court orders otherwise, a party will not be required to provide further information about the identity of the defendant's sources of information.

(Part 18 provides requests for further information)

Practice Direction – Defamation Claims
THIS PRACTICE DIRECTION SUPPLEMENTS CPR PART 53
CONTENTS OF THIS PRACTICE DIRECTION

General
1.   This practice direction applies to defamation claims.

Statements of case
2.1   Statements of case should be confined to the information necessary to inform the other party of the nature of the case he has to meet. Such information should be set out concisely and in a manner proportionate to the subject matter of the claim.

2.2   (1)   In a claim for libel the publication the subject of the claim must be identified in the claim form.

      (2)   In a claim for slander the claim form must so far as possible contain the words complained of, and identify the person to whom they were spoken and when.

2.3

      (1)   The claimant must specify in the particulars of claim the defamatory meaning which he alleges that the words or matters complained of conveyed, both
            (a)   as to their natural and ordinary meaning; and
            (b)   as to any innuendo meaning (that is a meaning alleged to be conveyed to some person by reason of knowing facts extraneous to the words complained of).

      (2)   In the case of an innuendo meaning, the claimant must also identify the relevant extraneous facts.

2.4   In a claim for slander the precise words used and the names of the persons to whom they were spoken and when must, so far as possible, be set out in the particulars of claim, if not already contained in the claim form.

2.5   Where a defendant alleges that the words complained of are true he must—
      (1)   specify the defamatory meanings he seeks to justify; and
      (2)   give details of the matters on which he relies in support of that allegation.

357

2.6 Where a defendant alleges that the words complained of are fair comment on a matter of public interest he must—
    (1) specify the defamatory meaning he seeks to defend as fair comment on a matter of public interest; and
    (2) give details of the matters on which he relies in support of that allegation.

2.7 Where a defendant alleges that the words complained of were published on a privileged occasion he must specify the circumstances he relies on in support of that contention.

2.8 Where a defendant alleges that the words complained of are true, or are fair comment on a matter of public interest, the claimant must serve a reply specifically admitting or denying the allegation and giving the facts on which he relies.

2.9 If the defendant contends that any of the words or matters are fair comment on a matter of public interest, or were published on a privileged occasion, and the claimant intends to allege that the defendant acted with malice, the claimant must serve a reply giving details of the facts or matters relied on.

2.10 (1) A claimant must give full details of the facts and matters on which he relies in support of his claim for damages.
    (2) Where a claimant seeks aggravated or exemplary damages he must provide the information specified in rule 16.4(1)(c).

2.11 A defendant who relies on an offer to make amends under section 2 of the Defamation Act 1996, as his defence must-
    (1) state in his defence—
        (a) that he is relying on the offer in accordance with section 4 (2) of the Defamation Act 1996; and
        (b) that it has not been withdrawn by him or been accepted, and
    (2) attach a copy of the offer he made with his defence.

Court's powers in connection with an offer of amends

3.1 Sections 2 to 4 of the Defamation Act 1996 make provision for a person who has made a statement which is alleged to be defamatory to make an offer to make amends. Section 3 provides for the court to assist in the process of making amends.

3.2 A claim under section 3 of the Defamation Act 1996 made other than in existing proceedings may be made under CPR Part 8 –
    (1) where the parties agree on the steps to make amends, and the sole purpose of the claim is for the court to make an order under section 3(3) for an order that the offer be fulfilled; or
    (2) where the parties do not agree–
        (a) on the steps to be taken by way of correction, apology and publication (see section 3(4));
        (b) on the amount to be paid by way of compensation (see section 3(5)); or

     (c)   on the amount to be paid by way of costs (see section 3(6)).
         (Applications in existing proceedings made under section 3 of the Defamation Act 1996 must be made in accordance with CPR Part 23)

3.3 (1) A claim or application under section 3 of the Defamation Act 1996 must be supported by written evidence.

    (2) The evidence referred to in paragraph (1) must include–
        (a)   a copy of the offer of amends;
        (b)   details of the steps taken to fulfil the offer of amends;
        (c)   a copy of the text of any correction and apology;
        (d)   details of the publication of the correction and apology;
        (e)   a statement of the amount of any sum paid as compensation;
        (f)   a statement of the amount of any sum paid for costs;
        (g)   why the offer is unsatisfactory.

    (3) Where any step specified in section 2(4) of the Defamation Act 1996 has not been taken, then the evidence referred to in paragraph (2)(c) to (f) must state what steps are proposed by the party to fulfil the offer of amends and the date or dates on which each step will be fulfilled and, if none, that no proposal has been made to take that step.

Ruling on meaning

4.1 At any time the court may decide–
    (1) whether a statement complained of is capable of having any meaning attributed to it in a statement of case;
    (2) whether the statement is capable of being defamatory of the claimant;
    (3) whether the statement is capable of bearing any other meaning defamatory of the claimant.

4.2 An application for a ruling on meaning may be made at any time after the service of particulars of claim. Such an application should be made promptly.

(This provision disapplies for these applications the usual time restriction on making applications in rule 24.4.1).

4.3 Where an application is made for a ruling on meaning, the application notice must state that it is an application for a ruling on meaning made in accordance with this practice direction.

4.4 The application notice or the evidence contained or referred to in it, or served with it, must identify precisely the statement, and the meaning attributed to it, that the court is being asked to consider.

(Rule 3.3 applies where the court exercises its powers of its own initiative)

(Following a ruling on meaning the court may exercise its power under rule 3.4)

(Section 7 of the Defamation Act 1996 applies to rulings on meaning)

Summary disposal

5.1   Where an application is made for summary disposal, the application notice must state—

    (1)   that it is an application for summary disposal made in accordance with section 8 of the Defamation Act 1996.

    (2)   the matters set out in paragraph 2(3) of the practice direction to Part 24; and

    (3)   whether or not the defendant has made an offer to make amends under section 2 of the Act and whether or not it has been withdrawn.

5.2   An application for summary disposal may be made at any time after the service of particulars of claim.

(This provision disapplies for these applications the usual time restriction on making applications in rule 24.4.1).

5.3   (1)   This paragraph applies where—

    (a)   the court has ordered the defendant in defamation proceedings to agree and publish a correction and apology as summary relief under section 8(2) of the Defamation Act 1996; and

    (b)   the parties are unable to agree its content within the time specified in the order.

    (2)   Where the court grants this type of summary relief under the Act, the order will specify the date by which the parties should reach agreement about the content, time, manner, form and place of publication of the correction and apology.

    (3)   Where the parties cannot agree the content of the correction and apology by the date specified in the order, then the claimant must prepare a summary of the judgment given by the court and serve it on all the other parties within 3 days following the date specified in the order.

    (4)   Where the parties cannot agree the summary of the judgment prepared by the claimant they must within 3 days of receiving the summary –

    (a)   file with the court and serve on all the other parties a copy of the summary showing the revisions they wish to make to it; and

    (b)   apply to the court for the court to settle the summary.

    (5)   The court will then itself settle the summary and the judge who delivered the judgment being summarised will normally do this.

Statements in open court

6.1   This paragraph only applies where a party wishes to accept a Part 36 offer, Part 36 payment or other offer of settlement in relation to a claim for –

    (1)   libel;

    (2)   slander.

6.2 A party may apply for permission to make a statement in open court before or after he accepts the Part 36 offer or the Part 36 payment in accordance with rule 36.8 (5) or other offer to settle the claim.

6.3 The statement that the applicant wishes to make must be submitted for the approval of the court and must accompany the notice of application.

6.4 The court may postpone the time for making the statement if other claims relating to the subject matter of the statement are still proceeding.

(Applications must be made in accordance with Part 23).

Transitional provision relating to section 4 of the Defamation Act 1952

7. Paragraph 3 of this practice direction applies, with any necessary modifications to an application to the court to determine any question as to the steps to be taken to fulfil an offer made under section 4 of the Defamation Act 1952.

(Section 4 of the Defamation Act 1952 is repealed by the Defamation Act 1996. The commencement order bringing in the repeal makes transitional provision for offers which have been made at the date the repeal came into force).

Appendix 5

Human Rights Act 1998, ss 12 and 13

1998 CHAPTER 42

12   Freedom of expression

(1)   This section applies if a court is considering whether to grant any relief which, if granted, might affect the exercise of the Convention right to freedom of expression.

(2)   If the person against whom the application for relief is made ("the respondent") is neither present nor represented, no such relief is to be granted unless the court is satisfied—

    (a)   that the applicant has taken all practicable steps to notify the respondent; or

    (b)   that there are compelling reasons why the respondent should not be notified.

(3)   No such relief is to be granted so as to restrain publication before trial unless the court is satisfied that the applicant is likely to establish that publication should not be allowed.

(4)   The court must have particular regard to the importance of the Convention right to freedom of expression and, where the proceedings relate to material which the respondent claims, or which appears to the court, to be journalistic, literary or artistic material (or to conduct connected with such material), to—

    (a)   the extent to which—

        (i)   the material has, or is about to, become available to the public; or

        (ii)   it is, or would be, in the public interest for the material to be published;

    (b)   any relevant privacy code.

(5)   In this section—

    "court" includes a tribunal; and

    "relief" includes any remedy or order (other than in criminal proceedings).

NOTES

Initial Commencement

    To be appointed: see s 22(3).

Appointment

    Appointment: 2 October 2000: see SI 2000/1851, art 2.

13   Freedom of thought, conscience and religion

(1)   If a court's determination of any question arising under this Act might affect the exercise by a religious organisation (itself or its members

collectively) of the Convention right to freedom of thought, conscience and religion, it must have particular regard to the importance of that right.

(2)   In this section "court" includes a tribunal.

NOTES
Initial Commencement
     To be appointed: see s 22(3).
Appointment
     Appointment: 2 October 2000: see SI 2000/1851, art 2.

Appendix 6

Solicitors Act 1974, ss 70–72

1974 CHAPTER 47

70   **Taxation on application of party chargeable or solicitor**

(1)   Where before the expiration of one month from the delivery of a solicitor's bill an application is made by the party chargeable with the bill, the High Court shall, without requiring any sum to be paid into court, order that the bill be taxed and that no action be commenced on the bill until the taxation is completed.

(2)   Where no such application is made before the expiration of the period mentioned in subsection (1), then, on an application being made by the solicitor or, subject to subsections (3) and (4), by the party chargeable with the bill, the court may on such terms, if any, as it thinks fit (not being terms as to the costs of the taxation), order—

    (a)   that the bill be taxed; and

    (b)   that no action be commenced on the bill, and that any action already commenced be stayed, until the taxation is completed.

(3)   Where an application under subsection (2) is made by the party chargeable with the bill—

    (a)   after the expiration of 12 months from the delivery of the bill, or

    (b)   after a judgment has been obtained for the recovery of the costs covered by the bill, or

    (c)   after the bill has been paid, but before the expiration of 12 months from the payment of the bill,

no order shall be made except in special circumstances and, if an order is made, it may contain such terms as regards the costs of the taxation as the court may think fit.

(4)   The power to order taxation conferred by subsection (2) shall not be exercisable on an application made by the party chargeable with the bill after the expiration of 12 months from the payment of the bill.

(5)   An order for the taxation of a bill made on an application under this section by the party chargeable with the bill shall, if he so requests, be an order for the taxation of the profit costs covered by the bill.

(6)   Subject to subsection (5), the court may under this section order the taxation of all the costs, or of the profit costs, or of the costs other than profit costs and, where part of the costs is not to be taxed, may allow an action to be commenced or to be continued for that part of the costs.

(7)   Every order for the taxation of a bill shall require the taxing officer to tax not only the bill but also the costs of the taxation and to certify what is due to or by the solicitor in respect of the bill and in respect of the costs of the taxation.

(8)   If after due notice of any taxation either party to it fails to attend, the officer may proceed with the taxation ex parte.

(9)   Unless—

(a)   the order for taxation was made on the application of the solicitor and the party chargeable does not attend the taxation, or

(b)   the order for taxation or an order under subsection (10) otherwise provides,

the costs of a taxation shall be paid according to the event of the taxation, that is to say, if one-fifth of the amount of the bill is taxed off, the solicitor shall pay the costs, but otherwise the party chargeable shall pay the costs.

(10) The taxing officer may certify to the court any special circumstances relating to a bill or to the taxation of a bill, and the court may make such order as respects the costs of the taxation as it may think fit.

(11) Subsection (9) shall have effect in any case where the application for an order for taxation was made before the passing of the Solicitors (Amendment) Act 1974 and—

(a)   the bill is a bill for contentious business, or

(b)   more than half of the amount of the bill before taxation consists of costs for which a scale charge is provided by an order for the time being in operation under section 56,

as if for the reference to one-fifth of the amount of the bill there were substituted a reference to one-sixth of that amount.

(12) In this section "profit costs" means costs other than counsel's fees or costs paid or payable in the discharge of a liability incurred by the solicitor on behalf of the party chargeable, and the reference in subsection (9) to the fraction of the amount of the bill taxed off shall be taken, where the taxation concerns only part of the costs covered by the bill, as a reference to that fraction of the amount of those costs which is being taxed.

NOTES

Initial Commencement

To be appointed: see s 90(2).

Appointment

Appointment: 1 May 1975: see SI 1975/534, arts 1(2), 2(b); for savings see Schedule thereto.

Derivation

Sub-ss (1)–(10), (12) derived from the Solicitors Act 1957, s 69.

See Further

See further: Administration of Justice Act 1985, s 9, Sch 2.

See further: the High Court and County Courts Jurisdiction Order 1991, SI 1991/724, arts 2(7), (8), 11, 12, Schedule, Part I.

Extent

This section does not extend to Scotland.

71   Taxation on application of third parties

(1)   Where a person other than the party chargeable with the bill for the purposes of section 70 has paid, or is or was liable to pay, a bill either to

the solicitor or to the party chargeable with the bill, that person, or his executors, administrators or assignees may apply to the High Court for an order for the taxation of the bill as if he were the party chargeable with it, and the court may make the same order (if any) as it might have made if the application had been made by the party chargeable with the bill.

(2)   Where the court has no power to make an order by virtue of subsection (1) except in special circumstances it may, in considering whether there are special circumstances sufficient to justify the making of an order, take into account circumstances which affect the applicant but do not affect the party chargeable with the bill.

(3)   Where a trustee, executor or administrator has become liable to pay a bill of a solicitor, then, on the application of any person interested in any property out of which the trustee, executor or administrator has paid, or is entitled to pay, the bill, the court may order—
(a)   that the bill be taxed on such terms, if any, as it thinks fit; and
(b)   that such payments, in respect of the amount found to be due to or by the solicitor and in respect of the costs of the taxation, be made to or by the applicant, to or by the solicitor, or to or by the executor, administrator or trustee, as it thinks fit.

(4)   In considering any application under subsection (3) the court shall have regard—
(a)   to the provisions of section 70 as to applications by the party chargeable for the taxation of a solicitor's bill so far as they are capable of being applied to an application made under that subsection;
(b)   to the extent and nature of the interest of the applicant.

(5)   If an applicant under subsection (3) pays any money to the solicitor, he shall have the same right to be paid that money by the trustee, executor or administrator chargeable with the bill as the solicitor had.

(6)   Except in special circumstances, no order shall be made on an application under this section for the taxation of a bill which has already been taxed.

(7)   If the court on an application under this section orders a bill to be taxed, it may order the solicitor to deliver to the applicant a copy of the bill on payment of the costs of that copy.

NOTES

Initial Commencement
    To be appointed: see s 90(2).

Appointment
    Appointment: 1 May 1975: see SI 1975/534, arts 1(2), 2(b); for savings see Schedule thereto.

Derivation
    This section derived from the Solicitors Act 1957, s 70.

See Further
    See further: Administration of Justice Act 1985, s 9, Sch 2.
    See further: the High Court and County Courts Jurisdiction Order 1991, SI 1991/724, arts 2(7), (8), 11, 12, Schedule, Part I.

Extent
This section does not extend to Scotland.

72 Supplementary provisions as to taxations
(1) Every application for an order for the taxation of a solicitor's bill or for the delivery of a solicitor's bill and for the delivery up by a solicitor of any documents in his possession, custody or power shall be made in the matter of that solicitor.

(2) Where a taxing officer is in the course of taxing a bill of costs, he may request the taxing officer of any other court to assist him in taxing any part of the bill, and the taxing officer so requested shall tax that part of the bill and shall return the bill with his opinion on it to the taxing officer making the request.

(3) Where a request is made as mentioned in subsection (2), the taxing officer who is requested to tax part of a bill shall have such powers, and may take such fees, in respect of that part of the bill, as he would have or be entitled to take if he were taxing that part of the bill in pursuance of an order of the court of which he is an officer; and the taxing officer who made the request shall not take any fee in respect of that part of the bill.

(4) The certificate of the taxing officer by whom any bill has been taxed shall, unless it is set aside or altered by the court, be final as to the amount of the costs covered by it, and the court may make such order in relation to the certificate as it thinks fit, including, in a case where the retainer is not disputed, an order that judgment be entered for the sum certified to be due with costs.

NOTES
Initial Commencement
To be appointed: see s 90(2).
Appointment
Appointment: 1 May 1975: see SI 1975/534, arts 1(2), 2(b); for savings see Schedule thereto.
Derivation
This section derived from the Solicitors Act 1957, s 71.
See Further
See further: Administration of Justice Act 1985, s 9, Sch 2.
Extent
This section does not extend to Scotland.

Appendix 7

Courts and Legal Services Act 1990, ss 58–58B

1990 CHAPTER 41

[58 Conditional fee agreements]

[(1)   A conditional fee agreement which satisfies all of the conditions applicable to it by virtue of this section shall not be unenforceable by reason only of its being a conditional fee agreement; but (subject to subsection (5)) any other conditional fee agreement shall be unenforceable.

(2)   For the purposes of this section and section 58A—

    (a)   a conditional fee agreement is an agreement with a person providing advocacy or litigation services which provides for his fees and expenses, or any part of them, to be payable only in specified circumstances; and

    (b)   a conditional fee agreement provides for a success fee if it provides for the amount of any fees to which it applies to be increased, in specified circumstances, above the amount which would be payable if it were not payable only in specified circumstances.

(3)   The following conditions are applicable to every conditional fee agreement—

    (a)   it must be in writing;

    (b)   it must not relate to proceedings which cannot be the subject of an enforceable conditional fee agreement; and

    (c)   it must comply with such requirements (if any) as may be prescribed by the Lord Chancellor.

(4)   The following further conditions are applicable to a conditional fee agreement which provides for a success fee—

    (a)   it must relate to proceedings of a description specified by order made by the Lord Chancellor;

    (b)   it must state the percentage by which the amount of the fees which would be payable if it were not a conditional fee agreement is to be increased; and

    (c)   that percentage must not exceed the percentage specified in relation to the description of proceedings to which the agreement relates by order made by the Lord Chancellor.

(5)   If a conditional fee agreement is an agreement to which section 57 of the Solicitors Act 1974 (non-contentious business agreements between solicitor and client) applies, subsection (1) shall not make it unenforceable.]

NOTES
Amendment
Substituted together with s 58A, for s 58 as originally enacted, by the Access to Justice Act 1999, s 27(1).
Date in force: 1 April 2000 (with savings in relation to existing cases): see SI 2000/774, arts 2(b), 5 and SI 2000/900, art 2.
Subordinate Legislation
Conditional Fee Agreements Order 1998, SI 1998/1860 (made under sub-ss (4),(5)).
Conditional Fee Agreements Regulations 2000, SI 2000/692 (made under sub-s (3)(c)).
Conditional Fee Agreements Order 2000, SI 2000/823 (made under sub-ss (4)(a), (c)).
Collective Conditional Fee Agreements Regulations 2000, SI 2000/2988 (made under sub-ss (3)(c)).
Extent
This section does not extend to Scotland: see s 123(1).

[58A Conditional fee agreements: supplementary]
[(1) The proceedings which cannot be the subject of an enforceable conditional fee agreement are—
   (a) criminal proceedings, apart from proceedings under section 82 of the Environmental Protection Act 1990; and
   (b) family proceedings.
(2) In subsection (1) "family proceedings" means proceedings under any one or more of the following—
   (a) the Matrimonial Causes Act 1973;
   (b) the Adoption Act 1976;
   (c) the Domestic Proceedings and Magistrates' Courts Act 1978;
   (d) Part III of the Matrimonial and Family Proceedings Act 1984;
   (e) Parts I, II and IV of the Children Act 1989;
   (f) Part IV of the Family Law Act 1996; and
   (g) the inherent jurisdiction of the High Court in relation to children.
(3) The requirements which the Lord Chancellor may prescribe under section 58(3)(c)—
   (a) include requirements for the person providing advocacy or litigation services to have provided prescribed information before the agreement is made; and
   (b) may be different for different descriptions of conditional fee agreements (and, in particular, may be different for those which provide for a success fee and those which do not).
(4) In section 58 and this section (and in the definitions of "advocacy services" and "litigation services" as they apply for their purposes) "proceedings" includes any sort of proceedings for resolving disputes (and not just proceedings in a court), whether commenced or contemplated.
(5) Before making an order under section 58(4), the Lord Chancellor shall consult—
   (a) the designated judges;

    (b)   the General Council of the Bar;

    (c)   the Law Society; and

    (d)   such other bodies as he considers appropriate.

(6)   A costs order made in any proceedings may, subject in the case of court proceedings to rules of court, include provision requiring the payment of any fees payable under a conditional fee agreement which provides for a success fee.

(7)   Rules of court may make provision with respect to the assessment of any costs which include fees payable under a conditional fee agreement (including one which provides for a success fee).]

NOTES

Amendment

Substituted together with s 58, for s 58 as originally enacted, by the Access to Justice Act 1999, s 27(1).

Date in force: 1 April 2000 (with savings in relation to existing cases): see SI 2000/774, arts 2(b), 5 and SI 2000/900, art 2.

Subordinate Legislation

Conditional Fee Agreements Regulations 2000, SI 2000/692 (made under sub-s (3)).

Collective Conditional Fee Agreements Regulations 2000, SI 2000/2988 (made under sub-s (3)).

Extent

This section does not extend to Scotland: see s 123(1).

[58B Litigation funding agreements]

[(1)   A litigation funding agreement which satisfies all of the conditions applicable to it by virtue of this section shall not be unenforceable by reason only of its being a litigation funding agreement.

(2)   For the purposes of this section a litigation funding agreement is an agreement under which—

    (a)   a person ("the funder") agrees to fund (in whole or in part) the provision of advocacy or litigation services (by someone other than the funder) to another person ("the litigant"); and

    (b)   the litigant agrees to pay a sum to the funder in specified circumstances.

(3)   The following conditions are applicable to a litigation funding agreement—

    (a)   the funder must be a person, or person of a description, prescribed by the Lord Chancellor;

    (b)   the agreement must be in writing;

    (c)   the agreement must not relate to proceedings which by virtue of section 58A(1) and (2) cannot be the subject of an enforceable conditional fee agreement or to proceedings of any such description as may be prescribed by the Lord Chancellor;

    (d)   the agreement must comply with such requirements (if any) as may be so prescribed;

(e)   the sum to be paid by the litigant must consist of any costs payable to him in respect of the proceedings to which the agreement relates together with an amount calculated by reference to the funder's anticipated expenditure in funding the provision of the services; and

(f)   that amount must not exceed such percentage of that anticipated expenditure as may be prescribed by the Lord Chancellor in relation to proceedings of the description to which the agreement relates.

(4)   Regulations under subsection (3)(a) may require a person to be approved by the Lord Chancellor or by a prescribed person.

(5)   The requirements which the Lord Chancellor may prescribe under subsection (3)(d)—

(a)   include requirements for the funder to have provided prescribed information to the litigant before the agreement is made; and

(b)   may be different for different descriptions of litigation funding agreements.

(6)   In this section (and in the definitions of "advocacy services" and "litigation services" as they apply for its purposes) "proceedings" includes any sort of proceedings for resolving disputes (and not just proceedings in a court), whether commenced or contemplated.

(7)   Before making regulations under this section, the Lord Chancellor shall consult—

(a)   the designated judges;

(b)   the General Council of the Bar;

(c)   the Law Society; and

(d)   such other bodies as he considers appropriate.

(8)   A costs order made in any proceedings may, subject in the case of court proceedings to rules of court, include provision requiring the payment of any amount payable under a litigation funding agreement.

(9)   Rules of court may make provision with respect to the assessment of any costs which include fees payable under a litigation funding agreement.]

NOTES

Amendment

Inserted by the Access to Justice Act 1999, s 28.

Date in force: to be appointed: see the Access to Justice Act 1999, s 108(1).

Extent

This section does not extend to Scotland: see s 123(1).

Appendix 8

Access to Justice Act 1999, ss 29–31

1999 CHAPTER 22

Costs

29 Recovery of insurance premiums by way of costs
Where in any proceedings a costs order is made in favour of any party who has taken out an insurance policy against the risk of incurring a liability in those proceedings, the costs payable to him may, subject in the case of court proceedings to rules of court, include costs in respect of the premium of the policy.

NOTES
Initial Commencement
　To be appointed: see s 108(1).
Appointment
　Appointment: 1 April 2000 (with savings in relation to existing cases): see SI 2000/774, arts 2(b), 5 and SI 2000/900, art 3.
Extent
　This section does not extend to Scotland: see s 109(6).

30 Recovery where body undertakes to meet costs liabilities
(1) This section applies where a body of a prescribed description under-takes to meet (in accordance with arrangements satisfying prescribed conditions) liabilities which members of the body or other persons who are parties to proceedings may incur to pay the costs of other parties to the proceedings.

(2) If in any of the proceedings a costs order is made in favour of any of the members or other persons, the costs payable to him may, subject to subsection (3) and (in the case of court proceedings) to rules of court, include an additional amount in respect of any provision made by or on behalf of the body in connection with the proceedings against the risk of having to meet such liabilities.

(3) But the additional amount shall not exceed a sum determined in a prescribed manner; and there may, in particular, be prescribed as a manner of determination one which takes into account the likely cost to the member or other person of the premium of an insurance policy against the risk of incurring a liability to pay the costs of other parties to the proceedings.

(4) In this section "prescribed" means prescribed by regulations made by the Lord Chancellor by statutory instrument; and a statutory instru-

ment containing such regulations shall be subject to annulment in pursuance of a resolution of either House of Parliament.

(5) Regulations under subsection (1) may, in particular, prescribe as a description of body one which is for the time being approved by the Lord Chancellor or by a prescribed person.

NOTES
Initial Commencement
To be appointed: see s 108(1).
Appointment
Appointment: 1 April 2000 (with savings in relation to existing cases): see SI 2000/774, arts 2(b), 5 and SI 2000/900, art 4.
Subordinate Legislation
Access to Justice (Membership Organisations) Regulations 2000, SI 2000/693 (made under sub-ss (1), (3)–(5).
Extent
This section does not extend to Scotland: see s 109(6).

31   Rules as to costs
In section 51 of the Supreme Court Act 1981 (costs), in subsection (2) (rules regulating matters relating to costs), insert at the end "or for securing that the amount awarded to a party in respect of the costs to be paid by him to such representatives is not limited to what would have been payable by him to them if he had not been awarded costs."

NOTES
Initial Commencement
To be appointed: see s 108(1).
Extent
This section does not extend to Scotland: see s 109(6).

Appendix 9

Conditional Fee Agreements Order 2000

SI 2000 No 823

Made   20th March 2000

Coming into force   1st April 2000

The Lord Chancellor, in exercise of the powers conferred upon him by section 58(4)(a) and (c) of the Courts and Legal Services Act 1990, and all other powers enabling him in that behalf, having consulted in accordance with section 58A(5) of that Act, makes the following Order, a draft of which has been laid before and approved by resolution of each House of Parliament:

1   Citation, commencement and interpretation
(1)   This Order may be cited as the Conditional Fee Agreements Order 2000 and shall come into force on 1st April 2000.
(2)   In this Order "the Act" means the Courts and Legal Services Act 1990.

NOTES
Initial Commencement
  Specified date: 1 April 2000: see para (1) above.

2   Revocation of 1998 Order
The Conditional Fee Agreements Order 1998 is revoked.

NOTES
Initial Commencement
  Specified date: 1 April 2000: see art 1(1).

3   Agreements providing for success fees
All proceedings which, under section 58 of the Act, can be the subject of an enforceable conditional fee agreement, except proceedings under section 82 of the Environmental Protection Act 1990, are proceedings specified for the purposes of section 58(4)(a) of the Act.

NOTES
Initial Commencement
  Specified date: 1 April 2000: see art 1(1).

4   Amount of success fees
In relation to all proceedings specified in article 3, the percentage specified for the purposes of section 58(4)(c) of the Act shall be 100%.

NOTES
Initial Commencement
  Specified date: 1 April 2000: see art 1(1).

Irvine of Lairg, C
Dated 20th March 2000

Conditional Fee Agreements Regulations 2000

SI 2000 No 692

Made	9th March 2000
Laid before Parliament	10th March 2000
Coming into force	1st April 2000

The Lord Chancellor, in exercise of the powers conferred on him by sections 58(3)(c), 58A(3) and 119 of the Courts and Legal Services Act 1990 and all other powers enabling him hereby makes the following Regulations:

1 Citation, commencement and interpretation
(1) These Regulations may be cited as the Conditional Fee Agreements Regulations 2000.
(2) These Regulations come into force on 1st April 2000.
(3) In these Regulations—
"client" includes, except where the context otherwise requires, a person who—
    (a) has instructed the legal representative to provide the advocacy or litigation services to which the conditional fee agreement relates, or
    (b) is liable to pay the legal representative's fees in respect of those services; and
"legal representative" means the person providing the advocacy or litigation services to which the conditional fee agreement relates.

NOTES
Initial Commencement
Specified date: 1 April 2000: see para (2) above.

2 Requirements for contents of conditional fee agreements: general
(1) A conditional fee agreement must specify—
    (a) the particular proceedings or parts of them to which it relates (including whether it relates to any appeal, counterclaim or proceedings to enforce a judgement or order),
    (b) the circumstances in which the legal representative's fees and expenses, or part of them, are payable,
    (c) what payment, if any, is due—
        (i) if those circumstances only partly occur,

(ii)   irrespective of whether those circumstances occur, and
(iii)   on the termination of the agreement for any reason, and

(d)   the amounts which are payable in all the circumstances and cases specified or the method to be used to calculate them and, in particular, whether the amounts are limited by reference to the damages which may be recovered on behalf of the client.

(2)   A conditional fee agreement to which regulation 4 applies must contain a statement that the requirements of that regulation which apply in the case of that agreement have been complied with.

NOTES
Initial Commencement
Specified date: 1 April 2000: see reg 1(2).

3   Requirements for contents of conditional fee agreements providing for success fees

(1)   A conditional fee agreement which provides for a success fee—

(a)   must briefly specify the reasons for setting the percentage increase at the level stated in the agreement, and

(b)   must specify how much of the percentage increase, if any, relates to the cost to the legal representative of the postponement of the payment of his fees and expenses.

(2)   If the agreement relates to court proceedings, it must provide that where the percentage increase becomes payable as a result of those proceedings, then—

(a)   if—

(i)   any fees subject to the increase are assessed, and
(ii)   the legal representative or the client is required by the court to disclose to the court or any other person the reasons for setting the percentage increase at the level stated in the agreement,

he may do so,

(b)   if—

(i)   any such fees are assessed, and
(ii)   any amount in respect of the percentage increase is disallowed on the assessment on the ground that the level at which the increase was set was unreasonable in view of facts which were or should have been known to the legal representative at the time it was set,

that amount ceases to be payable under the agreement, unless the court is satisfied that it should continue to be so payable, and

(c)   if—

(i)   sub-paragraph (b) does not apply, and
(ii)   the legal representative agrees with any person liable as a result of the proceedings to pay fees subject to the percentage

increase that a lower amount than the amount payable in accordance with the conditional fee agreement is to be paid instead,

the amount payable under the conditional fee agreement in respect of those fees shall be reduced accordingly, unless the court is satisfied that the full amount should continue to be payable under it.

(3) In this regulation "percentage increase" means the percentage by which the amount of the fees which would be payable if the agreement were not a conditional fee agreement is to be increased under the agreement.

NOTES
Initial Commencement
Specified date: 1 April 2000: see reg 1(2).

4   Information to be given before conditional fee agreements made
(1) Before a conditional fee agreement is made the legal representative must—
    (a)   inform the client about the following matters, and
    (b)   if the client requires any further explanation, advice or other information about any of those matters, provide such further explanation, advice or other information about them as the client may reasonably require.
(2) Those matters are—
    (a)   the circumstances in which the client may be liable to pay the costs of the legal representative in accordance with the agreement,
    (b)   the circumstances in which the client may seek assessment of the fees and expenses of the legal representative and the procedure for doing so,
    (c)   whether the legal representative considers that the client's risk of incurring liability for costs in respect of the proceedings to which agreement relates is insured against under an existing contract of insurance,
    (d)   whether other methods of financing those costs are available, and, if so, how they apply to the client and the proceedings in question,
    (e)   whether the legal representative considers that any particular method or methods of financing any or all of those costs is appropriate and, if he considers that a contract of insurance is appropriate or recommends a particular such contract—
        (i)   his reasons for doing so, and
        (ii)   whether he has an interest in doing so.
(3) Before a conditional fee agreement is made the legal representative must explain its effect to the client.
(4) In the case of an agreement where—
    (a)   the legal representative is a body to which section 30 of the Access to Justice Act 1999 (recovery where body undertakes to meet costs liabilities) applies, and

(b)   there are no circumstances in which the client may be liable to pay any costs in respect of the proceedings,
paragraph (1) does not apply.

(5)   Information required to be given under paragraph (1) about the matters in paragraph (2)(a) to (d) must be given orally (whether or not it is also given in writing), but information required to be so given about the matters in paragraph (2)(e) and the explanation required by paragraph (3) must be given both orally and in writing.

(6)   This regulation does not apply in the case of an agreement between a legal representative and an additional legal representative.

NOTES
Initial Commencement
Specified date: 1 April 2000: see reg 1(2).

5   Form of agreement

(1)   A conditional fee agreement must be signed by the client and the legal representative.

(2)   This regulation does not apply in the case of an agreement between a legal representative and an additional legal representative.

NOTES
Initial Commencement
Specified date: 1 April 2000: see reg 1(2).

6   Amendment of agreement

Where an agreement is amended to cover further proceedings or parts of them—

(a)   regulations 2, 3 and 5 apply to the amended agreement as if it were a fresh agreement made at the time of the amendment, and

(b)   the obligations under regulation 4 apply in relation to the amendments in so far as they affect the matters mentioned in that regulation.

NOTES
Initial Commencement
Specified date: 1 April 2000: see reg 1(2).

7   Revocation of 1995 Regulations

The Conditional Fee Agreements Regulations 1995 are revoked.

NOTES
Initial Commencement
Specified date: 1 April 2000: see reg 1(2).

[8 Exclusion of collective conditional fee agreements]

[These Regulations shall not apply to collective conditional fee agreements within the meaning of regulation 3 of the Collective Conditional Fee Agreements Regulations 2000.]

NOTES
Amendment
　　Inserted by SI 2000/2988, reg 7.
　　Date in force: 30 November 2000 (in relation to agreements entered into on or after that date): see SI 2000/2988, regs 1(1), 2.

Irvine of Lairg, C
9th March 2000

Appendix 11

Access to Justice (Membership Organisations) Regulations 2000

SI 2000 No 693

Made	9th March 2000
Laid before Parliament	10th March 2000
Coming into force	1st April 2000

The Lord Chancellor, in exercise of the powers conferred on him by section 30(1) and (3) to (5) of the Access to Justice Act 1999 and all other powers enabling him hereby makes the following Regulations:

1   Citation, commencement and interpretation
(1)   These Regulations may be cited as the Access to Justice (Membership Organisations) Regulations 2000.
(2)   These Regulations come into force on 1st April 2000.

NOTES
Initial Commencement
　　　Specified date: 1 April 2000: see para (2) above.

2   Bodies of a prescribed description
The bodies which are prescribed for the purpose of section 30 of the Access to Justice Act 1999 (recovery where body undertakes to meet costs liabilities) are those bodies which are for the time being approved by the Lord Chancellor for that purpose.

NOTES
Initial Commencement
　　　Specified date: 1 April 2000: see reg 1(2).

3   Requirements for arrangements to meet costs liabilities
(1)   Section 30(1) of the Access to Justice Act 1999 applies to arrangements which satisfy the following conditions.
(2)   The arrangements must be in writing.
(3)   The arrangements must contain a statement specifying—
　　　(a)   the circumstances in which the member or other party may be liable to pay costs of the proceedings,
　　　(b)   whether such a liability arises—
　　　　　(i)   if those circumstances only partly occur,

        (ii)   irrespective of whether those circumstances occur, and
        (iii)   on the termination of the arrangements for any reason,
   (c)   the basis on which the amount of the liability is calculated, and
   (d)   the procedure for seeking assessment of costs.

(4)   A copy of the part of the arrangements containing the statement must be given to the member or other party to the proceedings whose liabilities the body is undertaking to meet as soon as possible after the undertaking is given.

NOTES
Initial Commencement
    Specified date: 1 April 2000: see reg 1(2).

4   Recovery of additional amount for insurance costs

(1)   Where an additional amount is included in costs by virtue of section 30(2) of the Access to Justice Act 1999 (costs payable to a member of a body or other person party to the proceedings to include an additional amount in respect of provision made by the body against the risk of having to meet the member's or other person's liabilities to pay other parties' costs), that additional amount must not exceed the following sum.

(2)   That sum is the likely cost to the member of the body or, as the case may be, the other person who is a party to the proceedings in which the costs order is made of the premium of an insurance policy against the risk of incurring a liability to pay the costs of other parties to the proceedings.

NOTES
Initial Commencement
    Specified date: 1 April 2000: see reg 1(2).

Irvine of Lairg, C
9th March 2000

Appendix 12

Collective Conditional Fee Agreements Regulations 2000

SI 2000 No 2988

Made	7th November 2000
Laid before Parliament	8th November 2000
Coming into force	30th November 2000

The Lord Chancellor, in exercise of the powers conferred upon him by sections 58(3)(c), 58A(3) and 119 of the Courts and Legal Services Act 1990 hereby makes the following Regulations:

1   Citation, commencement and interpretation
(1)   These regulations may be cited as the Collective Conditional Fee Agreements Regulations 2000, and shall come into force on 30th November 2000.
(2)   In these Regulations, except where the context requires otherwise—
"client" means a person who will receive advocacy or litigation services to which the agreement relates;
"collective conditional fee agreement" has the meaning given in regulation 3;
"conditional fee agreement" has the same meaning as in section 58 of the Courts and Legal Services Act 1990;
"funder" means the party to a collective conditional fee agreement who, under that agreement, is liable to pay the legal representative's fees;
"legal representative" means the person providing the advocacy or litigation services to which the agreement relates.

NOTES
Initial Commencement
Specified date: 30 November 2000: see para (1) above.
Modification
A registered European lawyer may provide professional activities by way of legal advice and assistance or legal aid, and these Regulations shall be interpreted accordingly: see the European Communities (Lawyer's Practice) Regulations 2000, SI 2000/1119, reg 14.

2   Transitional provisions
These Regulations shall apply to agreements entered into on or after 30th November 2000, and agreements entered into before that date shall be treated as if these Regulations had not come into force.

NOTES
Initial Commencement
Specified date: 30 November 2000: see reg 1(1).

3   Definition of "collective conditional fee agreement"
(1)   Subject to paragraph (2) of this regulation, a collective conditional fee agreement is an agreement which—
 (a)   disregarding section 58(3)(c) of the Courts and Legal Services Act 1990, would be a conditional fee agreement; and
 (b)   does not refer to specific proceedings, but provides for fees to be payable on a common basis in relation to a class of proceedings, or, if it refers to more than one class of proceedings, on a common basis in relation to each class.
(2)   An agreement may be a collective conditional fee agreement whether or not—
 (a)   the funder is a client; or
 (b)   any clients are named in the agreement.

NOTES
Initial Commencement
Specified date: 30 November 2000: see reg 1(1).

4   Requirements for contents of collective conditional fee agreements: general
(1)   A collective conditional fee agreement must specify the circumstances in which the legal representative's fees and expenses, or part of them, are payable.
(2)   A collective conditional fee agreement must provide that, when accepting instructions in relation to any specific proceedings the legal representative must—
 (a)   inform the client as to the circumstances in which the client may be liable to pay the costs of the legal representative; and
 (b)   if the client requires any further explanation, advice or other information about the matter referred to in sub-paragraph (a), provide such further explanation, advice or other information about it as the client may reasonably require.
(3)   Paragraph (2) does not apply in the case of an agreement between a legal representative and an additional legal representative.
(4)   A collective conditional fee agreement must provide that, after accepting instructions in relation to any specific proceedings, the legal representative must confirm his acceptance of instructions in writing to the client.

NOTES
Initial Commencement
Specified date: 30 November 2000: see reg 1(1).

5 **Requirements for contents of collective conditional fee agreements providing for success fees**

(1) Where a collective conditional fee agreement provides for a success fee the agreement must provide that, when accepting instructions in relation to any specific proceedings the legal representative must prepare and retain a written statement containing—

    (a) his assessment of the probability of the circumstances arising in which the percentage increase will become payable in relation to those proceedings ("the risk assessment");

    (b) his assessment of the amount of the percentage increase in relation to those proceedings, having regard to the risk assessment; and

    (c) the reasons, by reference to the risk assessment, for setting the percentage increase at that level.

(2) If the agreement relates to court proceedings it must provide that where the success fee becomes payable as a result of those proceedings, then—

    (a) if—

        (i) any fees subject to the increase are assessed, and

        (ii) the legal representative or the client is required by the court to disclose to the court or any other person the reasons for setting the percentage increase at the level assessed by the legal representative,

    he may do so,

    (b) if—

        (i) any such fees are assessed by the court, and

        (ii) any amount in respect of the percentage increase is disallowed on the assessment on the ground that the level at which the increase was set was unreasonable in view of facts which were or should have been known to the legal representative at the time it was set

    that amount ceases to be payable under the agreement, unless the court is satisfied that it should continue to be so payable, and

    (c) if—

        (i) sub-paragraph (b) does not apply, and

        (ii) the legal representative agrees with any person liable as a result of the proceedings to pay fees subject to the percentage increase that a lower amount than the amount payable in accordance with the conditional fee agreement is to be paid instead,

    the amount payable under the collective conditional fee agreement in respect of those fees shall be reduced accordingly, unless the court is satisfied that the full amount should continue to be payable under it.

(3) In this regulation "percentage increase" means the percentage by which the amount of the fees which would have been payable if the agreement were not a conditional fee agreement is to be increased under the agreement.

NOTES
Initial Commencement
Specified date: 30 November 2000: see reg 1(1).

6   **Form and amendment of collective conditional fee agreement**
(1)   Subject to paragraph (2), a collective conditional fee agreement must be signed by the funder, and by the legal representative.
(2)   Paragraph (1) does not apply in the case of an agreement between a legal representative and an additional legal representative.
(3)   Where a collective conditional fee agreement is amended, regulations 4 and 5 apply to the amended agreement as if it were a fresh agreement made at the time of the amendment.

NOTES
Initial Commencement
Specified date: 30 November 2000: see reg 1(1).

7   **Amendment to the Conditional Fee Agreements Regulations 2000**
After regulation 7 of the Conditional Fee Agreements Regulations 2000 there shall be inserted the following new regulation:—

8   **"Exclusion of collective conditional fee agreements**
These Regulations shall not apply to collective conditional fee agreements within the meaning of regulation 3 of the Collective Conditional Fee Agreements Regulations 2000.".

NOTES
Initial Commencement
Specified date: 30 November 2000: see reg 1(1).

Irvine of Lairg, C
Dated 7th November 2000

Appendix 13

Notice of funding of Case or Claim Form N251

Notice of Funding of Case or Claim	In the	
	Claim No.	
	Claimant (Include Ref.)	
	Defendant (Include Ref.)	

Notice of funding by means of a conditional fee agreement, insurance policy or undertaking given by a prescribed body should be given to the court and all other parties to the case:
- on commencement of proceedings
- on filing an acknowledgment of service, defence or other first document; and
- at any later time that such an arrangement is entered into, changed or terminated

Take notice that in respect of [all claims herein][the following claims   ]
the case of   *(specify name of party)*

[is now][was] being funded by:
(Please tick those boxes which apply)

☐ a conditional fee agreement dated   which provides for a success fee;

☐ an insurance policy issued on *(date)*   by *(name of insurers)*   ;

☐ an undertaking given on *(date)*   by *(name of prescribed body)*   in the
   following terms

The funding of the case has now changed:

☐ the above funding has now ceased

☐ the conditional fee agreement has been terminated

☐ a conditional agreement dated   which provides for a success fee has been entered into

☐ the insurance policy dated   has been cancelled

☐ an insurance policy has been issued by *(name of insurer)*
   on *(date)*

☐ the undertaking given on *(date)*   has been terminated

☐ an undertaking has been given on *(date)*   by *(name of prescribed body)*
   in the following terms

Signed   **Date**
Solicitor for the (claimant) (defendant) (Part 20 defendant)
(respondent) (appellant)

The court office at

is open between 10 am and 4 pm Monday to Friday. When corresponding with the court, please address forms or letters to the Court Manager and quote the claim number.
N251 Notice of funding of case or claim (7.00)   *The Court Service Publications Unit*

387

Appendix 14

Solicitors' Practice Rules 1990

[with consolidated amendments to 1 December 2001]

© The Law Society

Rule 1 (Basic principles)

A solicitor shall not do anything in the course of practising as a solicitor, or permit another person to do anything on his or her behalf, which compromises or impairs or is likely to compromise or impair any of the following:

    (a)   the solicitor's independence or integrity;

    (b)   a person's freedom to instruct a solicitor of his or her choice;

    (c)   the solicitor's duty to act in the best interests of the client;

    (d)   the good repute of the solicitor or of the solicitor's profession;

    (e)   the solicitor's proper standard of work;

    (f)   the solicitor's duty to the Court.

Rule 8 (Contingency fees)

(1)   A solicitor who is retained or employed to prosecute or defend any action, suit or other contentious proceeding shall not enter into any arrangement to receive a contingency fee in respect of that proceeding, save one permitted under statute or by common law.

(2)   Paragraph (1) of this rule shall not apply to an arrangement in respect of an action, suit or other contentious proceeding in any country other than England and Wales to the extent that the local lawyer would be permitted to receive a contingency fee in respect of that proceeding.

Rule 15 (Costs information and client care)

Solicitors shall:

    (a)   give information about costs and other matters, and

    (b)   operate a complaints handling procedure,

in accordance with a Solicitors' Costs Information and Client Care Code made from time to time by the Council of the Law Society with the concurrence of the Master of the Rolls, but subject to the notes.

NOTES

    (i)   A serious breach of the code, or persistent breaches of a material nature, will be a breach of the rule, and may also be evidence of inadequate professional services under section 37A of the Solicitors Act 1974.

(ii)   Material breaches of the code which are not serious or persistent will not be a breach of the rule, but may be evidence of inadequate professional services under section 37A.

(iii)   The powers of the Office for the Supervision of Solicitors on a finding of inadequate professional services include:

(a) disallowing all or part of the solicitor's costs; and

(b) directing the solicitor to pay compensation to the client up to a limit of £1,000.[*]

(iv)   Non-material breaches of the code will not be a breach of the rule, and will not be evidence of inadequate professional services under section 37A.

(v)   Registered foreign lawyers practising in partnership with solicitors of the Supreme Court or registered European lawyers, or as members of recognised bodies which are limited liability partnerships, or as directors of recognised bodies which are companies, although subject to Rule 15 as a matter of professional conduct, are not subject to section 37A. However, such solicitors, registered European lawyers and recognised bodies are subject to section 37A for professional services provided by the firm.

[*]   [Law Society note: This limit has now been raised to £5,000.]

Rule 18 (Application and interpretation)

. . .

(2)   (Interpretation)

. . .

(c)   'contingency fee' means any sum (whether fixed, or calculated either as a percentage of the proceeds or otherwise howsoever) payable only in the event of success in the prosecution or defence of any action, suit or other contentious proceeding;

Solicitors' Costs Information and Client Care Code 1999

[with consolidated amendments to 6 April 2001]

© The Law Society

Code dated 3rd September 1999 made by the Council of the Law Society with the concurrence of the Master of the Rolls under Rule 15 of the Solicitors' Practice Rules 1990, regulating the English and Welsh practices of solicitors, registered European lawyers, registered foreign lawyers and recognised bodies in giving information to clients and operating complaints procedures.

1. Introduction

(a) This code replaces the written professional standards on costs information for clients (see paragraphs 3 – 6) and the detail previously contained in Practice Rule 15 (client care) (see paragraph 7).

(b) The main object of the code is to make sure that clients are given the information they need to understand what is happening generally and in particular on:

(i) the cost of legal services both at the outset and as a matter progresses; and

(ii) responsibility for clients' matters.

(c) The code also requires firms to operate a complaints handling procedure.

(d) It is good practice to record in writing:

(i) all information required to be given by the code including all decisions relating to costs and the arrangements for updating costs information; and

(ii) the reasons why the information required by the code has not been given in a particular case.

(e) References to costs, where appropriate, include fees, VAT and disbursements.

2. Application

(a) The code is of general application, and it applies to registered foreign lawyers as well as to solicitors of the Supreme Court and registered European lawyers (subject to note (v) to Practice Rule 15). However, as set out in paragraph 2(b), parts of the code may not be appropriate in every case, and solicitors should consider the interests of each client in deciding which parts not to apply in the particular circumstances.

(b) The full information required by the code may be inappropriate, for example:

    (i) in every case, for a regular client for whom repetitive work is done, where the client has already been provided with the relevant information, although such a client should be informed of changes; and

    (ii) if compliance with the code may at the time be insensitive or impractical. In such a case relevant information should be given as soon as reasonably practicable.

(c) Employed solicitors should have regard to paragraphs 3 – 6 of the code where appropriate, e.g. when acting for clients other than their employer. Paragraph 7 does not apply to employed solicitors.

(d) Solicitors should comply with paragraphs 3 – 6 of the code even where a client is legally aided if the client may have a financial interest in the costs because contributions are payable or the statutory charge may apply or they may become liable for the costs of another party.

(e) The code also applies to contingency fee and conditional fee arrangements and to arrangements with a client for the solicitor to retain commissions received from third parties.

3. Informing the client about costs

(a) Costs information must not be inaccurate or misleading.

(b) Any costs information required to be given by the code must be given clearly, in a way and at a level which is appropriate to the particular client. Any terms with which the client may be unfamiliar, for example 'disbursement', should be explained.

(c) The information required by paragraphs 4 and 5 of the code should be given to a client at the outset of, and at appropriate stages throughout, the matter. All information given orally should be confirmed in writing to the client as soon as possible.

4. Advance costs information – general

The overall costs

(a) The solicitor should give the client the best information possible about the likely overall costs, including a breakdown between fees, VAT and disbursements.

(b) The solicitor should explain clearly to the client the time likely to be spent in dealing with a matter, if time spent is a factor in the calculation of the fees.

(c) Giving 'the best information possible' includes:

    (i) agreeing a fixed fee; or

    (ii) giving a realistic estimate; or

    (iii) giving a forecast within a possible range of costs; or

(iv)   explaining to the client the reasons why it is not possible to fix, or give a realistic estimate or forecast of, the overall costs, and giving instead the best information possible about the cost of the next stage of the matter.

(d)   The solicitor should, in an appropriate case, explain to a privately paying client that the client may set an upper limit on the firm's costs for which the client may be liable without further authority. Solicitors should not exceed an agreed limit without first obtaining the client's consent.

(e)   The solicitor should make it clear at the outset if an estimate, quotation or other indication of cost is not intended to be fixed.

Basis of firm's charges

(f)   The solicitor should also explain to the client how the firm's fees are calculated except where the overall costs are fixed or clear. If the basis of charging is an hourly charging rate, that must be made clear.

(g)   The client should be told if charging rates may be increased.

Further information

(h)   The solicitor should explain what reasonably foreseeable payments a client may have to make either to the solicitor or to a third party and when those payments are likely to be needed.

(i)   The solicitor should explain to the client the arrangements for updating the costs information as set out in paragraph 6.

Client's ability to pay

(j)   The solicitor should discuss with the client how and when any costs are to be met, and consider:-
   (i)   whether the client may be eligible and should apply for legal aid (including advice and assistance);
   (ii)   whether the client's liability for their own costs may be covered by insurance;
   (iii)   whether the client's liability for another party's costs may be covered by pre-purchased insurance and, if not, whether it would be advisable for the client's liability for another party's costs to be covered by after the event insurance (including in every case where a conditional fee or contingency fee arrangement is proposed); and
   (iv)   whether the client's liability for costs (including the costs of another party) may be paid by another person e.g. an employer or trade union.

Cost-benefit and risk

(k)   The solicitor should discuss with the client whether the likely outcome in a matter will justify the expense or risk involved including, if relevant, the risk of having to bear an opponent's costs.

5.   Additional information for particular clients

Legally aided clients

(a)   The solicitor should explain to a legally aided client the client's potential liability for the client's own costs and those of any other party, including:

   (i)   the effect of the statutory charge and its likely amount;

   (ii)   the client's obligation to pay any contribution assessed and the consequences of failing to do so;

   (iii)   the fact that the client may still be ordered by the court to contribute to the opponent's costs if the case is lost even though the client's own costs are covered by legal aid; and

   (iv)   the fact that even if the client wins, the opponent may not be ordered to pay or be capable of paying the full amount of the client's costs.

Privately paying clients in contentious matters (and potentially contentious matters)

(b)   The solicitor should explain to the client the client's potential liability for the client's own costs and for those of any other party, including:

   (i)   the fact that the client will be responsible for paying the firm's bill in full regardless of any order for costs made against an opponent;

   (ii)   the probability that the client will have to pay the opponent's costs as well as the client's own costs if the case is lost;

   (iii)   the fact that even if the client wins, the opponent may not be ordered to pay or be capable of paying the full amount of the client's costs; and

   (iv)   the fact that if the opponent is legally aided the client may not recover costs, even if successful.

Liability for third party costs in non-contentious matters

(c)   The solicitor should explain to the client any liability the client may have for the payment of the costs of a third party. When appropriate, solicitors are advised to obtain a firm figure for or agree a cap to a third party's costs.

6.   Updating costs information

The solicitor should keep the client properly informed about costs as a matter progresses. In particular, the solicitor should:

(a)   tell the client, unless otherwise agreed, how much the costs are at regular intervals (at least every six months) and in appropriate cases deliver interim bills at agreed intervals;

(b)   explain to the client (and confirm in writing) any changed circumstances which will, or which are likely to affect the amount of costs, the degree of risk involved, or the cost-benefit to the client of continuing with the matter;

(c)   inform the client in writing as soon as it appears that a costs estimate or agreed upper limit may or will be exceeded; and

(d)   consider the client's eligibility for legal aid if a material change in the client's means comes to the solicitor's attention.

7.   Client care and complaints handling

Information for clients

(a)   Every solicitor in private practice must ensure that the client:

(i)   is given a clear explanation of the issues raised in a matter and is kept properly informed about its progress (including the likely timescale);

(ii)   is given the name and status of the person dealing with the matter and the name of the principal, or director (in the case of a recognised body which is a company), or member (in the case of a recognised body which is a limited liability partnership) responsible for its overall supervision;

(iii)   is told whom to contact about any problem with the service provided; and

(iv)   is given details of any changes in the information required to be given by this paragraph.

Complaints handling

(b)   Every principal in private practice (or, in the case of a recognised body, the body itself) must:

(i)   ensure the client is told the name of the person in the firm to contact about any problem with the service provided;

(ii)   have a written complaints procedure and ensure that complaints are handled in accordance with it; and

(iii)   ensure that the client is given a copy of the complaints procedure on request.

Appendix 16

Bar Council CFA Guidance

January 2001

General Introduction

It will be apparent to anyone reading this Guidance that conditional fees and the legislation governing them are complex, that they raise novel practical problems, and that they have significant potential pitfalls for the Bar, whose risk profile is different to that of solicitors. The reforms of 2000, which primarily permitted the recovery of success fees from losing parties, have served to increase the complexity.

Therefore any barrister who carries out, or who is considering carrying out, CFA work, must be fully conversant with the relevant source materials governing practice under CFAs, which are:

1. Statute
2. Statutory instruments
3. The CPR, Pre-action Protocols, and the Costs Practice Direction
4. Case law
5. The Code of Conduct and the Ethical Guidance contained in this Guidance
6. Any chambers protocols
7. The requirements of the BMIF
8. Relevant Specialist Bar Association model agreements and guidelines
9. Barmark requirements (where applicable)

Equally, no barrister should carry out CFA work unless his/her chambers have established systems for handling CFA cases that are compliant with these guidelines. This is important not only to ensure the efficient handling of cases, but also to permit the overall monitoring of CFA work.

This Guidance is an attempt to give the Bar the best advice currently available, but we welcome any suggestions from practitioners for improvements.

John Grace QC
Chairman, Bar Council CFA panel
January 2001

Part 1: Ethical Guidance

1. Introduction

This Part is intended to provide guidance only on the ethical problems which may arise from the operation of Conditional Fee Agreements ('CFAs'). It does not form part of the Bar's Code of Conduct. However, it is strongly advised that barristers should follow the advice set out here, which is intended to ensure compliance with the Code of Conduct. The Practical Guidance section of the Bar Council's CFA Guidance should be referred to for guidance on practical matters.

2. General

Paragraph 405 of the Code of Conduct permits a barrister in independent practice to charge for any work undertaken by her/him (whether or not it involves an appearance in court) on any basis or by any method s/he thinks fit provided that such basis or method is permitted by law; and does not involve the payment of a wage or salary. It is the responsibility of any member of the Bar who enters into a CFA to ensure that:

 1.2.1 he or she is familiar with the statutory provisions and regulations and orders made thereunder (see paragraphs 3 to 5 of Practical Guidance, and note in particular the distinction between 'old' and 'new' CFAs, and the different legislative regimes applicable thereto);

 1.2.2 he or she at all times acts in accordance with the Code of Conduct (relevant extracts of which are included in part 3 of the Guidance). For example, the barrister, before entering a CFA, must bear in mind the provisions of paragraph 603 of the Code, namely, that 'A practising barrister must not accept any brief or instructions if to do so would cause him to be professionally embarrassed', and the subsequent sub paragraphs of the Code defining circumstances in which such professional embarrassment may arise;

 1.2.3 the terms of the CFA comply with the requirements of the law and the Code. Compliance with the Code will be ensured if a Bar Council approved CFA is used.

3. The 'cab rank' rule

The 'cab rank' rule does not apply to CFAs. In other words, counsel cannot be compelled to accept instructions upon a CFA basis. See § 604(c) of the Code.

4. Internal agreements and arrangements between barristers

Some barristers and some chambers will find it appropriate to enter into standing agreements with each other or to establish practices whereby they will work under CFAs as a chambers or in groups. However, there are many barristers and sets of chambers who will not consider it appropriate to work under CFAs at all, or who will only consider it appropriate to work under them on a one off basis agreed for each particular CFA. The considerations to be taken into account when considering such internal arrangements are as follows:

 1.4.1 It is important to ensure that no arrangement or agreement is entered into which compromises or appears to compromise a barrister's integrity or independence, which creates or may create a partnership, or which creates or appears to create a conflict of interest (see Code §§ 104(a)(i), 301, 303, 306, 307(a), 603(e)). The Professional Standards Committee are presently considering whether any form of fee or profit sharing arrangements within a CFA team are or should be permitted under the Code of Conduct. Even if any such arrangement is or will be permitted, counsel who has such an arrangement with another counsel could not appear in front of that other counsel (acting as a judge or arbitrator) and could not act against that other counsel, in any action to which the fee or profit sharing arrangement applies: to do so would give rise to irresolvable conflicts of interest.

1.4.2 However, leaving aside the position of the Bar Council, there remains a likelihood that a court or arbitral institution would conclude that such an arrangement created a conflict of interest or the appearance of such a conflict, such that counsel involved should not be permitted to act against each other or as judge or arbitrator in any case. Pending guidance from the Professional Standards Committee, the Bar Council CFA Panel advises against any fee-or profit-sharing agreement, or any agreement which provides for a subsidy to be paid by chambers or a CFA group to members in respect of lost CFA cases. In our view, the better policy is to reduce the financial risks of CFAs by proper risk assessment and screening procedures (see Practical Guidance).

1.4.3 The Professional Standards Committee are also considering the implications of arrangements between counsel whereby they agree to accept each others' return CFA briefs and whether, in those circumstances, they would be precluded from acting against each other in any action to which such arrangements applied or from appearing in front of a counsel who was a party to such arrangements (acting as a judge or arbitrator).

5. Screening

If chambers operate a form of screening of CFA cases whereby one or more members of chambers read the papers in a case sent to another member with a view to deciding whether or not that case should be accepted on a CFA basis, the screener could not, in future, act on the other side, or as judge or arbitrator, in that case. Barristers acting as screeners should therefore keep records of the cases they have screened, and a record must be kept in each case of the identity of the screener. If screening would involve the disclosure of confidential information to the screener, consent to screening should be obtained in advance of the screening.

6. Forms of CFAs

There is no form of CFA prescribed by the Bar Council or any other body or specialist association; but see the guidance relating to insurance and the BMIF in paragraph 1.7 below. There is an approved form of CFA for use in personal injury and clinical negligence cases, and in chancery cases; draft model forms of agreement are under preparation for employment cases and commercial cases. These forms of CFA have been approved by, or are being prepared by, the relevant specialist bar associations, and barristers and their clerks would be well advised to make use of these forms. It is for the barrister entering into a CFA to be satisfied that the form of agreement used is appropriate and lawful. In any case where a barrister proposes or is asked to enter into a CFA with a solicitor upon terms which materially depart from any form of agreement approved by a specialist bar association, the barrister should ensure that such departure is lawful, fair to the lay client and reasonable in the particular circumstances of the case before agreeing to act on such terms. In particular, the barrister should ensure that no term increases or tends to increase inappropriate pressure on the lay client to reach a settlement. Although currently most CFAs are expressed not to intend the creation of legal relations, there is no objection to barristers entering into contractually binding agreements. If a barrister proposes or is asked to enter a CFA which is intended to be a binding legal agreement, the barrister should ensure that the agreement does not contain any clause inconsistent with the Code.

7. Insurance
Under §§ 204(b) and 402.1 of the Code, every barrister must be covered by insurance against claims for professional negligence, and be entered as a member with BMIF. Many standard form CFAs, including the APIL/PIBA model, provide for an indemnity in favour of the solicitor in the event that counsel's breach of duty causes the solicitor to suffer a loss of fees. The BMIF has agreed (subject to financial limits) to indemnify barristers against this type of claim, provided it has approved the form of the relevant agreement. A barrister will therefore not be insured against such a claim by the solicitor if he/she has entered into an agreement on a form not approved by the BMIF.

8. Inducements
The payment by barristers or their chambers of commissions or inducements is strictly prohibited by the Code: see §§ 307(d) and (e). Thus, for example, the payment of 'introduction' or 'administration' fees to an insurer or claims organisation is not permissible. Barristers may also be invited to enter into a CFA upon the basis that a concession will be given by the barrister in relation to fee levels on that CFA in the expectation of receiving further CFA instructions in other cases in the future. The request for the concession is likely to originate from the insurer of the lay client's costs exposure. Such arrangements are objectionable as they undermine the barrister's independence of judgment (both apparent and real) in assessing and dealing with the inevitable conflicts of interest that arise in relation to CFAs

9. Impartiality/conflicts of interest
Having accepted instructions to act under a CFA, a barrister shall thereafter give impartial advice to the lay client at all times and take all reasonable steps to identify and declare to the lay client and to the instructing solicitor any actual or apparent conflict of interest between the barrister and the lay client.

10. Advice and interests of lay client
During the currency of a CFA, the barrister should use his/her best endeavours to ensure that:
  (a)   any advice given by the barrister in relation to the case is communicated and fully explained to the lay client;
  (b)   any offer of settlement is communicated to the lay client forthwith;
  (c)   the consequences of particular clauses in the solicitor/lay client agreement and the solicitor/barrister agreement are explained to the client as and when they become relevant, particularly after an offer of settlement has been made.
This last obligation applies in particular to the financial consequences which may arise from the making of an offer to settle the case including consideration of (1) any increase in the offer of settlement; (2) 'conventional' costs consequences; and (3) the success fees which are or may become payable.

11. Advising on settlement
When advising on a settlement of the action the barrister should at all times have in mind his/ her obligation under paragraph 303 (a) of the Code to

'promote and protect fearlessly and by all proper and lawful means the lay client's best interests and do so without regard to his own interests or to any consequences to himself or to any other person (including any professional client or other intermediary or another barrister)'.

The barrister's duty must be, when advising the client on a settlement or on a payment in or Part 36 offer, to advise as to the best course of action from the lay client's point of view only.

12. Disagreement over Settlement
Difficulties may arise when the lawyers disagree about the wisdom of continuing the case or accepting an offer, whether that disagreement is:
  (a)   between them on the one part and the lay client on the other; or
  (b)   between solicitor and counsel; or
  (c)   between leading and junior counsel.
In such event careful consideration must be given to the lay client's interests. Every effort should be made to avoid unfairly putting the lay client in the position where having begun proceedings s/he is left without representation. However, where, for example, counsel has been misled about the true nature of the evidence or the lay client is refusing to accept firm advice as to the future conduct of the case, the terms of the CFA may permit counsel to withdraw. Before taking this serious step the barrister will have to check carefully whether s/he is entitled to withdraw.

13. Withdrawal from the case
The barrister may withdraw from the case in any of the circumstances set out in the CFA agreement, but only if satisfied that s/he is permitted to withdraw pursuant to part VI of the Code. In the event that the CFA agreement does

not contain a term that the barrister may withdraw from the case in particular circumstances, but the Code requires the barrister to withdraw in those circumstances, the Code takes priority over the agreement.

14. Disclosure of existence and terms of CFA

The fact that the action is funded by means of a CFA, and the terms of a CFA, should not be disclosed to the other parties to the action without the express written permission of the lay client, or save insofar as such disclosure is required by the court, the CPR, statute, rule, order, or Practice Direction.

Appendix 17

Press Complaints Commission Code of Practice

The Press Complaints Commission is charged with enforcing the following Code of Practice which was framed by the newspaper and periodical industry and ratified by the Press Complaints Commission, 1st December 1999.

All members of the press have a duty to maintain the highest professional and ethical standards. This code sets the benchmark for those standards. It both protects the rights of the individual and upholds the public's right to know.

The Code is the cornerstone of the system of self-regulation to which the industry has made a binding commitment. Editors and publishers must ensure that the Code is observed rigorously not only by their staff but also by anyone who contributes to their publications.

It is essential to the workings of an agreed code that it be honoured not only to the letter but in the full spirit. The Code should not be interpreted so narrowly as to compromise its commitment to respect the rights of the individual, nor so broadly that it prevents publication in the public interest.

It is the responsibility of editors to co-operate with the PCC as swiftly as possible in the resolution of complaints.

Any publication which is criticised by the PCC under on of the following clauses must print the adjudication which follows in full and with due prominence.

1   **Accuracy**
(i)   Newspapers and periodicals must take care not to publish inaccurate, misleading or distorted material including pictures.
(ii)   Whenever it is recognised that a significant inaccuracy, misleading statement or distorted report has been published, it must be corrected promptly and with due prominence.
(iii) An apology must be published whenever appropriate.
(iv)   Newspapers, whilst free to be partisan, must distinguish clearly between comment, conjecture and fact
(v)   A newspaper or periodical must report fairly and accurately the outcome of an action for defamation to which it has been a party.

2   **Opportunity to reply**
A fair opportunity for reply to inaccuracies must be given to individuals or organisations when reasonably called for.

3*   Privacy
(i)   Everyone is entitled to respect for his or her private and family life, home, health and correspondence. A publication will be expected to justify intrusions into any individual's private life without consent
(ii)   The use of long lens photography to take pictures of people in private places without their consent is unacceptable.
Note – Private places are public or private property where there is a reasonable expectation of privacy.

4*   Harassment
(i)   Journalists and photographers must neither obtain nor seek to obtain information or pictures through intimidation, harassment or persistent pursuit
(ii)   They must not photograph individuals in private places (as defined by the note to clause 3) without their consent; must not persist in telephoning, questioning, pursuing or photographing individuals after having been asked to desist; must not remain on their property after having been asked to leave and must not follow them.
(iii) Editors must ensure that those working for them comply with these requirements and must not publish material from other sources which does not meet these requirements.

5   Intrusion into grief or shock
In cases involving personal grief or shock, enquiries must be carried out and approaches made with sympathy and discretion. Publication must be handled sensitively at such times but this should not be interpreted as restricting the right to report judicial proceedings.

6*   Children
(i)   Young people should be free to complete their time at school without unnecessary intrusion.
(ii)   Journalists must not interview or photograph a child under the age of 16 on subjects involving the welfare of the child or any other child in the absence of or without the consent of a parent or other adult who is responsible for the children.
(iii) Pupils must not be approached or photographed while at school without the permission of the school authorities.
(iv)   There must be no payment to minors for material involving the welfare of children nor payments to parents or guardians for material about their children or wards unless it is demonstrably in the child's interest.
(v)   Where material about the private life of a child is published, there must be justification for publication other than the fame, notoriety or position of his or her parents or guardian.

7* **Children in sex cases**

1. The press must not, even where the law does not prohibit it, identify children under the age of 16 who are involved in cases concerning sexual offences, whether as victims or as witnesses.
2. In any press report of a case involving a sexual offence against a child –
    (i)   The child must not be identified.
    (ii)   The adult may be identified.
    (iii) The word 'incest' must not be used where a child victim might be identified.
    (iv)   Care must be taken that nothing in the report implies the relationship between the accused and the child.

8* **Listening Devices**
Journalists must not obtain or publish material obtained by using clandestine listening devices or by intercepting private telephone conversations.

9* **Hospitals**
(i)   Journalists or photographers making enquiries at hospitals or similar institutions must identify themselves to a responsible executive and obtain permission before entering non-public areas.
(ii) The restrictions on intruding into privacy are particularly relevant to enquiries about individuals in hospitals or similar institutions.

10* **Reporting of crime**
(i)   The press must avoid identifying relatives or friends of persons convicted or accused of crime without their consent.
(ii) Particular regard should be paid to the potentially vulnerable position of children who are witnesses to, or victims of, crime. This should not be interpreted as restricting the right to report judicial proceedings.

11* **Misrepresentation**
(i)   Journalists must not generally obtain or seek to obtain information or pictures through misrepresentation or subterfuge.
(ii)   Documents or photographs should be removed only with the consent of the owner.
(iii) Subterfuge can be justified only in the public interest and only when material cannot be obtained by any other means.

12 **Victims of sexual assault**
The press must not identify victims of sexual assault or publish material likely to contribute to such identification unless there is adequate justification and, by law, they are free to do so.

13   Discrimination
(i)   The press must avoid prejudicial or pejorative reference to a person's race, colour, religion, sex or sexual orientation or to any physical or mental illness or disability.
(ii)   It must avoid publishing details of a person's race, colour, religion, sexual orientation, physical or mental illness or disability unless these are directly relevant to the story.

14   Financial journalism
(i)   Even where the law does not prohibit it, journalists must not use for their own profit financial information they receive in advance of its general publication, nor should they pass such information to others.
(ii)   They must not write about shares or securities in whose performance they know that they or their close families have a significant financial interest without disclosing the interest to the editor or financial editor.
(iii)   They must not buy or sell, either directly or through nominees or agents, shares or securities about which they have written recently or about which they intend to write in the near future.

15   Confidential sources
Journalists have a moral obligation to protect confidential sources of information.

16*   Payment for articles
(i)   Payment or offers of payment for stories or information must not be made directly or through agents to witnesses or potential witnesses in current criminal proceedings except where the material concerned ought to be published in the public interest and there is an overriding need to make or promise to make a payment for this to be done. Journalists must take every possible step to ensure that no financial dealings have influence on the evidence that those witnesses may give.
(An editor authorising such a payment must be prepared to demonstrate that there is a legitimate public interest at stake involving matters that the public has a right to know. The payment or, where accepted, the offer of payment to any witness who is actually cited to give evidence should be disclosed to the prosecution and the defence and the witness should be advised of this).
(ii)   Payment or offers of payment for stories, pictures or information, must not be made directly or through agents to convicted or confessed criminals or to their associates – who may include family, friends and colleagues – except where the material concerned ought to be published in the public interest and payment is necessary for this to be done.

The public interest

There may be exceptions to the clauses marked * where they can be demonstrated to be in the public interest.

1. The public interest includes:
   (i) Detecting or exposing crime or a serious misdemeanour.
   (ii) Protecting public health and safety.
   (iii) Preventing the public from being misled by some statement or action of an individual or organisation.
2. In any case where the public interest is invoked, the Press Complaints Commission will require a full explanation by the editor demonstrating how the public interest was served.
3. There is a public interest in freedom of expression itself. The Commission will therefore have regard to the extent to which material has, or is about to, become available to the public.
4. In cases involving children editors must demonstrate an exceptional public interest to over-ride the normally paramount interest of the child

Broadcasting Standards Commission Code on Fairness and Privacy

June 1998

Preamble

1   In any democratic society, there are balances to be struck between the citizen's right to receive information and ideas, and the responsibilities of broadcasters and journalists to behave reasonably and fairly and not to cause an unwarranted infringement of a citizen's basic right to privacy.

The guidance in this Code cannot resolve that dilemma. But it sets out what the Broadcasting Standards Commission considers are the principles to be observed and practices to be followed by all broadcasters (including the providers of teletext services) to avoid unjust or unfair treatment in radio and television programmes, and to avoid the unwarranted infringement of privacy in the making and broadcasting of such programmes. Broadcasters and broadcasting regulatory bodies should reflect this guidance in their own codes and guidelines.

The Commission will, as required by the Act, take the provisions of this Code into account as it considers complaints and the Code will be revised, as necessary, in light of its experience. But the guidance in a code can never be exhaustive. Whether the needs of fairness and privacy have been met can only be judged by considering each particular case in light of the information the broadcaster had available after diligent research at the time the programme was made or broadcast.

Fairness

General

2   Broadcasters have a responsibility to avoid unfairness to individuals or organisations featured in programmes in particular through the use of inaccurate information or distortion, for example, by the unfair selection or juxtaposition of material taken out of context, whether specially recorded for a programme, or taken from library or other sources. Broadcasters should avoid creating doubts on the audience's part as to what they are being shown if it could mislead the audience in a way which would be unfair to those featured in the programme.

Dealing Fairly with Contributors

3   From the outset, broadcasters should ensure that all programme-makers, whether in-house or independent, understand the need to be straightforward and fair in their dealings with potential participants in factual programmes, in particular by making clear, wherever practicable, the nature of the programme and its purpose and, whenever appropriate, the nature of their contractual rights. Many potential contributors will be unfamiliar with broadcasting and therefore may not share assumptions about programme-making which broadcasters regard as obvious.

4   Contributors should be dealt with fairly. Where they are invited to make a significant contribution to a factual programme, they should:

(i)   be told what the programme is about;

(ii)   be given a clear explanation of why they were contacted by the programme;

(iii)   be told what kind of contribution they are expected to make – for example by way of interview or as part of a discussion;

(iv)   be informed about the areas of questioning, and, wherever possible, the nature of other likely contributions;

(v)   be told whether their contribution is to be live or recorded; and, if recorded, whether it is likely to be edited;

(vi)   not be coached or pushed or improperly induced into saying anything which they know not to be true or do not believe to be true;

(vii)   whenever appropriate, be made aware of any significant changes to the programme as it develops which might reasonably affect their original consent to participate, and cause material unfairness; and

(viii) if offered an opportunity to preview the programme, be given clear information about whether they will be able to effect any change in the programme.

The requirements of fairness in news reports pose particular challenges. The speed of newsgathering means that it is not always possible to provide contributors to news reports with all the information mentioned above. However, that does not absolve journalists from treating contributors fairly or ensuring that the reports compiled meet the needs of fairness and accuracy.

5   Broadcasters should take special care that the use of material originally recorded for one purpose and then used in a later or different programme does not create material unfairness or unwarrantably infringe privacy. The inclusion of such material, should be carefully considered, especially where this involves instances of personal tragedy or reference to criminal matters. This applies as much to material obtained from others as to material shot by the broadcaster itself.

6   All reasonable steps should be taken to ensure that guarantees given to contributors, whether as to content, confidentiality or anonymity, are honoured.

407

Accuracy

7   Broadcasters should take special care when their programmes are capable of adversely affecting the reputation of individuals, companies or other organisations. Broadcasters should take all reasonable care to satisfy themselves that all material facts have been considered before transmission and so far as possible are fairly presented.

8   Broadcasters should also be alert to the danger of unsubstantiated allegations being made by participants to live 'phone-ins and discussion programmes and ensure that presenters are briefed accordingly.

9   Contemporary drama which is based on the lives and experience of real people or organisations should seek to convey them fairly. It should be made clear in advance to the audience whether the drama is loosely based on the events it describes or rather purports to be an accurate account of what happened. In neither case should drama distort the verifiable facts in a way which is unfair to anyone with a direct interest in the programme. Care should also be taken not to convey through characterisation, or casting, or on-air promotion an unfair impression of the characters on whom the drama is based.

Correction and Apology

10   Whenever the broadcaster recognises that a broadcast has been unfair, if the person affected so wishes, it should be corrected promptly with due prominence unless there are compelling legal reasons not to do so. An apology should also be broadcast whenever appropriate.

Opportunity to Contribute

11   Where a programme alleges wrongdoing or incompetence, or contains a damaging critique of an individual or organisation, those criticised should normally be given an appropriate and timely opportunity to respond to or comment on the arguments and evidence contained within that programme.

Non-Participation

12   Anyone has the right to refuse to participate in a programme, but the refusal of an individual or organisation to take part should not normally prevent the programme from going ahead. However, where an individual or organisation is mentioned or discussed in their absence, care should be taken to ensure that their views are not misrepresented. (See also paragraph 25).

Deception

13   Factual programme-makers should not normally obtain or seek information or pictures through misrepresentation or deception, except where the disclosure is reasonably believed to serve an overriding public interest (see also paragraphs 14, 16, 18, 23, 26, 27, 28, 31, 32, 33) and the

material cannot reasonably be obtained by any other means. Where the use of deception is judged permissible, it should always be proportionate to the alleged wrongdoing and should wherever possible avoid the encouragement of conduct which might not have occurred at all but for the intervention of the programme-maker. Prior editorial approval at the most senior editorial levels within the broadcasting organisation should be obtained for such methods. The programmes should also make clear to the audience the means used to obtain access to the information, unless this places sources at risk.

Privacy

General

14   The line to be drawn between the public's right to information and the citizen's right to privacy can sometimes be a fine one. In considering complaints about the unwarranted infringement of privacy, the Commission will therefore address itself to two distinct questions: first, has there been an infringement of privacy? Second, if so, was it warranted? An infringement of privacy has to be justified by an overriding public interest in disclosure of the information. This would include revealing or detecting crime or disreputable behaviour, protecting public health or safety, exposing misleading claims made by individuals or organisations, or disclosing significant incompetence in public office. Moreover, the means of obtaining the information must be proportionate to the matter under investigation.

15   Privacy can be infringed during the obtaining of material for a programme, even if none of it is broadcast, as well as in the way in which material is used within the programme.

16   For much of the time, the private lives of most people are of no legitimate public interest. It is important that when, for a short time, people are caught up, however involuntarily, in events which have a place in the news, their situation is not abused or exploited either at the time or in later programmes which revisit those events. When broadcasters are covering events in public places, they should ensure that the words spoken or images shown are sufficiently in the public domain to justify their broadcast without the consent of the individuals concerned. When filming or recording in institutions, organisations or agencies where permission has been given by the relevant authority or management, broadcasters are under no obligation to seek the individual consent of employees or others whose appearance is incidental or where they are essentially anonymous members of the general public. However, in clearly sensitive situations in places such as hospitals or prisons or police stations, individual consent should normally be obtained unless their identity has been concealed. Broadcasters should take similar care with material recorded by CCTV cameras to ensure identi-

fiable individuals are treated fairly. Any exceptions to the requirement of individual consent would have to be justified by an overriding public interest.

17 People in the public eye, either through the position they hold or the publicity they attract, are in a special position. However, not all matters which interest the public are in the public interest. Even when personal matters become the proper subject of enquiry, people in the public eye or their immediate family or friends do not forfeit the right to privacy, though there may be occasions where private behaviour raises broader public issues either through the nature of the behaviour itself or by the consequences of its becoming widely known. But any information broadcast should be significant as well as true. The location of a person's home or family should not normally be revealed unless strictly relevant to the behaviour under investigation.

The Use of Hidden Microphones and Cameras

18 The use of secret recording should only be considered where it is necessary to the credibility and authenticity of the story, as the use of hidden recording techniques can be unfair to those recorded as well as infringe their privacy. In seeking to determine whether an infringement of privacy is warranted, the Commission will consider the following guiding principles:

(i) Normally, broadcasters on location should operate only in public where they can be seen. Where recording does take place secretly in public places, the words or images recorded should serve an overriding public interest to justify:

- the decision to gather the material;
- the actual recording;
- the broadcast

(ii) An unattended recording device should not be left on private property without the full and informed consent of the occupiers or their agent unless seeking permission might frustrate the investigation by the programme-makers of matters of an overriding public interest.

(iii) The open and apparent use of cameras or recording devices on both public and private property, when the subject is on private property, must be appropriate to the importance or nature of the story. The broadcaster should not intrude unnecessarily on private behaviour.

19 When broadcasting material obtained secretly, whether in public or on private property, broadcasters should take care not to infringe the privacy of bystanders who may be caught inadvertently in the recording. Wherever it is clear that unfairness might otherwise be caused, the identity of innocent parties should be obscured.

20 Broadcasters should apply the same rules on material shot secretly by others as they do to their own recordings in taking the decision whether to broadcast the material.

21 When secret recording is undertaken as part of an entertainment programme, care should also be taken to prevent the unwarranted infringement of privacy. Those who are the subjects of a recorded deception should be asked to give their consent before the material is broadcast. If they become aware of the recording and ask for it to stop, their wishes should be respected. In a live broadcast, especial care should be taken to avoid offence to the individuals concerned.

Telephone Calls

22 Broadcasters should normally identify themselves to telephone interviewees from the outset, or seek agreement from the other party, if they wish to broadcast a recording of a telephone call between the broadcaster and the other party.

23 If factual programme-makers take someone by surprise by recording a call for broadcast purposes without any prior warning, it is the equivalent of doorstepping (see paragraphs 25, 26, 27) and similar rules apply. Such approaches should only take place where there is reason to believe that there is an overriding public interest and the subject has refused to respond to reasonable requests for interview, or has a history of such failure or refusal, or there is good reason to believe that the investigation will be frustrated if the subject is approached openly.

24 Other recordings of telephone conversations for broadcast purposes made with the agreement of one of the parties but without the knowledge of the other party are to be assessed by the criteria which apply to secret recording on private property. (See paragraph 18).

Doorstepping

25 People who are currently in the news cannot reasonably object to being questioned and recorded by the media when in public places. The questions should be fair even if they are unwelcome. If the approach is made by telephone, the broadcaster should make clear who is calling and for what purpose. Nevertheless, even those who are in the news have the right to make no comment or to refuse to appear in a broadcast. Any relevant broadcast should make clear that a person has chosen not to appear and mention such person's explanation, if not to do so could be materially unfair. (See also paragraph 12).

26 Outside the daily news context, different considerations apply. But surprise can be a legitimate device to elicit the truth especially when dealing with matters where there is an overriding public interest in investigation and disclosure. Doorstepping in these circumstances may be legitimate where there has been repeated refusal to grant an interview (or a history of such refusals) or the risk exists that a protagonist might disappear.

27 Repeated attempts to take pictures or to obtain an interview when consent has been refused can, however, constitute an unwarranted infringement of privacy and can also constitute unfairness. Care must

411

also be taken not to make it easy to locate or identify the refuser's address unless it is strictly relevant to the behaviour under investigation and there is an overriding public interest.

Suffering and Distress

28   Broadcasters should not add to the distress of people caught up in emergencies or suffering a personal tragedy. People in a state of distress must not be put under any pressure to provide interviews. The mere fact that grieving people have been named or suggested for interview by the police or other authorities does not justify the use of material which infringes their privacy or is distressing. Such use is justified only if an overriding public interest is served. Broadcasters should take care not to reveal the identity of a person who has died, or victims of accidents or violent crimes unless and until it is clear that the next of kin have been informed.

29   Programme-makers should also be sensitive to the possibility of causing additional anxiety or distress when filming or recording people who are already extremely upset or under stress, for example at funerals or in hospitals. Normally, prior consent should be obtained from the family or their agents.

- At funerals, programme-makers should respect their requests to withdraw.
- No attempt should be made to enter wards or other places of treatment in hospitals without clear and informed authorisation from the medical staff and the individuals concerned or those acting on their behalf.

Broadcasters should also respect any reasonable arrangements made by the emergency services to supervise media access to victims of crime or accident or disaster, or their relatives, in the immediate aftermath of a tragedy.

30   Broadcasters should ask themselves whether the repeated use of traumatic library material is justified if it features identifiable people who are still alive or who have died recently.

Revisiting Past Events

31   Programmes intended to examine past events involving trauma to individuals, including crime, should try to minimise the potential distress to surviving victims or surviving relatives in retelling the story. So far as is reasonably practicable, surviving victims or the immediate families of those whose experience is to feature in the programme, should be informed of the programme's plans and its intended transmission. Failure to do this might be deemed an unwarranted infringement of privacy, even if the events or material to be broadcast have been in the public domain in the past.

Children

32   Children's vulnerability must be a prime concern for broadcasters. They do not lose their rights to privacy because of the fame or notoriety of their parents or because of events in their schools. Care should be taken that a child's gullibility or trust is not abused. They should not be questioned about private family matters or asked for views on matters likely to be beyond their capacity to answer properly. Consent from parents or those in loco parentis should normally be obtained before interviewing children under 16 on matters of significance.

Where consent has not been obtained or actually refused, any decision to go ahead can only be justified if the item is of overriding public interest and the child's appearance is absolutely necessary.

Similarly, children under 16 involved in police enquiries or court proceedings relating to sexual offences should not be identified or identifiable in news or other programmes.

Agency Operations

33   Broadcasters should be clear about the terms and conditions upon which they are granted access to police operations and those of other law enforcement agencies, emergency services or bodies working directly with vulnerable people. When accompanying such operations, crews should identify as soon as practicable for whom they are working and what they are doing. If asked to stop filming on private premises by the property owner or occupier, or to leave, they should do so unless there is an overriding public interest. Bystanders caught on camera should have their identities obscured, where unfairness might arise.

Appendix 19

ITC Programme Code

January 2002

Section 2: Privacy, Gathering of Information, etc.

2.1 General

The principles of the right to respect for private and family life and the right to freedom of expression are reflected in Article 8 and Article 10 of the European Convention on Human Rights, incorporated into UK law in the Human Rights Act 1998. As a public authority, the ITC must seek to ensure that the guidance given throughout this Code is consistent with Convention principles.

Article 8

Right to respect for private and family life
1. Everyone has the right to respect for his private and family life, his home and his correspondence.
2. There shall be no interference by a public authority with the exercise of this right except such as is in accordance with the law and is necessary in a democratic society in the interests of national security, public safety or the economic well-being of the country, for the prevention of disorder or crime, for the protection of health or morals, or for the protection of the rights and freedoms of others.

Article 10

Freedom of expression
1. Everyone has the right to freedom of expression. This right shall include freedom to hold opinions and to receive and impart information and ideas without interference by public authority and regardless of frontiers. This Article shall not prevent States from requiring the licensing of broadcasting, television or cinema enterprises.
2. The exercise of these freedoms, since it carries with it duties and responsibilities, may be subject to such formalities, conditions, restrictions or penalties as are prescribed by law and are necessary in a democratic society, in the interests of national security, territorial integrity or public safety, for the prevention of disorder or crime, for the protection of health or morals, for the protection of the reputa-

tion or rights of others, for preventing the disclosure of information received in confidence, or for maintaining the authority and impartiality of the judiciary.

Licensees may make programmes about any issues they choose. However, the method of treatment is limited by the obligations of fairness and a respect for truth, two qualities which are essential to all factually based programmes.

2.1(i)   *The Public Interest*
There will be occasions when an individual's right to respect for private and family life, or a licensee's right to freedom of expression, may be restricted in the public interest. Any act that relies on a defence of public interest must be proportional to the actual interest served. This will be a balancing exercise which will depend on the individual circumstances of each case. Where, for example, there is a significant intrusion into an individual's private affairs, particularly where that individual is innocent of any offence and/or where there is a significant risk of distress, an important public interest is likely to be required. Examples of a public interest which may justify an intrusion into an individual's privacy include: (i) detecting or exposing crime or a serious misdemeanour; (ii) protecting public health or safety; (iii) preventing the public from being misled by some statement or action of an individual or organisation; (iv) exposing significant incompetence in public office. Where freedom of expression is to be restricted, examples of public interest include ensuring the fair conduct of judicial proceedings or protecting public morals.

2.1(ii)   *The Public Domain*
In considering the application of the Code, the ITC will have regard to the extent to which material has, or is about to, become available to the public.

2.2   Filming and recording of members of the public

2.2(i)   *In public places*
When coverage is being given to events in public places, editors and producers must satisfy themselves that words spoken or action taken by individuals are sufficiently in the public domain to justify their being communicated to the television audience without express permission being sought from the individuals concerned. This applies in particular to material from closed-circuit television cameras of which the individual is unlikely to have been aware.

2.2(ii)   *In semi-public places*
When permission is received to film or record material in an institution, such as a hospital, factory, or department store, which has regular dealings with the public, but which would not normally be accessible to cameras without such permission, it is very likely that the material will include shots of individuals who are themselves incidental, rather than

central, figures in the programme. The question arises how far and in what conditions such people retain a right to refuse to allow material in which they appear to be broadcast. As a general rule, no obligation to seek agreement arises when the appearance of the persons shown is incidental and they are clearly random and anonymous members of the general public.

When their appearance is not incidental, where they are not random and anonymous or where, though unnamed, they are shown in particularly sensitive situations (for example as psychiatric or intensive care patients), individual written consents to use this material should be sought. Any exceptions should be justifiable in the public interest.

When by reason of age, disability or infirmity a person is not in a position either to give or to withhold agreement, permission to use the material should be sought from the next of kin or from the person responsible for their care, unless a decision to proceed without such permission can be justified as a matter of important public interest.

2.2(iii)   Filming on police operations

When permission is given to film police or similar official operations of any kind (e.g. Customs and Excise, Trading Standards) involving members of the public in other than public places (e.g. visits to homes under warrant, raids on licensed premises, etc) it is the responsibility of the producer or senior crew-member to make his position known to the members of the public involved and to identify the licensee or programme maker for whom he or she is working as soon as practically possible. If asked to leave premises by the person responsible for the premises or by police, he/she should normally comply. In such cases it must be recognised that there may have been a trespass. If asked to stop filming by the person responsible for the premises or by police, programme-makers should normally comply. In any event, reference should be made before transmission to the licensee's most senior programme executive or the designated alternate, who will need to be convinced that showing any of the material serves the public interest.

Programme-makers should also make reasonable endeavours either to inform persons in advance of transmission of any material in which they are prominently featured, or disguise their identities in any material broadcast, where not to do so would be unfair. In cases where those filmed have been found guilty of the offence which gave rise to the raid it may not be necessary to inform them of the transmission or disguise their identities. When in doubt, licensees should take legal advice.

Filming of private individuals, without their consent and in their own home, is likely to constitute a breach of Article 8(1) of the European Convention on Human Rights, and therefore may have to be justified by reference to the provisions of Article 8(2) of the Convention.

A licensee must also be aware of the reporting restrictions on pre-trial investigations into an alleged criminal offence in the United Kingdom where persons under the age of 18 are involved in the offence. These are dealt with in more detail in Section 2.11 below.

2.2(iv)   In circumstances of distress
The individual's right to privacy at times of bereavement or distress must be respected. Care should be taken to ensure that sources of information are the most reliable and verifiable which are available at the time.
Scenes of human suffering and distress are often an integral part of any news report of the effects of natural disaster, accident or human violence, and may be a proper subject for direct portrayal rather than indirect reporting. But before presenting such scenes a producer needs to balance the wish to serve the needs of truth, the desire for compassion and the public interest against the risk of sensationalism and the possibility of an unwarranted invasion of privacy. This applies both to individuals personally involved and, in the event of death or serious injury, to members of the immediate family. Insensitive questioning not only risks inflicting additional distress on the interviewee; it may also offend many viewers.

2.3   Fairness in revisiting past events
In non-news programmes concerning a natural disaster, accident, human violence or a serious crime, producers should assess the likelihood of personal distress arising from the programme and, where practicable, contact at an early stage any central figures involved (including members of the immediate family of any who have died) and give due consideration to their perspectives, taking account of how recently the event took place, the nature of the portrayal of those concerned, the extent to which the event continues to attract wider media attention, and the extent to which an important public interest is to be served, as distinct from public curiosity alone. In particular, where innocent parties are involved, special care should be taken not to present them in an unfair light. In any event, producers should, where practicable, inform all such people of times of intended transmission of programmes and when programme trails will start to be transmitted.

2.4   Secret filming and recording
The use of hidden microphones and cameras for the filming or recording of individuals who are unaware of it is acceptable only when it is clear that the material so acquired is essential to establish the credibility and authority of a story where this cannot or is unlikely to be achieved using 'open' filming or recording techniques, and where the story itself is equally clearly of important public interest. When, in the considered judgement of the producer, such a case arises, he or she must, wherever practicable, obtain the explicit consent of the licensee's most senior programme executive or the designated alternate before such material is recorded. Consent is required again before any material obtained by secret recording is transmitted. This applies whether the material was produced or commissioned by the licensee or acquired from an external

source. Licensees must ensure full records are kept of the consultation process followed in each case and of any material recorded and transmitted. The ITC may ask to see such records which must be retained for 18 months after transmission.

The requirements in the preceding paragraph also apply to the secret recording of telephone conversations where these are intended for transmission.

2.5 Fairness in the conduct of interviews

Interviewees should be made adequately aware of the format, subject matter and purpose of the programme to which they have been invited to contribute, and the way in which their contribution is likely to be used. Written confirmation should be provided if requested and in all cases where allegations of criminality or other serious wrongdoing are to be put to an interviewee. Interviewees should also be informed of any significant changes to the programme as it develops, which might reasonably affect their original consent to participate, and cause material unfairness.

For programmes dealing with political or industrial controversy or current public policy, interviewees should also be told the identity and intended role of other proposed participants in the programme, where this is known.

2.5(i) Editing of interviews

Fairness and impartiality apply equally to the editing of interviews as to their conduct. Editing to shorten recorded interviews must not distort or misrepresent the known views of the interviewee.

Interviews held on library tapes should be checked before use to see whether the views expressed are still valid, and where necessary captioned to show the date they were originally recorded.

2.6 Interviews without prior arrangement

Impromptu interviews with public figures and people in the news are a normal and usually unproblematic part of newsgathering. However interviews sought on private property without the subject's prior agreement should not be included in a programme unless they have a public interest purpose. The same consideration applies to restaurants, churches and other places where the subject would reasonably expect personal privacy. Interviews in which criminal or other serious allegations are put to individuals should not be attempted without prior warning unless a previous request has been refused or received no response, or where there is good reason for not making a prior approach. Particular care needs to be taken where the person approached is not the subject of the allegations, for example a relative, friend or associate, to avoid the risk of unwarranted invasion of their privacy. Reporters and crews should leave 'media scrums' unless there is a continuing public interest in their presence.

2.7 Opportunity to take part

Where a programme alleges wrongdoing or incompetence, or contains a damaging critique of any individual or organisation, those concerned should normally be offered an opportunity to take part or otherwise comment on the allegations. If a statement is offered, and the licensee considers it necessary to edit this, editing should be done in such a way as to represent its original content as fairly as possible. If the proposed contributor is unable or unwilling to participate, this need not prevent the programme going ahead, but care must be taken to give as fair an account as possible of his/her position. Reference to his/her absence should be made in a fair and appropriate manner.

2.8 Set-up situations

Set-up situations where members of the public or celebrities are featured without their knowledge or without prior warning are an established part of some entertainment programmes. Nevertheless, the use of such situations should always be carefully considered, and safeguards used to prevent unwarranted invasions of privacy.

Where material is recorded, the consent of the subjects should be obtained before transmission. In live situations, particular care should be taken to avoid offence to the individuals concerned. Requests to leave private property or stop filming should be complied with promptly.

A different kind of set-up situation is one where the subject consents to being recorded for a different purpose from that covertly intended by the programme makers. With unsuspecting members of the public, the use of such material without the subject's permission can only be justified if it is necessary in order to make an important point of public interest. With celebrities and those in the public eye, material should not be used without similar public interest justification if it is likely to result in unjustified public ridicule or personal distress. In all cases, consent to proceed should, where practicable, be given before recording by the licensee's most senior programme executive or the designated alternative. Such consent is required again before transmission.

2.9 Later re-use of material

Licensees should consider carefully whether unfairness to contributors results from re-use of material in later and different programme contexts, for example re-use of material recorded for a factual programme in an entertainment context. Particular care should also be taken where personal tragedy or criminal matters are involved.

2.10 Involvement of children in programmes

Children are involved in programmes in a number of ways and programme makers must have due regard to their welfare at all times. Particular care should be taken to avoid causing any distress or alarm to

children involved in programmes. Under no circumstances may children be put at physical or moral risk, for example in factual programmes concerning criminal activity.
Any interviewing of children requires care. The consent of a parent or guardian, as well as the child should normally be sought beforehand, with exceptions only for the least sensitive interview topics. Children should not be questioned to elicit views on confidential family matters, nor asked for expressions of opinion on matters likely to be beyond their judgement. Programme makers should consider consulting appropriate professionals if they are in any doubt about a child's capacity to understand or express him/herself.
Performances by children under 16 are controlled by the Home Office and administered by the Local Education Authorities. Exemptions are defined under the Children and Young Persons Acts (see Appendix 4).

2.11 Reporting of sexual and other offences involving children

Where children are or have been involved in police enquiries or court proceedings concerning sexual offences, special care needs to be taken to avoid the so called 'jigsaw effect'. This happens when several reports in different media give different details of a case which, when pieced together, reveal the identity of a child involved.
Particular care needs to be taken when reporting sexual crimes within a family. Naming the accused and describing the crime can have the effect of identifying the victim. Giving information about an accused person's address may contribute to the jigsaw which identifies the victim.
In 1993 most of the media agreed in principle to name the accused/ convicted person (provided this is not a child) and not to name the victim. The ITC expects licensees to abide by this principle. The offence should be described as 'a serious sexual offence'. If the accused and victim are related the victim should be described as 'a young woman' or 'a child' and so on.
When covering any pre-trial investigation into an alleged criminal offence in the UK, licensees should pay particular regard to the potentially vulnerable position of any person under 18 involved as a witness or victim, before broadcasting their name, address, identity of school or other educational establishment, place of work, or any still or moving picture of this person.
Particular justification is also required for the broadcasting of such material related to the identity of any person under 18 who is involved in the offence as a defendant or potential defendant.

2.12 Impartiality and fairness in drama and drama-documentary

Where proposed subject matter relates to political or industrial controversy, or current public policy, this section should be read in conjunction with the provisions contained in Section 3.

Drama is by definition the work of a creative imagination and the impartiality due in respect of a play is not the same as that required of a current affairs programme. Nevertheless, questions of impartiality and fairness may arise in the area of drama, particularly drama-documentary, when the boundaries between what is fact and what is fiction may become blurred. For this reason, a clear distinction should be drawn between plays based on fact and dramatised documentaries which seek to reconstruct actual events. Much confusion may be avoided if plays based on current or very recent events are carefully labelled as such, so that the fictional elements are not misleadingly presented as fact.

The dramatised documentary which lays claim to be a factual reconstruction of events is bound by the same standards of fairness as those that apply to factual programmes in general. It is inevitable that the creative realisation of some elements (such as characterisation, dialogue and atmosphere) will introduce a fictional dimension, but this should not be allowed to distort the known facts.

The evidence on which a dramatic reconstruction is based should be tested with the same rigour required of a factual programme. Sequences which are based on extracts of court proceedings or other matters of public record must be fair and accurate.

Care should be taken in scheduling drama and drama documentary programmes portraying controversial matters covered by the Act. Impartiality may need to be reinforced by providing an opportunity for opposing viewpoints to be expressed. This might take the form of a studio discussion following the drama itself, or a separate programme providing a right of reply within a reasonable period.

2.12(i)   Dramatised 'reconstructions' within factual programmes

The use of dramatised 'reconstructions' in factual programmes is a legitimate means of obtaining greater authenticity, so long as it does not distort reality.

Whenever a reconstruction is used in a documentary, current affairs or news programme it should accurately reflect the known facts and be labelled unless there is no possibility of viewers being misled.

2.12(ii)   Simulated news bulletins

Any simulation of a television news bulletin or news flash to be included in any programme should either be subtitled or produced in such a way that there can be no reasonable possibility that it could be taken to be an actual news bulletin.

2.13   Provision of tapes and transcripts to others

When a person or organisation can establish a reasonable claim that something derogatory has been broadcast about them, or that they are affected by alleged criticism, unfairness or inaccuracy, and request a recording or transcript, it should normally be provided.

The licensee may, however, feel it is more appropriate, as a first step, to attempt to satisfy the complainant in some other way, for example by a letter of explanation or apology. It may be necessary to establish the complainant has a proper interest in the matter at issue. A recording or transcript may also be delayed where there is clear legal advice that the particular circumstances or a request make provision inadvisable.

Index